FISHING

FISHING

How the Sea
Fed Civilization

BRIAN FAGAN

Yale
UNIVERSITY PRESS

NEW HAVEN AND LONDON

Published with assistance from the Louis Stern Memorial Fund.

Yale University Press books may be purchased in quantity for educational, business, or promotional use. For information, please e-mail sales.press@yale.edu (U.S. office) or sales@yaleup.co.uk (U.K. office).

Designed by Nancy Ovedovitz. Set in Adobe Caslon type by Integrated Publishing Solutions. Printed in the United States of America.

Library of Congress Control Number: 2017934016
ISBN 978-0-300-21534-2 (hardcover : alk. paper)

A catalogue record for this book is available from the British Library.

This paper meets the requirements of ANSI/NISO Z39.48-1992 (Permanence of Paper).

10 9 8 7 6 5 4 3 2 1

Frontispiece: Men apart. Danish fishermen with the sea etched in their faces. Michael Ancher, *To Fiskere Ved en Bad* (Two fishermen beside a boat), 1879. Courtesy Staten Museum for Kunst/SMK Foto.

To

Brian Walter and Mary Gwendoline Margaret Fagan

My late father and mother, with love and gratitude

———————

Deo patriaeque fidelis

And with thanks to Earl Viau, who gave us the plate,

so it could return home

CONTENTS

CONTENTS

PREFACE

My only accomplishment as a fisherman is that once, many years ago in a placid English stream, I tickled a trout with my fingers and then caught it. My only experience with rod and line dates to when I was nine. Some friends and I tried our luck in a small local river. All we caught were eels, once a much-favored food but rejected with disgust by my mother. I enjoy a delicious fish dish as much as anyone but not what the immortal Izaak Walton called "The Art of Angling." I have neither the patience nor the powers of observation, qualities I much admire in others, to be a recreational fisherman. So this is a history of fishing written by a nonfisherman. With the exception of the North Atlantic cod trade, there are almost no books or even popular articles that cover the history of fishing from a global perspective.

Fishing has played an important and overlooked role in human history. Of the three ancient ways of obtaining food—hunting, plant foraging, and fishing—only the last remained important after the development of agriculture and stock raising some twelve thousand years ago. Wild plant gathering is economically significant nowhere in the world today. Hunting exists mainly as illegal poaching for the illicit ivory and traditional medicine trades, and secondarily in North America as a means of controlling wild populations. Fishing, however, not only survived but expanded to provide rations for pharaohs, provisions for Norse sailors, and, today, food for millions of us. Yet fisherfolk and their communities have almost entirely escaped notice. They held their knowledge close to their chests and seldom gave birth to powerful monarchs or divine rulers. Because they lived and died in quiet obscurity, writing their history means drawing on a wide range of esoteric and specialized sources.

Much history vanishes with those who lived it. The problem is especially acute with fishing people. Their past unfolded with the help of unwritten knowledge passed from one generation to the next by word of mouth. Much of it came from tough times at sea. The Danish artist Michael Ancher painted fishermen from Skagen in northern Denmark during the late 1870s, when fishers still worked the North Sea under sail. One painting shows two fishers leaning against a boat and gazing into the teeth of the wind, the land at their back. The meaning of the ocean is etched into their faces: bearded, weather-beaten, stern, and unyielding. Fishers are people who draw their living from a hard, uncontrollable world that is perfectly indifferent to their fortune and suffering. This history is an effort to show what such fisherfolk did to help create our modern world.

The earliest fishing arose out of the fundamental human quality of opportunism. Careful observation, combined with grabbing chances when they arose, started our ancestors fishing two million years ago or so. Lifting marooned catfish from shallow African pools required nimble hands and careful stalking to avoid casting a shadow on the water. The art lay in knowing when and where to look, exactly the same skill used to collect honey, scavenge lion kills, and run down small antelope. The only difference was that these prey were in shallow water. One can hardly call this fishing, more a form of opportunistic hunting that persisted for tens of thousands of years.

The same observation can be applied to mollusks, although they are much easier to take than fish. Clams, limpets, oysters, and whelks cluster in dense patches, the variables being accessibility and currents or tides. Like fish, they served as a supplemental food, usually not a favorite one. From a hunter-gatherer's point of view shellfish were a predictable food, the kind of resources that became the anchors of life on the move. People visited the mollusk beds when other foods were in short supply, often in late winter and spring.

Opportunistic fish and mollusk collecting became an integral part of annual journeys through hunting territories, whether large or small. Skipjack tuna swimming inshore were prey for people on East Timor forty thousand years ago. Both the Neanderthals and modern late Ice Age hunters took fish and mollusks when the need or opportunity arose. By fifteen thousand years ago people living along the Vézère River in southwest France and elsewhere harvested spring and autumn salmon runs. Artists carved the fish on reindeer antler and engraved them on cave walls.

No one "invented" fishing. Everyone knew fish were there for the taking at specific times and places. I'm struck by the ways in which they were caught, even harvested in considerable numbers, with no startling technological innovations. Spears with barbed wood or antler tips were used as much on land as they were against fish in shallow water. Pointed antler, bone, and wooden gorges and, later, hooks were also ideal for catching birds. The nets and traps deployed against small game worked in water, too. Artifacts used for fishing remained startlingly unchanged through history, even if there were also specialized hooks and larger nets. The fisher's observational skill is the major tool and always has been.

In the sense that we are familiar with it today, fishing came into its own with the natural global warming that ended the last Ice Age glaciation after fifteen thousand years ago, especially after about six thousand years BP, when sea levels finally stabilized. Climbing temperatures, retreating ice sheets, and rising sea levels transformed northern environments. People moved to coasts and riverbanks, to lakeshores and lagoons. This is when fishing became a central part of subsistence, especially for groups living on newly productive coastlines, where shallow-water fish and mollusks abounded. For the first time the dynamics of human existence changed. Many communities now dwelt in the same locations either permanently or for many months of the year.

As local populations rose, territories became more closely defined. Mollusk beds and fisheries became depleted. Competition for marine resources sometimes erupted in violence, as it did among the Chumash of southern California and the Ertebølle people of Scandinavia. Here and elsewhere, societies reliant on mollusks, plant foods, and rich fisheries developed an increasing elaboration. Important kin leaders became individuals of authority, with special ties to the supernatural world through revered ancestors.

These were not divine rulers like pharaohs or Sumerian leaders in Mesopotamia. Their power depended on individual charisma and experience, on the loyalty of their followers, always a fickle thing. No fishing society ever developed into a civilization with cities and standing armies. They had no means of doing so. Their leaders enjoyed prestige and wealth, distributed their riches in food surpluses and exotic, prestigious objects such as ornaments, but they could never become kings because the resource base of fisheries was too fickle. Fishers always remained on the margins of preindustrial civilizations.

Much of the history of fishing is concerned with movement, not only with the dynamics of fishing itself but also with interactions between fishing communities and others who relied on them. Fishing was a major spur to the development of boats, a technology that facilitated trade, migration, and exploration. People were afloat and fishing off Southeast Asia before forty-five thousand years ago and in the Bismarck Archipelago of the southwest Pacific fifteen thousand years later. Survival on Pacific islands depended on expert pilotage and lagoon fishing, as canoes traveled to the Society Islands, Rapa Nui, and Hawaii by AD 1200.

The Jomon fishing communities of northern Japan depended heavily on salmon runs and ventured offshore to the stormy waters of the Kuril Islands and even Kamchatka in extreme northeast Asia. Jomon fishers caught almost the same species that the first Americans took when they settled on Alaskan coasts. In the far north, on the Bering Land Bridge that joined Siberia and Alaska until about eleven thousand years ago, fishing and sea mammal hunting were part of broad-spectrum adaptations that depended on mobility and finely developed opportunism.

Subsistence fishing with the aim of producing food surpluses at the household and village level is one thing, but harvesting vast numbers of fish as a commodity is another. Fish harvesting was commonplace in the ancient world, but its yields were for domestic consumption, even if some of the catch was traded to other communities near and far. Controlling salmon runs was a major source of economic and political power in the Pacific Northwest, as it may also have been among the Jomon. Fishers on the Danube harvested enormous sturgeon when they came into shallow waters to spawn. All these kinds of subsistence farming depended on efficient preservation methods such as drying, salting, and smoking, techniques used by hunters for hundreds of thousands of years.

Local subsistence fishing, even in well-organized seasonal harvests, was qualitatively different from the large-scale fishing that produced rations of dried fish for ancient Egyptians working on the Pyramids of Giza. Fishing on this scale required armies of scribes and petty officials to keep records of catches contracted from full-time fishers working large seine nets. Those catches, gutted, cleaned, butterflied, and dried by the thousands, had many advantages as rations for workers laboring in preindustrial economies. The product was light, easily carried in baskets, and kept for a long time. When fish became rations, the scale of the fishery changed. Fish as rations were a logical outcome of growing populations of nonfarmers, the appearance of city markets, and a need for nourishing rations for armies and sailors.

No one invented aquaculture either. When demand for fish mushroomed to the point that the local supply became overfished, people had limited options. One was to intensify fishing with long lines and other devices; another was to seek more distant fishing grounds. A third was to turn to aquaculture, or fish farming. This was a logical strategy for people concerned about smaller catches and also a way of corralling larger fish. The Chinese domesticated Amur carp as early as 3500 BC. Wealthy Romans delighted in showing off their farmed trophy fish at lavish banquets. In medieval Europe monastic houses took up fish farming in part because of Christian doctrine that prescribed increasing the number of meatless holy days for the devout.

Once a pagan symbol of death, fish became an appropriate meal to represent Christ and his suffering on the cross. For two thousand years Fridays have been obligatory days of abstinence from meat for Catholics, when the penitent faithful ate grains, vegetables, and fish instead. By the thirteenth century nearly half the days of the year were meatless. An insatiable demand for sea fish, notably herring and cod, created an international trade in salted herrings and cod that extended from Bergen, Norway, and the Baltic states across Europe. The fifteenth century saw North Sea fishers taking cod off southern Iceland. After John Cabot's voyage to Newfoundland in 1497, cod fisheries off North America and on the offshore banks boomed. Remarkably, the technology of the cod fisheries remained basically medieval until the eighteenth century.

The new technologies of the nineteenth century transformed fishing into an industrial enterprise. Falling catches led to long lines and larger gillnets and to the first bottom trawls that devastated the seabed. Then came steam engines, after that gasoline power, and finally the diesel, which took trawlers into ever-deeper waters and brought on the fisheries crisis we confront today.

The crisis of the fisheries ultimately merges with the much larger environmental disaster of today's oceans and climate. This last problem, which presents a truly existential threat to civilization, is already the subject of whole libraries of books, and I have neither the qualifications nor the desire to add one more. But I fervently believe that we need a historical perspective on humanity's last major source of food from the wild. When fish cease to play that role, a significant link with our long history will have been severed.

AUTHOR'S NOTE

Dates

All radiocarbon dates are calibrated against calendar dates. The AD, BC, and BP (before present) convention is used. Dates earlier than 10,000 BC are quoted as BP or years ago for convenience.

Place-Names

Modern place-names refer to the current most commonly used spellings. Where appropriate, widely accepted ancient usages are employed.

When referring to an area which is now in a modern country like, for example, Iran or Peru, I use such terms for convenience without the assumed prefix "now known as." As is obvious, many modern country names are of recent vintage.

Measurements

All measurements are given in metric, this now being common scientific convention.

Fisherman/Fisher/Fisherfolk

I have used the terms *fisherman, fisher,* and *fisherfolk* interchangeably throughout the book, again for convenience and in an intended gender-neutral way. In ancient and traditional modern societies men did most of the fishing, while women tended to gut, clean, and either prepare or preserve the fish. Women were responsible for mollusk collecting in most societies. Given the flexibility of these roles and for convenience, I've elected to use *fisherman* and *fisher* as terms covering the two sexes, which were clearly both part of the enterprise.

Recreational Fishing

For reasons of limited space this book does not cover the fascinating history of recreational fishing, which began with the pharaohs and perhaps even earlier.

Maps

In some instances locations that are obscure or minor or that are in or very close to modern cities have been omitted from the maps.

FISHING

Bountiful Waters

When I found some fish bones in a one-thousand-year-old farming village in Central Africa many years ago, my colleague threw them away. "Useless," he said. "We can't identify them." I was helping him out on his dig. Being very new to the game, I could say nothing. I'm sure he forgot the fragments at once, but his words remain with me nearly sixty years later. My interest in ancient fishing dates back to that long-completed excavation.

My own excavations into African farming villages during the early 1960s yielded no evidence of fish. Their inhabitants were cereal farmers and cattle people who hunted game and foraged for edible wild plants on the side. Only one dig involved hunters and plant gatherers, a place called Gwisho hot springs far north of my farmers. Three thousand years ago a small band camped by the springs, which overlook the Kafue River floodplain. The summer flood spills over this huge plain, then recedes, leaving behind shallow pools.[1]

My Belgian colleague Francis Van Noten and I were lucky at Gwisho. The site was waterlogged. We recovered wooden spear points, a digging stick, numerous antelope bones, plant remains—and fish bones, which we asked Graham Bell-Cross, a Zambian fisheries officer, to examine. Almost all were from catfish, easily speared in shallow pools as a flood recedes. We had no idea how much was known about their bones and were astounded when he told us that the most complete bones came from fish weighing between two and three kilograms, about the same as modern-day catfish in the Kafue. Fish were an unimportant part of the Gwisho diet of three thousand years ago. In retrospect, the people clearly took them opportunistically at the end of the flood, when the fish were easy to spot and kill in the shallows. They may even have caught some by hand.

Over the years I've visited modern fishing villages in Africa and elsewhere, pored over ancient fish bones, which I found hard to identify, and talked to fisherfolk working many different waters, deep and shallow. I was dazzled by salmon runs in the Pacific Northwest, where the fish crowded rapids and shallow pools. That's when you realize just how bountiful the world's fisheries once were. But only in recent years have archaeologists and historians turned serious attention to one of the oldest means of human subsistence.

Fishers have always been anonymous folk, usually on the margins of society, far from pharaohs' courts and teeming urban markets. Their catches must have arrived silently almost every day—a predictable food supply if one allowed for the seasons. To a scholar the illiterate fishing people of the past are elusive, and the history of their trade is a challenging puzzle of clues. Our knowledge of fishing must be assembled from many sources, including archaeology, anthropology, history, marine biology and oceanography, and also paleoclimatology, to mention only a few.

Since there are almost no firsthand accounts that date from before the eighteenth century, finding historical records of fishing involves searching through such esoteric sources as court records, information on fish landings for urban markets, manor and monastic diaries, and the occasional treatise on the subject. Fortunately, anthropological studies of modern-day subsistence fishing and mollusk collecting add a rich dimension to the documents and offer an invaluable perspective on the thousands of fragmentary and often minute fish bones found at archaeological sites.

Nineteenth-century Scandinavian archaeologists were the first to take prehistoric fish and mollusks seriously. This is hardly surprising: they found huge shell heaps (middens) surrounding many archaeological sites on Baltic shores. Then their careful cataloguing of fish bones and mollusk shells passed into obscurity. In the early twentieth century most excavators who discovered fish bones considered it sufficient to say that the inhabitants fished. They compiled no lists of species or information on ages and weights of the catch, and their reports provided little assessment of whether fish or mollusks had any importance to the people who ate them.

Everything changed during the 1950s, when archaeologists realized there was far more to studying an ancient community than counting stone artifacts or comparing potsherds. They turned to animal bones and plant remains and, later, to fish for the information they could yield. This is one of the reasons archaeological excavation today is far slower than it was even a generation ago. By the 1970s excavators were passing samples of occupation deposits through fine-mesh screens and water, especially to recover inconspicuous plant remains and fish bones. Wet sifting, often called flotation, has produced a surge of knowledge about ancient fisheries. The finer the screen, the better. At the nine-thousand-year-old Norje Sunnansund site in southeastern Sweden, the use of a 5-mm sieve, as opposed to a 2.5-mm size, reduced fish bone recovery by 94 percent.[2]

The identification of these tiny bones, by comparing them against modern fish skeletons, has become a well-refined, if esoteric, practice. Today fish specialists can also tease out answers to far subtler questions than size and species. What ages were the fish? Were they caught only in spawning season or year-round? What role did they play in the diet? What butchery and preservation methods were used? The list of questions and answers is limited only by the imagination and ingenuity of the excavators. For instance, the development of stable isotope analysis for bone chemistry has contributed much to our understanding of ancient diets. One can now use samples from human bones to discover how much of the diet came from maritime versus terrestrial foods.

Researchers can also marry archaeological and historic information with newly acquired insights into the habits of different fishes. They now know much more about species like bluefin tuna in the Mediterranean, which come inshore to spawn and were slaughtered by the hundreds. Thanks to marine biologists, the habits of anchovies, herring, salmon, sturgeon, and many other fish are far better known than they were a generation ago. These findings are invaluable grist for the archaeologist's mill.

Paleoclimatology, the study of ancient climate change, is slowly revealing the constant fluctuations of ocean ecosystems, molded by major and minor climate change. These shifts, both more complex and less visible than those ashore, can trigger major changes in fish populations. So can human destruction of habitats, especially in inshore waters. Large and small variations in global sea levels can have significant impacts on shallow-water fisheries. For instance, minute changes in local sea levels along southern Florida's west coast over the past four thousand years are clearly visible in the fish and mollusk catches of the Calusa Indians.[3]

Climate change on a larger scale had major impacts. The North Sea, the English Channel, and the Irish Sea are among the world's most productive fisheries. The local people exploited these waters from the end of the Ice Age, some fifteen thousand years ago and perhaps even earlier. Like all ocean waters these were dynamic, ever-changing ecosystems. Major climatic changes molded these systems, rising sea levels, El Niños, and epic storms among them. Overharvesting by humans altered habitats.

One major player in fish history is the North Atlantic Oscillation, or NAO, created by differences in atmospheric pressure between Iceland and the Azores. A high NAO index creates strong westerly winds and mild European winters. A low index brings weaker westerlies. Cold Siberian air descends over Europe, bringing bitterly cold temperatures. A low NAO index could make fishing harbors freeze over. A high index, with strong westerlies, could cause savage gales to descend without warning. On a fine night in July 1881 a fleet of more than thirty open fishing boats were shooting baited long lines for cod far off the Shetland Islands, north of Scotland, when a brutal storm blew up within minutes. Ten boats foundered. Thirty-six fishermen drowned, leaving thirty-four widows and fifty-eight orphans.[4]

NAO's unpredictable shifts also affected the size of herring shoals reaching the North Sea and coastal waters each year. Smoked or salted herring was a medieval staple, especially on holy days. The most robust herring landings in the English Channel and North Sea and as far south as the Bay of Biscay coincided with a low NAO index.

Fishermen of the past were well aware that their catches were irregular, even if they did not know why. In the western English Channel, for example, herring fed on a form of arrow worm that preferred colder conditions. When a different arrow worm species arrived in warmer cycles, most of the herring left, their places taken by the pilchard. People were happy to eat either, but the ratios of pilchard to herring tell us whether they were living through a hard winter or a mild one.

While the NAO is the oscillation we know the most about, similar periodic changes occurred worldwide. Anchovy populations off the north coast of Peru fluctuated with the rise and fall of El Niños, climatic events that could weaken powerful states and help overthrow kings and emperors. I don't want to stress this unduly: the complex history of people and fisheries almost never yields simple explanations. But fish were (and still are) an important food, and the abundance or scarcity of food has played a role in all sorts of social changes, large and small, good and catastrophic.

We've come a long way from the pioneering researches of the Scandinavian shell mound excavators of the mid-nineteenth century. They were generations ahead of their colleagues in recognizing the great importance of fish and mollusks to ancient societies. A century and a half later, fine-grained excavation and high technology science are producing startling insights into just how significant such foods were in the past. In earlier times, before the development of state-organized civilizations and cities, subsistence fishing and mollusk collecting tended to be seasonal occupations. Intensive fishing occurred, perhaps for a few days or weeks, when catfish were marooned in receding Nile pools or when salmon spawned in Pacific Northwest rivers during the spring. Fishing was, for the most part, an opportunistic part of human subsistence. Hunter-gatherer societies along Peru's North Coast spent much of the year inland, then came to the ocean to harvest anchovies. Shellfish collectors in northern Europe ate mollusks seasonally, when other foods were in short supply.

Such opportunistic harvesting of marine and river foods is almost as old as humanity itself. Sometimes people collected fish and mollusks in enormous numbers, but they were part of much more complex food-getting strategies that also encompassed big game, small animals, and edible plant foods. The most profound change came with the development of urban civilizations. Rulers like the pharaohs or Cambodian kings in Southeast Asia may have thought of themselves as divine leaders, but they had to feed enormous numbers of people laboring on their palaces and public works. Like grain, fish became rations, issued in preserved form to teams of pyramid workers or reservoir builders. Fish now became an anonymous, standardized commodity, just as they were for the Norse seaman who explored the North Atlantic millennia later. Nile catfish and Atlantic cod were like beef jerky for ocean sailors. Roman fishers harvested hundreds of large tuna in mass slaughters in spring. In nearly every civilization fishing became a commercial enterprise. The scientific advances are still in their infancy but offer enormous potential. Thanks to major advances in fish bone analysis we can now identify Lofoten Island cod from northern Norway that were decapitated and dried for export, even calculate their average weight from their bones. DNA studies of cod in English medieval markets are beginning to identify the changing trends in the international fish trade of the day.

Fisheries biologists and archaeologists are developing a mirror that reflects a hitherto unknown past—that of fishers and their catches, the people who labored anonymously in the shadow of cities and powerful civilizations. For the first time the new science is allowing us to think differently about pyramids and pharaohs, about the food surpluses of Angkor Wat, and about the profound importance of anchovies and fish meal to the Moche of coastal Peru. Fishing may not have created civilization, but it helped it to endure.

I would argue that people have been catching fish for nearly two million years, perhaps longer. I also believe that the earliest fishing was nothing more than shrewd opportunism, a matter of grabbing a catfish in a shallow African lake or river pool and not letting it slither away or bite you. Such foraging for fish was as routine as hunting and gathering edible plant foods. Opportunism is a fundamental human quality, the ability to adapt to changing circumstances and turn them to one's advantage. One could describe humans' earliest approaches to fishing as a matter of discovering and pursuing opportunities as they arose. This element never entirely departed from the practice, no matter how mechanized it later became.

Opportunism was hardly unique to fishing. Human ancestors practiced it every day when they scavenged lion kills or collected honey from a beehive. Picking up spawning catfish marooned by receding floods was more a matter of timing than skill. (I've grabbed a few myself as they lay helpless in muddy African shallows.) So was collecting mollusks during low tide at familiar spots. For hundreds of thousands of years fishing was a form of opportunistic hunting, as instinctive as stalking small antelope. Then, some fifteen thousand years ago, as sea levels began to climb rapidly over the great continental shelves, fishing came into its own.

The ten million or so people living on earth at the end of the last ice age had to adapt to an unimaginably changed world. Most became what experts call broad-spectrum hunters and foragers, living off smaller mammals, birds, and plants. Rising oceans flattened river gradients, making their streams more sluggish; they deposited silt and created swamps, deltas, and estuaries, all of which drew abundant birds, fish, edible plants, and shellfish. These food-rich, diverse landscapes inevitably attracted humans as well. Fishing became part of much broader based hunting economies than those of earlier times. A food-gathering strategy that had largely relied on opportunism based on careful observation now became something more complex and demanding. In the richer environments of seashores, lakes, and rivers people began to devise more complex and specialized tools for taking different foods. It was during these millennia of rapid climate change that fishing became significant as part of broad-based ways of survival. The three ancient ways of getting food—hunting, gathering, and fishing—thrived on opportunism.

They also depended on another fundamental human strategy: mobility. Food of all kinds, whether on the hoof, on trees and shrubs, or underwater, was unevenly distributed across territories, however compact or enormous. To acquire nourishment one had to take advantage of fish runs, game migrations, mollusk beds, or ripening acorns. This required frequent moves, often depending on experience passed verbally through countless generations.

In a world where humans lived in tiny populations of mobile, widely scattered bands, the average person might encounter only about thirty to fifty people in an entire lifetime. Yet this does not mean people could live without interacting with neighbors. Everyone had something to trade. We know from studies of trace elements in rocks that some bands exchanged lumps of fine-grained toolmaking stone or finished artifacts like spear points. Others traded baskets of acorns from local oak groves, deer hides, or exotic seashells. All of these commodities were passed hand to hand, sometimes over surprisingly long distances.

The ties of kin, the meat and drink of interaction, also extended far beyond the band and provided links with others, often across considerable distance. From such ties one acquired marriage partners and, sometimes even more important, intelligence about foods over the horizon.

Modern-day studies of hunter-gatherer bands in such landscapes as the Kalahari Desert and the Canadian arctic reveal that membership constantly ebbed and flowed. Such movements were the natural dynamics of hunter-gatherer life. A daughter would marry outside the band. A dispute might cause the loser to move away. A son and his wife would leave their band to explore a nearby valley and form their own band. The constant search for new hunting grounds or fishing streams could mean that people covered enormous areas within their brief lifetimes. Think of the rapidity with which people moved southward from Alaska after first settlement: it most likely took humans just two thousand years to travel the nearly sixteen thousand kilometers to the southern tip of South America. Where there were easily harvested fisheries there were fishers in season. Along Peru's north coast, shallow-water fishing was alive and well before 9200 BC.[5] Here and elsewhere mobility and opportunism went hand in hand.

Things changed first in southwestern Asia, but agriculture developed independently in several places, including China and Central America. About twelve thousand years ago some hunter-gatherer bands in the Middle East turned from foraging to agriculture and from hunting to animal husbandry. The reasons have been debated for generations, but they may be partly connected to drought cycles that devastated nut-bearing trees and wild cereal grasses. Food production spread like wildfire. Within a few millennia most people on earth were farmers or herders. Farming villages became small towns, then cities; some powerful chiefdoms became the world's first civilizations. Irrigation agriculture, cities, literacy, trade, and institutionalized warfare launched humanity on the trajectory that has brought us to the breakneck population growth and megacities of today.

Hunting and plant foraging faded in importance. Gathering of grains and other wild plants is not economically important anywhere in today's world. Hunting may be more important for recreation, pest control, and the illegal ivory trade than for food. Only subsistence fishing survived the changeover to remain a major economic activity.

As global populations climbed, the pressure on fisheries rose. The individual catch for one's family or a small band inevitably gave way to fishing for commerce. Fish became a commodity to be harvested. Since the Industrial Revolution the strategy of intensified fishing to feed more people has mushroomed into a major international industry. The diesel trawler and deepwater trawls, invented to meet the demand from vast cities, have devastated much of the world's fisheries.

Subsistence fisherfolk were concerned with feeding themselves, with harvesting a large enough catch that some of it could be dried or smoked and then eaten during the desolate months of winter and spring. This was fine while population densities remained relatively low. But as their numbers rose, people intensified their fishing, often by using large seine nets or developing seaworthy canoes to reach less accessible fishing grounds. By the time sea levels stabilized, around 4000 BC, intensified fishing was growing common. Anadromous salmon, which return to freshwater to spawn, and dense shoals of migrating fish like herring or mackerel began to yield enormous catches.[6] A visitor to a salmon run in the Pacific Northwest in AD 1000 would have seen a stout weir of posts and thick wattle spanning a shallow, frothing creek. The water is alive with salmon crowding upstream, so thick that they rub against one another as they swim. As they encounter the fence they collect by the hundreds, milling in confusion. Above them, the fishers stand on stout plat-forms holding long-handled nets. They dip them into the teeming fish, and when they lift, the net bulges with the weight of salmon, each weighing up to fourteen kilograms. Each fisherman casts his catch into a waiting basket, then dips the net again. Canoes upstream of the weir carry the laden baskets to shore.

As the male fishers brought in salmon by the hundreds, the women gutted and butterflied the catch, then smoked or dried the carcasses on wooden racks. The harvest fed dozens of people for months, but even in abundant years it could fall short, forcing the people to fall back on shellfish. Mollusks played the same role as wild plant foods in farming villages when cereal crops failed.

In a densely populated place like the Pacific Northwest this kind of inten-sified subsistence fishing led to major political and social changes. The need for large numbers of people to shoot nets and gather the harvest, the complex infrastructure required for catching and preserving thousands of salmon in spawning season, and the logistics of storing and transporting the catch cre-ated a degree of social complexity. A successful fishing operation rested on kin ties, social obligations within and outside the group, and supervision by au-thority figures. Powerful kin leaders often emerged, men and women of ability and charisma who acquired the loyalty of followers, assumed important ritual responsibilities, and had the power to distribute both food and wealth to oth-ers. These individuals presided over feasts and interceded with the ancestors and forces of the natural world. Their followers perceived them as having spe-cial powers that linked the living and the supernatural realms—powers that did not necessarily pass from father to son or mother to daughter. What mat-tered in fishing communities was experience against elusive, often fast-moving quarry.

The catch became further commodified with the appearance of civiliza-tions. After about 3000 BC, growing town and city populations created an intensifying demand for fish. Preindustrial civilizations like those of Egypt and Mesopotamia required large numbers of people engaged in tasks other than feeding themselves, and these workers had to be fed. The ancient Egyp-tian state built massive public works. The artisans, priests, and commoners who erected the Pyramids of Giza subsisted on a diet of bread, beer, and mil-lions of dried Nile fish.[7] This food had to be carefully rationed, which created still another class of worker: one can imagine white-clad officials counting the catch as a bulging seine net is hauled to the bank. They tally each basket of fish as it reaches the drying racks, and again as the fish are carried to the work sites, where kitchen workers prepare and apportion the rations. Fish were by then a routine commodity, as they were in contemporary Mesopotamian cities and later under the Roman Empire.

One can decry the decadence of wealthy Roman feasters singlehandedly eating three-kilogram mullet, but the fish's real value was in the city marketplace and the military commissary. During the heyday of the Roman Empire lesser species like mackerel were routine fare for sailors and soldiers, in part because they were light and easily carried in bulk. Humble fishing communities, socially the lowest of the low, caught enormous numbers of these smaller fish for sale to commoners in cities. Part of the harvest was made into garum, the ubiquitous fish sauce of the Roman diet. Garum was a staple of the imperial economy, traded as far north as Britain. Meanwhile, the fishers kept their knowledge within their own communities. Roman records also mention, but scarcely document, the ichthyophagi, the "fish eaters," in communities along the Indian Ocean and Red Sea, who supplied dried catches to passing merchant ships. According to the sparse written records, they were independent, difficult people who were vital to the Indian Ocean trade.

By Roman times fish were long established as a commodity to be fed to slaves as rations or sold in bulk. Properly smoked or salted, fish proved superior to other dried foods such as beef and hardtack, and it fed pharaohs and commoners, laborers, slaves, soldiers, and sailors. As portable food, it encouraged mobility by allowing sailors to spend months at sea. When Christian doctrine proclaimed meatless diets on holy days and during Lent in the midfirst millennium AD, fish became a staple of medieval and later economies. But intensified exploitation was not enough. As early as five thousand years ago another strategy came into common use, namely, fish farming, commonly known as aquaculture.

Farming the Catch

Just as no one invented fishing, no one invented fish farming either. Anyone who observed fish stranded in a shallow pool by a stream knew that they would remain there if corralled by a low dam. This was a very simple form of risk management but certainly not aquaculture in any classic sense. More formal fish farming began in China about 3500 BC. Chinese farmers in the Lower Yangzi valley had long created ponds to keep carp alive as monsoon floods receded. Carp are particularly easy to farm, and they grow fast in captivity. Yields could be enormous, especially if the fish were allowed to swim in large ponds. Aquaculture became an important element in China's rural life.

Ancient Egyptians, needing to feed growing populations in the Nile Valley, caught tilapia for rations and soon farmed them intensively as part of their irrigation agriculture. They introduced immature fish (and shellfish) into humanly created environments that encouraged their growth. Classic examples of ancient fish farming also come from the Bay of Naples: wealthy Romans maintained ostentatious fish ponds where they raised large mullet, rare in the wild, for eating or sometimes just for display at elaborate banquets. Aquaculture was important in late medieval Europe, partly to feed ecclesiastical houses and provision large households and also for the devout on meatless holy days. But the fish were expensive, and when cheaper sea fish became available much of the industry collapsed.

Some of the most successful ancient fish farming took hold in Hawaii, after the first settlement of those islands in the thirteenth century AD. The Hawaiians created seawater ponds by building seawalls at water's edge. Ingenious systems of grates and canals allowed immature fish to enter the ponds but kept mature individuals from swimming into the ocean to spawn. Water cycled through the ponds with the rise and fall of the tides with little human assistance.

These are but a few examples of ancient aquaculture, which declined worldwide after the Industrial Revolution and the start of highly destructive ocean trawling. Today, however, with accelerating population growth, densely populated cities, and persistent overfishing of both shallow water and deep ocean fish stocks, aquaculture is again on the rise. Today it produces nearly half the seafood consumed by humans.

Astonishingly, the technology used both for subsistence fishing and for catching tens of thousands of anadromous fish (that is, marine fish that return to freshwater to spawn), including Pacific salmon and the giant sturgeon of the Danube, has changed little in ten millennia. The simple double-ended gorge (see glossary), the bone- or wood-tipped spear, the barbed harpoon, nets and traps of many kinds—almost all of these devices developed out of hunting weapons used to dispatch terrestrial game and birds thousands of years ago. As fishers adjusted to the unique challenges of their fisheries they modified fishhooks and other weaponry for specific purposes.

But behind the history of fishing lies far more than simple if effective technology. Catching fish also relies on a constellation of uniquely human qualities. The quiet skills of acute observation and stalking of one's prey as well as innovation and careful planning applied as much to catching fish as to hunting deer. These behaviors came together in the conservative milieu of fishing societies throughout the world, in every kind of watery landscape imaginable. They supplied cities and civilizations, passing merchant ships, and entire armies and navies. To people inland, theirs was an alien, unfamiliar world, defined for thousands of years by exotic seashells that traveled long distances from the oceans where they once lived.

Seashells from Afar

I always feel a mild sense of shock when I find seashells hundreds of kilometers from any ocean. I've unearthed them in the remains of African villages that flourished on the Central African plateau over a thousand years ago. The shells were small cowries, identical to those I'd seen abandoned in huge piles on Indian Ocean beaches. Strings of them had traveled inland, passed from hand to hand. This far inland there were usually but one or two, once prized as hair decoration or carefully sown to clothing. I wondered about their symbolism, the value placed on cowries, a prestige associated with them that perhaps set their owners apart. (Such shells are found even in Tibet, about as far inland as one can travel.) Quite apart from mollusks' value as food, exotic and colorful shells had great appeal. Neanderthals living far from the sea kept them as early as fifty thousand years ago. European hunters of seventeen thousand years ago wore perforated marine shells as ornaments, as did people living in the shallow river valleys of the Ukraine.

There was something sensuous about carefully polished shells from afar that gave their owners status in what were basically egalitarian societies. Seashells like the tubular *Dentalium* appear in the graves of early farmers in Southwest Asia. More recently *Dentalium* ornaments formed the valuable wampum belts of Iroquois tribes. Few shells were as highly prized as the conical *Conus* shell from the East African coast. Prized for their circular bases and spiral insides, they were passed in precious strings for hundreds of kilometers up the Zambezi River in the hands of itinerant traders. The missionary explorer David Livingstone reported in 1853 that in one Central African kingdom two such shells could buy one a slave. A trader buried atop a low ridge named Ingombe Ilede in the Middle Zambezi valley in AD 1450 wore a necklace of no fewer than nine *Conus* shells, one backed with a thin plate of eighteen-carat gold.[8] His wealth must have been enormous, his seashells collected by a fisherman over 950 kilometers away.

Unlike precious metals, shells were easy to collect and process. On the East African coast and the North American Gulf Coast exotic shells virtually guaranteed that fishing societies would engage in long-distance trade. Mollusks were an abundant, renewable resource, valued long before the rise of agriculture or animal husbandry or crowded cities. Their value lay far more than merely in the shell's aesthetic appeal. Exchanges of such shells sometimes had profound symbolic importance, linking individuals and distant kin in ties that lasted for generations. The spectacular *Strombus* conch shells of Central America and the Andes served as both status symbols and ritual trumpets and were endowed with intense symbolic power.[9] Among the Maya they symbolized the Moon Goddess.

Ancient fisheries remind us that the ocean is not uniform but as complex and ever-changing as environments on land. In 1653 Izaak Walton remarked in his immortal treatise *The Compleat Angler,* "The *Water* is more productive than the *Earth.*"[10] At the time he may have been right, but no longer. Three and a half centuries after Walton, industrial-scale fishing has devastated the rivers and seas upon which humanity depended for so long. The story of how this happened began some two million years ago, almost surely by accident.

PART ONE

Opportunistic Fishers

Subsistence fishing, what one might informally call fishing for one's dinner, is almost as old as humanity. It probably began with hominins plucking catfish from drying ponds and river pools in tropical Africa, an activity so important to hominin survival that I was tempted to call part I "How Catfish Created Civilization." I didn't because that title would obscure a much more complex historical reality. But as the most durable of all human ways of getting food, fishing really did help create the modern world.

This first part of the book dwells on three fundamental human qualities: curiosity, observation, and opportunism. Our survival as hominins, archaic humans, and then _Homo sapiens_ has always depended on restless curiosity and acute awareness of our surroundings. In the predator-rich environments in which they evolved, our ancestors were both hunters and hunted. They had an intimate knowledge of their landscapes, the seasons of plant foods, and the movements of food and predator alike. They had to be accomplished opportunists, ready to scavenge lion kills or steal honey from bees' nests. They were well aware that catfish lurking in shallows at the end of the rainy season were food for the taking, not for long maybe but predictable when the landscape dried after the rains.

15

At first, fish must have been a transitory food, for they spoil rapidly in tropical climates. They remained so for hundreds of thousands of years, as did the fresh- and saltwater mollusks that could be readily gathered from shallow-water beds. A human band's survival depended on how foods were distributed across the landscape and how adept the humans were at finding it. Fish and mollusks were essential foods of opportunity for many bands in a sparsely populated world, gathered by hand, probably eaten when fresh, a small part of increasingly complex hunting and gathering lifeways.

At first, the technology of hunter-gatherer life was elemental, heavily dependent on careful observation and expert stalking that enabled hunters to spear big game at very close quarters. This was the world of the wooden, later stone-tipped, spear, a close-quarters weapon even in the best circumstances. Our remote forebears had only their hands, their careful watchfulness, and their ability to carry in their heads a sophisticated map and guidebook of their territory.

About 1.9 million years ago—the date is controversial—people tamed fire, and in the process may have revolutionized fishing. Fire provided warmth, enabled hunters to cook food, and may have helped them realize that their catches could be dried. Dried fish have enormous advantages. They are light to carry, can be stacked in compact skin bags, and are easy to eat raw or to cook at short notice. They were provisions for people on the move, a form of beef jerky except that the meat came from the water, not the land. From the moment fire was tamed, fish began its transition from an opportunistic food to something more.

By the late Ice Age, some twenty thousand years ago, many hunting groups in Africa, Asia, and Europe were fishing on an irregular basis. The most skilled of them had fished and traveled between the islands off Southeast Asia to New Guinea and Australia beginning some forty-five thousand years ago. At the time, the last great cold snap of the Ice Age had lowered global sea levels by about ninety meters, exposing vast continental shelves and creating land bridges that joined Siberia to Alaska, Britain to the Continent. As global warming took hold after fifteen thousand years ago, rising seas inundated the low-lying coasts and caused rivers to pond, creating extensive shallows and rich fisheries and mollusk beds. It was during these millennia of rapid climate change that subsistence fishing came into its own in areas blessed with deltas, estuaries, and swamps, where birds, fish, and mollusks abounded. For the first time the archaeological record reveals tools specifically designed to catch fish: artifacts such as fishhooks and barbed spears, shallow-water traps, and nets modified from those used against terrestrial game. By about 8000 BC increasingly elaborate societies greatly dependent on fish flourished along Baltic shores, in major river valleys, and in northern Japan. As their populations rose, some groups founded permanent settlements, which they occupied for many generations.

Still, except in the richest maritime landscapes most human societies still relied on mobility for their survival. Even those in rich fisheries moved from place to place, carefully timing their annual round to take advantage of catfish spawns along the Nile or salmon runs in northern Japan, Siberia, and western North America. The carrying capacity of even richly endowed landscapes was never high, which meant that hunting and fishing territories were large and people moved over long distances in their lifetimes. It was after the Ice Age, too, that watercraft became catalysts of migration. The search for fish enabled these migrations in two ways: it spurred continual technological refinement of boats and it gave people a reason to undertake long journeys.

Subsistence fishing was a significant element in the first human settlement of the Americas, there now being widespread agreement that the first human settlers moved southward from Alaska along the Pacific coast rather than down the center of North America. In the most favored territories, along the Pacific Northwest coast, in the San Francisco Bay area and the Santa Barbara Channel of southern California, also in the fertile river valleys of the Midwest and along the northeast and southern Florida coasts, population densities inevitably rose. Greater competition for mollusk beds and rich fishing grounds meant territories became more circumscribed, relationships between groups more competitive. People lived longer in one place. Inevitably, society became more complex, moving beyond the simple family connections that had unified small bands and communities for thousands of years. Now there were important kin leaders, individuals who led by example from positions of prestige and who were entrusted with ritual powers. These were never divine rulers who held absolute power. Some inherited their positions through the generations, others did not. They depended heavily on the loyalty of their kin and other followers and on their generosity and careful attention to other kin leaders. Many were what one anthropologist called "Great Men"—an apt description of shadowy ancient leaders from predominantly fishing societies along Baltic coasts, in northern Japan, some Northwest Coast chiefs, and the Chumash *wots* of southern California.

All the peoples described in these chapters were subsistence fishers and mollusk eaters, much of whose food came from local territories. They may have traded dried or smoked fish to neighbors, but this trade was not commerce in any modern sense. People donated food to those who needed it, in the certain knowledge that the donors would someday need the same charity. Commerce would come later.

One of the most striking things about subsistence fishing is just how little the methods and technology have changed over thousands of years. The net, the spear, the hook and line, and the trap were the fishing tools of prehistory; they are still the tools today. What mattered were experience, careful observation, knowledge of the environment, and familiarity with the potential catch. This was the closely held expertise that passed from generation to generation, rarely to others. And this is why, after 3000 BC, fisherfolk were people apart on the ever more complex stage of the early civilizations.

Subsistence fishing continued to thrive even after farming societies sprang up throughout the world. Fishers were anchored to fishing grounds, not to the finite boundaries of fields or grazing grounds. They often lived in fishing camps on banks and by sheltered bays, where farmers could not thrive. Unlike those who cultivated the soil or herded animals, fisherfolk had ready access to canoes and other watercraft, to the broad swathes of coastal waters that defined fishing grounds or shell beds. Some of them, like the Jomon people of northern Japan, may have engaged in some agriculture. Others, like the Chumash in coastal California and the Calusa of southern Florida, were well aware of farming but did not practice it, or practiced it only on a limited scale. They did not need to farm. Even in years when fisheries were decimated by short-term events like El Niños, they could fall back on mollusks and edible plants or catch less familiar fish.

Theirs was a world on the edge. They lived in intimate relationship with coasts and estuaries, shallow waters and deep, an alien, supernatural realm they could pass over but never inhabit, peopled by mythic creatures and powerful creators. Subsistence fishers exist on the edge of history as well, but their brilliant adaptations helped spread the human species throughout the world.

Beginnings

Olduvai Gorge, Tanzania, 1.75 million years ago: The waters of the receding lake shimmer in the brilliant sunlight, the afternoon temperatures so hot that the shoreline recedes every day. A band of short-statured hominins moves watchfully along the shallows, where catfish lie marooned in rapidly shrinking pools. Oblivious to the fetid smell, they make their way through a jumble of beached, rotting fish. A male reaches down quickly into the water and grabs a large fish, which he deftly jerks onto dry ground where his companion clubs it to death with a heavy stick. Some of the band wade into another pool. They stand quietly until they feel the fish moving around their feet. With practiced skill they grab exposed fish tails and cast their owners onto dry land. Well aware that their catch spoils rapidly in the heat, adults and young alike butcher the carcasses and cram the fresh fillets into their mouths. Meanwhile, hyenas and jackals move in to scavenge the decaying carcasses.

Fishing is as old as humanity, a statement that seems to fly in the face of the conventional assumption that our earliest ancestors subsisted on game and plant foods. Small bands of very early humans most likely helped themselves to trapped catfish. We often forget that they were omnivores who consumed a broad range of foods, adapting their diets with the seasons and varying opportunities. The Olduvai catfish, an example of such opportunistic eating, are known from a scatter of tiny bones among artifact clusters and animal bones on archaeological sites in the gorge. Almost certainly some of the fish bones at

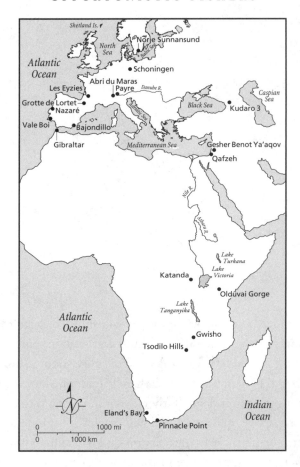

1. African, European, and Middle Eastern sites from the earliest times to the end of the Ice Age discussed in chapters 2 and 3.

Olduvai resulted from catches of live fish, although that argument still relies on incomplete evidence.[1] Preindustrial fishing, in whatever form it took, was always in large part a matter of watching for opportunities and then seizing them—the key to survival for the three million years or so that humans lived before beginning to grow food. It should not come as a surprise that fish were on the menu. Those who hefted them out of shallow creeks and pools knew their edible landscapes intimately. Easy-to-take foods like spawning catfish were obvious quarry, for their marooning was as predictable as the ripening of wild fruit or wildebeest migrations on the nearby Serengeti.

Our early ancestors must have learned that fish were edible by watching hyenas, leopards, even baboons scavenge them from shallow pools during the dry season. Seasonal food shortages affected browsers, grazers, and predators alike. Both people and their prey became fat-depleted in droughts, when plant protein levels are also low. Modern hunter-gather societies routinely turn to fish and mollusks to tide them over in lean times, typically late winter and early spring.

Taking fish required few tools, perhaps only wooden clubs and stone blades for cutting. At some point of intellectual development people would have learned that meat need not be eaten right away but could be dried in the sun, making for easily carried sustenance on the move, and that catfish fillets could be prepared the same way. The catch was nourishing, too. Fisheries researchers have shown that a forty-centimeter-long catfish provides almost a kilogram of flesh, sufficient fat- and oil-laden eating to sustain a family over several days. Kilogram for kilogram, a catfish contains more fat than a grazing mammal.

The Olduvai fish bones are not necessarily definitive proof of deliberate catching, however likely that may seem, rather than simply picking up of stranded fish. Nor are the 1.95-million-year-old catfish bones recently found at a hominin site near Lake Turkana in northern Kenya. Purists may call what these hominins did opportunistic scavenging, which it technically was. But it was persistent and widespread for hundreds of thousands of years and sufficiently routine to hunting groups that one can legitimately call it true fishing, especially after spears and other devices came into play.

The earliest absolutely definite evidence for human consumption of aquatic resources comes from a lowland coastal plain of lagoons, rivers, and swamps at Trinil, in Java's Solo Basin.[2] The Dutch fossil hunter Eugène Dubois found the first specimen of an archaic human, *Homo erectus,* here in 1894, dating to between a million and seven hundred thousand years ago. His excavations and those of others yielded the bones of terrestrial animals and of fish as well as numerous mollusks. Catfish thrive in turbid coastal mangrove swamps with brackish water and other wet environments, and their bones abound at Trinil. It is not known for sure whether the Trinil hunters caught catfish—the bones show no signs of human activity such as cut marks from cleaning bony carcasses, but they could easily have been taken during spawning season with simple spears or clubs or even by hand.

Pseudodon, a large-bodied freshwater mussel, came from the same levels as the human remains. Their shells are of an unusually uniform large size, suggesting that they were deliberately collected for their meat. The clincher comes from the shells of another freshwater mollusk, *Elongaria orientalis,* which was routinely broken open at its most fragile posterior end. Just like the Olduvai hominins, the *Homo erectus* groups at Trinil were ecological generalists, using a form of foraging behavior that endured for hundreds of thousands of years—because it kept them fed.

Seven hundred and ninety thousand years ago Lake Hula in Israel's northern Jordan Valley was lush and green, teeming with game, fish, and plant foods. Freshwater crabs and mussels were there for the taking. Here, opportunism paid off handsomely. With such a broad diversity of foods close to hand and human populations sparse, each band in the region must have needed only a relatively small territory. One of their regular locations is today known as Gesher Benot Ya'aqov.[3]

Human visitors to Gesher Benot Ya'aqov exploited not only the land but also the shallow waters of the lake, where careful observation provided ample food, especially during spawning season. The hunters preyed on Cyprinidae— barbel and carp—both of which spawn in shallow water, just as they did at Olduvai and Trinil. An observant hunter with a fire-hardened throwing spear could stand motionless in the water, allow the fish to come close, then impale them with lightning speed.

Like hunting on land, spearing barbel and carp required patience but not the exquisite stalking ability needed when tracking nervous antelope. The fish were readily accessible only for a few days at a time at certain times of the year. The hunters, who clearly knew this, returned year after year to the same locations, where preserved bones reveal that their hauls were bountiful, mostly large carp more than a meter long. Most of the bones lay in two concentrations, one near a hearth where catches may have been cooked or dried for later consumption.

Gesher Benot Ya'aqov is remarkable for its superb preservation conditions, which allowed the excavators to recover the most delicate remains. But the site cannot be unique: there were doubtless many other opportunities to spear fish in both clear and muddy shallows. Like Olduvai, Trinil, and other locations, Gesher Benot Ya'aqov confirms that the harvesting of fish and mollusks was a routine practice to our omnivorous ancestors and not something thought up by *Homo sapiens.*

Pinnacle Point Cave, South Africa, lies among tumbled cliffs that overlook an arid coastal plain. One hundred sixty-two thousand years ago you might have watched two hunters butcher a small antelope in front of their temporary camp near the cave entrance. A strong southwesterly wind barreling across the dusty continental shelf sends dust and sand cascading across the flatlands. Between the gusts the hunters can hear the distant roar of great breakers on the beach some kilometers away. The moon is full, bringing extreme tides that are at their ebb at midday. A few women and children from the group walk barefoot close to the breakers, feeling with their toes for buried sand mussels. Every few moments they bend and dig one out, to add to others in nets or skins carried over their shoulders. The older women, knowing that the tide is rising fast, keep a close eye on the surging waves. Soon they retreat to slightly higher ground and carry the mussels to the cave.

Most likely the people who camped at Pinnacle Point were anatomically modern and looked pretty much like people do now. Everyone agrees that our modern ancestors evolved in Africa, perhaps 150,000 to 200,000 years ago These first moderns did not necessarily possess the cognitive skills of *Homo sapiens* today, nor is much known about the first movements of our forebears out of Africa into Asia. Also unknown is when modern humans developed their full range of intellectual abilities: articulate speech; the ability to conceptualize, plan, and think ahead; the power of imagination. A common estimate is about 75,000 years ago. But artifacts found in South African caves, such as bone awls and refined spearheads, hint that some behavioral changes, including more adept ways of getting food, were under way much earlier. These gradual changes make Pinnacle Point Cave an unusually important site because it provides us with a remarkably fine-grained portrait of mollusk collecting 165,000 years ago.[4] The use of shells as personal adornment is the earliest known sign of the changes that resulted in today's cognitive skills.

Pinnacle Point Cave 13B (the archaeological nomenclature) lies on the central south coast of South Africa just west of the town of Mossel Bay, where cliffs with many caverns overlook the sea. In the past a vast continental shelf extended the land as far as 120 kilometers into what is now the confluence of the Atlantic and Indian Oceans. Long before Pinnacle Point was occupied people must have hunted and foraged on these now-submerged flatlands, attracted by, among other things, the mollusks in local tide pools. Climate change played a significant role in Pinnacle Point's history: sea levels rose and fell with the retreat and onset of northern hemisphere glaciers. Ten years' worth of excavation at the cave by Curtis Marean and others have painted a portrait of systematic mollusk collecting over thousands of years.

One hundred sixty thousand years ago the ocean was about five kilometers from the cave. The people who visited these caverns lived on the border between two ecological zones that provided diverse, reliable food sources. They hunted along one of the richest coastlines in the world, where the massive upwelling of the Benguela Current coming north from Antarctica converges with the powerful Agulhas Current flowing down the east side of Africa. The mixing of cold and warm water results in a diverse and dense shellfish population concentrated on the rocky intertidal zones of the shoreline. Inland from the cave lay what is now called the Cape Floral Region, which supports nearly nine thousand plant species of great diversity and a variety of small mammals. Larger animals are rare, which meant that local hunting bands depended heavily on plant foods and small game. At the same time, the coast, with its mollusks, was a reliable food source even during long droughts.

Donax serra, the sand mussel the Pinnacle Point women searched out with their toes, is an unlikely player on the historical stage. So is the brown mussel, *Perna perna,* another species taken by the same women. But they are two of the earliest systematically collected mollusks known to science. Mollusks are practically ubiquitous in the world's waters, often clustered in tidal pools or low-lying rocks where someone with a sharp-edged stone knife can pry them loose and toss them into a net or leather bag. Other species thrive in deeper water and are accessible only by divers, and yet others, like *Donax,* burrow into the sand. Harvesting them requires no great skill, just knowledge of the tides. Those who collected mollusks at Pinnacle Point knew the seasons when shellfish were rendered toxic by the harmful algal bloom known as red tide and the seasons when violent storms made coastal foraging dangerous. Mollusks tend to occur in clusters, which is just as well since several hundred are needed to make a satisfying meal. No human societies ever lived off mollusks alone, but they were a valuable supplement when game was scarce, fish weren't running, or plant foods were in short supply.

Intertidal mollusks, which are exposed during low tide, are the most common species around Pinnacle Point. The largest tides coincide with full and new moons, and this may have been when Cape bands foraged most intensively. Modern hunter-gatherer groups show a strong preference for spring tide foraging, and the Pinnacle Point people likely had the same preference.

While most of the Pinnacle Point shells come from easily foraged mollusks, there are some fascinating exceptions. The foragers also collected helmet and dog cockle shells, from mollusks that live in deep water accessible only to divers. Several specimens display slight wear, as if they had lain on the beach for a while and been sorted by waves. Some were turned into pendants.

Unfamiliar shells of great beauty from deeper water were treated differently from the more prosaic ones. They appear to have been worn, perhaps as adornment or as a mark of an elder. We will likely never know, and there are no known examples of shells from this period that were traded to more distant camps. Yet their presence here foreshadows the habitual exchange of seashells over long distances.

Far to the north, Qafzeh Cave in Israel's Lower Galilee lies in an area where food of all kinds was abundant.[5] Deer hunters visited the cave as early as one hundred thousand to eighty thousand years ago. They also collected marine bivalves—*Glycymeris insubrica*, still found in the Mediterranean today— and brought them to the cave from about forty kilometers away. Seven complete bivalves found at the site had natural holes in them, and four of these displayed notches that suggest wear caused by suspension from something like a leather thong. Most likely the Qafzeh people were collecting the perforated shells in order to thread the leather through them. Some of the Qafzeh shells were also stained with red and yellow ocher, brought from as far as sixty kilometers away. Although the shells keep silent about their use, it seems most likely that these objects were created for personal adornment, and that eighty thousand years after Pinnacle Point we can see the full emergence of human self-awareness—and its corollary, vanity.

"It Can Never Be Fully Learnt"

Izaak Walton remarked of fishing that it "may be said to be so much like the Mathematicks, that it can never be fully learnt."[6] He attributed success to a combination of careful observation and experience. Ancient hunters were certainly able to observe fish in shallow water, but to catch such an elusive and usually fast-moving quarry was far harder, except when a shoal of them became trapped in a drying pool or when salmon spawned so thickly in river shallows that one could simply reach into the water and grab one.

At first, such fishing must have been a transitory activity, taking up a few days or weeks in a group's annual routine. It required scheduling, but that was not new to hunter-gatherers, who monitored game migrations and knew when edible fruit and nuts would be ripe for harvesting. Early fishing was an opportunistic adaptation that came about in many places, especially along rivers where spawning fish congregated in large numbers in the shallows. Pursuing an elusive quarry day after day, month after month throughout the year or in deep water far from shore was a very different activity.

The use of spears made fishing a much more serious business. This simple technology began as a pointed stick with a fire-hardened tip, used by archaic humans in Europe at least half a million years ago. A spear has obvious advantages for fishers, for it allows them to reach more distant quarry, often at slightly greater depth. Using a spear in water is not as easy as it is on land. The user has to allow for refraction whether fishing in daylight or after dark with the aid of a flaming brand or bright light, probably an ancient artifice. Australian Aborigines used wooden spears with fire-hardened tips right into modern times, but other materials came into use in many places, among them antler, bone, ivory, stone, and, eventually, metal. Terrestrial hunters at Schoningen, in northern Germany, used wooden spears with long shafts about four hundred thousand years ago. Even the earliest fishers must have realized the advantage of these shafts, especially in deeper or more turbid waters or under ice. You could throw harder and farther.

Fish are slippery and wriggle when impaled, so barbs were an early innovation, probably developed initially for use against terrestrial game but soon seen to work against underwater prey as well. Barbed spears played a crucial role in fishing eighty thousand years ago in the Semiliki Valley, which runs north-northeast along the floor of the Great Rift Valley in Central Africa from Lake Rutanzige to Lake Mutanzige in eastern Zaire.[7] In the climate of the time, cooler and drier than today's, the river flowed through open savanna grassland, its banks lined by dense gallery forest and swamps. The Semiliki River was a magnet for human settlement and for wildlife large and small. It also witnessed some of the earliest known fishing.

Shallow-water spearfishing probably was done eighty thousand years ago exactly as it is done by aboriginal people today. Picture a group of large catfish lying almost motionless in the warm shallows, scarcely visible in the shadows of overhanging trees. Two men stand silently in knee-deep water, bone-tipped spears poised at the ready. Another acts as watchman on the bank, alert for crocodiles. The fishermen ignore the flies buzzing around their heads and keep their eyes on the riverbed. A fish moves its tail slightly, as if about to glide out of range. With effortless skill one of the hunters casts his spear into the water and impales the fish on the barbed point. The fish thrashes violently. Its assailant reaches down, pulls it off the spear, and casts it ashore, where the watchman clubs it to death. The water stills and the wait resumes. The two men stand motionless until the fish return to the pool.

At Katanda, about six kilometers north of the town of Ishango, where the Semiliki leaves Lake Rutanzige, the archaeologists John Yellen and Alison Brooks discovered dense concentrations of tools and fragmentary animal and fish bones that they believe to have been the remains of three campsites used during short periods. The animal remains came from both swampy environments and the drier savanna, while the many fish bones were almost all large catfish, some of them over two meters long, such as are known to frequent the Semiliki shallows at spawning season.

The Katanda fishermen used spear points with well-defined barbs on one side of the head, fashioned from the bones of large mammals. By attempting to replicate the makers' methods, Brooks and Yellen discovered that the bone was trimmed with some form of stone grinder, the edge shaped and then notched obliquely to form a series of barbs. Where they survived, the butt ends of the points had been grooved, presumably for fitting onto a wooden shaft.

From the extent of the artifact and bone concentrations it's clear that fishing was not a onetime occurrence. One or more bands may have visited the same location year after year for many years, most likely during catfish spawning season. This simple form of fishing endured with little apparent change for tens of thousands of years. Some twenty-one thousand to seventeen thousand years ago, just seven kilometers upstream, other hunters took more catfish, also using barbed bone spear points. The only change in some two hundred generations is that some points now have barbs on both sides. All of this is evidence for an enduring tradition of seasonal fishing for catfish during their spawning periods at carefully chosen locations.

Barbed bone points remained sporadically in use into much later times. Far north of Katanda, in the Atbara region of the Sudan near the confluence of the Atbara and Nile Rivers, lie three important sites that date from about 6600 to 5500 BC.[8] They were quite large settlements located in dry savanna on river terraces, occupied at a time when the annual rainfall was somewhat higher than today. Each location was chosen to avoid the flooding during the annual inundation, and, perhaps more important, each site lay close to small wadis whose shallow water made spearing fish or even catching them by hand an easy matter.

The fishers caught as many as thirty species of river fish and collected three types of edible mollusk. Many of the fish were the usual shallow-water species such as catfish, but others came from the main river channel, including very large Nile perch and also the striped Nile puffer, a fish with poisonous intestines that have to be removed immediately after capture. How the main channel fish were caught remains a mystery, but spears could have been used during the dry season, when the river was shallower. The people may have also used fiber nets, which would have made them the first Africans to do so.[9]

By then, people were fishing with spears with points of barbed bone over an enormous tract of Africa. These points appear in northern Kenya during a period of higher rainfall and higher water levels in Lake Turkana known to have been between about 7420 and 5735 BC, where the people who made them subsisted almost entirely on fish for more than two thousand years. Similar points occur in Ethiopia's Omo River Valley and at Gamble's Cave near Lake Nakuru. In the Tsodilo Hills of northern Botswana, fragments of barbed points span an immensely long period of time, from the third century AD to maybe as early as twenty thousand years ago.[10]

Similar fishing practices dominated everywhere in Africa. During the spawning season catfish bred in very shallow, grassy floodplains and were easy to catch with spears or bare hands. Perch could be speared or captured in their nests in shallow inshore waters. They might also have been taken in basket traps, nets, or even by poisoning the water in shallow pools with toxic plants. Immediately south of the Tsodilo Hills, geological deposits of the time include freshwater mollusks and diatoms that hint at the existence of a shallow lake a few meters deep that may have covered an area of eight by five kilometers. Oral traditions talk of fishing in a nearby valley until quite recent times.

African bone points with their sawtooth barbs are signs of opportunistic fishing that came into play whenever rainfall increased. Such artifacts are by no means unique to Africa but come from much of the world, including North and South America. They are not found in Australia or, surprisingly, South Africa. Judging from anthropological observations, they were multipurpose artifacts elsewhere, but in Africa they are invariably associated with fish bones.

The incomplete trail of fish bones, bone points, and mollusks from Africa is a growing archive, documenting a tradition that extends from the beginnings of the human species all the way to modern times. Even today African tribesmen spear and club flailing catfish during the spawning season. Walton was right. Opportunism is a fundamental quality of successful fishermen, who saw no need to change their technologies when the catch was easy to get.

3

Neanderthals and Moderns

Two fur-wrapped Neanderthals squat on water-smoothed boulders above a stream feeding into a river that will someday be named the Danube. Their stone-tipped spears close to hand, they peer into the clear, shallow water. The shadows of salmon flit across the sand and gravel bottom. Occasionally a large fin sends ripples across the calm water. The Danube salmon are preparing to spawn. Some are enormous, almost the size of a man, too large to heft from the water with one's hands even if one could catch them. The two men remain motionless for a long time but finally decide that the salmon are too active. Spawning has not yet begun. The hunters leave empty-handed but with a better sense of when they can harvest their prey. They'll hover near the pool for several more days, then return with their band.

Homo neanderthalensis were the indigenous Europeans who thrived in both Europe and parts of western Asia between three hundred thousand and about forty thousand years ago. (Their dates are much debated.) Squat, beetle-browed, agile, and immensely strong, they survived dramatic climate changes that included thousands of years of bitter cold, when nine-month winters were commonplace and subzero temperatures were often the norm. They possessed well-developed intellectual abilities and at least some speech. Until recently, many archaeologists assumed that these tough people were consummate big-game hunters, relying on formidable hunting skills, brute strength, and simple weapons against the largest of Ice Age game.[1]

Neanderthals did indeed hunt this magnificent bestiary, but they were also skilled omnivores. They had to be, for life in the intensely cold environments of the late Ice Age was never easy. Survival depended on fire, some form of skin clothing, and adequate winter shelter. Some of the densest Neanderthal populations thrived in the sheltered river valleys of southwestern France, where they hunted migrating reindeer in spring and summer before moving out into more open country during the warmer months. There was never enough fresh meat, especially during long winters. Their broad-based diet included salmon.

The Atlantic salmon (*Salmo salar*), which breeds in rivers from Portugal to Norway and along the North American East Coast, is among the largest of the salmonids. Young salmon spend between one and four years in the river of their birth, during which they smoltify, or undergo physiological changes that allow them to live in seawater. These changes include trading their stream-adapted camouflage for shiny sides more suited to the ocean. When they reach the sea, between March and June, the smolt follow surface currents and feed on plankton or fry from other fish species such as herring. After one to four years of good growth they return to their natal river, which they find by smell. Now quite large, they cease eating and swim upstream to spawn in quiet gravel beds in late fall. Unlike Pacific salmon, which die after spawning, Atlantic species are capable of spawning more than once, although few do.

In ancient times the annual runs up- and downstream would have involved thousands of fish congregating in shallow pools, leaping rapids, and crowding fast-flowing narrows. The salmon runs never failed. The number of fish might vary, but they always took place, providing about as predictable a source of food for hunters as one could imagine. As Africans witnessed tropical predators catching fish hundreds of thousands of years earlier, the Neanderthals would have seen bears and birds grab salmon at rapids or in shallows, as these animals do in Alaska today. It was easy enough to follow suit. Even a moderately competent Neanderthal hunter could impale a salmon in a pool with a stone-tipped spear and cast it ashore before quickly clubbing it.

Other fish could also have been valuable, among them the sturgeon, a large, anadromous fish found throughout Europe and Eurasia and probably a rare catch owing to its size. Then there were brown trout, *Salmo trutta*, freshwater fish that thrive in cool, clear lakes and rivers. Closely related to salmon, brown trout prefer shallow riffles with fast currents, where they feed in morning and evening. They also frequent dark pools, resting there in the middle of the day. Nearly ubiquitous, trout are smaller than salmon, lightning fast when disturbed, and almost impossible to impale with a spear. Neanderthals might have mastered the art of trout tickling, rubbing the fish's underbelly with one's fingers until the gentle massage sends the trout into a trancelike state, at which point it can be thrown onto land.

Even in Neanderthal times such elemental ways of fishing must have had a long history. Much later, Aelian, a Greek author from about AD 230, wrote in his *De Natura Animalium* of fishers who trampled sand in the shallows to create resting places for their prey. "After a short interval, the fishermen enter and . . . capture flat fish asleep."[2] In Shakespeare's *Twelfth Night,* Olivia's servant Maria is about to play a trick on the approaching steward, Malvolio. She says to her companion, "Lie thou there, for here comes the trout that must be caught with tickling."[3] Tickling is easily described but hard to master. The fisher, seeing the tip of a fin or a moving tail near a rock in the water, kneels and passes his fingers under the rock until he feels the fish's tail. Then he tickles his prey's underside with his forefinger, moving his hand along the body with infinite care. When his fingers are under the gills and the fish is in a trancelike state, he grabs it and jerks it out of the water. Known in the United States as noodling, fish tickling is a subtle art, no doubt first learned by chance. It would have been entirely within the abilities of a Neanderthal.

Like the early humans at Pinnacle Point, the Neanderthals were never full-time fishers or shellfish collectors. Their exploitation of aquatic food extended beyond salmon and other easily accessible fish to mollusks. At Bajondillo Cave in southern Spain—actually a long shelter in cliffs once near the rocky Mediterranean shore, now within the city of Torremolinos—they set up camp again and again to collect mollusks (see map 1 in chapter 2).[4] They first arrived some 150,000 years ago, when the climate was somewhat warmer than today's, sea levels were high, and mollusk-covered rocks abounded close to the shelter.

For tens of thousands of years people took advantage of this readily available food supply. They collected at least nine species of marine invertebrates, including barnacles, all easily foraged in large numbers at low tide. The foragers carried the mollusks back to the shelter, well clear of high tidelines, fractured them, ate the meat, and discarded the shells. This routine never changed for millennia, even if the frequency of visits fluctuated from year to year. Only when the Mediterranean receded with the onset of the last glaciation, sometime after one hundred thousand years ago, did mollusks almost vanish from the occupation levels.

At Bajondillo shellfish were part of a varied diet, not overwhelmingly central except in rare circumstances. Fish, being much harder to take than mollusks, seem to have been rarely, if ever, eaten. But at Payre another Neanderthal cave used sporadically by generations of visitors between about 250,000 and 125,000 years ago, things were quite different (see map 1 in chapter 2).[5] Payre lies on a promontory above the Rhône in a fabulous location for people subsisting on a highly varied diet that included large and small animals as well as plants. The excavators found no fish bones, but they used binocular microscopes to peer closely at artifacts and bones, looking for telltale signs of edge wear. They identified a dull, greasy polish in linear streaks on some tools that may have resulted from fish processing. Experiments with scaling and butchering modern fish replicated the patterns. And the researchers found minute traces of scales and fish bone fragments, even muscle, on the working edges of the artifacts, which came from occupation levels with no fish bones whatsoever. This may mean that the fishers processed their catch and ate it off-site, bringing back only their tools.

Returning again and again to the same location was a flourishing tradition throughout the Neanderthal world, from Spain to Poland and the shores of the Black Sea. About 89,000 years ago, during a period of significant cooling, Neanderthal bands occupied the Abri du Maras rock shelter, in a small valley close to the Ardéche River, a tributary of the Rhône (see map 1 in chapter 2).[6] Unlike Payre, Maras contained the bones of chub, which frequent calm pools, and European perch, which spawn at the end of April and in early May. The body weights calculated from the Maras bones were between 500 and 862 grams, much too large for the average animal predator to carry. It seems likely these fish were deliberately taken by Neanderthals. Far to the east, at the Kudaro 3 cave in the Caucasus Mountains (see map 1 in chapter 2), a band of Neanderthals ate salmon culled from local rivers about 48,000 to 42,000 years ago.[7] During a short stay at the Rock of Gibraltar 41,800 years ago, people collected large numbers of estuarine mollusks near Vanguard Cave, heated them to open the shells, then ate them.[8]

Meanwhile, On the Other Side of the World

The first habitual use of canoes and rafts for fishing most likely took place in tropical environments in Southeast Asia, where ocean temperatures were warm enough to allow people to fish while standing in shallow water for hours on end. The low sea levels of the late Ice Age caused a huge continental shelf

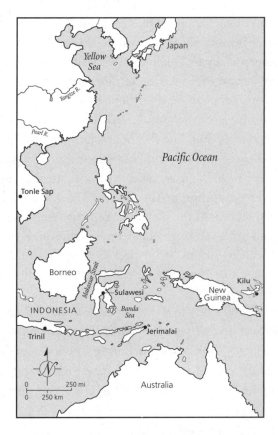

2. Early Southeast Asian sites from early times to the late Ice Age discussed in chapter 3.

off of mainland Southeast Asia to emerge as dry land, known to geologists as Sunda.[9] Only a hundred kilometers off its southern shore, across a narrow passage called the Makassar Strait, was the arid coastline of another, now largely submerged continental shelf that geologists call Sahul, which incorporated both New Guinea and Australia. Core drilling tells us that these shelves were complex landscapes of river deltas, floodplains, and coastal mangrove swamps. People living near the shore must have taken both shellfish and shallow-water fish from the mangroves and their environs. At some point they developed simple rafts, which could be readily made from local materials and had the advantage of being relatively stable fishing platforms. Here fishing must have been a continual activity involving the use of nets and spears, but unfortunately the fishers' settlements are now deep beneath the ocean.

Around fifty-five thousand years ago a raft or possibly a canoe crossed the strait to Sulawesi. Carrying cargoes or small groups of people across open water would have required at least a raft or, more likely, some form of outrigger canoe that would provide stability in ocean swells. Whatever the cause of their voyaging, those who ventured offshore were expert fishers who acquired much, if not most, of their diet from maritime sources. By forty-five thousand years ago watercraft had passed through the islands in the Banda Sea and landed on New Guinea. From there they ventured far and wide. Only a tantalizing mosaic of artifact scatters provides fleeting clues to their passing, mainly from caves and rock shelters.

The Jerimalai rock shelter lies on the eastern end of East Timor, at a spot where raised coralline terraces lie parallel to the present shoreline. When the Australian archaeologist Sue O'Connor and her colleagues dug test pits into the shallow shelter they recovered stone tools and 38,687 fish bones, which formed more than half the animal remains they found.[10]

The earliest Jerimalai occupation extended from forty-two thousand to thirty-eight thousand years ago. The inhabitants exploited at least fifteen fish types, nearly half of them varieties of skipjack tuna. Skipjack are fast, voracious fish that hunt along the surface for anchovies and other small fish commonly found near islands. They migrate in large, hungry shoals, frequent shallow water, and spawn in areas where the sea temperature rarely falls below 28 degrees C.

Most fishers catch skipjacks close to shore with a pole and line. One traditional method involved trolling lines equipped with elaborate barbed hooks behind canoes. Bone points made from large fish spines appear at Jerimalai between seventeen thousand and nine thousand years ago. These may have been parts of composite fishhooks used for trolling or else used as spears.

Jerimalai's people probably also had bamboo rafts. In the Philippines raft fishing for tuna persists even today, the raft forming a shadowy platform that attracts fish, especially when bait is attached to the underside. Today's raft-based skipjack fishing is most effective with juvenile fish. Significantly, most of the Jerimalai tuna bones also came from juveniles, perhaps attracted to rafts with their shade and bait, then hooked and dispatched with clubs. Tuna are warm-blooded and spoil rapidly, so in a world without freezers it would have made more sense to catch smaller fish.

As sea levels fell between thirty-eight thousand and twenty-four thousand years ago, at the height of the last glacial cold snap, Jerimalai became virtually deserted, but it was reoccupied as sea levels climbed after seventeen thousand years ago. For the next eight thousand years the occupants once again took tuna, but inshore fish such as groupers and triggerfish became more important, presumably because they were more accessible in the shallows and on reefs. Perhaps this is a reflection of warmer shallow waters and higher post–Ice Age temperatures.

Parrot fish and unicorn fish, with their distinctive hornlike appendages, thrive on reefs and in rocky shallows, where they could have been speared or taken with small fiber nets. They are grazers, living off algae and plants, while grouper, snapper, and trevallies are predatory, which means they would have been best caught with a baited hook and line, the most common method for taking them today. Surprisingly, only two barbless shellfish hooks have come from Jerimalai, one dating to between twenty-three thousand and sixteen thousand years ago, the other from about 9000 BC. They were made from large *Trochus niloticus* sea snail shells, which have a thick inner layer of nacre and are much prized today for making mother-of-pearl buttons. The appearance of the hooks coincides with an increase in the number of grouper and trevally in the deposits. The Jerimalai fishhooks are the earliest such artifacts known, but, judging from the bones in earlier levels, the classic hook-and-line technology they document must have existed much earlier. The use of hooks would have required strong fiber lines, which means that the fishers were certainly capable of making netting, also useful for catching rodents and small game on shore.

The rafts and canoes used for fishing also encouraged migration. By thirty-five thousand years ago people were catching tuna and sharks on New Ireland in the southwestern Pacific. At least thirty thousand years BP the inhabitants of Kilu rock shelter on Buka Island were catching mackerel, tuna, and other pelagic fish. Colonizing the island would have required open-water journeys of between 130 and 180 kilometers. Most food on these islands lay on the shoreline or below water—fish and mollusks. Here, terrestrial hunting was opportunistic while fishing was the staple, the opposite of what happened in Africa. Unfortunately, the first settlers are historical ghosts. They arrived in canoes or on rafts, camped for a while, sometimes under convenient rocky overhangs, then moved on, perhaps when local mollusk beds were picked clean or better fishing grounds called. Here, as would be true elsewhere, successful fishing depended on carefully planned movement dictated by water and weather conditions and by constantly moving prey.

Salmon and Shellfish in Western Europe

The reindeer depicted on an antler fragment in the Grotte de Lortet, in France's Haut Pyrénées (see map 1 in chapter 2), look as if they are swimming in a river. The last one in the line looks over his shoulder, a doe in front of him. Between their feet large salmon cavort happily, in a close juxtaposition of the two most important foods for western Europeans during the last cold spell of the Ice Age. No one can decipher the symbolic meaning of this fragmented scene, meticulously carved on bone seventeen thousand years ago. We can only see two animals they thought it important to depict.

Fully modern humans first settled in Europe about forty-four thousand years ago. They arrived in small numbers from Southwest Asia or possibly Eurasia during a brief period of somewhat warmer conditions. The newcomers—often called Cro-Magnons, after a rock shelter near Les Eyzies in southwestern France where they were first identified (see map 1 in chapter 2)—came into contact with the indigenous Neanderthal population as they spread across the continent.[11] The two species' first encounters in that sparsely populated region must have been fleeting and sporadic. Whether they were friendly or hostile must be left to the imagination. We know only that the Neanderthals were extinct by at the latest thirty thousand years ago. Well before the peak of the last Ice Age the moderns had Europe to themselves.

Like their predecessors, the newcomers soon acquired an expert knowledge of local landscapes, but there were significant differences. These were people

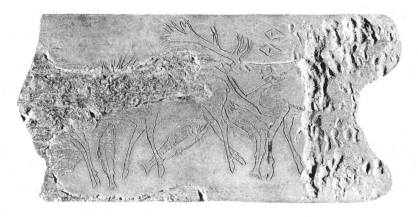

Reindeer and salmon. A Magdalenian engraving from Grotte de Lortet, France, c. seventeen thousand years old. Musée des Antiquités Nationales, St. Germain-en-Laye, France/Bridgeman Images.

who thought ahead and possessed technologies that were far more versatile than the Neanderthals' stone-tipped spears, scrapers, and clubs.

The best way to grasp the early Europeans' approach to technology is by thinking of a Swiss army knife: they had a variety of tools all emerging from a single hinged chassis. The European toolmakers created carefully shaped lumps of lustrous flint, then struck off thin, sharp-edged blanks from this chassis, which they converted into all manner of artifacts, including delicate awls, knives, spear points, scraping and woodworking tools, and, most important of all, what archaeologists call burins, or gravers. Their burins allowed them to groove reindeer antler and bone, fashion delicate ivory needles for making tailored, layered clothing, and create a broad range of hunting weapons, including lethal spears with barbed points fashioned from antler. Some of these have projections on their bases, to which a hunter could tie a thong and create a revolutionary weapon, the harpoon. When cast with a throwing stick, another innovation that extended a spear's range and impact force, the harpoon could break from the shaft inside the prey's body but remain attached to the shaft by the thong.

With such weaponry and their growing strategic abilities fishing and mollusk foraging gradually became far more than opportunistic. From about twenty-four to twelve thousand years ago people visiting the Vale Boi site near the Sagres Peninsula in southern Portugal collected both edible and ornamental mollusks (see map 1 in chapter 2).[12] Their shells form layers through the settlement, densely packed together with numerous rabbit bones and large numbers of bone points, which were probably used for fishing.

This was a prime location for both fish and mollusks. The coast of western Iberia lies next to a rich upwelling zone, which supports today's productive Portuguese fisheries. Anyone living along this coastline had access to a diverse range of marine mammals and shellfish because the powerful upwelling brought deep, colder water infused with seabed nutrients to the surface, supporting marine life of all kinds. Deep-sea cores off northern Portugal and southern Morocco reveal exceptionally high productivity during the last glacial maximum, around eighteen thousand years ago, when a northern extension of South Atlantic currents helped increase upwelling intensity and nutrient levels. During the coldest millennia the Portuguese coast was a very rich environment that could more than feed the small human population for thousands of years. Marine productivity declined sharply during warm periods and is much lower today.

Other Portuguese sites, many of them open-air camps located on sand dunes near tidal flats, show that their inhabitants had a similar taste for shellfish. Some ornamental shells from this area moved as much as twenty kilometers inland to a site known as Lagar Velho, where they lay both in the occupation deposits and with a child burial. Elsewhere, some one hundred kilometers northeast of Lisbon and fifty kilometers from the Nazaré coast, excavations in two caves have yielded unequivocal signs of both fishing and shellfish collecting (see map 1 in chapter 2).[13] These various sites confirm that marine foods formed a significant part of coastal Iberian diets as early as twenty-five thousand years ago, along with birds, rabbits, and other small terrestrial animals.

The accomplished hunter-gatherers who inhabited central and western Europe after eighteen thousand years ago, named Magdalenians by archaeologists after the La Madeleine rock shelter in southwest France, are famous for their magnificent cave art and richly decorated portable objects like the swimming reindeer of the Grotte de Lortet. Omnivorous hunters and foragers, the Magdalenians were remarkable innovators at a time when the climate was cycling irregularly between colder and more temperate conditions. These perturbations may be one reason they developed a broad array of specialized hunting weapons for use not only on land but also in rivers and streams.

As the climate warmed, Magdalenian bands adapted to the changing landscapes. Some groups spent lengthier periods on the open steppes in the north, following reindeer as they always had. Others remained in more forested territories, where their food quest intensified and became more varied. Innovations perfected on land were adapted to catching fish as well. Magdalenians had always taken rabbits and other small game, prolific quarry that multiplied so fast there was no danger of overhunting. The development of fiber nets, snares, traps, and lightweight weapons brought the ability to harvest them in larger numbers. Whereas the Neanderthals and earlier moderns had speared or trapped salmon, their Magdalenian successors applied much more sophisticated weaponry. A harpoon could spear fish in deeper water or near the surface, then haul them ashore with the line attached to a detachable harpoon head. Some fishers probably used leisters, spears with two barbed heads that faced one another, allowing them to grip larger fishes more effectively. All of these innovations, perfected on land, came into use in rivers and lakes to catch Atlantic salmon.

Salmon became crucial to the human diet in much of Europe, especially after the climate began to warm irregularly sometime after eighteen thousand years ago. As sea levels rose and river gradients flattened, huge spring and fall salmon runs thronged strategic rapids in rivers like the Garonne and Vézère. This period of profound environmental change also seems to have witnessed an explosion in ritual and in sophisticated spiritual belief that intensified the already close relationships between people and their prey and added to the hunters' knowledge of the bestiary around them.

The Magdalenians must also have harvested salmon runs, presumably on a much larger scale than the Neanderthals, if for no other reason than that they had more people to feed. Teeming shoals of fish in narrow channels at spawning time could be speared, trapped, or netted by the hundreds, but doing so required careful planning, not only to catch the fish but also to process and dry them. Even a modest harvest would have required closely knit teams of men and women and efficient ways of drying and smoking fish, to say nothing of structures for storing them. Far more was going on in Magdalenian camps than merely grabbing a chance to catch fish. The people would have returned to the same locations generation after generation, erecting hide tents close to abandoned drying racks from previous years and repairing them before using them again. The Laugerie Haute rock shelter, near Les Eyzies, lies close to the salmon-rich Vézère River. Here, generations of visitors combined fishing with harvesting reindeer herds at a nearby ford. The women and children would have gutted and filleted the catch, laying the butterflied carcasses on racks or drying them before large fires. Local bands probably cooperated for the days of the run, or each camped by its own rapids and pools. By the time the run was over, each band would have accumulated hundreds or thousands of salmon, dried for eating during the hungry months of late winter, when game was in poor condition and plant foods were unavailable.

While it seems something like this must have happened, it is inferred from very limited evidence. Did the Magdalenians actually harvest salmon on a large scale? Fish hover in the artistic and archaeological background of our knowledge. The Lortet reindeer scene and other engravings include some salmonids, but they hardly tell a tale of intensive annual harvest. Many of the artifacts used to catch and process the fish would have been made from perishable materials like wood and fiber. The fishers may have speared their catch with wooden spears, which do not survive. Antlers preserve better. Just as African fishers developed barbed bone points, so the Magdalenians used barbed antler harpoons that modern experiments have shown to be more than capable of impaling fish.

Quite apart from transitory artifacts, the fish camps set up near salmon rivers cannot have survived long. Rivers flood and channels shift. One of the reasons there are so few fish bones in caves and rock shelters may be that the fishers processed their salmon at the river and threw the debris into the water. The salmon fishers of the Pacific Northwest often did this until quite recently.

Some of the best evidence for Magdalenian fishing comes from a team of scholars in northern Spain who have inventoried fish remains from Asturias province, where at least eighty-eight sites have been excavated.[14] Only three of these excavations have reported complete details of fish remains, which is a testament to the challenge of researching prehistoric fishing. There seems little doubt that fish were an important food resource, especially along rivers, where people took advantage of salmon and trout runs. In neighboring Cantabria salmon vertebrae testify to such activity at least forty thousand years ago. Most bands took salmon and other freshwater species, for marine fish are completely absent during the height of the last glacial maximum, when low sea levels put most of the sites much farther from the ocean than they are today.

Despite these isolated clues, the archaeology remains an enigma. It is extraordinarily difficult to assess just how important fishing was to Magdalenians. The Les Eyzies region, one classic center of Magdalenian societies, is more than 150 kilometers from the Atlantic. Anadromous salmon were the only marine food available to these inland hunters. Bone collagen tests show that marine resources were a small part of most peoples' diets, with a gradual increase through time—but only a few samples have been tested.

Most likely, human exploitation of fish changed profoundly after about seventeen thousand years ago. People may not have taken salmon systematically before the very end of the Ice Age. But when conditions started to warm, the Magdalenians' traditional game species grew rarer and the landscape became more forested. The antler harpoons and depictions of salmon on artifacts and cave walls may reflect the beginning of a new era, when hunting cultures accustomed to cold-loving game had to adapt to new circumstances. Part of this adaptation involved modifying terrestrial hunting weapons for new purposes. No fishhooks, net weights, or other specialized fishing gear appear in Magdalenian sites. But as rapidly changing landscapes, rapid warming, and rising sea levels radically transformed food supplies people began to harvest large numbers of fish and to subsist off them as a fundamental resource year-round.

The Magdalenians were fumbling their way toward full-time, intensive fishing, but they remained more hunters than fisherfolk. Their successors would continue the transition. Some six thousand years after the Ice Age, coastal populations along the Baltic coast would derive about 90 percent of their diet from marine sources.

4

Shellfish Eaters

No one who has experienced a North Sea gale in a small boat ever forgets it. Sullen gray clouds hover near the surface; dark, steep-sided waves assault from several sides at once; the wind shrieks across the deck. One feels helpless in the face of the pitiless elements, with no defense other than to lie to the storm and hope to stay well offshore. Thousands of fishermen have perished in such storms over time. It can be almost inconceivable that the very spot where one is fighting to keep from being washed overboard was once dry land.

The North Sea is only about seventy-five hundred years old—nothing in geological terms—a product of global warming after the Ice Age ended fifteen thousand years ago and dramatic environmental changes that transformed entire landscapes throughout northern and western Europe. The people who settled the newly deglaciated terrain encountered a complex environmental tapestry. In 10,000 BC the region that would become the North Sea was a patchwork of salt marshes, swamps, rivers, streams, and small lakes.[1] The estuaries and wetlands that defined this low-lying world must have been an environment of plenty, rich in fish, eels, and wildlife for the hunting bands that ebbed and flowed across the landscape. They would have camped on slightly higher, better-drained land or at the backs of small bays or creeks where dugout canoes could land and unload their catches. A wisp of campfire smoke, the soft chipping of an adze shaping a dugout, or the scraping sound of a woman cleaning a deer skin pegged out on the ground—humanity would have made

3. Post–Ice Age European sites from the Danube to the Baltic discussed in chapters 4 and 5.

a light imprint in a world where everyone lived at the mercy of the inexorably rising ocean. Rivers would overflow their banks and alter course without warning, familiar bays and safe canoe landings would disappear within generational memory.

Century by century the North Sea slowly became an archipelago of low islands and then the shallow, capricious body of water it is today. The gray waters with their short, vicious waves covered a vanished landscape dimly remembered in oral traditions. But what remained were the lowlanders' fishing skills; they must have spent most of their lives in dugouts, possibly birch bark canoes or skin boats. Their expertise endured as the bands moved to higher ground or settled along the rapidly changing coastline of another new patch of ocean, the Baltic Sea.

Complex geological processes formed the Baltic basin, with its lakes, marshes, and rivers. Deglaciation, uplift of the earth's crust, and major sea level changes all shaped its topography.[2] As the Scandinavian ice sheet retreated, a glacial lake formed along its southern rim, dammed by low hills along the north German and Polish coasts. When the weight of the ice lightened, the land rose. The interplay of rising land and rising seas turned the ocean into lake, then back into a brackish lake. Around 5500 BC seawater finally broke through the land bridge between Denmark and Sweden, forming the direct ancestor of the modern Baltic Sea. The warming brought a much greater diversity of sea mammals and waterfowl. Both marine and anadromous fish thrived in the changing water temperatures and variable salinity of the ever-shifting landscape. So did many shellfish species.

People first colonized the new Baltic environments as early as 10,500 BC. Between about 8000 and 2000 BC the maritime and terrestrial foods available to humans were exceptionally rich and variable.[3] Human settlement flourished, with locally quite dense populations and a strong preference for marine foods. The hunters became so reliant on seals, waterfowl, fish, and mollusks that many groups maintained base camps at the same locations for centuries or even millennia. But life was not necessarily easy. The Baltic coasts experienced marked seasonal contrasts. Some fish and waterfowl were abundant only for short periods, especially in spring and autumn. For the rest of the year coastal people relied on game, inshore fish, and, crucially, mollusks. Shellfish were always available, easy to collect in large numbers, especially at low tide. Mollusks were predictable, reliable food, even if they were a supplement to everyday diet, as was the case in so many ancient societies. Shellfish assumed such importance in Baltic societies that huge shell dumps surrounded major encampments. In some places people even built dwellings on them.

To the first archaeologists who studied them, shell heaps large and small defined the earliest inhabitants of Baltic shores. Nineteenth-century excavators called them kitchen middens. A Danish zoologist, Japetus Steenstrup (1813–97), a professor of zoology at the University of Copenhagen, was the first to study the hundreds of prehistoric shell heaps that dotted the Danish landscape. The *kojokkenmoedinger*, or "kitchen middens" (*midden* comes from the Danish word meaning "kitchen leavings"), were so named by Steenstrup. This gifted zoologist identified changes in mollusk-collecting habits in the kitchen middens through time, something that did not take hold in wider archaeological circles for generations.

Steenstrup and his colleagues looked back at the past through a lens of well-established evolutionary doctrines of racial superiority. They worked at a time when descriptions of exotic, non-Western societies were adding new perspectives to scientific understanding of human diversity. The English archaeologist John Lubbock was one of those who searched for living examples of shellfish collectors. Lubbock drew on Charles Darwin's description of the Fuegian Indians of Tierra del Fuego in *The Voyage of the Beagle:* "The inhabitants, living chiefly on shellfish, are obliged constantly to change their place of residence, but they return at intervals to the same spots, as is evident from the piles of old shells, which must often amount to many tons of weight." In an era that viewed biological and social evolution in strictly linear terms, neither the Fuegians nor the early Scandinavian foragers received flattering descriptions. "To knock a limpet from the rock," Darwin wrote, "does not require even cunning, that lowest power of the mind."[4] He compared the Fuegian shell foragers' skills to those of animals.

Archaeologists have long investigated shell middens in many parts of the world, from Japan to South Africa, the Pacific Northwest and California coasts of North America, Europe, Australia, and New Zealand, to say nothing of Peru and Tierra del Fuego. Captain Cook observed Maori shell middens in New Zealand in 1769. Early travelers in eastern North America remarked on large shell mounds accumulated by Indian foragers. Few early archaeologists followed Steenstrup's or Lubbock's example. Shell midden excavations were crude, reports on them usually confined to sterile lists of the shell species found in the trenches or, sometimes, a record of change in species through time. There was none of the glamour, indeed fascination, of studying ancient hunting in shell mounds. The lingering stereotypes of simplicity and primitiveness associated with shellfish collectors lingered in the academic literature. Many, until recently, would have agreed with the eminent British prehistorian Grahame Clark, who wrote in 1952 that "a diet in which shellfish are the mainstay is normally associated with a low level of culture. . . . It is noticeable that among communities which pursued hunting and fishing at sea with vigour shell-fish occupied only a subsidiary place."[5]

To give Clark his due, he later changed his mind: in a more recent book he discussed why shellfish had become significant in ancient Scandinavian diet. Unfortunately, anthropological studies of living shellfish foragers were extremely rare, so much so that there was a wide assumption that shellfish were little more than a survival food collected in times of hunger. This is nonsense, for far from being a sign of "primitive" culture, a diet with a large component of shellfish had profound advantages. The food was close to hand and usually abundant, and, above all, it was a reliable food source for hunters and fishers during the lean months of the year, quite apart from being a valuable source of protein.[6]

The evidence from Steenstrup's kitchen middens alone testifies to the great importance of mollusks in early Scandinavian diet. The huge shell middens at Ertebølle and other Danish sites accumulated over centuries, if not millennia, of long- and short-term visits. The inhabitants exploited shellfish throughout the year but especially during seasons when cockles, mussels, and oysters became staples when other resources were in short supply. To quote only one example, the inhabitants of Norsminde, on the east coast of Jutland in eastern Denmark, lived from about 4500 to 3200 BC in a settlement near a deep channel of an inlet where there were also extensive shallows.[7] They ate oysters, especially during the early spring. Oysters thrive in shallow water, usually below low-tide level, and the people who collected them would have had to scoop them from the bottom in bitterly cold water. This could have been a challenging task at slightly greater depths even at low tide, meaning that for much of the time oysters were effectively inaccessible to people who probably were not divers. The greatest tidal range is at the March and September equinoxes. Tides in the Baltic today are negligible, but there is evidence that the range was much greater at the time when Norsminde was occupied.

"Many Dead Shells"

After more than a century and a half of shell midden research, we now know that at least some mollusk collecting was routine in a vast range of coastal societies dating to the past ten thousand years. Thanks to the Pinnacle Point excavations in South Africa and research in Spain, we know that shellfish were an opportunistic food during the late Ice Age. Almost certainly, however, intensive shellfish consumption became commonplace as sea levels rose after the Ice Age. Why, we don't know, but it may in part be due to the extensive shallows close inshore formed by rising sea levels along low-lying coastlines like Scandinavia and elsewhere.

Almost all shellfish consumed by humans divide into two molluscan classes, Pelecypoda (bivalves) and Gastropods. There were other shellfish, such as chitons and dentalium, but many of their shells tended to serve sometimes as much-valued ornaments. Gastropods include such common mollusks as abalone, limpets, conches, whelks, and snails. Bivalves include estuarine and marine mussels, clams, cockles, and oysters. All of the most commonly exploited marine mollusks occupy habitats close to shore, often in intertidal zones, some in rocky bottoms, others in mud or sand.

To human predators, mollusks are small meat packages sealed in heavy, inedible shells. Almost invariably the logistics of carrying and eating shellfish meant that the foragers tended to locate their camps close to collecting spots. If they did not, they would process the shells at the shore, then carry the meat inland. They are far from ideal food for several other reasons. Extracting the meat can be energy-intensive, and the caloric value tends to be low. The amount of meat relative to weight is generally small, except for a few large exceptions like conches. Shellfish processing could be less labor-intensive than one might imagine because mass boiling or roasting saved a great deal of time. Protein values are especially high in oysters, which compare favorably to sunflower seeds and pecans. Much more important was the predictable concentration of mollusk beds, especially in estuaries. They were available year-round and were a way of reducing the risk of hunger when other foods were in short supply. In most societies, whether ancient or modern, shellfish collecting was women's and children's work. The flesh from the shells provided a continual supply of protein, which helped maintain good health, especially during pregnancy and in early childhood. Like edible plants, mollusks were static food resources that were predictable for people who relied heavily on game or fish for their subsistence.

For those who write narratives of ancient times, shellfish collecting is a prosaic activity by the standards of big-game hunting or the exploiting of salmon runs. This is probably why we know so little about traditional shellfish exploitation. Fortunately, there is one significant exception. A landmark study of the foraging practices of the Gidjingali Aborigines of northern Australia draws back the curtain on this prosaic activity, which did far more to shape history than has long been suspected. For the Gidjingali and many other Australian Aboriginal groups, mollusks were far from a survival food.[8]

The Gidjingali inhabit a large territory in northern Australia that includes a coastline of sand dunes and mangrove swamps. The heart of their land lies in the coastal plain of the Blyth River, known to the Aborigines as An-gatja Wana, "big river." An-gatja has a wide mouth where it meets the sea in Boucaut Bay. Here, sixty kilometers of sandy beach lie between two headlands. Extensive sand and mud banks lie exposed at extreme low tide and extend off-shore at least three kilometers from the beach. An ever-changing coastline of old river channels, swamps, and sand dunes makes foraging here a challenge. The Gidjingali look for quiet locations where the availability of food supplies has a degree of permanence. The strategy works: midden excavations in neighboring areas chronicle at least six thousand years of shellfish collecting.

The Australian anthropologist Betty Meehan studied Gidjingali foraging in the early 1970s, when there were about four hundred Aborigines living in four loosely knit communities.[9] She spent most of her time with the Anbarra group, who resided at the mouth of the An-gatja Wana. Because of the bountiful food supply they seldom moved their home bases, but they were intensely mobile, walking up to twenty kilometers a day. The population density was about two square kilometers per person, or, if you count just the coastal strip, six people to a kilometer, a very high density for Aboriginal Australia.

This is monsoon country, with well-defined wet and dry seasons. The rains usually fall between November and March, then the dry season lasts until September, when the northeast winds fill in as a prelude to the rains' return. The Gidjingali knew their weather and its nuances. They named at least five winds and knew the cycles of the moon and tides in detail, the latter because they were vital to the operation of the canoes in which they moved loads, fished, and foraged for shellfish.

Anbarra home bases were never static. Much like the Danish shellfish people, they moved dwellings and hearths all the time and deposited garbage of all kinds on the periphery of their hearth complexes. Debris of all kinds accumulated irregularly. Fires were sometimes set over larger piles to clear off grass or to deter the hordes of flies congregating around them. Not all the detritus was fresh. Older shells and other rubbish were added to the growing heaps. The Anbarra called the middens *andjaranga anmama*, "many dead shells." There were lesser sites, too, some of them eating places with cleared areas and a couple of hearths, again with piles of shells and other discards piled at the margins. Most cooking was done close to the mollusk beds, on fires lit over carefully piled shells. The foragers set the newly collected mollusks atop the hot shells and covered them with green branches and bark to steam them open, which took but two or three minutes.

Shellfish were a constant in the eclectic Gidjingali diet. Modern Gidjingali sometimes described their shoreline as a supermarket. They exploited three major shellfish environments, mainly the open sea beaches with their sand and mudflats. The species changed as one walked out toward the edge of the sublittoral zone. To collect shellfish here required an intimate knowledge of spring and neap tides and of the waxing and waning of the moon that determined their cycles. Equinoctial tides, known today as king tides, exposed the greatest extent of mollusk beds. This was a crucial time of year, for the largest gastropods were accessible only during the lowest tides.

Knowing the tides was but the start. They also had to observe complex environmental factors such as the movements of sandbanks, changes in local current patterns, and the effects of rough weather, which can decimate long-established shell beds for kilometers. *Tapes hiantina,* a clam that lives buried in sand within a few centimeters of the surface, was the favorite and formed 61 percent of the beach catch. Another was *Batissa violacea* (18 percent), a large brackish-water bivalve with a heavy shell, so weighty that the catch was cooked near the collecting site and only the flesh was carried back to camp. *Crassostrea amasa,* a variety of oyster, congregated in clumps on rocks and were lifted as a compact mass and then cooked or separated nearby. Upriver, where extensive mangrove stands lined mudflats and tidal creeks, mussels were plentiful, as they were in beds inundated by tides farther upstream. Collecting among mangroves required knowing the microenvironments where different species were found.

During Meehan's research period the Anbarra collected twenty-nine shellfish taxa but only gastropods and bivalves. Women did most of the collecting, accompanied by their children; they were highly selective, carefully planning each excursion to focus on only one species and talking with one another to modify their collecting strategy as they worked. There was nothing random about it except after extensive storm damage in January and February, when the foragers collected a greater variety of quarry.

Most gathering expeditions lasted about two hours. Children remained close by, and as they grew older they could help and learn. Shellfish gathering required knowledge but no particular skill or special physical strength and only the simplest artifacts: a wooden digging stick or a probe and woven dilly bags or string containers in which to hold the catch. The women would test an area with their fingers or a stick. If the tide was out and the sand was damp, they dug a hole, sifting the sand with their hands, discarding immature shells, and washing the chosen mollusks in saltwater ponds. They used the same method when collecting in a few centimeters of water as they often did in rising or falling tides. Often they took their dogs with them to scare away the sharks that abounded in shallow water.

Anbarra women and their children collected mollusks throughout the year but most consistently during the heaviest part of the wet season. The frequency varied for a variety of reasons, including the distance from mollusk beds and the number of shellfish needed. Visits were commonplace and were occasions when gifts of shellfish flesh, game, or plant foods were passed from band to band. Ceremonial obligations required greater numbers of mollusks to feed large groups attending rites, such as Kunapipi, an initiation of boys that always ended at the full moon. Groups living closest to the water collected shellfish on about 70 percent of days, while those dwelling inland did so less often.

The rhythm of foraging revolved around the king tides of October, the end of the dry season, and the onset of the northwest monsoon. Januarys were wet and very hot, and the Anbarra exerted themselves less and also ate less. They spent much of the month sitting in the shade. This was the only time when shellfish could be considered vital; indeed the Anbarra call this period shellfish time. But overall, gathering mollusks was a very regular activity; the four Gidjingali communities did it on 58 percent of the days of Meehan's study period, as often as they went fishing. The bands relied more heavily on fish and mollusks than on game or plants. Meehan estimated that the Anbarra collected at least sixty-seven hundred kilograms of shellfish during her partial year with them, yielding about fifteen hundred kilograms of edible flesh. She estimated the total annual catch at seventy-three hundred kilograms and calculated that this would create about eight cubic meters of midden if the shells were all gathered in one place. When we consider that people carried on essentially the same lifeways for several millennia of prehistory, we begin to see why shell middens are so conspicuous in many hunter-gatherer territories.

Meehan's Anbarra study showed that a diet with a sizable quantity of shellfish had profound yet inconspicuous advantages. The testimony of shell mounds from many parts of the world places shellfish at the heart of ancient human subsistence. To exploit mollusks was smart risk management, whether one lived in temperate estuaries or in tropical lagoons. In a real sense they were the silent elephant in the subsistence room long before people became farmers or moved into cities. If we are looking for why humans were able to inhabit such a wide range of environments, shellfish must be a central part of the answer. They were vital to almost every ancient fishing society discussed in this book.

5

Baltic and Danube After the Ice

The major environmental changes at the end of the Ice Age after fifteen thousand years ago brought not only rising temperatures, shrinking ice sheets, and climbing sea levels but also profound changes to human societies in all parts of Asia and Europe. This was when humans first crossed from Siberia into North America, when continental shelves flooded and great rivers ponded and flowed slower. Above all, these were the millennia during which the descendants of earlier hunting groups diversified their lifeways as the great herds of Ice Age big game thinned and many species became extinct. Many hunter-gatherer bands settled along coasts and rivers, on lake shores, and by coastal lagoons. Nowhere in Europe were the changes more profound than in Scandinavia.

Between about 8000 and 2000 BC the maritime and terrestrial foods available to humans over much of coastal northern Europe were exceptionally rich and variable.[1] There were major challenges. In the north, Baltic coasts experienced marked seasonal contrasts. Some fish and waterfowl were abundant only for short periods, especially in spring and autumn. For the rest of the year coastal people depended on game, inshore fish, and mollusks. They also relied heavily on fish preserved for later consumption.

Drying and salting game meat was certainly routine in Ice Age societies that were constantly on the move and lived through long, severe winters. Fish presented a somewhat different challenge, for their flesh spoils rapidly, espe-

cially that of oily species like herring. Drying was easy in cold northern landscapes, especially in spring, when the sun shone and strong winds dried out
fish like cod laid out on wooden racks. As we shall see, dried cod from the
Lofoten Islands of northern Norway was a staple in medieval and later times.
But drying and smoking large catches in cold but wetter northern environments was often impracticable owing to the prevailing damp and short fishing
seasons. Thanks to a fortunate discovery, we now know that early Scandinavian fishers turned to fermentation.[2] The Norje Sunnansund site, occupied
twice between 7600 and 6600 BC, lies on the shore of an ancient lake in
southeastern Sweden, close to an outlet to the Baltic. People lived here most
of the year, especially during the colder months, at a time when winter temperatures were about 1.5 degrees C cooler than today. They consumed large
quantities of freshwater fish, many of which archaeologists recovered from a
narrow gutter the people had dug into underlying clay. The site lay at the lake's
edge, excavated on a slight slope that ended up in a pit, and was full of fish
bones. Unlike the rest of the site, where perch and pike were common, the pit
contained 80 percent roach. Roach are small and bony, hard to eat unless the
bones are softened. The Norje Sunnansund people most likely used some fermentation process to make the roach edible.

In modern times a broad swathe of circumpolar people from Greenland to
Kamchatka fermented fish without using salt. To minimize transporting the
catch many groups buried it in a hole dug into underlying clay close to water.
This seems to be what the Norje Sunnansund people did. They may also have
fermented roach in airtight sealskin or wild boar bags, parts of which were
found in the gutter. Stake holes around the gutter hint at a relatively permanent structure to keep out predators. Judging from the enormous numbers of
bones, enough fish were being fermented to support large numbers of people,
allow food surpluses to accumulate, and foster more sedentary settlement.

The vagaries of preservation mean that shellfish survive more commonly
in archaeological sites than traces of fish fermentation. This traditional method
of fish preparation was far more important than one might assume, it being
one of the few methods beyond drying and salting that prevented spoiling.
Most likely it was commonplace soon after the Ice Age. When climates were
too wet for drying, fermentation provided a way of treating such fatty fish as
salmon, trout, herring, and arctic char. Fermented fish and their by-products
were the ancestors of the numerous fish sauces of the ancient and modern
world, notably Roman garum that fermented fish blood and intestines in a salt

brine. The garum trade was a huge industry throughout the Roman Empire. Currently there's a revival of interest in traditionally fermented foods such as fish, which add unique flavors and nutrients to the diet.

The newly exposed Baltic environments supported a wide variety of human societies, which depended heavily on fishing and other maritime resources. Several thousand years of increasingly sophisticated Baltic fishing and foraging societies culminated in a distinctive culture, known by archaeologists as the Ertebølle (after a site in northern Denmark [see map 3 in chapter 4]), which appeared around 4500 BC. Whereas their predecessors were more mobile and lived in larger territories, Ertebølle people tended to maintain the same base camp for many generations, while moving out to temporary camps at specific times of year to harvest fish or mollusks. Their base camps, remarkable for their thousands of fish bones and mollusk shells, came into being when the marine environment was saltier, warmer, and more nutritious than today. There was also a greater tidal range than what we have today, giving access to more extensive mollusk beds at low water.

From studying more than a hundred thousand fish bones from fourteen settlements, archaeologists know that coastal Ertebølle people lived off a broad range of species, mostly smaller individuals, not only roach, stickleback, and other small forms but also larger fish like cod, predominantly between twenty-five and thirty-five centimeters long, and plaice or flounder, the latter rarely longer than thirty centimeters.[3] Virtually all the bones come from coastal fish, some of which, like bullhead, spend their entire lives in eelgrass close to shore. Others, like garfish, come inshore during the summer to breed, then hunt other fish in shallow water. Judging from the bones, almost all Ertebølle fishing took place during the summer months, when garfish and mackerel appear in local waters and small cod are not far offshore. The diversity of this large sample suggests that the fishers did not concentrate on a few species but instead took whatever fish were present during the summer.

How did the Ertebølle folk catch such a variety of fish? Topographical studies have shown that almost all of their settlements were established in places suitable for large, stationary fish traps—locations with strong currents such as river mouths, islets, and headlands where the seabed is relatively steep. Several locations have yielded the remains of ancient basket traps and weirs. One Ertebølle trap found in southern Sweden still held the remains of a forty-five-centimeter cod. Some of these traps were large-scale, permanent structures, often constructed with hazelwood stakes. The fishers also used bone hooks

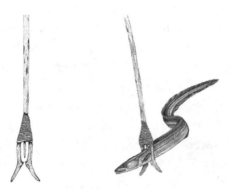

Reconstruction of an eel leister from near Lolland, Denmark. Courtesy Museum Lolland-Falster.

and barbed, multipronged spears (often called leisters), but hooks and spears could not have brought in the varied catches that appear in the middens. Traps were almost certainly the mainstay of the inshore fishery. Still, a site at Grisby on the rocky shores of Bornholm island, southeast of Sweden, yielded the bones of larger cod that were almost certainly caught with hook and line because the topography was unsuitable for traps (see map 3 in chapter 4).

Eel traps are often shaped like bottles; others are conical or spherical. Wooden potlike traps are used on the bottom, set alone or in groups on their sides. Some fishers even fix wicker traps under rafts. Many Danish fishermen still use bag-shaped netting traps called fyke nets, kept tensioned with wooden frames or with posts dug into the bottom. Today, fyke nets can be found on e-bay. Such nets can be deployed in rows, with their chambers combined, to create large systems capable of trapping great numbers of fish.

Inland Ertebølle sites are rarer, but almost all of them lie next to lakes and contain fish such as pike and large perch, which prefer heavily vegetated water with soft bottoms. At Ringkloster, in Jutland, long hazelwood stakes point to the use of weirs (see map 3 in chapter 4). The bones include many large pike, easily taken on warm summer days when they lie near the bottoms of shallow lakes.[4] An old lake at Kunda in Estonia has yielded numerous pike skeletons, two of them impaled with barbed points (see map 3 in chapter 4). Pike finds are plentiful at Svaerdborg in the Danish archipelago (see map 3 in chapter 4), where many head bones come from decapitated individuals, the carcasses of which were then dried, as people did in much later times with Atlantic cod.

The fishing methods invented and refined by the Ertebølle people persisted until the Industrial Revolution. They seem to have hardly differed in medieval times: an account written by J. Scheffer in 1674 tells us that the Lapp people's "way of fishing alters with the season, in the Summer usually with drag nets between two boats, or else with spears like Tridents, but that they have more teeth. With these they strike pikes, especially when they lye sunning themselves near the top of the Water: they do the same by Night burning dry wood at the brow [of the boat], which light the Fish are enticed thither."[5]

Inland fish, heavy reliance on large, stationary traps and weirs, apparently no deepwater fishing—these are all conservative, low-risk practices. Inshore and lake fishing was mostly a summer activity. How did Ertebølle people survive the rest of the year, especially during the winter? They were certainly expert terrestrial hunters, and they collected enormous numbers of hazelnuts in autumn. For much of the year they would have relied heavily on dried and carefully stored fish and nuts.

They also, as we know, collected enormous numbers of mollusks. The huge shell middens at Ertebølle and other sites testify to the enormous importance of mollusks in local diets: the shells clearly accumulated over centuries, if not millennia, of long- and short-term visits. Cockles, mussels, and oysters were important staples when other resources were in short supply.

Ertebølle populations rose steadily after about 4000 BC, and territories became more constricted. Whether people liked it or not, the ways they moved across the land changed significantly. Even in as rich a coastal landscape as the western Baltic there were limits to the number of people the fisheries and shell beds could support over the long term. Interactions between neighboring bands became more important and more complex. Judging from the enormous shell middens they accumulated, many groups either spent much of the year in permanent settlements or else habitually visited the same locations at certain times of the year—in the case of Norsminde in eastern Denmark (see map 3 in chapter 4)—to collect oysters in the spring. Permanent settlements also permitted ties of kin and marriage to cement links among communities.

The assumption that early Baltic coastal societies were nomadic goes back to Charles Darwin.[6] A century and a half later the archaeological community has a more nuanced view of hunter-gatherer life. Pacific Northwest Indians and a wide range of other ancient groups developed very complex societies, often with powerful chiefs and elaborate social institutions. While this complexity did not require a dramatic reduction in mobility, it did change its character. Was the same true of Ertebölle society? We don't yet really know.

Every community, however large or transitory, depended on food sources that came and went with the seasons. Migrating waterfowl were a dependable source in spring and autumn, shot and trapped by the hundreds, then dried for winter use. Herrings, mackerel, salmon, and many other species had their weeks, even months of abundance. Survival in any Ertebølle territory, however large, required exquisite timing, at least some movement, and constant intelligence about inshore fish, acquired through generations of careful observation from the shore and from boats.

The widely differing sizes of hunting territories must also have played a decisive role in survival. At one extreme, recorded in Scotland, people ranged across only about one hundred kilometers. Other territories involved journeys of as much as one thousand kilometers, still quite a manageable distance by boat or on foot. All kinds of factors helped determine the size of a band's territory: the nature of the landscape, the local environment and its food resources, and the number of people living within each territory. People certainly moved around a great deal, to trade, perhaps to contract marriages, or in search of fisheries.

The question is not whether people moved—they did—but how regularly they returned to the same locations. These were landscapes they knew intimately. They observed the subtle shifts in vegetation and cloud formations that marked changes in the seasons, understood the rhythm of tides, knew where currents ran strong and where to take refuge when caught out on the water by a sudden gale. They understood the local fish and animals as well as they knew other people. Mobility was not an unchanging routine but a carefully thought out strategy, implemented by individuals, families, kin groups, and entire bands. This intricate landscape knowledge was passed from one generation to the next by example, through oral recitation and chants, and through rituals surrounding what were believed to be supernatural beings. The most powerful presence in fishers' mobility was the power of their ancestors and the hidden spiritual forces for which the ancestors served as intermediaries.

Even a superficial glance at European societies between 9000 and about 6000 BC, when the first farmers arrived, reveals bewildering diversity. The Ertebølle peoples of the Baltic region were unusual in their strong focus on fish and mollusks, but this is no surprise given the cold climate, which tended to inhibit agriculture in the north until after 3000 BC. Fish and mollusks were the most readily available food source.

Sturgeon at the Iron Gates

Baltic societies exploited a broad range of fish from lakes, rivers, and the sea, but nothing caught there rivaled the giant sturgeon of the Danube River's Iron Gates, a 230-kilometer series of gorges between the Carpathian and Balkan Mountains where the water once flowed at speeds of up to 18 kilometers an hour (see map 3 in chapter 4). (The Iron Gates have been affected by hydroelectric dams since the 1970s.) In the most confined of these gorges, the Great Kazan, the river was 150 meters wide and reached a depth of 53 meters. With their dynamic water-level changes, fast currents, and varied depths, the Iron Gates were rich in nutrients, aquatic plants, insects, and invertebrates that sustained large and diverse fish populations. The king among them was the sturgeon.[7]

European sturgeon are members of the genus *Acipenser*, large, long-lived fish that are olive-black with a white belly.[8] Swimming near the river bottoms with their four barbels dragging the murky substrate, sturgeon are unusual both for their size and for their bony plated armor, or scutes. They spawn in freshwater and then mature in the ocean, preferring estuaries and their muddy bottoms. Once adult, they return to freshwater to spawn.

In the Black Sea sturgeon enter rivers like the Danube between January and October, the peak migration occurring during high water in April and May. A second, smaller migration downstream peaks in October. Five sturgeon species occur in the Danube. *Huso huso*, the Beluga sturgeon famous for its caviar, can live as long as 118 years and weigh as much as 250 kilograms, reaching a length of up to 6 meters. Truly enormous fish of more than 1,500 kilograms and 7 meters appear in nineteenth-century records. *Huso huso* lays eggs in holes in the riverbed along only two stretches of the Danube: the last few kilometers before the river drains into the Black Sea and far upstream in the Iron Gates. This is where Gates people lived. They were serious fishers. Stable isotope samples from human skeletons at two sites, Vlasac and Schela Cladovei, show that between 60 and 85 percent of their diet came from aquatic sources.

Lepenski Vir, on the river's Serbian bank, was the largest settlement. Four or five families lived there as early as 9500 BC on a narrow terrace backed by cliffs and facing the Danube.[9] By 6300 BC, several centuries after the climate stabilized and the river slowed, the first settlement had become a substantial village with two wings of dwellings and a central open space, linked to about ten satellite settlements, including Padina and Vlasac. Over time at least seven versions of Lepenski Vir rose on the same site, the later ones with trapezoid dwellings. Each had a plaster floor and a large central fireplace constructed of stone blocks. A small shrine of sculptures carved from river boulders lay against the rear wall. Everything faced the river, which was the focus of daily life and of the community's elaborate religious beliefs. Its symbolism revolved around the sturgeon.

Life at Lepenski Vir focused on the coming and going of the great fish. Sturgeon could swim against the most powerful currents, an ability that may have cast them as influential guardians of those who preyed upon them. One of the stone statues at Lepenski Vir has a crest of dermal scutes carved along its back. Other statues have bulging eyes and frightening facial features that do not recall sturgeon but may have been representations of mythic ancestors or of fish gods that were thought to ward off evil. The British archaeologist Clive Bonsall has argued that the Lepenski Vir statues were protectors against unpredictable, sometimes catastrophic floods.

The first fishing camps along the river may have stemmed from the usual restless opportunism that defines all hunting societies, but the opportunism eventually gave way to what we might call a piscatorial and spiritual obsession. This is hardly surprising, for a large sturgeon swimming in shallow water is a spectacularly awesome sight. At migration time the gorges would have been packed with them. Catching sturgeon in the Iron Gates was river fishing at its most strenuous and dangerous: even a glancing blow from a large sturgeon's tail could be fatal.

The technology to catch fish was still rudimentary, so what really worked was the peoples' intimate knowledge of fish behavior. Close to the banks at Lepenski Vir the water was shallow, but starting just ten meters from the bank it descends into deep gullies about thirty meters deep. Here, large whirlpools diverted the migrating fish away from the rapids and into the shallows, where the fishers waited for them. Judging from traditional nineteenth-century practice, the fishermen would have used dams, V-shaped traps, and also stout nets weighted with grooved stone weights to corral the sturgeon, and then clubbed them to death. The sites where sturgeon bones abound have yielded numerous heavy stone clubs or mallets, most of which show signs of wear at one end, as if they were used to pound fish on the head.

Most Danube fish spawned during spring and early summer. Along with sturgeon bones, the archaeological sites along the gorges yielded considerable numbers of large catfish, wild carp, and pike as well as a broad range of smaller fish.

As was true everywhere, droughts and variations in flood rates would affect spawns unpredictably, but it appears that the Iron Gates fisheries were so rich and varied that there was never a compelling reason to leave the gorges. Sturgeon predominates at Lepenski Vir, catfish at the satellite settlement of Padina, and carp at Vlasac. Perhaps each settlement specialized in a different quarry—this may in fact be the reason for the satellite settlements.

By 6000 BC Lepenski Vir was no more. Farmers lived in the open areas near the Iron Gates, and thousands of years of isolation came to an end. One telling sign that local fishing communities had become part of a wider cultural universe comes from the bone chemistry of three people among the many buried at Lepenski Vir. They had consumed much more terrestrial protein than others buried around the same time, as if they had spent much of their lives among farmers. We do not know if they were male or female. Had they married into the group? Or did they just work among the farmers for some time? Still, the ancient tradition of sturgeon fishing continued on an ever-larger scale, with methods little changed from the remote past. As recently as the twentieth century Iron Gates fishers would set traps and nets at rapids or whirlpools. Men in boats would then pull in the nets, stunning the catch with strong blows to the head delivered with massive wooden clubs. They would catch large sturgeon swimming upstream in spring and downstream in autumn. The trapping and killing may have reached frenzied heights, just like the fierce tuna killings in the Mediterranean.

In later times, as we know from medieval archives in Hungary, yields became enormous. In 1518, following ancient tradition, the city of Komárum in northern Hungary acquired the rank of Royal Sturgeon Fishing Grounds (see map 3 in chapter 4). By that time it required large shipments of oak logs and the labor of entire villages of serfs working under a *magister clausurae* to maintain the sturgeon weirs. Only well-organized estates could afford them.

Seventy-seven sturgeon were caught in one day in 1553. Two centuries later, along just one fifty-five-kilometer stretch of the Danube, the annual catch was twenty-seven tons. In 1890, records state, "50–100 sturgeons were caught and butchered daily" on an island just downstream from Orsova at the upper end of the Iron Gates (see map 3 in chapter 4). The wooden weirs eventually gave way to stout nets made of hemp and vertical gillnets that caught the fishes' pectoral fins. Fishers also used sharp hooks strung on a line stretched from bank to bank across smaller rivers. No bait was needed. The sturgeon, fascinated by the shiny hooks, were caught by their curiosity.

By the twentieth century sturgeon sizes were shrinking because of overfishing. Add pollution and the two Iron Gates dams, which restricted the fishes' access to spawning grounds, and the recipe for extinction is in place. There are efforts to release young sturgeon in the wild in the hope that they will spawn, but the millennia-old tradition of sturgeon fishing is most likely gone forever.

Subsistence fishing had assumed great importance over much of Europe long before the first farmers arrived in the Danube Basin about 6000 BC and in Scandinavia about two thousand years later. In landscapes of exceptional diversity with rich fisheries and shellfish beds like those of the southern Baltic, population densities rose and more complex societies emerged from patchworks of small bands. In a way such emerging complexity was a preadaptation for the sedentary villages and changing social institutions that came with farming and stock raising. But as earlier societies gave way to farmers and herders and adopted the new economies, at least in part, the ancient traditions of subsistence fishing persisted and endured, albeit in much modified forms, right into the nineteenth and early twentieth centuries.

6

Rope-Patterned Fisherfolk

Just as in Europe, fishing developed in East Asia along much the same cultural trajectory. Some groups in northern Japan may have been fishing during the inhospitable millennia of the late Ice Age, but this was probably a sporadic, perhaps seasonal, activity that coincided with salmon runs and other predictable events. Then global warming at the end of the Ice Age brought major environmental changes in both China and Japan. In northern China a handful of archaeological sites show evidence of people adapting to warmer conditions while still living in relatively open country. They used lightweight weaponry, including bows and stone-tipped arrows, their constant movements dictated by the availability of diverse foods. But the most intensive fishing activity centered on northern Japan and developed as early, if not somewhat earlier, than in Scandinavia on the other side of the world.

As sea levels rose Japan became an archipelago. Rising Pacific waters created many islands and tidal flats as the ocean flooded estuaries and bays. The long coastlines that resulted nurtured great biotic productivity. The rugged terrain inland, with mountains up to three thousand meters high, provided another kind of productive landscape. This was the setting in which the Jomon culture flourished for at least ten thousand years. With such a wide range of animal species, an abundance of shellfish on extensive tidal flats, rich inshore fisheries, and plentiful autumn harvests of nuts and other plant foods, they had few incentives to change a lifeway that originated in the immediate after-

4. Long-lasting fishing societies: Jomon and other archaeological sites in Japan discussed in chapter 6.

math of the Ice Age or perhaps earlier. The name Jomon, which means "rope-patterned," refers to the distinctive cord-impressed pottery found in their earliest settlements.[1]

Most experts believe the Jomon emerged when the indigenous people of what is now northern Japan were joined or perhaps invaded by small numbers of hunter-gatherers moving southward from mainland Asia at least fourteen thousand years ago, perhaps driven by rising sea levels.[2] Almost certainly the early Jomon moved among various locations to exploit seasonal foods in the increasingly diverse landscape. Fish were crucial from the beginning. Jomon fishers visited Yunosato in southern Hokkaido as early as 8000 BC and repeatedly for thousands of years. Excavations have revealed at least fifteen pit dwellings and ceremonial areas marked by stone alignments. The dwellings contained fireplaces whose ashy soils yielded bones of dog salmon of spawning age, carp, and sardines.

By 7000 BC the number of Jomon sites had increased dramatically, for reasons we do not know. The fishers lived in larger settlements, many with semisubterranean pit dwellings set into the soil. One site, at Musadhidai in Tokyo City, has yielded an arc of nineteen pit dwellings, a circular arrangement of houses that was characteristic of larger Jomon settlements for thousands of years. This site was occupied during a period of warmer conditions, when deciduous forests with acorn-bearing oak trees spread widely. As they did elsewhere in the world, acorns became a staple for Jomon groups.

Sites with pit dwellings located near tidal flats chronicle rising population densities in the Kanto region around Tokyo Bay. As early as 7450 BC, when the seas were rising rapidly and spreading into river valleys, inhabitants at the Natsushima shell midden in Yokosuka Bay collected oysters and ribbed cockles, both of which live in muddy-bottomed inshore waters.[3] As sea levels stabilized, the mud gave way to sand, where clams thrived; they are commonly found in later midden accumulations at Natsushima. The inhabitants took tuna, mullet, sea bass, and other familiar species, apparently with antler hooks and fiber lines. All were caught inshore. The fishers on Oshima Island, about fifty kilometers south of the Tokyo region, focused on deeper waters. One of their settlements was covered by thick deposits of volcanic ash, preserving the bones of open-water species such as tuna, moray eels, rock bream, mackerel, and parrot fish as well as sea turtles and dolphins. With the wide array of animal species, an abundance of shellfish on extensive tidal flats, rich inshore fisheries, and bountiful harvests of nuts and other plant foods, the island had all the ingredients for steady population growth.

In such favored locations the Jomon population rose steadily to a peak between 3000 and 2000 BC. The landscape became a lattice of well-defined territories, leading inevitably to more complex societies and perhaps to large permanent settlements.

Where did fish fit into the equation? In 1947 the archaeologist Sugao Yamanouchi proposed a "salmon hypothesis" for Jomon subsistence. Yamanouchi was familiar with salmon-fishing societies on the west coast of North America and with the Ainu people of Hokkaido, who relied heavily on salmon runs.[4] He argued that Jomon communities near rivers in northeastern Japan similarly depended on salmon runs for sustenance, just as people in eastern Siberia did. The primary Jomon diet came from nuts such as acorns, different varieties of chestnuts, and walnuts, all harvested in the autumn and carefully stored for later use. But almost as essential, Yamanouchi asserted, were the dog salmon that ran up numerous rivers each fall. Easily harvested and smoked, they were one of the primary Jomon food sources. Yamanouchi countered the criticism of his more conservative colleagues, who noted the lack of salmon bones at his sites, by pointing out that salmon bones do not preserve well in acid soils and shell middens. Furthermore, since many of the fish were almost certainly dried and then pulverized, the bones would have been eaten along with all other parts of the gutted carcasses. The archaeological community was not convinced.

Today it looks as if Yamanouchi was right. Recovery methods have improved dramatically, thanks to the practice of wet-sieving excavated deposits. Archaeologists have found fragments of salmon vertebrae in both coastal and lakeside Jomon settlements. When fresh, these bones are high in lipids (fat), but they soon break apart when the soft matter decays. Many of the sites where salmon remains occur lie away from the riverside locations where the fish were caught. The bones show signs of burning, as if the fish were filleted and then preserved before being carried to the settlement.

An early Jomon site at Maedakouchi is a case in point.[5] On a terrace of the Tama River, which flows into Tokyo Bay, excavators uncovered a dwelling dating to about 9000 BC. The fill of the house contained enormous numbers of charred salmon and small mammal fragments. At least sixty to eighty fish came from the dwelling; salmon heads were far more common than back-bones. It appears that the inhabitants first cut off the fishes' heads, then opened the bodies and removed the inner spines and ribs as they cleaned the abdomen. They dried the open bodies over a fire, which charred and broke the bones. This dwelling may have been used purely for fish harvesting.

On the Noto Peninsula on the Sea of Japan coast, on a coastline dotted with calm bays, people living at the Mawaki site hunted dolphins, a practice that continued into historic times.[6] Eyewitness accounts depict springtime catches of more than a thousand dolphins that took two days to kill after the fishers drove them into an encircling net. A Jomon site at the same location, occupied from perhaps 9000 BC into medieval times, has yielded the remains of at least 285 dolphins, some of them *Lagenorhychus obliquidens*, the Pacific white-sided dolphin, which migrates northward in April and May in schools of a thousand or more. Catching agile quarry like *L. obliquidens* requires strong nets or permanent barriers set close inshore, into which the creatures can be driven. More docile short-beaked dolphins, also found at the site, are easily shocked when driven into the shallows and could have been landed even by hand. Mawaki was a kill site, where the catch was butchered. An intact backbone survives from a fish of a size that could be easily carried, the flesh transported while still adhering to the vertebrae to share with neighboring communities, perhaps with the people who took part in the hunt.

The archaeologists developed what they called a Jomon calendar, which laid out the seasonal cycle observed by many groups over thousands of years.[7] The calendar assumes that the people relied on four major subsistence activities. During the summer they fished and pursued marine mammals. Salmon runs became focal at many locations in fall, when the nut harvests also produced storable food for the winter. Terrestrial mammals were quarry during the winter months. During the lean times of late winter and spring shellfish assumed a central role. Fishing, like other activities, was closely tied to such factors as mobility, social organization, the varying complexity of society from one community and location to the next, and the religious beliefs that governed the food quest. In historic times a calendar like this was common to the Ainu people of Hokkaido, Sakhalin, and the southern Kuril Islands. Each community had its well-defined river territory, where fishers used weirs and traps to catch cherry salmon in summer and dog salmon in autumn as well as smaller fish such as dace. They smoked much of their catch and kept it in storehouses for the lean months.

Jomon societies are also remarkable for their clay vessels, some of the earliest in the world. The earliest ones, small, round-bottomed cooking pots, were in use as early as 14,700 BP in the south and may have been introduced from mainland China.[8] What were these for? Many vessels bear scorching marks or traces of soot, suggesting they were used for cooking. Picture an ash-filled hearth containing a couple of clay vessels surrounded with red-hot embers. Fish and nuts simmer in the cooking pots, forming a hot stew that was easy to prepare and keep warm, an imperative consideration for fishers who had spent the day wading in bitterly cold water to harvest oysters or set fish traps. The historical Ainu hunters and fishers of northern Japan, whose ancestry may lie at least in part among the Jomon, used deep clay pots set among hot embers in hearth pits to cook fish stews. The staple of Ainu diet—and this is where the pots come in—was a soup known as *ohaw* or *rur*. The pots could remain on the fire for days at a time, providing a continual supply of warm

Reconstruction drawing of a late Jomon village, c. 2500 BC. Artist unknown.
De Agostini Picture Library/Bridgeman Images.

soup enriched with meat or fish as well as boiled wild plants and gruels of wild
grains. No one knows whether Jomon groups followed the same practice, with
cooking pots constantly simmering, but the continuity in early Japanese fishing practices may reflect a diet that also made extensive use of fish- and meat-
based soups. Not all Jomon pots were for stews. In later times elaborately
decorated shallow bowls and spouted vessels adorned many graves.

The more than eleven thousand known Jomon sites of varying size and
complexity make it hard to generalize about their society. The people exploited
a wide range of coastal and inland environments, dwelling in some landscapes
that were densely populated and others that were not.[9] But a number of distinctive features distinguish them from contemporary fishing societies over
an enormous swath of the North Pacific world after the Ice Age. Above all,
Jomon was a strikingly fluid society of broad-spectrum hunter-gatherers
and, later, farmers that thrived in a world of remarkable biotic diversity. From
the often enormous shell middens they accumulated, many of them surrounding fairly large communities, we can get a sense of their remarkable risk-
management skills. These may have been permanent settlements, but much

of the Jomon population was constantly on the move, practicing a lifeway that required exquisite awareness of nut seasons, salmon runs, and the breeding seasons of waterfowl. Mollusks were the anchor for every group.

Any Jomon community near the ocean or by freshwater must have spent a great deal of time on the water. Fish runs and inshore fishing as well as occasional offshore catches supplied much of the year's food. Tending traps, setting nets, spearing fish, and collecting oysters all required mobility afloat. Ties of kin linked communities near and far, and imports like exotic mollusks and volcanic obsidian testify to widespread connections, many of which would have required watercraft. At least fifty dugout canoes have come to light in wet Jomon sites. The oldest, from the waterlogged Torihama site close to Lake Mikata in Fukui Prefecture, dating to about 3500 BC, was about sixty centimeters wide and more than six meters long and was fashioned from half a Japanese cedar tree. Cedar paddles were found at the same site. The Torihama canoe is by no means the largest Jomon vessel; an example from near Kyoto was at least ten meters long.

It is impossible to separate the development of Jomon society from the use of boats or fishing. There must have been a connection between more intensive fishing activity, the development of more elaborate technologies for the purpose, and more complex Jomon societies. The growing complexity of the Jomon world over the millennia is marked by the rapid development of specialized sites, such as the locations near Tokyo where horseshoe or ring-shaped shell middens lay close to or over large concentrations of pit dwellings. Whether these are signs of an intensive reliance on marine foods or of many years of seasonal visits remains to be established. Certainly an increasing reliance on watercraft, perhaps even planked boats, to catch fish in deeper water would have required specialized artisans and individuals who owned and perhaps captained what were now larger fishing craft.

Jomon might have flourished indefinitely had rice farming not been brought to Japan from Korea.[10] How swiftly it spread northward through the archipelago is a matter of debate, but ancient fishing traditions survived in the north among the ancestors of the modern-day Ainu, and fish remain of great consequence in Japanese society. Matoba is a fishing village of the eighth and ninth centuries AD that lies in modern-day Nagata City on a coastal sand dune formed by the Shinano River.[11] Spearheads, net sinkers, and wooden floats have come from the site as well as many wooden writing tablets (*mokkan*), which recount that much of the salmon catch from the river was beheaded, filleted, and preserved and then sent to Kyoto as tax payments. Kusado Sen-gen, on the Asida River, was a medieval port in southern Japan that was destroyed by floods in the fifteenth century AD. The waterlogged deposits abounded in fish remains from the Sea of Japan. Several complete salmon vertebrae came from garbage pits but cannot have been caught locally, as salmon did not thrive in the Inland Sea. Most likely they arrived from some center like Kyoto or Osaka, either by sea or over the mountains. That the vertebrae are all complete suggests that the fish may have been salted, as many modern salmon are in Japan today.

Written records testify to centuries of importance of salmon in Japan. It became a high-ranking food for emperors, nobles, and their families. The *Engishiki,* a ninth-century legal manual, recorded that the imperial family ate many salmon. One estimate places the number of salmon transported to the capital at Kyoto as more than twenty thousand annually. By the eighth century AD the demand for fish in the imperial palace was so strong that fish were raised in ponds to satisfy it. Sixteenth-century fishers sowed oysters on the sea-bed in the Sea of Japan. Not that this aquaculture was revolutionary: the Chinese had been practicing it since before 3500 BC.

Jomon and the Wider World

The Jomon of northern Japan enjoyed a terrestrial and maritime lifeway based not wholly on fish and mollusks but on risk-averse, broad-spectrum hunt-ing and gathering. In this sense they were similar to the early Scandinavians, who exploited a remarkably wide range of foods. Such lifeways were a logical, opportunistic response to rapidly changing environmental conditions, espe-cially rising sea levels. Jomon was a quintessential Japanese society, as distinc-tive as the Ertebølle of the distant Baltic. But one can argue that they were in touch with a far wider world that extended deep into Northeast Asia as far north as Kamchatka, within striking distance of the Bering Strait. This raises a fascinating question: Did the Jomon people play a role in the first settlement of North America?

Both genetics and the realities of late Ice Age geography make it certain that the journey into the Americas began in Northeast Asia. In later times, after the Ice Age, a broad sweep of cultural similarity existed across the far north, from northern Japan, the adjacent Asian mainland, even the Kuril Is-lands, into coastal Alaska. People across this enormous region exploited the same resources, among them salmon, sea mammals, and bears, and often used the same fishing methods. The cultural and emotional ties still persist. The modern Ainu people of northern Japan, the putative successors of the Jomon, still feel a strong pull toward this vast area and think of their culture as being closely related to the peoples of the North Pacific, including even Northwest coast groups and Eskimo tribes across the Bering Strait in North America. This intangible pull must have extended far back into the past. Did it extend back to Jomon times? We do not know.

There are, however, some intriguing realities. Jomon groups were so well adapted to the complex environmental conditions of their homeland that their culture thrived for more than ten thousand years. Inevitably their social organization became more complex and their contacts with neighboring areas intensified. During the earlier Jomon the groups living on northern Hokkaido maintained lasting contacts with people living along the Amur River on the Siberian mainland, contacts based on trade and other interactions.

Even during the late Ice Age extensive fish-rich kelp beds thrived in the Sea of Okhotsk and farther north, around the Kamchatka Peninsula and extreme northeastern Siberia. Kelp fish were a key food source along the Pacific coast and perhaps along the shores of the land bridge that connected Siberia and Alaska as well. Hunting of sea mammals assumed greater importance as people intensified their search for food along coasts and on the water. This resulted in increased maritime contacts with other Japanese islands to the south and to the first known settlement of the Kuril Islands north of Hokkaido, which form a chain that extends as far as Kamchatka. Some settlements from this period in sheltered Kuril bays and coves contain reindeer bones and antlers. Reindeer were hunted on Kamchatka but did not dwell on the Kurils, so some island hunters ventured that far north.

The close links with Siberia are not surprising, for Hokkaido and Sakhalin are only forty-two kilometers apart. Sakhalin, in turn, lies only twenty kilometers from the mouth of the Amur River on the mainland. The Tatar Strait that separates the islands from Asia is shallow and covered by ice for much of the winter, which makes it easy to cross. As a result, cultural influences from as far away as the Trans-Baikal region in western Siberia extended into the Jomon homeland through links that were forged as early as late Ice Age times. Unfortunately, the key cultural landscapes of Northeast Asia are still among the least known archaeologically in the world, so Jomon's contribution to the first settlement of the Americas remains an intriguing mystery.

What is striking is the remarkably similar response to the environmental changes spurred by global warming in northern latitudes—a significant intensification of subsistence fishing that developed far beyond the traditional opportunism of earlier times. That this new emphasis on fish and also mollusks played a major role in one of history's defining moments, the first settlement of the Americas, seems ever more likely as we learn more about the first Americans.

7

The Great Journey Revisited

The Bering Land Bridge, twenty thousand years ago: A howling northerly wind drives thick snow before it, causing the gray clouds to billow and twist, blurring land and sky. Within the huddle of domed huts that squat in the shallow valley like low hillocks, people lie half asleep, swathed in thick furs under layers of musk ox hide, the storm but a murmur in the background. They have lain there for days, comfortable except when they leave the dwelling to relieve themselves. Fat-burning lamps flicker in the gloom as a shaman tells a story of the mythic creators who shaped the land and formed animals and people. Everyone has heard the story many times, but it always varies slightly, a source of reassurance and comfort in an unimaginably harsh cosmos.

The first Americans are mysterious people, the little-known heroes of some of the greatest migrations in the human past. Their untracked movements amid hostile, ever-changing northern landscapes began more than twenty thousand years ago, during the so-called Last Glacial Maximum (LGM), when the last Ice Age glaciation deep-froze most of the far north. The story of first settlement is not a tale of fisherfolk or bold seafarers skirting ice floes between Siberia and Alaska, as some scholars hypothesize. Rather, the human migrations that colonized the Americas unfolded over forbidding terrain where the only means of survival was to exploit a very broad spectrum of food resources: everything from big game to edible plants, mollusks, sea mammals, and fish. Many years ago I wrote a book on the first settlement of the Americas entitled *The Great Journey*.[1] This chapter is an update of a changing narrative that puts coastal settlement in the forefront.

Few issues in archaeology provoke more controversy than the first Americans. Only now, after nearly a century of scientific inquiry, are some tentative scenarios emerging from a morass of claims and counterclaims. The latest researches involve long-term teamwork among archaeologists, anthropologists, botanists, ecologists, geneticists, geologists, paleoclimatologists, and even experts on Ice Age beetles. Their researches show that fisherfolk were some of the people at the ancient table. Usually hunter-gatherers whose lives encompassed the harvesting of salmon runs and other such events, they were significant players in one of the most important and complex migrations in human history.

Both genetics and late Ice Age geography tell us that the journey into the Americas began in Northeast Asia. In later times, after the Ice Age, a broad cultural similarity spanned the far north, from northern Japan, the adjacent Asian mainland, and the Kuril Islands into coastal Alaska. People across this enormous region exploited the same resources, including salmon, sea mammals, and bears, and often used the same fishing methods. The cultural and emotional ties persist today. As noted earlier, the modern Ainu people of northern Japan, the putative successors of the Jomon, still think of their culture as being closely related to those of North Pacific peoples, including Northwest coast groups and Eskimo tribes in North America.[2]

Beringia and Broad-Spectrum Lifeways

Logically, then, the best place to start is with the Jomon of northern Japan, whose remarkable land-based and maritime lifeway was based not wholly on fishing and mollusks but also on broad-spectrum hunting and gathering. They were so well adapted to the complex environment of their homeland that their culture thrived for more than ten thousand years. Inevitably their social organization became more complex, and contacts with neighboring areas intensified. In chapter 6 I described how earlier Jomon groups in northern Hokkaido developed ties with people living along the Amur River in Siberia.

Fish-rich kelp beds from the late Ice Age were widespread in the Sea of Okhotsk, around Kamchatka, and off the low-lying plains between Siberia and Alaska exposed by low sea levels. Sea mammals and kelp fish were an important food source along the Pacific coast and perhaps along the shores of Beringia as well. The intense search for food along the coasts and on the water brought increased maritime contacts with Japan and led to the first known settlement of the Kuril Islands, which, as noted earlier, form a chain that extends as far north as Kamchatka. Some settlements from this period, perhaps twelve thousand years old, in sheltered Kuril bays and coves contain reindeer bones and antlers. Island hunters must have taken them on Kamchatka and brought the meat back to the Kurils. The entire coastal region of the extreme northwestern Pacific was a lattice of irregular cultural contacts, even between people living considerable distances apart.

Were people with Jomon ancestry the first Americans? For a long time established scholarly opinion described the first people to cross from Siberia to Alaska as big-game hunters. Images of spear-throwing humans attacking mammoths enmired in treacherous swamps still linger in the popular imagination. They probably never did this, any more than sea mammal hunters and coastal fishers settled North America by canoe or skin boat. But it is certain that broad-spectrum hunting and foraging like that practiced by the Jomon and various mainland groups had a long ancestry over a large area of Northeast Asia before the intense cold of the LGM. The latest scenario for first settlement assumes that environmental realities virtually dictated that those who lived in the north had to subsist on a broad range of foods. Jomon may represent the kind of broad-spectrum lifeway that supported the first settlers, but they were almost certainly not the ancestral first Americans.

Almost everyone agrees that the ancestral Native Americans were descendants of Siberian peoples who crossed to Alaska over a low-lying land bridge.[3] The genetic structure of samples of modern Native American populations and a handful of ancient skeletons confirms that all American Indians came from a monophyletic group that diversified into two main branches. One represented Amerindians from North America south of the Ice Age ice sheets, also from Central and South America. The other comprises inland groups in the north like the Athabaskans, Paleo-Eskimos, and Inuit.

Genetically, the first split between Siberians and Native Americans of both branches is thought to have occurred around twenty-three thousand years ago.[4] By about 13,000 BP ancestral Native American populations had fully diverged into their northern and southern branches, the former including ancestors of present-day Athabaskans and northern groups such as the Chipweyan, Cree, and Ojibwa. The celebrated Kennewick man, a skeleton found at Kennewick, Washington, in 1996, gives strong evidence of genetic continuity between ancient and modern Native American populations in some parts of the Americas going back at least to 6500 BC, when Kennewick Man lived. Research on this subject is a landscape of shifting sands, but at this point the genetic evidence points reasonably firmly to a single migration eastward sometime during the late Ice Age, twenty to fifteen thousand years ago. This offers a baseline for taking a closer look at the people behind the migration and the ways they might have lived.

The story of what happened begins in the extreme cold of the LGM, at its height twenty-one thousand years ago.[5] Temperatures were 5.1 degrees C lower than those of today, and ice sheets covered the northern latitudes. Widespread aridity expanded deserts and shrank grasslands at all latitudes. Plant and animal productivities fell to levels that could not sustain human populations, forcing people living in what are now temperate and semiarid regions to retreat to warmer, better-watered areas. A scatter of pre-LGM sites in Northeast Asia shows that cold-adapted hunters, who had expanded into northern Eurasia between forty thousand and twenty-eight thousand years ago, abandoned much of that range in the face of extreme cold between 24,000 and 21,000 BP.

Quite apart from the aridity and extreme cold, the harsh landscape would have been largely treeless, making firewood unavailable. Modern experiments have shown that at least some timber is needed to kindle fires even if people are able to rely on mammoth limb bone "logs" scavenged from predator kills or dead beasts and other bone fuel. The only recourse was to move south into warmer, if still severe, environments or to a refugium. This seems to have been what happened. Unlikely as it may sound, one such refuge was in the heart of Beringia.

Beringia was a vast swathe of northern lands that extended from Siberia's Lena River and Verkoyansk Mountains to the Mackenzie River in Canada's Northwest Territories. Its southern boundary includes all of the Kamchatka Peninsula, which was much larger during the height of the late Ice Age, when sea levels were far below today's.[6] The region's heart was the low-lying Bering Land Bridge that once joined Siberia and Alaska. Paleoecologists once assumed that the land bridge was a bitterly cold place covered by a virtually uninterrupted swathe of steppe-tundra that extended from Eurasia across into Alaska, with shallow river valleys inhabited by sparse numbers of giant herbivores—

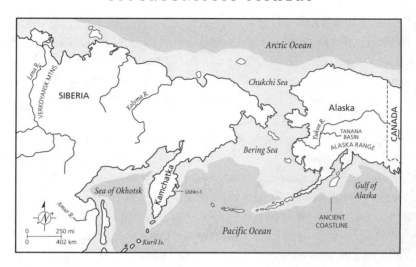

5. The far north during first settlement of the Americas: Beringia and the Bering Land Bridge when fully exposed, as discussed in chapter 7.

a dry, dusty, windy, and inhospitable land. From this bleak portrait stemmed another one, of tiny bands from Siberia who survived by hunting big game in one of the harshest landscapes on earth.

Core borings into the islands and seabed of the Bering Strait have upended this chilly portrait. Temperatures in much of Beringia during the LGM were not much lower than they are today, although many parts were considerably drier. Far from being a landscape of unremitting severity the land bridge was a diverse tapestry of environments, a slightly more temperate landscape bounded to the west by the extreme cold of mainland Northeast Asia and to the east by the great ice sheets that mantled huge tracts of North America. The steppe plant communities of the land bridge supported a remarkably high biomass of large mammals, many of which had been hunted by Ice Age peoples in western Siberia and Eurasia for millennia. The heart of the Bering Land Bridge became an unlikely refugium above 60 degrees north. Cores bored into the now-submerged land surface reveal scrub tundra vegetation and occasional trees. This landscape stood in sharp contrast to those in what is now Siberia and Alaska, which were either ice-covered or extremely cold. The refugium existed because of the North Pacific circulation. Much like the Gulf Stream, which today allows palm trees to grow in parts of Scotland, the North Pacific circulation brought moister and warmer conditions to the heart of the land bridge.[7]

Were there humans in the refugium during the LGM? It is certain that there were, not because of known archaeological sites but because of newly acquired genetic data from modern populations. Native Americans are descended from groups that lived in the refugium and were isolated from their mainland Siberian ancestors during the LGM. This scenario has groups of hunter-gatherers living there during the coldest millennia. As the climate warmed up after sixteen to seventeen thousand years ago, animal and plant productivity throughout Beringia soared, allowing people to expand into hitherto uninhabitable areas. They followed the expanding scrub tundra east and west, not only back into Siberia but also into Alaska. A few archaeological sites on higher ground on either side of the Bering Strait document a human presence fourteen to fifteen thousand years ago. On the American side, much population movement depended on the retreat of the gigantic ice sheets that had covered most of northern North America from the Atlantic to the Pacific. This scenario, which envisages a human population of perhaps as many as ten thousand people but perhaps far fewer confined to the land bridge refugium, is known as the Beringian Standstill Hypothesis. It is unproven but seems to dovetail with the known facts.[8]

By all indications the inhabitants of both Northeast Asia and Alaska during the warming millennia lived in small, highly mobile bands. Most of them relied on lightweight tool kits and used tiny, razor-sharp stone blades (microblades) as barbs for highly portable weapons, reflecting a lifeway that involved constant movement and the obtaining of food from all manner of sources in arid landscapes with widely dispersed food and water supplies. By this time, too, some groups were using quite complex bone and ivory artifacts. At the Ushki I site on Kamchatka the Russian archaeologist Nikolai Dikov unearthed a badly preserved burial and several structures dating to thirteen thousand years ago; he also uncovered lethal stone points, bird bones, and some traces of salmon caught by people with an elaborate but unfortunately poorly preserved bone-and-ivory tool kit.

The renewed settlement took hold around fifteen thousand years ago, a time when mean summer temperatures were rising in much of Beringia. Evidence for this comes from fossil beetles, creatures that are sensitive to temperature change and a rise in moisture, which caused the shrub tundra to give way to scattered beech and aspen/poplar tree coverage. At about the same time, many larger grazing mammals, like the mammoths and wild horses of earlier times, became completely extinct.

On the Alaskan side, undisputed very early sites are extremely rare. By around 13,800 years ago, when lake levels rose and shrub tundra became widespread in the northern foothills of the Alaska Range, there was sparse but widespread human occupation in eastern Beringia. The Tanana Basin in central Alaska has yielded three sites, the earliest levels of which date to around 14,000 and 13,400 years ago. Here, microblades duly appear, largely identical to those from Siberian sites. One of the Tanana locations, known as Broken Mammoth, has yielded the bones of large and smaller game as well as those of birds and a few poorly preserved salmon remains. The inhabitants of the Tanana sites practiced a broad-based hunting and foraging economy in which fish played a minor, opportunistic part, especially easily taken salmon, presumably in spawning season. Judging from these locations and from Ushki 1 on Kamchatka, the first Alaskans were broad-spectrum hunters and foragers. They must have eaten everything from caribou, musk ox, and elk to small mammals, birds, and fish.

What role did fishing play in the first settlement of both Beringia and the Americas? The population movements out of the Beringian refugium resulted from warmer temperatures and greater ecological productivity, rising sea levels that encroached on the low terrain, and the classic penchant of hunter-gatherers to explore new territories over the horizon in an endless cycle of opportunism. Given that they lived in a heterogeneous, arid, windy landscape that was under siege, it's no wonder the Beringians were on the move. The land bridge vanished completely around 11,600 years ago. As sea levels continued to rise, the waters flooded river valleys and created coastal shallows that could have been rich environments for fish and mollusks, especially in areas where kelp beds flourished. There may also have been salmon runs. Could the first Americans have been coastal fishing people rather than the terrestrial hunters assumed by earlier scenarios?

In theory land bridge coasts could have abounded in marine foods of all kinds, including sea mammals, but the ice-strewn, often ice-covered waters were hazardous to navigate except possibly in the summer months. The inhabitants could exploit spawning fish populations and collect mollusks from the shore, but any serious fishing and sea mammal hunting would have required watercraft, which in these landscapes with stunted tree growth would have meant skin boats, the remote ancestors of Eskimo kayaks—fast, maneuverable, and remarkably seaworthy vessels. There is ample evidence that the Ainu of the Kuril Islands and the Eskimo of the Bering Strait were expert sea

fishers in later times. The strands of commonality among maritime populations across the far north make it tempting to think that the Beringians might
have been sea fishers as well, but the question remains: How soon after the Ice
Age did this focus on the ocean and on fishing take hold?

No one can doubt that those who first settled Beringia were well aware of
sea mammals and salmon runs and of other fish that could be caught, perhaps
in kelp beds near to shore. Whether these foods were taken opportunistically,
at certain seasons of the year, or systematically remains a mystery. Judging
from the very sparse archaeological signature, the first people over the Bering
Land Bridge were broad-spectrum hunters who consumed fish and mollusks
when the opportunity arose. To hypothesize that the first settlement of Alaska
was purely in the hands of fisherfolk using skin boats stretches the little existing evidence to the breaking point.

The earliest known evidence of salmon fishing in Alaska comes from the
Upward Sun River site, located not at the coast but about fourteen hundred
kilometers from the mouth of the Yukon River, near where it meets the Tanana
River. Bones from a hearth associated with a structure date to about 11,500
years ago, from fish caught long after humans entered Alaska.[9] Using stable
isotope analysis and DNA from the fish vertebrae, the researchers identified
them as chum salmon.

Chum are a North Pacific species that travel enormous distances up rivers
on both sides of the Bering Strait, up the Amur as well as the Yukon, and also
spawn in Korean and Japanese waters. They are known as far south as California. In Alaska they journey upstream for spawning in June and August. Their
runs, which apparently go back to just after the Ice Age if not earlier, are predictable and often abundant, making them ideal quarry for hunter-gatherers
constantly on the move. Exploiting chum salmon runs must have been a
seasonal activity, which would have allowed the people to dry or smoke large
catches for later consumption.

The deposits at Upward Sun also held the bones of ground squirrels,
grouse, and other birds and mammals, giving a picture somewhat like the one
from earlier Beringian sites: the inhabitants were broad-spectrum hunters, but
in this case their options included salmon, which had the advantage of being
abundant as well as predictable. These people were not fisherfolk in the classic
sense of a group that subsisted on fish to the virtual exclusion of other foods.
The time when intensive fishing to the virtual exclusion of other hunting and
foraging activities was far in the future.

A plausible scenario for the first settlement of extreme northern North America is thus slowly coming into focus. The first groups, which arrived about fifteen thousand years ago, may have once lived in the Beringian refugium and moved both east and west as rising sea levels began to inundate the land bridge's central lowlands. Their stone tool kits included tanged spear points like those found in both Kamchatka and Alaska, but perhaps not the efficient microblades of slightly later times.

The little that is known of the first settlers suggests that they were perfectly capable of harvesting salmon runs, as were the microblade users who followed in their footsteps as post–Ice Age conditions settled over Beringia. Everywhere, the hunters of earlier times adapted to rapidly warming conditions in which the large mammals of yesteryear were becoming extinct. What saved them was that they were never exclusively big-game hunters: they had always lived by broad-based hunting and foraging. As the large mammals grew scarcer, both waterfowl and fish became increasingly important elements in their diet.

Herein lies the essence of fishing's inception in North America. Just as it was in Africa and elsewhere thousands of years earlier, fishing was an opportunistic activity, practiced when the chance arose. As northern temperatures grew warmer, the harvesting of salmon-crowded rivers at spawning time assumed ever-greater importance, especially after the Younger Dryas, a one-thousand-year cold period that brought tundra conditions to the north beginning about eleven thousand years ago.

Knowledge of fishing, especially of the harvesting of anadromous species like salmon, was probably commonplace during the LGM, when fish and mollusks may have abounded on the southern shore of the land bridge. But such foods were most likely opportunistic quarry rather than the impetus that drove groups to move down the Bering coastline to a new home on the Alaskan side. Only later, as temperatures warmed and people lived habitually along newly inundated coasts and estuaries, did fish and mollusks form the main core of human diets in the Bering Strait, out through the Aleutian Islands, along the Southeast Alaskan coast, and into the Pacific Northwest.

Exactly when watercraft adapted to arctic waters came into use and how they were developed will probably always be a mystery. The remains of these early craft have long perished. Anyone who had fashioned a hide into a simple container would have known that it could be waterproof and would float. In river valleys like the Amur and on Kamchatka and the Kuril Islands such simple watercraft might have become commonplace soon after temperatures warmed. It would have been impossible to fish intensively in these fretted coastal environments without at least simple vessels. People who set out in such boats to find fish or sea mammals would inevitably have ventured across more open water on calm days, especially if they could see their destination on the horizon.

It's reasonable to assume that this technology did spread across the north into Alaska, but the knowledge of how to fashion such craft may have arrived faster than the vessels themselves. Paddling and fishing expertise may not have been immediately put to use by broad-spectrum hunters, whose main activities took place on land or on riverbanks and lakeshores. These were much more benign environments than a churning ocean, where strong winds and steep waves were constant hazards and the waters were cold enough to kill a swimmer within minutes. Only later, probably around the time the Bering Land Bridge finally vanished, did hunters on both sides of the strait begin spending more time afloat. Eventually, though, the knowledge was put into practice, and in some cultures, such as that of the Aleuts to the south, even young children spent most of their lives aboard skin craft. For these populations, most food came from the ocean and food-rich estuaries, where shallow waters provided spawning fish and plentiful mollusks.

To the South

The great North American ice sheets extended as far south as the Great Lakes and into the Seattle region. The two enormous glaciers, the Cordilleran in the west and the Laurentide in the east, merged about thirty thousand years ago, blocking any human access to areas to the south for millennia. Overland movement southward had to wait until about thirteen thousand years BP, when the ice sheets melted sufficiently to create what is famously known as the ice-free corridor between the two retreating masses. About five thousand years earlier, though, the Cordilleran ice had receded inland from the northwestern Pacific coast, leaving a potential shoreline route for humans to move southward into the heart of the uninhabited continent.

By all indications, the retreat of North American ice sheets brought a rapid movement of small numbers of human settlers southward into the heart of North America. The archaeological signature of these settlers before about eleven thousand years ago is meager at best, consisting mainly of small traces of brief stops at convenient locations, often near water or where a large mammal was killed and butchered.

The diverse landscapes south of the ice sheets were much warmer and more favorable than those of the far north, with reasonably plentiful food of all kinds. Human settlement of North, Central, and South America was astoundingly rapid. Scattered hunting bands penetrated as far south as Patagonia by at least thirteen thousand years ago. That some of these people ate fish is unquestionable, but controversy surrounds the pioneers' route. Did they penetrate to the heart of North America by crossing rugged interior terrain, then traversing the narrow ice-free corridor that developed between the two great ice sheets where food was scarce? Given the low carrying capacity of the land, they would have had to move through pretty fast in the hunter's normal response to resource-poor landscapes. Or did they slowly migrate down the Southeast Alaskan and British Columbian coasts, then move inland when they reached more temperate landscapes in the Pacific Northwest?

The western border of the Cordilleran ice sheet had begun retreating inland from the Pacific by seventeen thousand years ago, exposing some quite extensive areas of continental shelf that apparently supported shrub tundra until rising sea levels flooded them. The same rising ocean also drowned whatever human settlements lay at water's edge along the shelf. Without question there were human groups that settled on the exposed lowlands, where islands of higher ground created sheltered waters along much of the coast. Such channels and estuaries would have abounded with marine life. Perhaps it was here, on the eastern side of the North Pacific, that watercraft first came into their own, especially as people moved into the heavily forested landscapes of what is now the Pacific Northwest. Large wooden canoes with dug-out hulls and high ends, their sides raised with carefully split planks lashed together with strong plant fibers, would have been ideal for fishing, especially for large bottom fish such as halibut, which abound in these waters.

How fast and exactly when the first human settlers of the coast reached areas like Haida Gwaai (the Queen Charlotte Islands) of northern British Columbia is uncertain, not because the coast was uninhabited—far from it— but because their villages now lie underwater.[10] Only suggestive traces of their presence survive on higher ground. No sites earlier than about 13,300 years ago are known from along the coast. Two caves on Haida Gwaai date to around 12,800 years ago but with no surviving remains of fish.

The Kilgii Gwaai site, in the intertidal zone between Moresby and Kunghit Islands, was occupied about 10,700 years ago. Here, people caught rockfish like halibut and lingcod as well as sea mammals. Microblade users occupied On-Your-Knees Cave to the north on Prince of Wales Island in Southeast Alaska about 7200 BC. Human remains found in the cavern have stable isotope signatures that indicate a diet rich in maritime foods. Do these transitory occupations hint at a separate migration southward from Beringia along the Pacific coast? The notion receives significant support from a site far to the south, on the Channel Islands of southern California (see map 6 in chapter 8).

The Arlington Springs site, on Santa Rosa Island in the Santa Barbara Channel, dates to about thirteen thousand years ago and has yielded bird, fish, and sea mammal bones (see map 6 in chapter 8).[11] At that time the island was accessible from the mainland via a series of relatively short open-water voyages over what was often a calm Pacific. This site is a clear sign of rapid movement southward. Its presence in the Santa Barbara Channel, where natural upwelling created exceptionally rich coastal fisheries in later times, suggests that the settlers may have been sufficiently dependent on fish to look for such places—or at least to stop there when they found one.

The same pattern of rapid settlement, especially along richly endowed tropical coastlines, extended into South America. The Huaca Prieta site in northern coastal Peru has yielded traces of human habitation dating to about fourteen thousand years ago.[12] At the time it was occupied, the site lay at least twenty kilometers inland. The inhabitants caught fish, including such formidable prey as sharks, pursued sea mammals, and collected crabs and mollusks. Another location, Quebrada Jaguay on the southern Peruvian coast, was occupied a millennium later and also yielded fish and clams. The human populations may have been small, but the fisheries would have been very rich. People equipped with simple watercraft could exploit kelp beds and harvest anchovies near shore. Such plentiful food could well have fostered more permanent settlements, given that the extremely arid landscapes inland would not have encouraged exploration.

A plausible scenario asserts that the settlement of the Americas began with the movement of broad-spectrum hunter-gatherers out of Beringia onto higher ground. Then came rapid movements southward, probably both along the coast and inland, which depended to a considerable degree on watercraft and fishing expertise deeply embedded in the settlers' traditional knowledge. Beginning as a subsistence strategy deployed when the opportunity arose, fishing was later developed to a high pitch, as broad-spectrum hunting diversified into more intensive food quests with new focuses—smaller game, plant foods, and fish and mollusks. Eventually, rich fisheries and human ingenuity combined to create much more complex societies in the Americas.

Fishers on the Pacific Northwest Coast

No one knows when fishing and sea mammal hunting became truly important along Alaskan shores. Nor do we know when Alaskans first paddled out, island to island, from the mainland deep into the Aleutian chain. By about nine thousand years ago some remote ancestors of the modern-day Aleut lived at Anangula, an islet about 2.4 kilometers long off the western shore of Umnak Island, far out in the central Aleutians.[1] The small community lived in houses dug partly into the ground and entered through the roof. A semisubterranean existence was desirable in this environment of high seas and savage winds, where the only consistently available foods were fish, mollusks, and sea mammals. Even in the nineteenth century enormous halibut weighing as much as 136 kilograms were caught near the island.

Fishing these frigid waters required not only brilliant expertise in paddling small kayaks and hide boats, but also clothing able to combat immersion hypothermia. Survival depended on the sewing skill of Aleutian women and their forebears, who used fine bone needles to sew waterproof parkas made from sea lion or seal intestine lashed tightly at ankles and wrists. Bird-skin parkas made from thirty or forty cormorant or puffin skins lasted as long as two years and were lashed around cockpit rims to make paddler and kayak a single waterproof unit.

Aleut men spent much of their lives in their *baidarkas,* kayaks made of sea lion skin, which they began learning how to handle at the age of six or seven.[2]

6. Early fishing settlements in western North America discussed in chapters 8 and 9.

They became accustomed to paddling in rough water and were soon expert at spearing fish and sea mammals with a harpoon stowed aboard. Ancient Aleuts, who depended for food almost entirely on the Pacific and fast-flowing rivers, used the kayaks as devices for both fishing and hunting. The Aleuts enjoyed an intimate relationship with both inshore and deeper waters.[3] Their speech was a nuanced directory of the ocean that included dozens of words for wind and swell conditions. One of the world's most expert fishing and sea-mammal-hunting societies, the Aleuts over thousands of years adapted effortlessly to shifting climatic conditions and to unpredictable migrations of fish and sea mammals. A constant thread of cultural identity protected them. They lived in the heart of landscapes they invested with powerful spiritual meanings, including the belief that the souls of animals and humans were immortal and returned to the world in the body of a new beast or human after their owners died. This cycle of regeneration lay at the heart of their belief that new generations of living things would continue to nourish their communities.

The Aleuts placed a premium on kin relationships. The individuals and groups with the greatest wealth, the largest families, and the best access to important food sources enjoyed the highest status. This was basically a village-based society, although there were larger political alliances, details of which did not survive. Irregular warfare with neighbors on nearby islands or with people to the east on Kodiak Island or on the Alaska Peninsula was commonplace, both to avenge perceived insults and to obtain slaves. Some of the most elaborate settlements developed among salmon fishers and sea mammal hunters are those on Kodiak Island, especially after about two thousand years ago.

Such was the abundance of food along the islands that many settlements remained in use, on and off, for centuries. Some settlements, like the Hot Springs site at Port Moller on the Alaska Peninsula, were occupied from perhaps 2000 BC to AD 1000, the numerous houses dug partially into the ground. After about two thousand years ago the landscape, especially in the Kodiak region, became more crowded. During these centuries the spiritual foundations of maritime life became ever more important, with powerful shamanistic underpinnings, myths, and oral traditions. Important village leaders gained power and prestige across a competitive economic, political, and social landscape. Yet even the largest Kodiak and Aleutian communities never developed the elaboration and artistic flamboyance that marked the intricate cultural topography of the rugged coastline to the south.

With its rocky islands, forest-mantled coastlines, convoluted estuaries, and deep inlets fed by fast-flowing rivers, the Northwest coast from Alaska to the Columbia River was a bountiful homeland for fishing and sea mammal hunting societies for thousands of years. The broad-spectrum hunter-gatherers who first settled there would have been well aware of the rich fisheries and numerous sea mammals close at hand. Dozens of these species were already familiar to people across a broad arc of the North Pacific, from Siberia eastward. There were halibut, some weighing up to quarter of a ton; no fewer than five salmon species jammed rivers during the spawning season; and candlefish, herring, and other small fish that swarmed in coastal waters. Mollusks abounded; waterfowl, game, and plant foods were there for the taking. The predictability of the fisheries and mollusk beds provided a deep cushion of foods to fall back on throughout the year.

Vast stands of cedar, hemlock, spruce, and other trees grew to the water's edge, where island archipelagos protected much of the rugged coast and afforded smooth waterways for canoe travel, though often with strong tidal streams.[4] The damp coastal environment furnished abundant natural materials with which to create an elaborate fishing technology and material culture. Soft, straight-grained woods like cedar, fir, and spruce could be easily split and worked with polished-stone axes, adzes, and wedges and with shell knives. Planks from these trees formed the walls and roofs of the famed wooden dwellings of the Northwest coast. The same trees supplied the raw material for the most important artifact of fishing in these plentiful waters: dugout canoes.

Despite this abundance the coastal population remained sparse for thousands of years, perhaps because of the rapidly changing sea levels that continued to transform the coast until about 4000 BC, when the ocean stabilized at near-modern heights. A thousand years later rising coastal populations were intensively exploiting shell beds. Fishing also intensified. By the time of Christ, local fisherfolk preyed on a variety of fish large and small, using a wide range of simple technologies. Many early European visitors remarked on the local people's fishing skill. After surveying the region in 1885, the American naval officer Albert Niblack wrote, "There is little in the art of fishing we can teach the Indians."[5]

In more northern waters the halibut was all-important. Its average weight was something over fourteen kilograms, but hook-and-line fishers sometimes landed epic fish weighing as much as ninety-one kilograms.[6] The halibut, of the genus *Hippoglossos*, comes from the family of right-eye flounders. They are the largest of flat fish, dark brown on the upper side with an off-white underbelly. When young, they swim around like salmon, with eyes on both sides of their head. After six months one eye migrates over the top of the head to join the other, so that they resemble a flounder. They are omnivorous and are happy at shallow depths, but they spend most of their time near the seabed, hundreds of meters below the surface.

As halibut matured, wind-driven currents carried them onto the shallower continental shelf, where the ancient fishers could take them from canoes. Catching halibut required lines and baited hooks. Many local materials served as strong fishing lines, including bull kelp, a seaweed found in the upper tidal zone along most of the coast and out into the Aleutians. The solid part of the kelp formed a stem that could reach a length of twenty-four meters. Once soaked in freshwater, it became a tough, wirelike line that could be stretched and twisted. The women who made the lines joined shorter lengths with a special knot to form long coils that could reach considerable depths. They also made strong fishing lines from twisted inner cedar bark. These lines were especially effective for heavier catches and, in finer iterations, for making nets.

Hook making required consummate skill. Halibut fishhooks, fashioned from steamed and softened yew, spruce, or hemlock, were an art form. They were ingeniously designed so that no halibut could open its mouth wide enough to take more than the baited portion of the hook. The fishhook maker took extraordinary care to use tough wood, usually from knots where branches joined the trunk. A cedar-root lashing fixed a sharp bone barb to the hook, the end result, when baited, being an extremely effective, lethal hook. The fisherman often weighted the line so that it would sit on the bottom and then suspended hooks from each end of a light sapling. A large bladder on the surface marked the line as it rode with the waves.

Many halibut fishers used large hooks lashed into V shapes, one arm often carved with a symbolic figure such as an octopus or devil fish, in the belief that the depiction of such common bait would serve as a spirit helper for the fisher. The undecorated arm of the V was the hook that impaled the fish's mouth. The two-part hook also allowed its owner to replace damaged parts. Many surviving hooks show marks from the fierce biting of the halibut as it remained caught until the fisherman hauled in the line. A bladder marked the hook and line after it was cast in the water; an individual could watch over five or six such lines. Once a fish took the bait, he allowed plenty of time for it to get securely hooked before hauling it to the surface. Not that this was always straightforward. Raising a large halibut was a hazardous enterprise, since a very large one could easily swamp the canoe or overturn it.

Salmon were another staple, harvested by the thousand during spring and autumn runs. In many places the salmon and herring harvests involved constructing weirs in shallow water to capture large numbers of fish. Many weirs consisted of long rows of wooden stakes sunk into the seabed in intertidal zones, filled in with removable latticework that was renewed each season. Openings in the weir led to long, parallel-sided traps that were too narrow for the fish to turn around in. Others lay in shallow river waters, sometimes angled to guide the catch into waiting traps. Much depended on the fishermen's knowledge of their prey, especially in tidal waters, where fish would swim over traps as the tide was coming in and then be caught as the water receded. The fishers relied on the salmon's urge to overcome every obstacle as they made their way upstream to the spawning grounds.

Most large weirs belonged to an entire village, a reflection of the work involved in constructing them, and they sometimes created political and social complexities. Owners of downstream structures harvested before those up-river, and when they had caught enough fish the downstream harvesters would open the weir to allow more fish to reach the next village. A tardy opening, real or perceived, could cause angry complaints.

There were numerous variations on the weir theme. Some were adapted to fast-flowing rivers while others were designed to catch leaping fish or to trap them for spearing at leisure. Some weirs across shallow rivers had no openings but featured platforms set on stout tripods of poles, where the fishers would spear the confused, milling fish or catch them with dip nets.

By no means all salmon came from seasonal runs. Trolling with hook and line from canoes in sheltered bays and inlets could yield abundant catches. The fishermen baited their trolling hooks with small fish caught for use as bait. They fastened their lines, weighted with a light sinker, to their paddles, thus keeping the bait in constant motion as they moved along. The bait seemed alive; the salmon leapt at it, only to be flicked aboard with a quick paddle movement.

Great care went into making the leader for the hook. Often leaders were made invisible by using long strands of women's hair, light deer skin, or fine cedar bark twine. The hooks themselves were slender and lethal. When exploiting crowded runs, the fishers would use jigging hooks that snagged the fish and enabled the fisherman to haul them out quickly.

Spearfishing for salmon was an art in the Northwest, where it was generally done with a harpoon-style spear. The head came off the shaft when it struck a fish but remained attached by a line. Harpooning worked best with larger fish and was most effective in clearer water, where the fisher could watch his prey and allow it to swim around, thereby impaling the barbs more firmly into its body. Spears were most effective with smaller salmon, especially when the fish were concentrated by a trap or dam, where they could be taken quickly and be flipped onto the bank in seconds. Leisters were the most lethal spears of all. Used also by ancient Scandinavian fishers, the leister was equipped with reverse-angle barbs that held a fish firmly, especially when thrust vertically into prey lurking in shallow water. Northwestern fishermen speared salmon from canoes or from the banks of shallow streams. Gaff hooks used from platforms over rapids allowed fishermen to jerk the gaff upward, throwing the salmon ashore or into a canoe.

Then there was the sturgeon. In the major rivers of the Northwest, as in the Danube, they grew to great lengths and weights.[7] Northwest sturgeon are sluggish in winter and lie in deeper water, so they could have been taken in the cold months with twin-pronged harpoons attached to long poles. Sometimes fishers would allow a large sturgeon to drag a canoe into deep water, slowed by a heavy boulder tethered to the boat. Eventually the fish would tire and sink to the bottom; the line would become vertical, and the fishers would strike the fish with several more harpoons before eventually hauling it to the surface, where they would dispatch it with clubs. Then, with a deft maneuver, the fishermen tipped the canoe and rolled the dead sturgeon aboard, bailing out the water that came with it. Come spawning time, from April through summer, the sturgeon moved into shallow water. This was the prime season for taking them with dams, nets, and harpoons. Many fishermen caught sturgeon at night, tracking the phosphorescent trails they left in even quite deep water.

Prolific runs of schools of smaller fish like herring were often a family affair. The fish congregated in enormous numbers close inshore in early March for about three weeks. Husbands and wives would venture out in canoes bearing fire-hardened wooden rakes with sharp spikes fashioned from hard wood, bone, or even whalebone, mounted on long cedar shafts. While the wife steered the canoe, the fisherman worked from the bow, sweeping his rake through the dense mass of herring in one deft pass. The sweep worked like a paddle, impaling many herring or smelt with each stroke.

Eulachon (*Thaleichthys pacificus*), commonly called smelt or candlefish, were another vital catch. These small anadromous fish spend their youth in the ocean and then return to freshwater in late winter and early spring to spawn. They feed on plankton and occur from Southeast Alaska as far south as northern California. The Indians ate them fresh and also dried them. They were a welcome food when they ran inshore at winter's end.

Most eulachon were rendered down for their oil. They were caught by the thousands in long, fine-meshed nets attached to wooden poles that were set in river bottoms where tides ran strongly. Small camps by the riverbank processed the fish as they were brought ashore. The processors, mainly women, cast the eulachon into large pits covered with logs. The fish were then left to "ripen" for up to three weeks, the length of time depending on the weather.

When the processors deemed the contents of a pit ready, they transferred the rotted fish into bentwood boxes or even into a fisher's canoe. The processors then simmered the fish in water heated with hot stones, stirring and agitating the mixture to separate the oil from the carcasses. After several hours the mixture stood and cooled before the oil was skimmed off the surface. Then women levered or squeezed the residue into woven baskets. A highly prized commodity, eulachon oil was traded along the coast and far into the interior. It was used as an accompaniment to all kinds of meals and even stored with dried berries for winter use.

The relatively shallow inshore waters where most fishing was done were a mosaic of jealously guarded neighborhoods and fishing grounds. They were also a marketplace. The development of large, high-ended dugout canoes opened up long-distance trade routes through which everything from dried fish and eulachon oil to tool-making stone and exotic ceremonial objects were exchanged. Owning a large canoe meant power and prestige: one could visit neighbors, carry goods, and seek large halibut or pelagic fish in open water.

Coping with Unpredictable Fisheries

Northwestern fisheries were seemingly so abundant and predictable that one could easily assume that people everywhere enjoyed a degree of ease and even affluence. The reality was different. Many oral traditions talk of famines and food failure in years of paltry salmon or herring runs.[8] The unpredictability of these runs lay at the center of the northwesterners' traditional beliefs. The people believed that all living things, including fish, possessed spirits and that they could present themselves in abundance or opt to stay away. A fish run was seen as a voluntary act. The people believed that the goodwill of a fish's spirit, not the fisher's skill, caused it to be caught. Elaborate ceremonies, customs, and taboos surrounded fishing. Chants, prayers, and songs were the currency of these rituals, often uttered spontaneously and at other times acquired through dreams or intense spiritual experiences.

The First Salmon Ceremony was the most important ritual, an expression of reverence and respect when the run's first fish was caught.[9] Some groups honored the first salmon with a praise name. Often, shamans conducted elaborate ceremonies before the fish was butchered and served. Prayer and ritual also greeted the first eulachon or herring caught, an occasion for joyous celebration and renewal. The fishers recognized the natural cycle of human and animal life by clubbing the first fish with one blow and then honoring it with a prayer. The normal routines of butchering and cooking received exceptional care and attention. When the fish had been eaten, most groups threw the eating mats and bones into the sea, both to ensure that the salmon would become whole again and return and to let the other salmon know the first had been well treated so that they would duly proceed up the river. All prayers and rituals conveyed respect for the foods of river and ocean.

Still, the bountiful maritime environment was unable to support the rapidly growing coastal population. Each community had to adapt to constantly changing food supplies. Along the west coast of Vancouver Island there were such fluctuations in annual salmon runs that some communities might be in danger of starvation while people living not that far away had so many salmon they could not fully harvest them. To survive, less well-endowed communities joined alliances and participated in feasting ceremonies as a way of widening their contacts and mitigating food shortages.

Salmon runs have the advantage of appearing at regular places and times, even if the volume changes considerably. Larger rivers are less volatile than smaller ones; the variation can fluctuate with relative regularity of large runs, say, only every second to fourth year. To quote only one figure, in historic times the annual coho salmon run on the Columbia River, the richest of all salmon rivers, varied between about 1.5 million and 2.5 million fish. The chinook run ranged from 290,000 to 517,000.[10] In ancient times the size of the run may have been less important than the human equation, that is, having enough people to catch and process the harvest. Eventually, salmon runs alone could not support the increasingly complex societies that had developed along the coast. They required a constellation of fishing activities to exploit a wide range of species as well as mollusks, sea mammals, and terrestrial foods.

This was a world in which most food resources were available from spring to fall, often at the same time but in different locations. Only the most fortunate groups could remain in one place year-round. People dealt with unpredictable catches by staying on the move, taking advantage of ripening berry harvests inland while also harvesting salmon near the shore. Organizing work parties to exploit all these food sources required careful timing and organization as well as mobility. For instance, the Coast Tsimshian people, of the area around modern-day British Columbia's Prince Rupert, spent their winters at a sheltered canoe landing located where the city's harbor is now. In late February or early March many households traveled by canoe to the mouth of the

Interior of a Nootka house, Nootka Sound, Vancouver Island, by John Webber (1750–93), artist on Captain James Cook's last expedition. De Agostini Picture Library/Bridgeman Images.

Nass River, fifty kilometers north, for the eulachon runs. When the fish had been processed into oil, most people returned to the winter bases, where they fished locally and took shellfish on offshore islands. In late spring the Tsimshian dismantled their Prince Rupert houses down to the massive posts, which they left in place, and lashed the planks to canoes to form rafts for their possessions. Everyone moved to the nearby Skeena River, where they set up their villages for the salmon runs and summer fishing. In autumn they took everything back to their winter bases. Some groups in other areas moved far more frequently, while others stayed in one place year-round.

After 1800 BC major changes occurred along the coast. Populations rose, larger-scale storage became essential, and large seagoing canoes first appeared in significant numbers.[11] For the first time there are signs of social ranking in societies that had long been egalitarian. The hints of ranking are indirect: planked houses, for instance, where households engaged in specialized tasks such as axe making or canoe building. Households had long been the basic economic and social units along the coast. They were the way in which property and such important assets as ownership of fishing rights passed through the generations.

Households never functioned in isolation but belonged to much larger economic and social spheres. A village comprised several households, each with its individual territories that provided the members' food. These territories could consist of several places, occupied and exploited at different times of the year. Each household and settlement had wider connections, links based on political and social ties, through marriage, trade, and the activities of their chiefs. Chiefly prestige and rank assumed a central role in coastal societies, which became far from egalitarian as populations rose. The scale of a household's economic and social ties was a reflection of the chief's status in the social tapestry.

None of this would have been possible without permanent settlements, which were viable only when food resources were enough to support such communities. Along with more sedentary living came another necessity: the organization of labor to intensify the food quest and feed growing numbers of people. Along the Northwest coast, households could not operate with the labor of a few people but instead required many individuals working together on a wide variety of tasks, from fishing to carving dance masks. Think of a symphony orchestra playing a Sibelius composition, the players carrying out different roles as the work unfolds. In the Northwest a critical step toward more complex societies was taken when households organized themselves to perform many tasks simultaneously.

Larger Northwest settlements were wealthier because they could obtain more food, maintain wider trading connections, and produce more desirable goods. Typically, Northwest communities large and small consisted of a row of planked houses facing a beach or a canoe landing. The availability of water, the ease of landing and launching canoes, and the potential for mounting an effective defense were crucial factors in choosing a site. The largest houses were those of the highest-ranked households. The layouts of even the smallest villages reflected the social relationships among the inhabitants.

Getting power required having the political and social adeptness, first, to gain control of a household economy or several of them and then to divert the proceeds to one's own ambitions. Or one could participate in large-scale trade and exchange networks that extended through the coastal waterways and far into the interior. One could also gain control of access to the resources in one's own territory, something that was usually in the hands of high-status individuals with wide social connections. Many chiefs exchanged valuable goods for prestige, for status, and for the loyalty of numerous followers. These were the currency of coastal society.

Over many centuries, as population densities rose and small, kin-based communities gradually became large settlements housing several kin groups, household territories were increasingly circumscribed by locally dense populations, regular conflict, and the uneven distribution of good fisheries and other food sources. As the landscape became more crowded, a few individuals assumed control over the redistribution of food supplies and over political relationships between neighbors. Northwest societies became marked by intricate patterns of exchange, intense rivalry, and highly formalized systems for the redistribution of food and other goods throughout society. One such device was ceremonial feasting—the celebrated potlatch.

Northwest society regarded all wealth as the property of kin groups. An individual could acquire dried fish, pelts, canoes, or exotic objects, but ultimately they were group property, even if a chief or other leader spoke of them as his own. Wealth was for display and conspicuous consumption, a means of enhancing the group's prestige among its neighbors. Potlatches were dignified ceremonies held by a chief or his kin group and witnessed by other chiefs and their groups to mark a meaningful occasion: the marriage of an important person or the assumption of a title or a crest. These events were surrounded by intricate protocol, ritual, singing, and dancing as well as the expectation that those who attended would reciprocate in the future. Much of the rich ceremonial life of the Northwest involved the reenactment of myths and the constant reinforcement of ranks and titles, a process that redistributed food and wealth through society as a whole.

These cannot have been easy societies for the elite. A chief was surrounded by intense factionalism and shifting alliances, and he was required to retain, through charisma and generosity, the loyalty of his followers. He was not a divine ruler, like an Egyptian pharaoh, but a leader at the mercy of the shifting currents of public opinion and of the shamans who were the intermediaries between the living and the powerful, often malevolent forces of the supernatural realm. The volatile, prestige-obsessed nature of the Northwest fishing societies was their survival strategy in the face of the intricate realities that confronted them, conducted at a level of complexity that was as viable for long-term existence as a city or a civilization.

9

The Myth of a Garden of Eden

South of the Olympic Peninsula, the Pacific coast of North America was mostly steep cliffside, even when sea levels were ninety meters below those of today. There were occasional estuaries and offshore flatlands. After fifteen thousand years ago the rising ocean flowed inexorably into estuaries and river valleys, forming extensive marshes that were ideal for mollusks and shallow-water fish. But the human population remained sparse except in the most productive estuaries and coastal areas, where denser communities lived close to rich, shallow water.[1] Here, fish were easily taken from simple rafts or reed canoes, and mollusks of all kinds abounded. San Francisco Bay was a river valley opening into a wide coastal plain. Enormous shell mounds bore testimony to extensive mollusk harvesting in the bay for thousands of years.

Many bay-area shell mounds mark camps that were used in late autumn and winter but not in summer, when water supplies were limited. Others were bases for salmon harvesting or clam foraging. But they were also much more. Some were cemeteries where people sought contact with their ancestors. Close relationships linked home, food, and burials, for which local leaders organized feasts "to feed the dead." The great mounds stood out on the flat landscape and became symbolic markers in foraging and fishing societies with intricate mythic and supernatural beliefs and regular connections with a far wider world.[2]

The Chumash and Their Predecessors

Point Conception, the northern frontier of southern California, is the westernmost cape along the California coast (see map 6 in chapter 8). When the onshore wind blows hard out of the northwest, the full force of the open Pacific bursts onto the headland cliffs. But just south of Conception the wind drops, the swells even out, and the Santa Barbara Channel is like another world (see map 6 in chapter 8). The mainland takes a sharp turn eastward here, so that the channel faces south, protected on its offshore side by the four northern Channel Islands of Anacapa, Santa Cruz, Santa Rosa, and San Miguel, an extension of the mainland Santa Monica Mountains, which form an east–west line along the outer edge of the channel (see map 6 in chapter 8). These rugged islands are a frontier for some of the richest coastal fisheries on earth. They lack many of the mainland animals and plants but support highly productive sea mammal rookeries, bountiful shellfish beds, and rich kelp fisheries close inshore. This was the nexus of the Chumash Indian world when the Spanish made contact in the sixteenth century. How long ago they settled there is unknown, but it was far back in the past.

In the western part of the Santa Barbara Channel the cool northern California current meets the warm southern California countercurrent. The ecosystem created by this encounter promotes great biomass and species diversity. In addition, seasonal winds around Point Conception and in the channel create frequent upwellings, which force nutrient-laden deep-ocean water toward the surface, into the biologically rich zone less than 120 meters from the surface, where sunlight is able to penetrate. These concentrations of nutrients and macrozooplankton support unimaginably rich fish populations. Numerous fish species also inhabit the thick kelp beds that line much of the coast.[3]

When sea levels were at Ice Age lows the Channel Islands were a single landmass known to geologists as Santarosae, its nearest point just 9.6 kilometers from the low-lying mainland at what is now Point Hueneme. This short distance was navigable on calm summer days by canoes made of local bulrushes and paddled by men and women who chose their weather and did not mind getting wet during the crossing. Once on the other side they could dry out their partially waterlogged canoes in the sun so that they could get back to the mainland. When sea levels rose and the islands became more isolated, simple reed canoes were no longer safe for the crossing nor could they carry heavy loads. Despite the increasing separation, the Channel Islands were among the earliest locations to be settled in southern California.

Traces of human settlement on the islands date to about 13,000 years ago, perhaps earlier. The first visitors spent some weeks, perhaps months, hunting sea mammals, collecting mollusks, and catching the fish that abounded in the kelp beds close inshore, but the paucity of island water meant they probably could not stay year-round. Their scant archaeological signature consists of thin occupation layers in caves and occasional shell middens and artifact scatters on higher ground. Daisy Cave, on the northeast coast of San Miguel Island, has signs of occupation at least 11,500 years old, when people visiting the cave ate abalone, mussels, and other shellfish. The main focus was shellfish, but the cave also contained double-ended bone gorges—early substitutes for fishhooks that stuck in the mouth of the catch—and the debris resulting from making them as well as fragments of fiber cordage and basketry.

Throughout the islands and along the mainland coast most of what human visitors ate came from fish and mollusks. California mussels were a major prey, as were black abalone, along with plant foods, some terrestrial game, sea mammals, and fish. But since plant foods and game were scarce on the islands, visitors relied on the ocean. Daisy Cave yielded at least eighteen shellfish taxa as well as twenty-seven thousand bones from at least nineteen fish forms.[4] Most of them were from near-shore species like cabezon, sheepshead, and rockfish, which were fished consistently for the next two thousand years.

The still shadowy people who first fished the Santa Barbara originated, ultimately, from a very ancient tradition of broad-spectrum hunting and gathering, of which fishing was a part. Like every other hunter-gatherer group they were consummate opportunists who subsisted on a broad range of foods. Throughout the channel the major fishery was in the kelp beds that flourish in shallow rocky habitats mantling most of the island and mainland shores. These canopy-forming kelps grow with extraordinary rapidity and reach heights of well over ten meters, often much greater. The channel, with its ample sunlight, nurtured thick beds and, combined with the natural upwelling in the west as well as the minerals and organic materials from the rivers, these were highly productive waters. Readily accessible in reed canoes, the great kelp beds of the Channel were a treasure trove of marine foods.

The fishing technology consisted of little more than hooks and lines for halibut and other species, also nets, perhaps stabbing spears, traps, and cast nets suspended between two watercraft.[5] Yields were relatively predictable, especially in the western reaches where the natural upwelling was most vigorous. Even in later times, when people pursued pelagic fish like tuna, sharks, and swordfish, the staple was always kelp and surf fishing. Fishers used baskets full of ground-up cactus leaves to attract sardines by the hundreds. Many centuries later a Spanish soldier, Pedro Fages, remarked of the Chumash that their days were one continuous meal. Perhaps this is the earliest manifestation of the common belief that the Santa Barbara Channel was a paradise for the Indians who lived along its coasts. The myth has persisted, but it is belied by climate change.

Climate and Culture Change

The Santa Barbara Channel enjoys a climate that is a seemingly monotonous routine of morning fogs, afternoon sunshine, and irregular rainfall. In fact, those who fished its waters had to adapt to constant environmental change. Major cultural changes sometimes resulted. Fortunately, a deep-sea core drilled in the deep waters of the channel's Santa Barbara Basin documents many of these climatic shifts.

Dramatic environmental and temperature changes have affected the Santa Barbara Channel over the past fifteen thousand years. Rising sea levels inundated the mainland continental shelf and created today's four Channel Islands from a single landmass. The sparse numbers of people who lived through this dramatic transformation were broad-spectrum hunters and foragers, who probably relied heavily on kelp fish, taken from reed canoes, and on mollusks, which occur in shallow middens on San Miguel and other islands. Judging from the burial of the Arlington woman on Santa Rosa Island, the first human settlement took place about thirteen thousand years ago, not long after first settlement in the far north. The ensuing seven thousand years or so were ones of constant adjustments to changing landscapes, where hunting territories and fishing grounds could change within a few generations. Some of these transformations would have been potentially disastrous, such as the flooding of sea lion rookeries in confined waters or the destruction of kelp beds and freshwater ponds by severe winter storms. We will probably never learn of all the cultural changes that took hold in local environments where rainfall was unpredictable and food supplies were distributed unevenly over the landscape. As the available coastal land shrank in the face of the ocean there would have been constant social and political adjustments to be made in a changing world where even seemingly plentiful foods could become scarce.

Between about 11,000 and 6000 BC most human groups considered the coast part of their annual round, part of much wider foraging territories, even if they spent long periods of time by the Pacific. Apart from anything else, the shore provided an abundance of mollusks during hungry months as well as easy hunting of sea mammals, this apart from the inshore fishery. Here mollusks were a staple, except during periods of "red tide" in summer that turned their flesh toxic and inedible. For all this abundance, the Santa Barbara Channel was part of a much wider world of hunting and foraging. Its human visitors probably thought of the Pacific as an enormous, albeit salty, lake. They must have taken kelp fish with spears and nets, and many of them were predominantly terrestrial hunter-gatherers and opportunistic, seasonal fisherfolk.

By about 7000 BC local sea levels had basically stabilized at near-modern levels. A prolonged period of warmer conditions ensued, a time of technological innovation and intensive exploitation of inshore fisheries and shell beds. Enjoying relatively predictable foods at the coast, some groups began living at the same location for longer periods of time, a development that seems to have led to a greater emphasis on fishing and mollusks. Many larger settlements rose near rocky and sandy coastlines, often on headlands where kelp beds and other near-shore habitats lay close at hand. Their permanence was dictated by the availability of fish and mollusks: the more productive the nearby waters, the longer people stayed. Fishing technology changed little. Everyone still relied on bags, baskets, lines, spears, and nets, often made from sea grass.

Before 5000 BC well-established communities were present on the islands, communities which would not have been viable without regular economic and social contacts with the mainland and seaworthy watercraft to make visits and longer stays possible. This may have been when people began to waterproof their reed canoes with locally available asphalt (bitumen), which made at least limited excursions into deep water possible. By this time mussels, abalone, and sea mammals formed about 60 percent of the diet; fish constituted about 17 percent. Fish became ever more important before 3300 BC as people spent more time on the water. Shell middens at the western end of Santa Cruz Island dating to between 5000 and 3300 BC contain significant quantities of large red abalone (*Haliotis rufescans*), which live in much deeper subtidal waters. There is so much of the red variety that these shell heaps are often called red abalone middens. All these shell heaps also contain large quantities of California mussels, long a staple and so abundant they could be collected intensively without depleting the stock. Nevertheless, one site on Santa Cruz Island, known as SCRI-109 and mainly occupied around 3000 BC, has yielded telltale signs of diminishing mussel size through time, perhaps a sign of pressure on local mussel populations. Red abalone were taken as early as 5000 BC, if not earlier, but more intensive exploitation may have coincided with a rise in the number of dolphins taken around 3500 BC, when sea lions also became a more popular target. The climate was warm and relatively stable; populations rose, perhaps putting pressure on readily accessible fish and mollusk populations. This may have been one of the triggers that led people to venture some distance offshore, where they took more fish and dived for red abalone in deeper waters relatively close to land.

What do these shifts mean? Most likely, island populations were rising, and demand exceeded the limits of readily available mollusk beds and kelp fisheries.[6] There are some fleeting clues, among them several larger settlements on the islands and mainland. By 4000 BC pestles and mortars had appeared on the islands, as if the inhabitants were broadening their diet to include plant foods like acorns, which were nutritious and easily stored. Plants of all kinds had long been a staple on the mainland. For the first time there are signs that Santa Barbara Channel societies were developing greater complexity long before the much more elaborate economic, political, and social elaboration of later times—much earlier than once thought.

This social complexity is really the beginning of more nuanced adaptations to new environmental and human realities. Kelp fisheries are relatively predictable, but they don't come close to the scale of the vast salmon, herring, and eulachon runs of the Pacific Northwest. Northwestern catches and fish harvests were enormous, but the long-term viability of increasingly complex societies depended on constant interaction with other groups, near and far. For such contacts, watercraft were of vital importance. Distances between northwestern settlements and good fishing grounds were often long, but the fortunate happenstance of straight-grained trees turned small dugouts from earlier times into large, high-ended canoes capable of weathering rough water and carrying heavy loads over long distances. The challenges in the Santa Barbara Channel were strikingly different, yet in many respects similar. The Northwest had heavy rainfall and often severe winters. The channel had natural upwelling that nourished rich fisheries but lay in a semiarid environment plagued by irregular, often prolonged, drought cycles. Distances were shorter, but there were no tall, easily worked trees to shape into high-sided canoes. But here, just as in the Northwest, long-term survival depended on regular interaction and trade between communities that were often separated by open water.

The connections between islands and mainland were one of the catalysts for the much more elaborate societies of later times. They strengthened cooperative relationships, forged marriage alliances, and enhanced economic stability and interdependence. The quickened pace of trade, for instance, carried Catalina Island soapstone, valued for vessels and ornaments, northward from what is now the Los Angeles area. Ocher, pigments, and toolmaking stone also traveled widely. Most crucial of all, however, was the trade in island shellfish—not for eating but for beads.[7] For some reason—call it the caprice of fashion—mainland communities craved shell beads from offshore, and the Channel Islands developed into a major center of shell bead production, notably using the shell of *Olivella biplicata,* the purple olive sea snail. *Olivella* shell beads were in use from very early times as bodily decoration. Eventually they became so popular that they were traded as far inland as the Rio Grande and as far north as Oregon.

The climate may have been warm and more stable than usual for some centuries, but long-term survival also meant adjusting to constant, irregular climatic shifts. In the southern California world, the productivity of the fisheries depended on natural upwelling, which fluctuated dramatically when short-term climatic changes led to higher and lower water temperatures. Colder water produced vigorous upwelling and much higher productivity. Warmer surface temperatures meant less surface upwelling and poorer fishing.

Fortunately for archaeologists, a 198-meter core in the deep waters of the channel's Santa Barbara Basin documents climate change in sediments that accumulated at a rate of about 1.5 meters per millennium.[8] Combinations of changing marine foraminifera and ultra-accurate radiocarbon dates have yielded a portrait of maritime climate change in the region at twenty-five-year intervals over the past three thousand years, the very millennia during which channel societies underwent dramatic change.

James and Douglas Kennett, father and son, found that sea surface temperatures oscillated from warm to cold and back again on a millennial timescale, with cooling episodes of varying length occurring about every fifteen hundred years. They found that after about 2000 BC conditions became far less stable and sea surface temperatures varied by as much as 5 degrees C. This made human life much more complicated, since the productivity of coastal fisheries varies dramatically with water temperature. For example, between 1050 BC and AD 450, while population densities on the mainland and at the islands were rising and local societies changed rapidly, temperatures were relatively warm and stable. Inevitably, territorial boundaries between different groups shrank and became more rigid.

From 450 to 1300 sea temperatures cooled sharply to about 1.5 degrees C colder than the mean sea temperature of channel waters since the Ice Age. For three and a half centuries, from AD 950 to 1300—what in Europe is called the Little Ice Age—marine upwelling was exceptionally strong and the fisheries were highly productive. In contrast, the centuries after 450 were ones of un-predictable climatic shifts and sustained, often severe drought cycles. There were many more mouths to feed, perhaps to the point that some areas were overfished: we have no proof of this. The effects on fisheries and coastal com-munities would have been relatively minor, even when periodic El Niños brought violent storms and floods, shut down upwelling, and destroyed kelp beds. There is no archaeological evidence for the collapse of the maritime economy along the channel's coasts. The real trouble was in the mainland in-terior, where persistent droughts played havoc with acorn harvests and plants of all kinds. Close social ties knitted even widely separated communities into long-standing webs of interdependence. Food shortages and intergroup com-petition affected everyone, as did water shortages. Crowded into large coastal settlements, sometimes with as many as a thousand inhabitants, Chumash communities were ruled by chiefs who competed with one another.

Violence became commonplace, as did malnutrition. A study of several hundred human skeletons from the Channel Islands yielded strong evidence for malnutrition and for infections caused by unsanitary conditions in crowded villages. Another study of dead from both the islands and the mainland pro-duced numerous examples of people killed or wounded by projectiles, reach-ing a peak between about AD 300 and 1150, during stressful times. Then the violence subsided dramatically. About one thousand years ago the Chumash leaders, plagued by escalating violence and persistent hunger, seem to have paused and realized that survival depended on peace and interdependence at a time when the ocean warmed again. By 1550 upwelling had subsided, and marine productivity was again lower. In earlier times Chumash leaders were what one might call aggrandizers, men whose power depended on their ability to attract loyal followers. Now the social equation changed. Leadership be-came hereditary, vested in elite lineages headed by chiefly families, where power passed down the generations. By the time the Spaniards arrived in 1542 Chu-mash society had developed a more formal structure, mechanisms for con-trolling trade and resolving disputes and, above all, for distributing food in a world where a distance of only a few miles could make the difference between plenty and shortage. At Spanish contact there were an estimated fifteen thousand Chumash on the mainland and islands, their society sharply divided between a small elite and commoners. There developed an economic interdependence and firm control of trade across the channel, the larger settlements linked by kin ties and strategic marriages. There were quarrels and, occasionally, wars, but cooperative behavior between scattered communities over a large area and carefully observed ritual practices created fishing societies that were able to adapt to the constantly unpredictable climate of the Santa Barbara Channel.

Just a glance at the climatic curves reveals at once that neither the mainland nor the Channel Islands were a Garden of Eden. Quite the contrary, for while there were always kelp fish, sustained droughts and uncertain acorn crops plagued the bands that lived inland. Even in the absence of drought, acorn harvests varied greatly from year to year, making the social and economic ties that linked the people of the coast with their close and distant neighbors in the semiarid interior a critical reality. The same was true of the offshore islands, where the permanent inhabitants of later times relied almost entirely on fish and sea mammals, although some local plants were available. Thus interdependence and links between Chumash communities near and far were the core of local life in ways that were perhaps even more vital than in the Pacific Northwest. Exchange of prosaic commodities like acorns and dried fish, shell beads and exotic objects assumed ever-greater significance in daily life and in the political relationships between neighboring bands and communities, especially during times of the year when some foods were in short supply and stocks of stored acorns and other commodities were much reduced. The processing and storing of dried catches assumed great importance in Chumash communities. So did watercraft, which enabled people to acquire larger numbers of fish.

Tomols *and Widening Domains*

The first Spaniards to arrive in the Santa Barbara Channel region, in 1542, were astounded to find large, densely populated villages. Some twenty-five thousand Chumash lived on the mainland and islands when the Spanish reached the area. No one knows when the Chumash first settled there, but recent DNA research places their ancestry certainly thousands of years in the past. By the sixteenth century they enjoyed a highly adaptable and flexible culture that had survived, and usually thrived, in a harsh, drought-prone land-scape.[9] Their adaptations were owing to much earlier trends, as if their elaborate society was the culmination of survival strategies that developed in some cases soon after the Ice Age. Long before fish became really important around 1500 BC, the isolated hunter-gatherer communities that settled the area after the Ice Age had already begun the transformation into a more complex, broadly interconnected culture, with rising population densities, intensive exploitation of maritime and plant foods, larger settlements, and a significant increase in contacts with other communities near and far. Regular contacts across the Santa Barbara Channel between island and mainland communities depended on the most important of all the Chumash's technological innovations: the tomol, a planked canoe.

The tomol was one of the most remarkable watercraft in the ancient world: a planked canoe constructed from driftwood rather than from local trees.[10] Exactly when it first came into use is a matter of debate. Experts agree that the boats were in use by AD 400, but it is likely that simpler versions—essentially bulrush canoes but made of wood with built-up sides—were used much earlier for sporadic deepwater fishing and trade. When a canoe reached the end of its useful life, it was either left to rot away or its precious driftwood planks were recycled. All traces of the earliest ones are long gone.

The tomol is a simple concept. The bottom is a single heavy timber, with carefully split driftwood planks forming a flexible, sewn hull with high ends. The builders collected driftwood, which they split into planks with whalebone wedges and carefully thinned and smoothed with adzes and with sandpaper made of sharkskin. They caulked the planks with a bitumen mixture called *yop*, forming the hull and bracing it amidships with a beam. The ends of the uppermost planks remained open to hold fishing lines or pulling ropes; washboards at both ends deflected waves. These boats were fast and easily paddled, capable of venturing into deep water and traveling long distances during the calmer hours or on the not-uncommon windless days experienced in these waters. Almost certainly Chumash tomol captains chose their weather carefully and did much of their passage making in the early morning, when winds are normally calm.

Building a tomol was a long, expensive process, so much so that those who commissioned the builders were people of influence and wealth. Ownership of a planked canoe gave one access to impressive contacts near and far as well

Chumash Indians carry a tomol ashore. Lithograph by William Langdon Kihn
(1898–1957), 1948. National Geographic Creative/Bridgeman Images.

as control over the people and goods that were transported over open water.
Tomols opened up opportunities for lucrative exchange of such commodities
as pounded acorn meal from the mainland, soapstone vessels from Catalina
Island off present-day Los Angeles, and, above all, shell beads, manufactured
by the tens of thousands on Santa Cruz and Santa Rosa Islands. Tomol owners
could manage information about potential trading contacts and monopolize
load carrying between widely separated communities.

Quite apart from control of trade routes, the planked canoe also widened
the fishing domain to encompass deeper waters outside the kelp beds, where
pelagic species like bluefin tuna, yellowtail, and, most prestigious of all, the
mystical swordfish dwelt. Judging from sporadic finds of deepwater fish bones,
there had long been occasional catches of sardines and other species in deeper
water, especially off the islands. But with the emergence of wealthy canoe owners, deepwater fishing came to be controlled by small numbers of people who
drew their political and social power from transport and fishing. Canoe owners belonged to the Brotherhood of the Canoe and wore short bearskin capes,
a garment that only elite individuals like village chiefs were permitted to wear.

Long canoe voyages across the Santa Barbara Channel and along mainland
and island shores became commonplace, but a canoe's arrival at an isolated

community must have been an event. A heavily laden tomol approaching an island beach on a calm day would have been a sight to behold. The shell inlay on the high bow glitters in the morning sunlight. Paddling slows as the canoe approaches the kelp bed, while the skipper, dressed in his cape, stands in the stern. Digging deep, the paddlers maneuver the canoe through the seaweed, then head for the beach, chanting as they ride the gentle breakers onto the sand. Waiting villagers grab the sides as the crew leaps into the shallow water, and the group drags the tomol ashore. The skipper stands calmly as the canoe grounds, then steps ashore with quiet dignity. His crew carries baskets of shell beads, two tuna and a white sea bass, harpooned along the way, to the headman's dwelling.

All pelagic fish taken from tomols were prestigious catches, but nothing rivaled the swordfish. In 1926 David Banks Rogers of the Santa Barbara Museum of Natural History unearthed a spectacular burial on a headland overlooking the Pacific west of Goleta slough, part of which is now Santa Barbara airport. The skeleton of a man, later carbon-dated to about AD 600, lay crouched on its left side. The man wore a cape of carefully arranged abalone shells that extended over his shoulders and was attached to the split skull of a swordfish. The fish cranium encased the man's skull and pointed upward from his forehead. He had been a Swordfish Dancer, a figure who would have glittered with brilliant iridescence as he twirled and danced in the sunlight wearing his cape. Eugenia Mendez, one of the informants of the Smithsonian Institution anthropologist John Harrington a century ago, wrote, "When the man is dancing, you can see only his feather skirt and sticks, [you] cannot see his body. He is like an animal he dances so fast, making a whirring sound."[11]

Intense ritual and complex beliefs surrounded the swordfish, *Xiphias gladius,* said to be the "master of the animals."[12] Formidable prey, swordfish were known to attack canoes. They were said to have a house at the bottom of the sea surrounded by water, and the Chumash considered them the marine equivalents of human beings. When dancing, the Swordfish Dancer, a powerful shaman, was thought to have the power to assume the spirit of the fish. The spectacular mask transformed him into a supernatural being who honored a fish that was said to drive whales ashore and to provide good food in summer. Whether the attacks on whales occurred is uncertain, but the period of greatest food stress in Chumash country was the spring, the time when gray whales migrate north through the Santa Barbara Channel and strandings were most frequent. In the Chumash cosmology, thinking of these strandings as the work of a beneficent sea god is a sensible conclusion.

Swordfish fishing may have begun around AD 400, at a time of enhanced social complexity, when pelagic fish were becoming more important both as food and as objects of veneration. It was made possible by the advent of the barbed harpoon foreshaft and the planked canoe, at a time of slightly higher temperatures. *Xiphias* tends to travel alone or in small, widely separated groups. On calm days it often swims slowly close to the surface, its dorsal fin easily spotted. If paddled with great care, a tomol could have approached silently, gliding almost over the fish before the harpooner struck. On many occasions the fishers would bait a fragment of white textile, cast it into the water, then lure their prey close enough to the canoe for a strike. Once the fish was impaled, the fishermen played the catch with a line and floats until it tired.

One Chumash bone harpoon foreshaft—collected by George Goodman Hewitt, a surgeon's mate on George Vancouver's expedition, which visited the Santa Barbara Channel in 1792–93—had a chert stone point and a sharp bone barb lashed to the tip, all coated with asphaltum. An easily detachable cone-shaped base was set into the main shaft, carrying a line that came into play when the harpooner jerked the foreshaft free to play the catch. The barb of the head was apparently sufficiently large and sharp to keep the fish firmly impaled. These harpoons were light, easily thrown weapons that were highly effective against large pelagic fish, but they were useless against sea lions, porpoises, or baleen whales. The Chumash made long, three-ply fishing lines from horse nettle or hemp twisted on the maker's thigh. The lines could be seventy-five meters or more in length and were routinely carried aboard tomols in case they encountered a large fish. Even a small swordfish was an important catch. Apart from their flesh, the bones became dancer's masks and digging or throwing sticks; the large vertebrae served as cups, and their spines were effective awls, needles, or pins.

Canoe builders and skippers possessed expertise, wealth, and great prestige. Chumash society and its predecessors were already becoming more complex before the tomol assumed a central role in local life, serving as the catalyst that linked isolated communities and concentrated wealth among the few canoe owners and chiefs known as *wots*. This wealth came primarily from shell beads, which became so central to Chumash life that they were used as currency for centuries. Just as in Northwest society, those who controlled the wealth came to prominence, and people of prominence came to control wealth. Kin leaders (for society was still kin-based) and influential individuals with ritual connections and powers used their political ability and charisma to attract loyal followers in a society where prestige was the currency of power.

Over many centuries Chumash society became ranked, with broad echelons. At the top was a small, well-connected elite whose power came from the networks they developed, nurtured, and controlled. Personal wealth, prestigious artifacts, and warfare were the ingredients of chiefly power, especially in times of social stress caused by drought, growing populations, and food shortages. Sporadic fighting is well documented by war casualties buried in thousand-year-old Chumash cemeteries. The wots, clad in bearskin capes, controlled large, often closely packed communities of dozens of houses. Their power came from their control of fisheries and trade routes as well as from their unique forms of personal charisma and military prowess. Such qualities created the leaders of fishing societies in many environments around the world, especially those, like the Chumash, where food shortages and malnutrition stalked every community.

The seasonal round of ceremonial feasts honoring spiritual figures, who were believed to provide food sources, was meant to ward off such threats. Every major point in the calendar had a ritual organized around a food source. A ceremony held at the completion of the fall nut harvests paid homage to the earth, while one performed at the winter solstice venerated the sun. Specialists in astronomy maintained a twelve-month lunar calendar in order to determine the days for solstice ceremonies, to which people from far and wide brought gifts from their leaders to the host wot, who was responsible for organizing and orchestrating the ceremony.

These gifts confirmed political and social ties, but they had a competitive element as well, especially at mortuary events, when many shell beads and other precious items such as steatite vessels and mortars were destroyed. Wots and their family members belonged to the *'antap* society, a group of elite individuals and specialists who maintained cosmic balance, provided astrological information, and connected members of the elite over wide areas. A *paha* assisted the wot in organizing large ceremonies, the two working together to get and distribute goods, especially prestige items. They acquired both wealth and food stores, which they later redistributed through the community as a way of demonstrating prestige and political influence and thereby securing the chief's position. All of these practices served as an institution for redistributing re-sources, especially food, in a rich area that still faced great uncertainty.

Kin ties, alliances reinforced by strategic marriages, meticulous observation of the ritual calendar, and careful redistribution of commodities and wealth through society: these were the foundations of a society that depended heavily on fishing and on widespread networks. Just as in the Pacific Northwest, it was in these networks that the ultimate power lay. Such were the economics of coping with food shortages, adopting permanent settlement, and relying on rich, if patchy, fisheries through centuries of long- and short-term climate change.

The Calusa: Shallows and Sea Grass

The massive natural global warming that flooded the Bering Land Bridge and melted the great ice sheets of the north had far-reaching and often subtle effects on the rest of North America. River estuaries flooded, creating spawning grounds, and rivers slowed, their swampy backwaters and lush floodplains turning into rich fish habitats. As sea levels stabilized around 7000 BC, population densities rose in food-rich landscapes like river deltas and low-lying floodplains. Fishing and mollusks assumed importance in broad-spectrum subsistence economies, in which survival depended on careful risk management and relying on diverse food supplies. Some societies remained in a state of perpetual motion, notably in cooler environments with their dramatic seasonal contrasts. Others, like fishing societies in southern Florida, lived at or close to low-lying coastlines, where they were at the mercy of even minor changes in sea level.[1]

In the southern tracts of the Florida peninsula a huge mass of freshwater flowed sluggishly southward through a maze of salt grass and swamps, one of the great wetlands of North America. Lake Okeechobee, the most expansive area of open water, was almost twice the size it is today, before the southern end was drained in the late nineteenth century.[2] This was a waterlogged world in which dry land was in short supply. Most of southern Florida was effectively under water. Where dry land could be found, by the Gulf and Atlantic coasts or along major rivers like the Kissimmee and Caloosahatchee, Native

Americans settled, all of them hunters and fisherfolk who also foraged for plant foods. There are signs that some of them grew squashes, gourds, chili peppers, and papaya, but these efforts paled alongside their maritime adaptations.

The Calusa people lived along a subtropical coastline that enjoyed mild winters. In the northern areas of their homeland the people dwelt in the heart of an estuarine landscape, where a convex barrier reef system enclosed broad bays fringed with mangrove swamps. The southern part of this coast is sometimes called the Ten Thousand Islands, a lattice of mangrove islets forming a mosaic of narrow channels that can be navigated only by canoe. Up in the north the Pine Island Sound area is a tapestry of sea-grass meadows supporting numerous species of small fish and juveniles as well as innumerable bivalves and gastropods.[3] These shellfish provided not only meat but also shells that served as raw material for artifacts of all kinds, including fishhooks.

Pine Island Sound, whose average depths of about 0.5 meters extended over a large area, is an unusually productive seawater habitat. To the south, at the northern end of the Ten Thousand Islands, the people who lived on Marco Island had to contend with deeper waters and faster-running currents, making for a different kind of fishing. The Big Marco Pass River is fast-running, with depths up to 9.8 meters in the main channels, and home to numerous larger fish species, including shark and tarpon.

When the first Spanish conquistadors landed in Calusa country in the sixteenth century they found dense, sedentary populations whose leaders exercised political influence over much of south Florida. Spanish accounts tell of an elaborate society whose prosperity and power came from their maritime economy and from wide social and trading contacts. The origins of the Calusa lie among much earlier maritime societies. Archaeology traces coastal netfishers in this region back to at least 4000 BC. They and their successors lived in an estuarine environment that was unpredictable and far from homogeneous. Both short-term and longer-term climatic fluctuations caused local changes in topography and hence in fish and mollusk resources that may well have kept population growth in check. Food supplies were never homogeneous or evenly distributed. Nor were they even temporarily stable. Anyone who lived and fished in this ever-changing landscape was always vulnerable to sudden climate changes and devastating hurricanes. This was never the kind of coastal environment where societies flourished and progressed steadily over many centuries, achieving greater cultural and social complexity thanks to bountiful fisheries. The societies that developed here varied greatly in complexity and

7. Eastern North America, showing locations and sites mentioned in chapter 10.

elaboration. As in southern California, much depended on one's relationships not only with neighbors but also with groups who lived inland. What developed were decentralized ways of adapting to a subtropical aquatic environment that proved to be both flexible and effective. Everything depended on how people interacted with one another within the contexts of their own local surroundings and historical experience of it.

The Calusa faced some unique realities in their shallow estuary homeland. The archaeologist William Marquardt believes that they would have noticed sea-level changes within as short a time as a twenty-five-year generation and certainly within three of them.[4] Theirs was a coastline where freshwater discharged from three major rivers and where there were extensive sea-grass meadows, mangrove wetlands, and barrier islands separating it from the Gulf of Mexico. Some parts of Calusa territory enjoyed exceptional biological productivity, but, like the Gulf of Mexico, the region belongs in the enormous North Atlantic climatic system. As a result, broadly recognized climatic fluctuations such as the so-called Roman and Medieval Warm Periods and the Little Ice Age caused sea-level changes along parts of the Florida Gulf Coast. These were minor shifts that would have had little or no effect on groups living along the shores of deeper channels or estuaries. But people in shallow estuary settings would have been profoundly affected by rises and falls of even a few centimeters. This was a classic case of sea-level changes in shallow water, which have much more profound effects horizontally than vertically, as was also the case in the low-lying North Sea and the Nile Delta thousands of years earlier.

In areas like Pine Sound, a focus of much Calusa research, it is clear that people made decisions in response to even minor fluctuations in sea level. To give a modern example, the sea level in Pine Island Sound rose about twenty-five centimeters between 1850 and 1978, in an environment that is still shallow. The effects of such a rise on local fish and mollusk populations would have been dramatic.

The chronicle of local climate change will remain incomplete until a new generation of research, now under way, fills in gaps in our knowledge.[5] Sea surface temperature records from the Sargasso Sea, the Florida Straits, the Chesapeake, and even West African waters show that a period of cooling at about the time of Christ was followed by abrupt warming and wetter conditions between AD 1 and 150, then rapid warming until about AD 550. This warmer period coincides in general terms with the Roman Warm Period, when the Romans expanded their empire into Europe. The warmer conditions brought higher sea levels in Denmark and the Mediterranean as well as in South Carolina, where sea levels may even have been slightly higher than they are today. Similar significant transgressions are known from the Gulf of Mexico coast. In the Pine Island area, beach ridges document higher sea levels until about AD 450, with a rise of between 1.2 and 2 meters. Intense hurricanes washed storm deposits ashore that lie sandwiched between human occupations with potsherds. Five centuries with warmer temperatures and higher sea levels, punctuated by shorter-term relatively cool events, produced aquatic conditions that were often similar to today's. The Calusa responded by focusing on fishing, generally with nets, as well as the harvesting of mollusks.

Cooling followed from about AD 500 to 900 over a wide area of the tropical North Atlantic, when temperatures were sometimes lower. There were at least three abrupt sea-level retreats, interspersed with warmer conditions and sea-level rises. These were centuries when there was also considerable volcanic activity, especially around AD 535–36, but the extent to which it affected global climate in the long term is uncertain. However, significant drops in sea level are well documented in Denmark between AD 550 to 850, interspersed with occasional shorter rises. In the Pine Island Sound area the sea level fell as much as 2 meters around AD 550—about 0.6 meter below the twentieth-century mean. This, then, was a period of cooler temperatures and lower sea levels. Isotope analyses of two oyster shells reveal winters that were significantly colder than today's. Most likely it was consistently dry. Hurricanes are not recorded.

These retreats brought lower salinity in shallow waters. Oyster populations shrank; common crown conchs and whelks increased in numbers. In some places the lower sea levels shrank the shallow parts of Pine Island Sound, forcing the fish to the west and perhaps compelling some villages to move elsewhere. This may have been a time when people exploited more saltwater mollusks because fewer fresh ones were available, a choice driven as much by ecological changes as by preference. The consumption of shellfish was such that by this time large shell middens were accumulating.

To return to the climatic record from the Sargasso Sea in the Atlantic: it shows a warming that began in AD 850 and reached a peak in 1000 that continued until about 1100. This coincides in general terms with the Medieval Warm Period, well known for being the time when the Norse settled in Greenland. Sea levels rose over wide areas, including Denmark, the Red Sea, and South Carolina as well as the Gulf of Mexico, where there is evidence from geological deposits of increased storminess. The sea-level rises of the time inundated mangrove swamps and reached as high as the twentieth-century mean. Calusa communities responded by taking a great variety of catches, including small fishes like pinfish and pigfish as well as enormous quantities of whelks, conchs, and other marine snails as well as smaller numbers of oysters and clams. The centuries between AD 800 and 1200 were an apogee of Calusa culture, with hundreds, perhaps thousands, of people living in the immediate vicinity of Pine Island Sound. They left the greatest concentration of shell middens anywhere in North America.

In addition to accumulating huge shell middens, the Calusa constructed steep-sided shell mounds, causeways, ramps, and canals. Some of their middens are linear, snaking through mangrove swamps for hundreds of meters. One on Cayo Costa is 114 meters long and 4.6 meters high. Some communities expended much effort in building canals to aid canoe navigation. The largest, 7 meters wide and 1.5 meters deep, ran for 4 kilometers across Pine Island and was designed as a series of segments separated by small dams. This arrangement enabled a traveler to lift a canoe from one area of impounded water to the next, scaling a height of 3.9 meters as he or she crossed the island. It was, in effect, a canoe portage that was often a canal.[6]

Then came the Little Ice Age, a cooler period that, according to Sargasso Sea records, took hold around 1100 and actually was comprised of at least three cool periods separated by warmer intervals. Once again sea levels dropped, to a level as much as 0.6 meter below modern levels around 1450, with, however, some brief warmer spells. After 1850 dramatic warming occurred, which continues today. Large Calusa settlements remained in use and expanded right up to the seventeenth century, the height of the Little Ice Age, by which time European goods appear in the middens, as the Calusa traded with the Spaniards.

Coping with an Unpredictable World

The Calusa flourished in a maritime environment that offered both unusual opportunities and unpredictable environmental changes. At some sites shark remains are much more common than those of other marine animals. The people probably took these lethal fish with composite bone and wood hooks. They may also have used nets, since most local sharks frequent relatively shallow water.[7] Little is known about Calusa shark-fishing methods, but shark flesh is nutritious, and their teeth were useful as cutting tools and for piercing. The skin could serve as sandpaper. Then there were lightning and pear whelks, which could be collected by the tens of thousands on the sandy bottoms of shallow bays. One adult lightning whelk can yield as much as 0.9 kilogram of flesh. Many Calusa middens in Pine Island Sound contain millions of whelk shells, representing systematic, intensive collection over many centuries. Whelk shells, and perhaps the flesh, were also commodities in highly organized exchange networks, which allowed the Calusa to create a much more complex society than many other maritime groups.

The Calusa were so dependent on fish and mollusks that these two foods comprise most of every sample from their shell middens put through fine-mesh screens.[8] The proportions of fish and mollusks vary, with higher proportions of fish coming from sites nearer the ocean. One deeper inlet sample yielded 47 percent fish, while more estuarine sites had only between 7 and 1 percent. Not surprisingly, the largest fish came from sites by inlets. About half the bones at both shallow-water and inlet sites came from hardheaded catfish and mollusk-eating sheepshead.

In addition to these two staples, the Calusa caught three species of shark and smalltooth sawfish with their bladelike snouts as well as sea trout, lefteye flounders, needlefish, and burr fish. In the sixteenth century the Spanish explorer and geographer Juan López de Velasco witnessed Indians harvesting "a great fishery of [striped or black] mullet . . . which they catch in nets as in Spain."[9] Vast numbers of mullet congregate in estuaries during spawning season between late October and January, making them an attractive target for netting.

Like subsistence fishers everywhere, the Calusa developed a fishing technology that took advantage of readily available raw materials and local conditions. Small-meshed seine nets worked well near shore, where the fishers could walk a loaded net to land. Larger-meshed gill nets were effective in deeper water. Fragments of nets made of palm fiber cordage have been recovered from

Calusa Indians fishing with a net in a shallow estuary. Art by Merald Clark, courtesy Florida Museum of Natural History.

both Key Marco and Pineland. Rectangular net gauges, employed by almost all net-using fishing societies to standardize mesh sizes, have come from several locations. Here they were made of bone, stone, or wood.

Calusa sites also yield grooved-shell *columellae,* the central spires of spiral univalve shells that served as fishing sinkers for nets and lines. Those from Key Marco are larger than those from Pine Island, presumably a reflection of Key Marco's greater depth for fishing and the larger fish caught there. Deeper water usually involved hook-and-line fishing, which relied in some part on baited double-ended bone gorges, with a line lashed to the center. Such devices, called throat gorges, were also effective in shallower water. Some bone points were glued or lashed to shanks, making composite hooks. These were probably very effective when trolling from a canoe for fish that feed by striking, which are not readily taken in nets in either deep or shallow water. Only at sites close to deeper water does one find harpoons or barbed points.

Abundant shallow-water and deepwater fish, an exceptional abundance of edible shellfish, and an equable climate: all these were ingredients for a stable, prosperous existence based on aquatic foods. One could understandably assume that Calusa society developed steadily along a simple trajectory of ever-greater social and political complexity, supported by a reliably plentiful, unchanging but very diverse food base. The Calusa did indeed become a complex, well-organized society over many centuries, with connections across the Florida peninsula. But one subtle variable played a decisive role in their society. Here, more than almost anywhere else in the world, seemingly insignificant sea-level changes could play havoc with Calusa life.[10]

There was no such phenomenon as a stable sea level in this area of shallow waters. Even a rise or fall of a few centimeters could decimate a sea-grass fishery or destroy oyster and whelk beds. Even a minor sea-level change could have momentous consequences for those who relied on shallow-water fish or mollusk beds. The sea-level fluctuations caused by the Medieval Warm Period or the Little Ice Age might not have had much consequence in the deeper waters of the Maine or California coast, but the impacts were significant in the shallow-water estuaries of places like Pine Island Sound.

Pine Island Sound is never deeper than 1.2 meters, and most of it is shallower. The shallowness has endured for centuries, although the sound is now deeper than it was five hundred years ago. In human terms, sea-level changes affected not only the siting of houses but also the availability of firewood and food supplies, especially in cooler times when sea levels fell, as they did between AD 580 and 850. Increased social complexity was most likely a response to harder times.

Among the factors testifying to the growing complexity of Calusa life was greater reliance on watercraft, hinted at by an increase in the number of shell woodworking tools after AD 800. The elite probably controlled boatbuilding, for they needed larger canoes to maintain contacts with trading partners and potential rivals. This is also the period when major works like the Pine Island canal were undertaken and the long-distance trade in valuable stone increased. Cultural influences from powerful chiefdoms with distinctive religious beliefs far to the north may have come into play. Most likely, however, the social organization of Calusa society was never rigidly hierarchical before the arrival of the Spaniards.[11]

The Calusa depended on aquatic resources, and the only way to do so successfully was to live in compact, permanent settlements. In their landscape of low islands and water, the number of truly dry, higher locations was limited, making mobility a challenge and permanent settlement the most viable solution. By the same token, their social networks extended far beyond a single village in an environment where the power of different chiefs changed constantly as the abundance of fisheries fluctuated. Long-term storage was nearly impossible, so control over strategic foods was all-imperative, and reciprocal trade and exchange relationships benefited everyone. Calusa society may have become more complex during difficult times, not because a growing population had outstripped food supplies but because a network of local settlements was needed to balance out supply and demand. Given the impossibility of hoarding, the overwhelming advantage lay in redistributing one's excess to one's needy neighbors, in the expectation that they would do the same when positions were reversed.

The glue that held such diverse societies together must have lain partly in the realm of the intangible. Like other fishing societies, the Calusa enjoyed a complex ritual life in which ceremonial feasting, dancing, and other rituals as well as singing and oral recitations played a highly meaningful role. Almost nothing is known about these practices; we have only some chance discoveries of parts of wooden dancing masks preserved in waterlogged archaeological deposits. A whooping crane head crafted in cypress wood has come from Pineland and is dated to AD 865–985. The bill, which could be opened and shut to make a clacking sound, was clearly part of a dancer's mask.[12] Waterbirds were spiritually influential in Florida Indian society (as well as in many other places) from at least five thousand to six thousand years ago. For example, cranes were associated with shamans, who rode long distances on their backs in Northwest Coast Tlingit iconography. And Ainu girls in Japan have long performed and still perform an elegant crane dance.

The evidence of crane mythology associated with a mask becomes even more significant when combined with several wooden animal heads excavated from the waterlogged Key Marco site in 1895–96. The series includes masks depicting raccoons, rabbits, great horned owls, an eagle, and a falcon.[13] Some may have been parts of dance masks, others totem symbols. The designs would probably have allowed a dancer to produce dramatic special effects during his or her performance. Most likely the Calusa masked dancers performed dramatizations of the process of spiritual transformation, in which the audience participated. Their ancient myth dramas and legends have long vanished into oblivion, but the occasional discoveries of masks and other ceremonial regalia proclaim that the chasm between the living and the supernatural worlds was absolutely bridgeable by both animals and humans. The clacking crane mask of Pineland is a compelling witness.

When the Spaniards first landed in Florida there were about ten thousand Calusa, perhaps more, living over a wide area in the southwest of the peninsula. The explorer Juan Ponce de León explored the coast in 1513, his primary objective being to obtain slaves.[14] He landed just north of today's Cape Canaveral, then sailed south into Biscayne Bay near modern-day Miami. His ships were dirty and leaking, so he anchored in San Carlos Bay, near Fort Myers on the east coast, where he intended to caulk their hulls. The Calusa had never encountered Spaniards, but they had heard of them from fugitives who had fled from Cuba. Twenty, then eighty, Calusa canoes carrying archers with shields approached the ships aggressively. The Spaniards attacked, drove the Indians to shore, and destroyed some of their canoes. But the fierce Calusa warriors forced the visitors to withdraw. Four years later three Spanish ships anchored at the same location, but the Calusa drove off a well-armed landing party. Six Spaniards were wounded, one captured; thirty-five Indians reportedly perished.

In 1519 Spanish ships had reached the Mississippi delta, just when smallpox came ashore and began decimating local populations, with a mortality rate between 50 and 75 percent. Three years later Ponce de León returned to San Carlos Bay in an attempt to found a colony, with a force of two hundred men and fifty horses as well as European livestock. Once again Calusa warriors attacked the Spaniards, this time at close quarters, where their reed arrows were deadly compared with clumsy Spanish crossbows. Ponce de León himself was wounded in the thigh and subsequently died in Cuba.

Smallpox marched ashore ahead of an even stronger Spanish force headed by the brutal Pánfilo de Narváez, which landed north of the Calusa, near present-day Tampa in 1527. Narváez was merely interested in gold and a passage to Asia, but he ordered the public reading of a *requerimiento,* a legal document that bound the Indians to the Catholic church and the Spanish Crown as slaves, subject to savage punishments. This tendentious document was widely used by the Spaniards throughout the Americas to justify colonization. The Calusa would have nothing of it. They met Spanish incursions with deadly arrows. Nevertheless, they engaged in extensive trade in European goods, many of them salvaged from shipwrecks. They were a powerful political and economic presence in southwestern Florida. In 1566 Pedro Menéndez de Avilés described a Calusa town of four thousand people. The chief's house stood atop a tall mound. Eleven years later López de Velasco described a small island, now known as Mound Key, that at the time was the Calusa capital, ruled by a major chief. Mound Key lay behind a narrow, shallow pass that could be navigated only by small canoes.

The Calusa resisted the One True Faith even more forcefully. Dominicans attempted to missionize them in 1549 but withdrew in the face of unrelenting hostility. Jesuits tried in 1566 and 1567 but also failed. The Calusa persisted in their traditional beliefs until the eighteenth century. Their ferocious reputation and swampy homeland enabled them to escape much of the trauma of Spanish colonization until the seventeenth and early eighteenth centuries, when slave raiders from the north brought waves of smallpox epidemics that decimated their densely populated towns and villages. Eventually, the surviving Calusa retreated into more remote country to the south and east. Their descendants were resettled in Cuba during the eighteenth century, except perhaps for a few fishermen of Calusa ancestry in Cuban fishing camps along the southwestern Florida coast. In the end it was not climate change but the ravages of exotic disease that destroyed the Calusa and their distinctive fishing and foraging society. Otherwise, they would probably have survived alongside Europeans into modern times.

11

The Great Fish Have Come In

The Bismarck Archipelago, east of Papua New Guinea in the southwestern Pacific, 1400 BC: The double-hulled canoe lies still in the mirrorlike sea. The crew have lowered the sail. Their craft drifts in the hot sun, barely moving in the slight ground swell. Crude mats shade the men, but they are peering over the side. In the dark shadows cast by the hulls gray shadows lurk, moving sluggishly in the pellucid water. One of the men stands in full sunlight, spear at the ready, waiting for a chance. A brief swirl explodes alongside the canoe. A fin breaks the surface. The spearman thrusts with lightning speed, maintaining a grip on his weapon, but the fish dives as it spots his shadow. He waits patiently. The crew spot more swirling as several tuna swoop by close to the surface. Two spear thrusts impale two fish, who struggle furiously. Deftly, the fishers cast them aboard, where the crew dispatch them with clubs. While the fishermen dismember the catch, the steersman watches the horizon for signs of a breeze. An hour later a gentle air fills in as the trade winds resume from the northeast. While the canoe slips along under full sail, the men eat raw tuna steaks and hoist the rest of the gutted carcasses above the hulls to dry in the sun and wind.

Much of the history of fishing has involved journeys, usually, but not invariably, on water. Fishing took hold in many places when the opportunity arose—in Azania (the East African coast), in Mesopotamia, along the Indian coast, and in Sri Lanka—but it was people's mobility and their interaction with

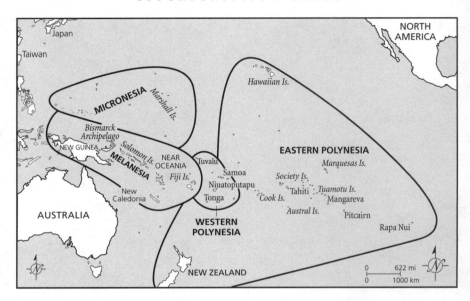

8. New Guinea, the Bismarck Archipelago, and offshore Pacific islands.

others that caused fishing to influence much greater developments. Fishing and voyaging also went hand in hand in Southeast Asia and across the Ice Age lands of Sunda and Sahul as far as the islands of the Bismarck Archipelago. Even farther eastward early fishers voyaged among islands in the Pacific, through Near Oceania and beyond.

The Lapita People

The Bismarck Archipelago forms a scatter of heavily forested islands that extend far south and west into the Pacific. They form a benign voyaging corridor with predictable winds and currents, sheltered from the tropical cyclone belts to the north and south. Using even rudimentary watercraft, late Ice Age seafarers had settled as far south and east as the Solomons by twenty-five thousand years ago. Wherever they paddled or sailed they clung to the islands in small camps and rock shelters, in tiny fishing communities. Island life was a matter of constant movement, of close interdependence between scattered fishing groups, as was the case in such societies in many other parts of the world.

For thousands of years the population of the Southwest Pacific remained tiny, constrained by the realities of the maritime landscape and by endemic malaria from the mainland, imported by the first settlers. Then newcomers in much larger canoes arrived from the west about 1300 BC, and more frequent inter-island voyaging began. Archaeologists call these newcomers the Lapita people, named after an archaeological site on New Caledonia.[1] Expert sailors, they seem to have appeared without warning, perhaps in fast-sailing canoes with much taller rigs quite unlike anything that had plied these waters before. Their crews were as much at ease on the water as they were on land, constantly on the move, apparently in a quest for trading opportunities and new fishing grounds. Fortunately, the extent of Lapita voyages can be traced from a distinctive kind of dentate, stamp-decorated pottery the group created, which serves as a marker for their deep-sea voyaging in the western Pacific. Some of the pots bear intricate designs, including stylistic representations of human faces, as if they were depictions of cultural identity among people who traveled from island to island over enormous distances. Thanks to this pottery and well over two hundred radiocarbon-dated Lapita sites scattered from the Bismarcks to the Solomons, Fiji, Tonga, and Samoa, archaeologists have a sense of this group's spectacular voyaging.

Starting from far to the west before 2000 BC Lapita seafarers migrated over Near Oceania in one of the most remarkable maritime explorations in history, all within a few centuries. Five hundred years later they had settled throughout Near Oceania, intermarrying with the indigenous population. Unlike their opportunistic predecessors on the islands, these immigrants were farmers, whose canoes carried seedlings, chickens, dogs, and pigs from island to island, the first domesticated animals to arrive in the southwestern Pacific. The new crops and animals brought a much-needed flexibility to island economies that relied heavily on fishing and wild plant foods, along with some limited hunting. Lapita farmers stored food, so their canoe skippers could carry taro and thus spend much longer periods at sea. Their greatest limitation was their ability to store drinking water, which they carried in gourds. Nevertheless, voyaging and inter-island contacts intensified, perhaps in the hands of relatively few people. Passage making may have become as much a social phenomenon as a matter of colonization, with powerful social and ritual underpinnings. None of this would have been possible without agriculture and fishing, which provided vital staples for dozens of isolated communities.

Oceanian and Polynesian islands have impoverished flora and terrestrial fauna. Such impoverishment becomes even more marked as one travels farther eastward. The best foodstuffs lie in the water. Coral reef communities, lagoons, and the pelagic waters around tropical Pacific islands support many kinds of edible fish, plus mollusks and crustaceans as well as echinoderms like sea urchins, starfish, and sea cucumbers and a wide variety of seaweeds.

Fishing in Pacific waters presented many challenges to human hunters, who were, after all, unsuited to hunting on the water, which is what fishing really entails. They faced many challenges that were unknown on land—the issue of buoyancy, waves and water turbulence, and the difficulties posed by refracting light when sighting fish below the surface, to mention only a few. This meant that island fishers refined technologies that were first developed in calmer waters off islands in Southeast Asia, including fish traps, hooks, and nets. The Lapita people were the first to venture truly offshore in the western Pacific. Just to survive and to adapt to the maritime and island landscapes of the region would have required expert fishing skill. They could not provision their canoes without dried or salted fish, even if they sometimes relied on fresh catches when under way. I have learned at first hand that fish in deep, open tropical waters prize shade. Lapita outrigger canoes may have provided shade for occasional catches speared or hooked from above, but the provisions stowed on board in advance were the sailors' staples, many of which were preserved catches taken in shallow water.

Lapita fishing methods remain a mystery, for no evidence of them except the bones of catches and the occasional more durable items such as net weights or fishhooks survive.[2] Just as in Southeast Asia, almost all the equipment used for fishing was highly perishable and often soon replaced. About the only way to paint a portrait of Lapita piscatory skills is to consider anthropological research carried out on modern communities that are still using traditional fishing methods. For example, today about a thousand people live on the small Tongan island of Niuatoputapu, which was colonized by Lapita people during the early first millennium BC. These modern inhabitants have been less influenced by Western culture than those on other Tongan islands, so their strategies for catching prey probably remain much the same as they were before Europeans arrived.

Niuatoputapu may be small, a mere fifteen square kilometers in area, but it is blessed with a remarkable diversity of marine ecosystems. These include a shallow, saltwater lagoon, reefs that lie to windward of the island, surge channels leading to the Pacific, and the open ocean. Even on the roughest days women and children can gather mollusks and catch small fish in rock pools, while the men can deploy nets in the sheltered lagoon. Niuatoputapu's fisheries are extremely rich. About four to five hundred fish species, known collectively as *'ika,* inhabit local waters. The most diverse fish populations lie on the outer reef slopes. The lagoon channels are also productive fisheries.

The archaeologist Patrick Kirch and his colleague Tom Dye identified no fewer than thirty-seven distinct fishing methods used by Niuatoputapu's inhabitants. Niuan fishers catch more fish with nets than by other methods, especially in the island's leeward tidal reef flat, which allows for the use of seines. By their very nature seines are communal nets. Seines are most effective when set at high tide; often quite large fish are caught in them as the tide recedes. Catches of over one thousand fish are possible when a seine is set overnight.

Angling with hook and line from reef's edge is not very productive, but fishing from canoes allows Niuan fishers to engage in skipjack trolling, which never takes place farther than seven kilometers from shore. Following tradition, the fishers use a bamboo pole about two meters long, to which they attach two or three lengths of line fitted with pearl-shell lures that have a turtle carapace lure attached to them. The fishers locate shoals by following flocks of birds preying on the small fish that are the skipjack's quarry. When a fish strikes, the fisher immediately jerks it into the boat, where it is dispatched in short order. The jerk is so violent and sudden that the fish sometimes hits the fisherman's chest.

Spearfishing works well on the reef flats located on both the windward and leeward sides of the island, especially at night. A flaming torch often attracts flying fish. Spearing along the windward surge channels is more of a hunt, conducted by men chewing coconut meat. When they see a fish after a wave has surged through, they leap onto a coral head and spit the coconut into the water. The oily sheen clears the water, allowing the spearman to see the bottom. He rapidly spears the fish before another wave enters the channel. This method works well with parrot fish, a popular catch. Poisoning is also widely used. The fishermen seal off the exits from the reef flats with seine nets and then shake the pounded roots of toxic plants from bags into the water, especially under coral heads and overhangs. The stunned fish rise to the surface or lie on the bottom within a few minutes, where they can be speared or simply picked up.

For all their knowledge of numerous species, the Niuans confine most of their fish eating to about thirty-one species but also consume lobsters, crabs, and edible gastropods. The largest number of fish come from inshore waters, especially from the reef flats. Only the much desired 'atu, or skipjack, comes from open water. Mollusks are considered a lowly catch, the domain of women and children, while men regularly take lobsters and crabs, a more prestigious prey.

Applying this information to a reconstruction of Lapita fishing is hampered at once by the paucity of artifacts. Only three shellfish hooks have come from the extensive Niuatoputapu middens. All three are very similar to examples from East Timor and to others found on the Solomon Islands. So far, just one other fishing artifact has come from the extensive middens on Niuatoputapu, a split cowrie shell commonly used as a weight for dip nets throughout Polynesia. Almost certainly most Lapita fishing was in lagoons and other inshore waters, where a wide variety of edible fish could be taken with seines and by angling. Open-water trolling for tuna must have been a matter of careful observation combined with skilled seamanship conducted relatively close to land.

Deep-sea fishing never played a major role in the long-distance voyaging that took the descendants of the Lapita people from Samoa eastward into the heart of Polynesia, to the Society Islands, and farther into the remote Pacific. Such voyages depended on carefully stored foodstuffs, not wholly on fish caught in open water. Shallow-water fisheries helped sustain the lengthy journeys that took canoes far offshore into Remote Oceania.

The Central Pacific

Imagine colonizing a random pattern of islands scattered over thousands of square kilometers of open water, and upwind in the teeth of the prevailing winds at that.[3] Such was the challenge facing the voyagers who sailed eastward beyond Samoa. Lapita seafarers had reached Tonga and Samoa by 800 BC. They stayed around Samoa and the Tonga archipelago for more than a thousand years. Then, suddenly, between about AD 1000 and 1300 Polynesian seafarers discovered and usually colonized nearly every other island in the eastern Pacific within a remarkably short time frame. No one knows why this sudden wave of exploration unfolded, but it may have been the result of a combination of improved deepwater canoes with better loading capacity, land shortages at home, and plain adventurous curiosity. Polynesian social structure revolved around cultivable gardens and access to the land, so many voyages may have been searches for territory that could be cleared, farmed, and then inherited by one's family.

There is no question that the explorers intended to return. Almost invariably they voyaged to the east against the prevailing winds, taking advantage of lulls in the trade winds, always with the guarantee that they could return with following breezes if they needed to do so. Vast reservoirs of traditional navigational lore using the stars and other phenomena came into play. Whatever the cause of this surge in colonization, both radiocarbon dates and artifacts confirm that it was a rapid process. Adzes and fishhooks in such widely separated locations as the Society Islands, the Marquesas, and New Zealand show close similarities, as if their common origin was within the recent past. Most Polynesians stayed at home, cultivated their fields, and fished lagoons. Passage making was a prestigious activity, for the ocean waters across Polynesia were not a barrier but a network of watery highways that connected each island to many others. With these pathways across the open Pacific came economic, social, and other ties, many of which endured for generations.

The arrival of people on remote Pacific islands led to immediate, often fundamental, environmental change and, frequently, to deforestation from agriculture. Widespread soil erosion followed, leading to the intensive hunting and ultimate extinction of many land and sea birds as well as animals like indigenous turtles. The islands became cultural environments. Ingenious and highly productive agriculture combined with fishing produced large food surpluses on islands like Tahiti, despite rising population densities. Inevitably, political and ritual power passed to those who owned the best land. By AD 1600 some Polynesian societies had developed elaborate chiefdoms headed by classes of chiefs, navigators, and priests. Factionalism and fierce rivalries led to vicious competition, slippery alliances, and war. Few kingdoms, aside from Hawaii, were as elaborate or powerful as those in the Society Islands, most notably on Tahiti.[4]

Early European visitors described traditional Tahitian fishing on an island that was a hub of long-distance voyaging. When the French explorer Louis-Antoine de Bougainville (after whom the well-known plant is named) anchored off Tahiti in 1767 he encountered a flamboyant island society apparently living in harmony with nature. The more phlegmatic Captain James Cook arrived six years later to observe a transit of the planet Venus across the sun. He returned on several occasions, during which he and his officers wrote voluminous accounts of Tahiti and its people. They gave an impression that the Tahitians were indifferent, even casual farmers but ardent and skilled fishers. This may or may not have been true.

Generations of writers, including anthropologists, have left us with quite detailed accounts of Tahitian fishing, the most technically developed of all their subsistence activities—and a vital source of protein. Fishing was also the nearest that the Polynesians came to participating in a sport. The missionary William Ellis wrote in 1829, "The smoothness and transparency of the sea within the reefs, favoured their aquatic sports, and a chief and his men, furnished with their spears (etc), often set out on their fishing excursions with an exhilaration of spirit equal to that with which a European nobleman pursues the adventures of the chase."[5] The more daring younger chiefs would pursue sharks. Older nobles would sit in their canoes and watch.

Tahitian fishers had access to a very broad range of seafood.[6] There were edible sea turtles that were easily captured when nesting on surrounding atoll beaches. Crustaceans included freshwater shrimp, langoustes, and crabs. Urchins were a common food, as were mussels, oysters, and the giant *Tridacna* saltwater clam (also widely eaten in Mediterranean lands). Gastropods abounded among the reefs and lagoons, while the shells were used for fashioning tools and ornaments. The Tahitians loved octopus, but fish were the most important food from the ocean. They took a broad range of species from reefs and in lagoons, everything from sharks and rays to eels. Then there were pelagic fish like tuna and bonito, even swordfish.

The islanders were omnivorous fish eaters, catching their prey large and small with an astounding array of methods. They tickled fish in shallow water, used small nets and sticks, speared and trapped lobsters and freshwater prawns. They are said to have avoided oysters to keep from cutting their feet on the sharp shells. The villagers also poisoned fish in still water with toxic leaves and roots. Much depended on an intimate knowledge of their prey, to which they adapted their methods. Turtles were a great delicacy. Their shells were used for fishhooks and ornaments, and their meat was offered to temples. Eels abounded in streams, lakes, and lagoons and were a considerable delicacy that figured prominently in local folklore and legend. Some eels were kept in large, shallow pools and grew to an enormous size in narrow defiles, emerging only when called by a shrill whistle to be fed.

The Tahitians excelled at net making. They made hand scoop and casting nets with fine mesh that they cast over shoals of small fish, sometimes enclos-

Fijians driving lagoon fish, shouting, singing, and splashing to scare the catch into a large seine net. Drawing by an unknown artist, 1973. Private Collection/© Look and Learn/Bridgeman Images.

ing most of them. The great seine nets, constructed of strong bark with communal effort, were the most impressive of all. Some were as much as 73 meters long and 3.65 meters deep. The bottom edge was weighted with stones, while the top was kept afloat with hibiscus-wood floats. Mainly used for lagoon fishing, the nets were hauled by men with canoes or were fixed to the bottom by swimmers, who also drove the fish into captivity. Even when the work was done from canoes, people in the water worked the net, catching fish when they tried to escape. If sharks intervened, men swimming beside the net goaded them ashore. Permanent and temporary weirs worked well when fish swam into streambeds and lagoons. Expert fishermen armed with simple or multiple-pronged spears jabbed at their catch while swimming or hurled their weapons from canoes or from rocks. Many fishers worked after dark by torchlight, using torches formed of bundles of dry coconut fronds. The fisherman would hold his torch in one hand, his spear in the other, ready to strike when a fish appeared.

Many Tahitian fishermen were expert anglers with rod, hook, and line, but they excelled above all at offshore fishing, a dangerous and challenging search for albacore, bonito, dolphin, sharks, and even swordfish. Centuries of experimentation and hard experience turned them into truly expert offshore fishermen, probably more so than any earlier Polynesians. Fortunately, Charles Nordhoff, a journalist, writer, and ardent fisherman, described Tahitian fishing methods during the 1920s.[7] Even after centuries of European influence their fishing methods had achieved such a level of perfection that they still survived more or less intact. Albacore, bonito, and dolphin were the primary catches, largely because they traveled in shoals. The fishers were bold men, tackling dolphins weighing forty-five kilograms or more as a matter of routine. According to the eighteenth-century *Bounty* mutineer James Morrison, the Tahitians always fished for dolphin while sailing against the wind, deploying long lines made of tough sword grass fitted with pointed wooden hooks fabricated of strong roots or ironwood. The hooks were baited with flying fish. Unlike Europeans who used hooks with barbs, Tahitian fishers never jerked the line to lodge the hook in a fish's mouth. Instead, they kept a steady tension on the line, allowing the fish to catch itself. The pull of the line caused the hook to revolve and to set deeper into the fish's jaw.

According to Nordhoff, an experienced older man helming a canoe would approach birds wheeling around a shoal from upwind. The old man flung bait into the sea to attract the fish. The young fishermen with him cast their baited lines into the water as the canoe luffed into the wind and lost speed. When a fish struck a hook, the fisher kept a steady tension on the line until the catch became tired. Then he held it steady some meters below the surface. Meanwhile, trolling resumed, on the assumption that the fish would swim away if the first one was taken into the canoe. Once a second fish was hooked, the first was cast into the canoe, then quickly triced up so it was helpless. The rapid fire routine continued until all the fish were in the boat.

Albacore came in several varieties, all known to the Tahitians as *'a'ahi*. They congregated fairly close to island reefs in areas where currents swept small fry into close quarters, allowing the albacore to feast on them. These so-called holes were in relatively calm waters; about a dozen were located off Tahiti alone. The fishermen caught smaller albacore with pearl-shell hooks. They also fished with deep, stone-weighted lines inside the holes, having cast chum into the water and baited the hooks.

To catch larger albacore, the Tahitians used what they called a *tira*. At the surface of the water between two canoes, the fishermen rigged a flat basketwork structure between them upon which to land fish. The tira, a long, curved pole with a bifurcating end, carried two lines with baited pearl-shell hooks, rigged so that they lay close to the surface of the water. The bifurcation secured the lines to the tira and then led to the stern of the canoe, where the fishers watched the hooks. Bunches of feathers attached to the pole dipped and twisted with the pitching of the canoe, mimicking the birds that followed the small fish on which the albacore preyed. The albacore followed the birds as much as they did the small fish, so they struck at the baited hooks. Once a fish was well hooked the fishers pulled on the line, using the tira as a cranelike device. As soon as the fish was on the basketwork platform, the fishers swung out the pole and chased after the shoal with frantic paddling. Tira fishing was so highly productive, especially for landing large fish, that communal fishing for albacore was held in much higher regard than the work of a solitary angler.

Nordhoff drew an analogy between a tira fisherman and an expert tennis player and wrote of fishers who were said to have two fish in the air at once. Each fisherman owned several hooks, which he changed at short notice depending on weather conditions. The pearl-shell shank, which also served as the lure, was a highly prized possession; each was given an individual name. A true expert used short, blunt hooks, adjusted and designed to just lift the fish out of the water before the hook came loose. By that time, the catch was shooting toward the canoe and the hook was almost immediately back at work. True masters of the technique were few and far between.

Bonito swim off Tahiti in large schools, chasing their smaller prey at high speeds that challenged canoe paddlers. They are voracious feeders, constantly moving rapidly to find and devour more food. Fishers had to be fit to catch up with a bonito school, which often took hours. Once among their quarry, the fishers had but minutes to make their catches and land them as they broke water around the canoe. The Tahitians used ingeniously designed hooks with carefully aligned points canted at the correct angle to set in the fish. The hooks were colored precisely to attract the bonito. Using a rod up to 5.5 meters long, the fisher would cast the hook and then jerk his catch quickly into the canoe.

The canoe skippers knew which fish they were pursuing from the species of birds that followed them. For example, boobies and terns hunting together were a sign that the former were hunting albacore and the latter were tracking bonito. The volume of fish lore was encyclopedic, as was canoe owners' knowledge of weather and winds. These skippers were expert at forecasting fishing conditions, the most favorable for bonito fishers being the *maoa'e,* the light north to northeast wind that blows steadily and warmly all day. The fish changed with the seasons, and most fishing took place during the summer, known to the Tahitians as *te tai,* or "the [open] sea," when calm conditions prevailed for much of the time. The stronger northeasterly trades of winter generated large swells, which made fishing dangerous. The American linguist Frank Stimson recorded some of the Tahitian songs associated with fishing, which incorporated centuries of oral lore, especially those associated with the phases of the moon. "*Tamatea.* The moon has begun to shine brightly, the great fish have come in from the deep sea upon the sand shallows. . . . A net is again the fishing method." And, on moonless nights, *Māuri-matĕ:* "Daylight has trodden on the moon, the moon has set; the fish, too, have gone to sleep; this [is] a very fishless night."[8]

To the North: Hawaii

A century or so after colonizing the Society Islands, Polynesians, probably from the Marquesas, ventured north into unknown waters. They colonized Hawaii sometime after AD 1000 as part of the rapid settlement of Remote Oceania. Some decades of sporadic voyaging ensued, commemorated in Hawaiian oral traditions that tell of great navigators like Mo'ikeha and Pa'ao. They are said to have sailed to a mythic homeland known as Kahiki, perhaps Tahiti, and returned safely. The great voyages ceased after 1300, when Hawaii became completely isolated from the rest of Polynesia, except for the symbolic return of an anthropomorphic god, Lono, who was said to journey to Kahiki and back. This was why the Hawaiians, when they learned that he had sailed from Tahiti in 1778, assumed that Captain Cook was Lono. Cook promptly became a revered ancestor. By this time at least 230,000 people lived on the Hawaiian Islands under the rule of powerful chiefs. For all their isolation, the Hawaiians had a profound sense of their maritime ancestry and a strong bond with the great ocean, whose fish gave them most of their protein.[9]

With human occupation Hawaii underwent fundamental environmental change. The Hawaiians achieved a remarkable level of agricultural production, including carefully nurtured taro cultivation, using irrigation and terraced hillsides. Fish and shellfish were the main source of protein for the Hawaiians. They were expert fisherfolk and had a profound knowledge of the ocean and its denizens. They relied on a wide range of fishing strategies, among them spearing, trapping, and netting as well as trolling and angling, methods introduced by early settlers and familiar throughout the Pacific. Unlike other Polynesians, the Hawaiians relied on bone rather than shell for most of their hooks.

Different ways of attaching the line, the size of the hook, and variations in the curvature of the shank—all reflected minor variations in design resulting from dissimilar environments and quarry. In general, however, the basic fishhook designs were remarkably like those from elsewhere in Polynesia, perhaps reflecting the rapid spread of colonists to the islands. The biggest two-piece hooks caught large game fish, such as tuna, and also sharks. Some fishhook makers used even human bone for their largest hooks, prized for their size and strength. Using the bones of a defeated enemy to make hooks was also a means of humiliating a foe's family or village. Some chiefs went to great lengths to disguise their burial places to prevent them from being violated by fishhook makers.

The islanders exploited a wide range of local environments. The shoreline was a rich source of shellfish, especially crabs and sea urchins, as well as of seaweed and some small fish. The leeward shores, with their smoother seas, were the most productive. Because of its well-developed reefs an inshore zone was the most productive of all marine ecosystems, and it was here the people fished most intensively. The so-called benthic zone, with waters from about 30 to 350 meters deep, was the deepest water regularly exploited. It had much lower fish populations but was a favorite place for taking rockfish like snapper. Here, people used the line, armed with ingenious, weighted lure hooks. Finally, there was the pelagic zone, where fishers trolled for much-prized skipjack tuna. These tuna, known as *aku,* were a high-status food reserved for chiefs and other people of rank.

The Hawaiians were unique in the Pacific for their extensive aquaculture, which was based not on weirs and traps but on an abundance of mostly walled fishponds. In Southeast Asia people both farmed fish and corralled much of their wild catches for later consumption. Aquaculture mitigated shortfalls in freshwater catches for everyone. In Hawaii fishponds became symbols of chiefly status and power. The ponds' yields fed chiefs' households and the chiefly penchant for conspicuous consumption. The mid-nineteenth-century Hawaiian sage Samuel Kamakau wrote, "Fishponds were things that beautified the land, and a land with many fishponds was called 'fat.'"[10] The ponds turned Hawaiian fishing into far more than a subsistence activity. Fish became a commodity with social meaning. The islanders entered the realm of intensive fish production and husbandry. Combined with large-scale taro irrigation in fertile valleys and extensive dry-land farming systems, several hundred fishponds throughout the islands enabled the Hawaiians to produce large food

Ancient Hawaiian fishpond on Molokai. Courtesy Gaertner/Alamy Stock Photo.

surpluses and to develop complex chiefdoms. Most ponds lay along the coast on shallow reef flats, where the owners could easily construct broad, semicircular barriers out from the shore. Such locations included Pearl Harbor on Oahu and the south shore of Molokai. Landowners also added walls and gates to natural spring-fed ponds in lava basins along the coast, which turned them into productive water holes.

The most important ponds were the arc-shaped coastal ones, known as *loko kuapa*, with walls constructed of basalt and coral blocks that projected about a meter above the highest tide level. The builders constructed gaps with carefully designed sluice gates that allowed seawater to flow in and out but prevented the fish from leaving. Such ponds varied in size from 0.4 to 212 hectares. Some of these coastal ponds are still in use on Molokai, but many are now buried from siltation. Most of the fish raised in these ponds were milkfish or mullet, both of which thrive in brackish water. Freshwater ponds inland were used to raise smaller fish and shrimp. A study conducted a century ago estimated that Hawaiian fishponds produced an average of 166 kilograms of fish annually, not an exceptionally large amount by modern standards but closely tied to social prestige and conspicuous consumption.

Everywhere from the Red Sea to remote Pacific islands, canoes and merchant ships relied on fish landed not in deep waters but close to shore. Dried, salted, and smoked fish provided sustenance for men sailing along distant shores and far offshore. Inconspicuous catches along these shores were a driving force of history as early civilizations traded over ever-longer distances in increasingly complex webs of connectedness.

PART TWO

Fishers in the Shadows

Without fisherfolk and their catches, the pharaohs could never have built the pyramids of Giza, and the stupendous temple of Angkor Wat in Cambodia would have been a shadow of its present self. Moche lords on the north coast of Peru depended so heavily on coastal anchovy fishers that their spectacular, gold-laden state might never have arisen without them. Most early civilizations flourished beside estuaries, lakes, and rivers or within easy reach of the ocean. Without the laden baskets and canoes of the fishing communities outside city walls, far from the great ceremonial centers, many ancient civilizations would never have come into being.

The world's first cities emerged in the eastern Mediterranean world around 3100 BC. Other preindustrial states developed independently somewhat later in Asia and in the Americas, but all of them had some common features. All were complex social pyramids with an all-powerful, usually divine ruler at the summit. Below him were carefully defined classes of nobles, officials of all kinds, and priests as well as specialized craftspeople and merchants. At the base of the pyramid were thousands of commoners, including farmers, herders, porters, small-time artisans, male and female—and fisherfolk. The entire superstructure of the state, whether Sumerian, Egyptian,

Roman, Shang, or Maya, depended on powerful ideologies that propelled the efforts of thousands of anonymous laborers, people who served on great estates, built temples, tombs, and public buildings, and produced the rations that fed not only the ruler but also his armies of officials. Some of the most essential and most anonymous of these laborers were the fishers, who, along with farmers, were the most vital of all food purveyors in states that had to feed large numbers of people engaged in public works.

Subsistence fishing fed families and kin groups, communities, and sometimes neighbors near and far. Much fishing was a solitary pursuit—a man or a woman with hook and line or standing on a convenient boulder with a barbed weapon. Cooperation was a rarer occurrence—when seine nets were deployed or a village was exploiting a catfish spawn or salmon run. Then the harvest required catching, gutting, and drying thousands of fish in a short time. This was something very different from subsistence fishing, even if the technology remained largely unchanged from earlier times. Increasingly as populations grew, fishers worked together, transporting their catches to small towns and then cities, bringing fish to markets and temples every day before dawn. Fish became a commodity rather than a food caught for individuals and their kin. For the first time, some communities became virtually full-time fishers, bartering or selling fish in town and village markets in exchange for other necessities. Their catches were recorded and taxed. In time, fish became rations of standard size issued to noble and commoner alike. The ruler and the state required hundreds, even thousands, of skilled and unskilled laborers. Their work might be a form of taxation, but the king had to support them in kind.

The earliest evidence of the use of fish for rations comes from Egypt, where Nile catfish were easily harvested, especially during the spawn, then gutted and dried in the tropical sun on large racks. The pyramid town at Giza includes a large fish-processing building. The authorities assigned teams of fishers to catch specific quotas within set periods, especially when the inundation was receding. The camps the fishermen used are long vanished, but paintings in nobles' tombs show that large seine nets provided much of the catch, deployed and hauled in by teams of villagers. Over many centuries Nile fishers helped feed those who labored on the public buildings, temples, and sepulchers of ancient Egypt. They were the harvest of the river, just as cereals were the produce of the fields.

Fish as rations had numerous advantages. Shallow-water species in particular could be taken in enormous numbers at predictable times of year. One has only to look at the Tonle Sap fishery in Cambodia, whose catfish fed thousands of Khmer laboring on Angkor Wat and its canals and reservoirs. Early European visitors who crossed the lake after the monsoon, as the water level was falling, reported catfish teeming so thickly that one could almost walk across the water on their backs.

Once people had mastered ways of preserving the catch, they had access to potentially enormous quantities of food that could readily be hefted on the backs of donkeys or in saddle packs, could be packed tightly even into small boats, and, above all, could be kept for some weeks or months without spoiling. Fish rations contributed to the great upsurge in mobility that resulted from an explosion in long-distance trade between long-isolated parts of the Mediterranean and Asian worlds. Like much later medieval travelers, both land-based merchants and ocean voyagers carried dried fish on the backs of their animals or in ships' holds. Dried fish were the food that first linked Egypt to the Indian Ocean and the waters of the Persian Gulf. They were not necessarily carried all the way from the Red Sea to, say, India. For centuries small camps of Fish-Eaters bartered fish as provisions for passing ships. On the other side of the world, along the arid north coast of Peru, the anchovy fisheries, nourished by natural upwelling from the seabed, yielded enormous numbers of small fish that, when dried and turned into fish meal, made a valuable food supplement for farmers. Caravans of llamas carried bags of fish meal high into the Andes, where it was a major economic prop of the Inka empire.

Great public projects like pyramid building and flood works along the

Indus River eventually caused inconspicuous but relentless overfishing. Just as hunter-gatherers in Southwest Asia and China turned from foraging to deliberate cultivation of wild cereals, so, inevitably, fishing communities became involved in aquaculture. At first this meant the corralling of marooned catfish in specially deepened ponds, as undoubtedly happened along the Lower Yangtze River in southern China, on the shores of the Tonle Sap, and in Egypt's Nile Delta and Faiyum Depression. But aquaculture soon became much more sophisticated. Those who oversaw ponds large and small learned about critical nutrients, about raising small fry introduced into enclosures, and about rotating the fish between ponds as they grew. Exactly when and where fish farming began is unknown, but it appears that Egyptians and Chinese were the first expert aquaculturists, perhaps as early as 2500 BC. At first, the most common farmed fish were various forms of carp, which were easily penned and bred in captivity. As expertise intensified, fish farmers grew mullet and other popular fish by the thousands.

Aquaculture was a response to rising city and rural populations, to the uncertainties of harvests, and to a growing demand for provisions on a scale large enough to feed armies and fleets of merchant vessels and warships. Over the centuries it became big business, largely because its products could be supplied reliably and predictably. Alongside dried fish there were fermented products as well. By Roman times a large international trade in the fish sauce known as garum, used as a condiment by rich and poor alike, extended from northern Europe to the empire's eastern frontiers. The garum industry relied on a wide range of fishes, mainly smaller species, to create an array of diverse sauces, some of remarkably high quality.

Fish and fish farming are quiet activities, carried out by men and women who jealously guarded their hard-won knowledge and passed it down to succeeding generations. The Fish-Eaters of the Red and Erythraean Seas were considered barbarians by the Greek writers who fleetingly described them. They were people apart, people who appeared with their catches at court kitchens, markets, and temples, then vanished quietly back to their small, often transitory villages in the hinterland. Perhaps it was the smell of fish that clung to them or the simple baskets, nets, and spears they used to harvest their catches that kept them isolated from the townsfolk. Or perhaps they preferred to be taken for granted. But their efforts helped create, feed, and link great civilizations for thousands of years.

12

Rations for Pharaohs

The Nile Valley, Upper Egypt, sixteen thousand years ago: A tiny cluster of reed shelters, a line of hearths, and simply constructed reed drying racks set on a dune in an arid wadi. For generations the hunting bands in these encampments have returned to these locations. They have watched for days while the brown, silt-filled waters of the summer inundation crept into the dry valley, creating pools and submerging valley dunes under deepening water. Each morning as the sun rises the elders watch the dawn mist hugging the valley, then the rising sun cloaking the low cliffs and desert outcrops in delicate pink. Their eyes are alert for movement in the shallows, for catfish feasting on low-flying insects. As the days pass, the shallow floodwaters reach into the desert and begin to teem with spawning fish. It is time to begin the harvest.

The Mediterranean Sea of sixteen thousand years ago stood far below modern levels. The mouth of the river that would later be called the Nile lay at least fifty kilometers offshore from where it is today. The river passed across a gently undulating near-desert dissected by numerous small channels. Thanks to the steeper gradient, it flowed much faster than it does today, bringing down more gravel than silt. Far upstream, wadis opened into the river, filled with dunes created by sand blown down from nearby low cliffs. Only a few thousand hunters and foragers dwelt in this harsh landscape. They survived by keeping close to the water, moving constantly in search of edible plant foods, game, and fish.

Wadi Kubbaniya is an inconspicuous valley that joins the west bank of the Nile about thirty kilometers south of Aswan in southern Egypt.[1] It has been dry for thousands of years except during rare heavy rainstorms, when it overflows with fast-moving water. A less promising landscape for human settlement is hard to imagine, yet sixteen thousand years ago small bands of foragers visited there at irregular intervals to feed on the catfish that abounded in the shallows created by the annual Nile inundation. Every summer rising floodwaters submerged the valley's lowermost dunes before slowly receding. These inundations brought small bands to Wadi Kubbaniya to camp amid its drought-tolerant scrub and occasional tamarisk trees. When the valley dried up, their search for food moved elsewhere.

During the 1960s the archaeologists Fred Wendorf and Romuald Schild plotted artifact scatters and bone fragments in a search for the visitors' temporary camps. The two archaeologists pieced together a complex mosaic of seasonal occupations over many centuries. Judging from the distribution of small stone artifacts and food remains, the Wadi Kubbaniya people exploited a long, narrow territory that extended at least 150 kilometers downstream.

Nile catfish begin to spawn with the start of flooding and finish in September as the waters recede. During the higher floods of sixteen thousand years ago the Nile's overflow extended far up the wadi. At first the people would camp on the escarpments overlooking the flooded valley or move up-wadi to harvest fish at the water's edge. As the waters receded, the fishers took more catfish and also some tilapia (another bottom fish) and eels from swales and cut-off ponds. Most catfish bones from the Wadi Kubbaniya sites come from adults harvested in enormous numbers and dried for later consumption. The catfish harvest of Wadi Kubbaniya is a classic case of opportunistic mobility.

Clarias, the Nile catfish, has a long dorsal fin and a bony head covered with distinctive bumps, qualities that make it relatively easy to recognize in archaeological sites.[2] As today's Nile fishers testify, *Clarias* tolerates conditions that kill most other species. They congregate in shallow, deoxygenated waters, which they can survive thanks to an elaborate oxygen breathing system that lets them move overland from one body of water to another, a trait that enables them to colonize swamps and backwaters with considerable speed. They are also said to burrow deep into the mud of temporary pools when they dry up until they flood once more.

Nile catfish spawn in teeming runs concentrated in small streams, making them an easy target for humans, just as they were for hundreds of thousands

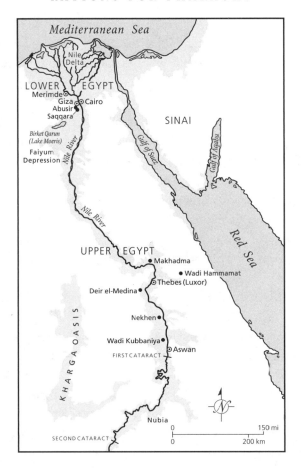

9. Upper and Lower Egypt, with major archaeological sites in chapter 12.

of years in tropical Africa. One can envision naked fishermen standing in shallow pools among the dunes, stabbing rapidly with bone-tipped spears, then flipping the wriggling fish onto the sand. Others in the band grab the fish and club them before quickly cutting them open and splaying the eviscerated carcasses along the backbone. Within moments the catfish are drying on reed racks in the hot sun. When the fish crowded the shallows, the fishers simply reached down and grabbed them, often feeling for them with their feet. Sometimes a band would form a close line across a drying pond and drive the fish into ever-shallower water, where they could simply be picked up.

The catfish harvest offered a temporary feast, but its real importance lay in the drying racks, which turned the fish into food for the lean months when other foods were scarce and elusive. Some groups used fire to smoke their catches. A twelve-thousand-year-old site at Makhadma in Upper Egypt has yielded thick garbage heaps with fish bones and abundant charcoal, including what were probably smoking pits.[3]

As sea levels rose and the Nile slowed, the inundations brought heavy silt loads that built up a large delta at its mouth. Water also overflowed into the arid Faiyum Depression, eighty kilometers southwest of Cairo, forming fish-rich Lake Moeris (now Birket Karun).[4] Its dunes, marshes, and reed beds made the depression a magnet for human settlement by at least eleven thousand years ago. Scatters of nine-thousand-year-old fish bones from camps along the north shore of the then-extensive lake have yielded numerous catfish bones. The lake also supported a diverse population of other shallow-water species, most of which were taken from the receding floodwaters at spawning season.

The Nile Delta, which would become the granary of the pharaohs, was also a bountiful fishery. Here, the floodplain extended to the horizon, a maze of scrubland, swamps, narrow, shallow channels, and reed-choked ponds that changed with each flood. This was the ancient Egyptians' Ta Mehu (land of papyrus), named for *Cyperus papyrus,* a wetland sedge that yielded its pith for the thin, paperlike sheets used by scribes. Like the Faiyum, the delta was a paradise for shallow-water fishers, a fishery so predictably rich that opportunism could give way to routine. The tools and weapons that had long dispatched terrestrial game and trapped birds—clubs, barbed spears, and simple nets—were more than sufficient in the shallows and at water's edge. Here, the fishing grounds were extensive and ever changing, the water often too deep for shore-based spearmen. At some unknown moment Egyptian fishers took to the water in boats constructed from the only raw material available in their treeless world, papyrus reeds.

The technology is simplicity itself and is known to have been in use in Kuwait by at least 7000 BC. Almost certainly Nile fisherfolk began using papyrus watercraft about the same time, for this is when the diversity of fish found in archaeological sites increases dramatically to include such deeper-water fish as mullet and Nile perch. The fishermen lashed papyrus stalks into tight bundles to form double-ended canoes with elevated ends. Using the same technique, they also built sturdy rafts that could be used for casting nets and carrying loads. The hot, dry climate worked to the fishers' advantage, for they could prolong the useful lives of their easily waterlogged canoes by laying them out in the sun to dry. Ancient fishers in southern California and coastal Peru did the same. Papyrus revolutionized Egyptian fishing, turning it from opportunistic foraging into a much more intensive form of subsistence and then into a sport. In much later times the Eighteenth Dynasty high official Userhat, who had the imposing title of scribe who counts bread in Upper and Lower Egypt, commissioned a painting in which he is shown spearing a fish from a papyrus boat, accompanied by his cats as his family looks on. Other nobles used this theme for their own vacation snapshots.

The delta and quiet backwaters farther upstream were ideal for papyrus craft and may have been the nursery of subsistence fishing. Two fish in particular became crucial: the Nile perch and the mullet. The Nile perch (*Lates niloticus*) is a silvery fish with a blue tinge that can grow quite large, sometimes weighing more than ninety kilograms.[5] Larger specimens had enough flesh to feed a great many people. It testifies to their importance that in later times they were frequently mummified.

Mullet (Mugilidae) are among the commonest coastal fish in temperate and tropical ocean waters.[6] The three species that occur along Egypt's Mediterranean coast all enter the Nile and swim far upstream. One species, *Mugil cephalus*, a gray mullet, is found as far south as the First Cataract, 1,850 kilometers from the delta. Today, along with tilapia, they are the most vital commercial fish in the country. Gray mullet congregate in large, easily caught schools in the delta, especially in deep water or where water plants are abundant, before leaving to spawn at sea.

A wide variety of artifacts, including tomb paintings and other art, depict ancient Egyptian fishing practices. The technology was simple and changed little over millennia. By the time the Giza Pyramids of the Old Kingdom were built, in the mid-third millennium BC, barbed spears and harpoons with bone, horn, or ivory points were in common use. Most of the time, fishers stabbed their prey, sometimes with bidents, or two-pronged spears. A tomb relief in the sepulcher of Kagemni, a vizier and judge of about 2335 BC, shows three fishermen impaling fish with barbed spears in shallow water.

Fishhooks have a long history in Egypt. The earliest, made of bone, ivory, and shell, date to long before the pharaohs. None have barbs. Copper hooks come into use around the time of unification in 3100 BC, but barbed hooks were unknown until about the Twelfth Dynasty (c. 1878 BC). A scene from the sepulcher of the Fifth Dynasty official Ti, from 2400 BC, shows a fisherman hauling in a large catfish, holding a club in his right hand ready to dispatch it.

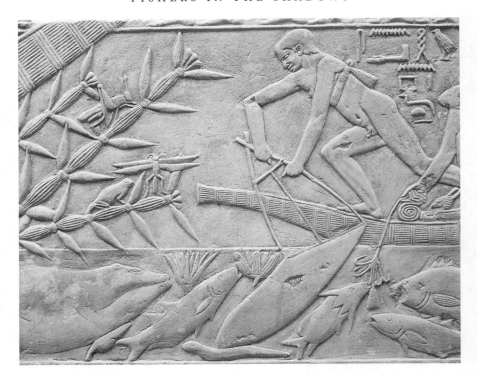

Egyptian Old Kingdom fishermen catching fish from a papyrus canoe in shallow
water. From the *mastaba* of Kagemni, Saqqara. Sixth Dynasty, c. 2300 BC.
Bridgeman Images.

Another tomb scene from Saqqara shows a fisherman in a papyrus canoe trapping a large catfish. Another fisher holds a line with his index finger extended
to feel a tug from a hooked fish. Underwater, five hooks lie in wait. One has
caught a catfish of the genus *Synodontis*, notorious for its bony spines. By
about 1950 BC tombs depict nobles seated in chairs fishing in artificial ponds
in their gardens. There is more to this scene than just sport. Invariably, they
are catching tilapia, a symbol of rebirth. Whether bait was used is unknown,
but it likely was. In many cases, however, fishermen would use a naked hook
and jig the line, the fish being attracted to the shiny metal.

Cooperation produced larger harvests. The reeds and shallows of both the
delta and the Faiyum were ideal environments for barricade traps. Using simple barriers of reeds and sticks, fishers could channel fish into shallow water,
where they could spear them or take them by hand. Unfortunately, no examples of such barricades have survived from ancient times, but in the early

twentieth century the archaeologist and natural historian William Leonard Stevenson Loat observed modern Egyptians capturing mullet by netting them in river channels leading to the ocean.[7] When villagers spotted a shoal moving downstream to spawn, they alerted the fishers, who set nets across narrow channels and encircled the fish.

Loat saw people living by Lake Qarun using a cone-shaped trap fabricated from dried reeds, known as a *garaby*. Each trap had a wide opening and a narrower one; the narrow end was tied with reeds and then opened to release the trapped fish into a waiting basket. The fishers fixed larger weirs in position with stakes set into the banks and with a large trap in the center whose entrance was supported by floats. The narrow end of the trap could be lifted from the water and the contents tipped into a basket. This required the fishers to keep several canoes rafted together while they emptied the traps.

Most subsistence fishing involved simpler devices, especially nets. A scene from the elaborate tomb of the vizier Mereruka of the Sixth Dynasty at Saqqara shows fishermen raising their catch in nets. Hand nets were ideal for taking small to medium-sized fish in shallower water. The fisherman would lash a pair of sticks near a handle, forming a V braced with a third stick, while a cord formed the third side of the triangle. He would attach a net to the triangle so that it could be manipulated by the cord. One can envision a man or woman standing in shallow water, casting the net and watching it gradually sink, pulled down by light weights. The fisher would then expectantly retrieve it, just as people do today.

By Old Kingdom times, which began about 2686 BC, Egyptian fishers were catching at least twenty-three fish species, all of which are found in Egyptian markets today. Saqqara tomb paintings hint that mullet were among the most prized, not only for their flesh but also for their roe. They are the most frequently represented, followed by catfish and Nile perch. While many fish were sold fresh, most were slit down to the backbone, cleaned, and laid flat or hung up to dry, with the head and backbone often left intact. A scene in the tomb of the vizier Teti of the Sixth Dynasty, who was responsible for the scribes of the royal documents, shows fishermen taking their catch to be recorded by clerks, a portion of it then being distributed to various officials. The fisher traded the rest for other commodities at reasonably constant rates: a mullet for a jug of beer, a basket of dried fish for an amulet.

Long before Egypt became a unified state, fish were already providing more than subsistence. During the late fourth millennium BC, Nekhen (Hierakonpolis) in Upper Egypt was the busy center of a major kingdom whose leaders played a major role in the unification. An impressive temple with a courtyard flourished here for centuries.[8] Throughout that time the priests dumped refuse from ceremonies involving animals into trash pits outside the wooden wall surrounding the court. These pits now yield enormous quantities of potsherds, wild and domestic animal bones, and the remains of huge Nile perch, some of them at least 1.5 meters long. Such large fish, which flourished only in the deepest part of the river, were very hard to catch and even harder to land, especially from a canoe. The pits contain their backbones but not their heads and fins, as if the fish were butchered off-site. Only the meatier parts of these extraordinary perch were brought to the temple, most likely as offerings to the gods.

When were they caught? Such large perch were most easily hooked when the river was low, in late June just before the annual flood arrived. This was also the best time for collecting Nile oysters, which also abounded in the pits. The ritual beliefs followed at Nekhen's temple are long forgotten. They may well have involved mastery over animals and other symbols of a chaotic world reduced to order by sacrifices to cosmic deities and the ruler.[9] The only certainty is that large Nile fish had a symbolic and ritual meaning beyond their use as food.

Fish Become a Commodity

For four or five thousand years Nile fishing involved small numbers of villagers feeding their families and drying much of their catch for later consumption. It is not known precisely when fish became a commodity to be bought and eaten by strangers—perhaps that shift was driven by rising populations.

By 4500 BC a small town at Merimde Beni-Salama, fifty kilometers northwest of modern-day Cairo, was a leading trading center with perhaps five thousand inhabitants and extensive contacts up- and downstream.[10] A growing population of artisans and traders relied on others—fishermen as much as farmers—for their food. Here as in much earlier Egyptian farming villages, ties of kin and of reciprocal obligation lay at the center of daily life. Exchanges based on such responsibilities inevitably developed units of value for diverse commodities, not in the sense of money but in terms of weight and other standard measurements. Bread and beer were fundamental to the Egyptian diet from very early times, to which communities like Merimde added fish, either fresh or, more likely, dried.

How did people who had been subsistence fishers begin catching fish on a near-industrial scale? Fishing along the Nile became a full-time occupation because some workers' settlements now required monthly fish deliveries. Although few records exist of these arrangements, it is certain that they were commonplace. Preindustrial states were social pyramids, with a supreme leader commanding a well-ordered hierarchy of nobles and officials. At the base were thousands of artisans and soldiers, village farmers and fishers, who lived under the close supervision of petty officials and scribes. Around 3250 BC they began building actual pyramids as well as temples, palaces, and estates.

The rations that fed these workers were a form of symbolic reciprocity between the ruler and the ruled, almost a social contract, which is one of the reasons Nile fish became as much a commodity as a subsistence food. The scale of public works would have been modest at first, but it accelerated after the unification of Egypt about 3100 BC, eventually requiring armies of laborers and huge amounts of food. Their needs demanded a change of mind-set. A fisherman had to think in terms of hundreds of fish, not just of a handful to feed his family. Catfish harvests were reliable during the inundation—indeed they were a staple of the ration cycle—but new technologies also came into play, notably the seine net. Such nets could yield enormous catches, which meant that large numbers of people had to be at hand to gut and prepare the fish for drying.

The seine net is what turned fish into a significant commodity. Ancient Egyptian seines were quite large and heavy enough that they required teams of fishers to operate them.[11] Tomb paintings show long strips of netting with parallel upper and lower support lines and tapered ends, with harness ropes at each end for hauling in the net. Sometimes the fishers wore broad woven bands around their waists, which they knotted around the harness rope to help them handle heavier catches. Stone or ceramic weights attached to the bottom support line kept the net vertical in the water, while triangular pieces of wood lashed to the upper line kept its top near the surface. Seine net teams usually worked from river or channel banks or else in deeper water from large rafts or boats.

The technology endured long past the pharaohs. Early twentieth-century fishermen used seine nets, paying them out while paddling slowly across the water until the net extended in a large arc. Sometimes a paddler would beat the water with an oar to scare fish toward the net. The ends would be brought together until the seine formed a large circle. Then the fishers would haul in

Fishermen work a seine on the Nile. Eleventh Dynasty, tomb of Meketre, Egyptian National Museum, Cairo/Bridgeman Images.

the end ropes, operating either from two boats or with one end of the net afloat and the other ashore. A model in the tomb of the Middle Kingdom vizier Meketre (c. 1980 BC) at Thebes shows two papyrus canoes heading to shore with a seine net suspended between them. This was mass-production fishing, frequently depicted in Old Kingdom art.

Feeding Workers at Giza

At any one time perhaps as many as twenty thousand skilled and unskilled workers were employed at Giza.[12] Teams of villagers moved stone blocks weighing up to fifteen tons using sledges and rollers. Most of the heavy work took place during the months of the inundation, when barges could carry massive boulders right up to the construction sites.

A nearby town housed artisans, priests, scribes, laborers, and their families. Those who died went to eternity in humble graves in a nearby necropolis. Just beyond the quarries, supply routes, and rock-cut harbor, in an area of low desert south-southeast of the Giza Plateau, lay the workers' settlement. The pyramid town may have lain close to a basin known as the *ra-she*, like the one described in a papyrus found in the archives of the Fifth Dynasty pharaoh Djedkare-Isesi (2414–2375 BC) from the pyramid field at Abusir, north of the

Saqqara necropolis, built nearly two centuries after Giza. The ra-she was a place for deliveries, production, and storage as well as for assembling rations. Inscriptions from the sun temple of another Old Kingdom pharaoh, Niuserre (2453–2422 BC), give an impression of the inflow of provisions: 100,800 bread, beer, and cake rations, 7,720 loaves of *pesen* bread, 1,002 oxen, and 1,000 geese arrived annually. And these goods were to supply workers building only a temple, a far less elaborate operation than the enormous organization at Giza.[13]

Each Egyptian pyramid had its complex of pyramid towns, but Giza is the best known. These settlements housed not only workers but also the officials and priests responsible for the offerings presented to the *ka,* or vital force, of the deceased pharaoh. Each settlement depended on bread and other rations provided by the state and by the owners of lavish estates that flourished nearby. The sepulcher of a later vizier, Meketre, contained models of estate workshops, including a bakery and a granary, part of an elaborate infrastructure that could produce and store enough grain to feed five thousand to nine thousand people a year.

In 1991 the Egyptologist Mark Lehner excavated two bakeries, including the vats for mixing dough and a cache of the large, bell-shaped pots used for baking bread. While bread and beer were the staples of the pyramid workforce, they also ate fish. No one knows how many workers labored on ration preparation, but the number may have been as high as two thousand. A huge mud-brick building adjacent to the bakeries, still incompletely excavated and of unknown size, contained troughs, benches, and tens of thousands of tiny fish fragments in the fine ashy deposit covering the floor.

Fresh catches had to be dried and preserved immediately. Lehner believes the fish were laid out on reed frames to dry on well-ventilated troughs and benches in a production line that provided protein for thousands of people. Precise estimates are impossible, but at its peak the line must have employed hundreds of people and processed thousands of fish per day. The fishermen must have been contracted to harvest enormous numbers of catfish in order to supply such an operation. The annual climax of pyramid building at Giza coincided each year with the inundation, so presumably fishing activity culminated with the early summer catfish spawn and the retreat of the floods, a six- to eight-week period when the entire Nile Valley became a shallow lake with thousands of gradually shrinking pools.

The fishers were thus only the first stage of an infrastructure of hundreds of people needed to process the fish, lay them out and turn them on drying racks, and store the dried catch for later consumption. The demands of this operation must have led to large, temporary fishing villages springing up at the same general locations every inundation season over many generations.

The commoners who built the pharaohs' pyramids and temples and labored in the fields of the nobility, led lives of ceaseless, repetitive toil. The peasant's life revolved around the timeless seasons of inundation, planting, and harvest. Fishing became part of this cycle, a frenzied harvest during the inundation, when seine nets gathered heavy catches for officialdom. Many artisans, scribes, priests, and petty officials lived by their skills rather than manual labor. Fisherfolk were not among them: their trade required both skill and muscle.

Fishers lived on the margins of Egyptian civilization. Judging from nineteenth-century observations, when fishing conditions were still remarkably similar to those of ancient times, the number of fishing craft was enormous. More than six thousand fishing boats operated in Egypt in the late nineteenth century. About as many must have operated in pharaonic times, for fish loomed large in official rations. They were a food with divine approval: the father of the Middle Kingdom pharaoh Merikare told his son in about 2010 BC that the gods made fish for humans to eat. Middle Kingdom pharaohs ordered the distribution of enormous quantities of fish to temples.

By the time the great New Kingdom ruler Seti I (1290–1279 BC) gave fish rations to his soldiers, fish had been used as provisions for centuries. His successor, Ramesses II (1279–1213 BC), boasted that his workers had their own "fishmen" to keep them supplied. The royal necropolis craftspeople at Deir el-Medina, on the west bank at Thebes, lived mainly on fish contractually supplied by twenty fishermen whose catches were divided among about forty people in the amounts determined by their rank. One record states that one fisherman could supply 130 *hekats* (882 kilograms) of fish over a six-month period, including tilapia and other species.[14] Ramesses III (1186–1155 BC) gave no fewer than 474,640 gutted, fresh, and pickled fish to the Amun festivals at Thebes over a period of thirty-one years as well as 129,000 to lesser shrines.

Fish also prompted desert expeditions. A stela in the arid Wadi Hammamat in the Eastern Desert records four expeditions to the area's quarries in search of stone for statues ordered by Ramesses IV of the Twentieth Dynasty (1151–1145 BC).[15] One group of 8,368 men, including 2,000 soldiers, contained 200 "officers of the court fishermen" who were responsible for obtaining "a plenty of fish" for the entourage, including the royal harem. By Ramesses IV's time, fish were being transported in huge quantities up and down the Nile by boat. A painting in the tomb of King Horemheb (1321–1293 BC), an earlier New Kingdom pharaoh, shows such a vessel with rows of fish drying in the rigging. The usual cargo was mullet, the most desirable catch and expensive enough to be worth transporting.

Notwithstanding the inundation-season harvests, much ancient Egyptian fishing was a solitary quest with a spear in shallow marshes or with hook and line in a papyrus boat or on a raft. There was endless casting of throw nets in shallow water, perhaps at dusk when the fish rose to catch mosquitoes and other bugs. The rhythm never altered, but what had changed profoundly with the formation of the state was the scale of the operation. Now there were quotas and taxes imposed by watchful scribes, labor carried out for the pharaoh and the state, a civilization dependent on the flood in all its capricious variability, living in fear of drought years, when the river would barely rise above its banks.

Fish continued to play a central role in Egypt long after the pyramids passed into history. Ships sailing down the Nile carried dried catfish and other species to ports along the Levantine coast. Some of the cargo may have been sailors' rations, but some was carried inland.[16] When faced with shortages, officials turned to fish farming, a pursuit that, like fishing, long outlasted the great pharaohs. In Greek and Roman times travelers remarked on the richness of the Nile fisheries. The Greek writer and geographer Diodorus Siculus wrote in the first century BC that "the Nile contains every variety of fish and in numbers beyond belief: for it supplies the native not only with abundant subsistence from the fish freshly caught, but it also yields an unfailing multitude for salting."[17] Herodotus remarked that every marsh dweller possessed a fishing net.

While it may have been home to the first society in which fish became a commodity, Egypt was by no means unique. All preindustrial states fed rations to those laboring on public works and serving in armies. Fish were part of the rations, so much so that they became a near-industrial commodity. The significant step from opportunism to commodification also took hold elsewhere in the Mediterranean world.

13

Fishing the Middle Sea

The Mediterranean, or the Middle Sea, has long been a deep basin with narrow continental shelves, only a fifth of it less than two hundred meters deep. Most of its waters come from the Atlantic. Summer heat evaporates them faster than rainfall or the three major rivers—the Nile, the Rhône, and the Po—can replenish them. A trickle comes from the Black Sea, but most of the shortfall is made up by a colder, less saline inflow from the Atlantic. This means that around Gibraltar and the Dardanelles as well as along the coast marine life is poor, except where lagoons or rivers inject nutrients into the ocean. Evaporation leaves salt, which sinks toward the deep-sea bed in concentrations that are too strong for many marine species. Most fish live in the upper levels of open water and are famously hard to catch, except when they come inshore to feed or, like the bluefin tuna, the signature fish of these waters, pass by during annual spawning migrations. Except for these migrations the Mediterranean has never been a highly prolific fishing ground by the standards of, say, the North Atlantic.

Neanderthals and moderns were opportunistic fishers along Mediterranean shores. The inhabitants of Nerja Cave, on the Bay of Málaga in southern Spain, took thirty mostly inshore species between about twenty-three thousand and twelve thousand years ago. Their prey included large freshwater-spawning sturgeon as well as Atlantic cod, haddock, and pollock that came through the Strait of Gibraltar in search of food.[1] Then came the warming.

Populations rose, and people rapidly settled into hitherto uninhabited environments. Fishing was still an opportunistic quest, undertaken when inshore
or migrating species could be taken easily. Almost everywhere the people who
caught these species were constantly on the move, exploiting increasingly diverse food sources, of which fish were only a small part.

The situation changed rapidly with the transition to farming and stock raising over a wide area of the eastern Mediterranean sometime after ten thousand years ago. In a warming, drying world with increasing populations, rich
concentrations of marine resources grew more and more attractive. Isotopes
from the skeletons of the inhabitants of the Grotta dell'Uzzo in northwestern
Sicily, settled from about eleven thousand years BP, reveal an increasingly
diverse diet rich in plant and sea foods. The earliest inhabitants collected
mollusks during the winter months. By the seventh and eighth millennia BC
they turned more intensively to fishing, catching such species as grouper and
mackerel. The site lies close to the great tuna spawning grounds in deep water
to the north and west. In later times the inhabitants harvested the fish close
inshore and then, when spawning ended, moved elsewhere. By 6000 BC these
people were fishing year-round.[2]

By that point the wooded Levantine coast in the eastern Mediterranean
was more densely occupied than in earlier times, especially by herding groups.
At Atlit-Yam, a now-submerged village of rectangular houses off northern
Israel, ten burials include four males with signs of ear damage caused by diving into cold, deep water. Almost all the fish bones at Atlit-Yam come from
gray triggerfish, which thrive at some depth. Presumably the divers were operating from boats, as the sea floor shelves gently for a considerable distance
from shore.

For the first time there are clear signs of long-term base camps by the
ocean, along the shores of the Adriatic, and elsewhere. Small fish were the
quarry. Far to the west, outside the entrance to the Middle Sea, Atlantic tides
ebbed and flowed through estuaries like those of the Tagus and other rivers,
where marine and terrestrial foods abounded in astounding variety. Band after
band settled along the inner reaches of these estuaries in villages where people
stored food, buried their dead, and ate enormous numbers of cockles, oysters,
and limpets, their diet changing from location to location depending on the
topography. Huge white shell heaps, remnants of their millennia-old villages,
still line these shores. Judging from the size of the middens, these settlements
were occupied continuously for many centuries.

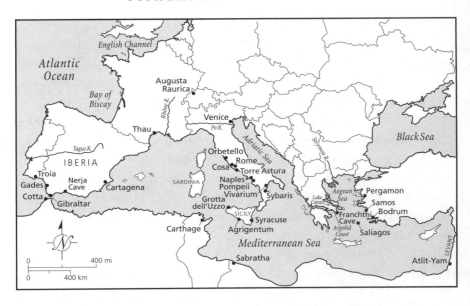

10. Major sites in the Mediterranean region discussed in chapters 12 and 13.

Harvesting Catches

Franchthi Cave, near the Aegean Sea in Greece, was occupied at least thirty-eight thousand years ago and was used sporadically for thousands of years. After taking shallow-water fish for thousands of years, people changed their habits dramatically during the mid-eighth millennium BC. Between 20 and 40 percent of the Franchthi bones from this time and later come from large tuna weighing up to two hundred kilograms. Specialized fishing implements such as stronger nets must have come into play (although none survive), together with razor-sharp obsidian artifacts, presumably to gut and fillet the catch. Fishing was changing profoundly throughout the Middle Sea during this millennium. While the old opportunistic methods never went away, the emphasis changed toward the harvesting of relatively predictable migrating fish, especially mackerel and tuna.

The Atlantic bluefin tuna (*Thunnus thynnus*) is native to much of the Atlantic and the Mediterranean and has been a much sought after food fish for thousands of years.[3] Today, industrial fishing has decimated tuna stocks, so much so that they are now under severe fishing pressure. Bluefins, dark blue above and gray below, are very strong fish that can reach enormous sizes. The largest on record, caught off Nova Scotia, was 3.7 meters long and weighed

679 kilograms. Tuna can reach speeds of 64 kilometers an hour and dive to depths of 305 meters. They can cover enormous distances, and massive schools of them regularly cross the Atlantic. Each spring millions of tuna enter the Mediterranean in search of warm, salty waters containing ample nutrients to support spawning and the hatching of their young. Most of them spawn around the Balearic Islands and Sicily, while smaller numbers reproduce in the Aegean and off Libya. They leave again in the fall, thin and hungry after breeding.

Tuna are voracious predators that feed on mackerel, sardines, and other small fish as well as invertebrates. They hunt by sight and seek food in relatively clear water. This means that great schools of them tend to swim close to shore, especially when winds blow them inshore. From the ancient fisher's point of view, tuna had the priceless advantages of being relatively predictable in a sea where fishing was difficult and of coming close to the beach, where they could be harvested from small boats.

Many communities harvested tuna as well as bonito and mackerel at strategic locations. As the British archaeologist Cyprian Broodbank has shown, early maritime activity in the Aegean opened up seaways for all kinds of trade, ranging from exotica such as volcanic obsidian for making sharp-edged tools to more mundane items like dried or salted fish, an ideal trade commodity because it is a light food that keeps well.[4] Tuna fishing was never a permanent lifeway here, for the fish were only seasonally bountiful and found only at strategic locations. At Saliagos, a small settlement on an island between Paros and Antiparos, fishermen of 4300 to 3700 BC took almost no fish but tuna, which they apparently hunted in large numbers during the spawning season with barbed arrows and stone-tipped spears fashioned from obsidian. The rest of the year they were farmers.

Fishermen did not have to pursue tuna in boats, as they could net their prey from shore and even spear them in the shallows. Annual harvests took hundreds of large fish that could be dried or salted for later use. All of these fisherfolk used technical knowledge about their prey acquired over many generations. Much of it depended on the kind of subtle observation that hunters practiced on land: spotting seabirds following migrating tuna, knowing that weather conditions or currents would send the fish toward shore, and even being aware that dolphins would sometimes drive fish into their nets, a collaboration noted in Roman times by Pliny the Elder and also seen in Brazil and the South Pacific.

Ancient Mediterranean fishermen not only knew their prey but also developed highly effective, simple equipment to catch fish of all kinds. They chose their materials so well that the same basic equipment and methods survived virtually unchanged into the twentieth century AD.[5] Take, for example, some lead fishing weights found in a Byzantine shipwreck of the eleventh century AD, excavated off the coast of Bodrum in southern Turkey. One of the sinkers contained organic fibers that turned out to be goat hair. When the archaeologists interviewed an elderly fisherman from Bodrum, they learned that goat hair is a good material for fishing lines because it is durable, has long fibers, and does not retain water. Women's hair was said to be even more useful. An Ottoman fishing net in the Bodrum museum with a weight line fashioned from goat hair confirms that it was a favored material for centuries, probably since antiquity. The same intelligent use of raw materials extended to everything from wicker basket nets used in lagoons to eel traps. Only with the advent of affordable synthetic equipment have tools such as fishing nets made of esparto grass or hemp become obsolete.

The equipment of ancient Mediterranean fishing began with hook and line, but large-scale operations involved fish traps and nets. The casting net, gill net, and seine deployed from a beach were commonplace, as were conical fish nets used in river fishing. Individuals fishing for their families often owned casting nets to snare small fish and juveniles. This net was common in marshy landscapes along the Nile and in Italian lagoons. Larger nets hung vertically, with floats suspending the upper edges and weights holding down their lower ones. Some were fixed, others were deployed from boats and then hauled to shore. The gill net was a netting wall, as it were, hanging vertically in the water in the hope that fish would entangle themselves in it by their gills, whence the name. Meshes varied in size according to the quarry.

Net makers used vegetable fibers, including hemp and flax, as well as various forms of twisted bark. Hemp was abundant in swamps, precisely the places where fish were plentiful. Long lines with multiple hooks hung on branch lines were in widespread use by Roman times and probably earlier. Volcanic ash buried a long line in a basket at Herculaneum, while a group of forty small bronze hooks from a rural villa near Pompeii are probably also from such a line. More exotic methods included the curious technique of tying a male fish by its gills, then letting it swim near the shore to attract females. Greek and Tunisian fishers used this tactic into the nineteenth century.

Carefully directed sounds could steer fish schools toward waiting nets.

Some fishers attracted tuna by slapping the water with paddles or oars to mimic the sound of leaping fish. Flaming torches reflected on the water drew fish to waiting boats, a method still used by modern fishers in the Adriatic and Mediterranean and employed off Sardinia to lure sardines.

Almost all large-scale fishing in the Middle Sea took advantage of seasonal fish migrations. But smaller fisheries also assumed great importance. Although now destroyed by nineteenth- and early twentieth-century land reclamation, in ancient times enormous tracts of the Mediterranean's coasts were marshy lagoons. These environments were priceless assets, not only for their potential for salt manufacture but also as pasture and for their plenitudes of fish and eels. Mullet and other species would swim into the lagoons in spring, grow quickly, and leave in the fall.

Armed with fishing nets and wicker or cane traps, fishermen could easily partition off segments of a lagoon, either temporarily or permanently depending on the topography, to catch the fish as they tried to return to sea. A well-managed lagoon was a valuable fishing ground, as much as twenty times more productive than the open ocean, especially on stormy nights when many fish would try to flee out to sea. Large lagoons like those surrounding Venice were partitioned with cane fences, which were also used elsewhere by the Romans to increase the productivity of fish farms.

In tidal waters such as those along Atlantic coasts, the ebb and flood could cause fish to move toward permanent barriers at any time of the year. Well-placed weirs could be prodigiously productive. Placed at the mouths of coastal lagoons, they could trap 1,000 kilograms of fish in a night, often anchovies and sardines. Such highly productive methods remained in use into the middle of the twentieth century. The Lagoon of Thau, west of the Rhône in southern France, covers seventy-five hundred hectares and once boasted of annual catches averaging 140,000 kilograms and of even greater yields of shellfish. Today, oyster farming is dominant, and wild fish catches are reduced.

Putting the Marine into Cuisine

The classical Greeks' passion for fish was almost an addiction. Not for them the Homeric warriors' feasts of roasted oxen. The ancient Minoans and Mycenaeans were certainly fish eaters; fish was probably a dominant part of the average person's diet. But if Homer is to be believed, fish were not for heroes. After surviving passage between Scylla and Charybdis, Odysseus and his followers landed on a green island where the sun god, Helios, kept his sacred cattle. Food ran short, so they were forced to "range for quarry with twisted hooks; for fish, birds, anything they could lay their hands on."[6] The crew mutinied and feasted off Helios's oxen. Zeus promptly destroyed the ship and the entire crew except for Odysseus.

Who first "put the marine into cuisine," as the classicist James Davidson puts it, is unknown, but the Greek obsession with seafood is clearly ancient.[7] As far as archaeologists can discern, gourmet fish cookery may have originated in the wealthy city of Sybaris, located on southern Italy's instep and famous for its eel fisheries. The Greek love of fish seems to have been largely inspired by the culinary culture of Sicily. One of the world's earliest known cookbooks comes from the hand of Mithaecus of Sicily. Only fragments remain, but it is certain that fish were prominent in his recipes. "Cut off the head of the ribbon fish [wrasse]" reads one recipe. "Wash it and cut into slices. Pour cheese and oil over it."[8]

Much of what we know about Greek fish consumption comes from Greek comedies, which feature shopping lists and even recipes, recited by comic chefs. A hierarchy of fish emerged that persisted into Roman times. Any form of preserved fish was looked down upon, except for a few specialties, including tuna steaks bottled at the correct season. Anchovies, sprats, and other small fish were for less affluent citizens, and disdain for them was a symbol of elitism. The great delicacies at the top of the hierarchy included eels, grouper, the mullets, and tuna as well as crayfish. Certain parts of the tuna, especially the shoulder and neck area, were highly prized.

But Greek seafood was ruled by the eel, as the fourth-century-BC author Archestratus from Syracuse testifies, praising the "large size and wondrous girth" of those caught in the Strymon River.[9] The eel, he wrote, commands the "field of pleasure" and is "the only fish with no backbone."[10] The best eels came from the waters opposite the straits of Messina. The Greeks caught them with hooks baited with worms or large fish and also with three-pronged spears.

Among the numerous panegyrics extolling fishers is an epigram by Leonidas of Tarentum from the third century BC. He wrote of a man named Diophantus, whose equipment included an anchor and long spears, a horsehair fishing line, and carefully made baskets for holding what he brought in. Diophantus also wisely carried a pair of oars. Fishermen might have lived on the margins of society, usually far from the city, bringing their wares to the market before dawn, but their seductive catches sometimes inspired passion and desire. Not that anyone liked the rapacious fishmongers, who were de-scribed by the early Hellenistic writer Lynceus of Samos as "the unblinking ones, the unyielding-on-price ones," with whom the best negotiating tactic was loudly delivered rude remarks about their fish to scare off fellow shoppers.[11]

Mattanza!

The Italians, who call the massive slaughtering of migrating tuna in spring and fall the mattanza, thought the tuna kill was invented by Arab fishermen who introduced it into Sicily and Spain during medieval times.[12] There is no question that the annual tuna migrations were the highlight of the Mediterranean fishing year for many centuries. Much earlier net systems, set out "like a city" with gatekeepers, are described by the Graeco-Roman author Oppian in a poem on fishing from the second century BC: "The tuna rush quickly on, in rows, like phalanxes of men."[13]

Offshore fishing, while not unusual, was not performed on any sizable scale. Phoenician fishers are known to have sailed four days outside the Strait of Gibraltar looking for tuna along the Atlantic tidal zone. They caught remarkably large fish, which they salted and exported as far east as Carthage. For the most part, however, tuna fishing was shore based. Great fish schools favored the same coastal routes in ancient times that were familiar until the industrial fishing of the late twentieth century. Tuna fisheries and salting facilities lay at key locations along the coastline, especially in North Africa, where the fishermen erected fixed nets placed at right angles to the shore. Even today, small-boat sailors have to be careful when sailing inshore at night, for tuna nets and barriers extend quite far offshore.

A century ago the mattanza was a dramatic, bloody business. Complex systems of fixed and anchored nets trapped and guided the tuna into chambers. When migrating tuna encounter a barrier on their route, they swim along it trying to continue their journey. Eventually they end up in carefully sited antechambers, where they are corralled until enough of them are trapped. Then the fishermen open the net that blocks the entrance to the death chamber, the *tonnara*. They surround the nets and haul in fish as fast as they can. Increasingly hemmed in, the tuna panic and swim frantically, charging the sides of the net, even wounding one another. The fishers haul the net to the surface. The tuna that remain enmeshed in the net are hauled into the boats with gaffs, many of them already half dead from their experience in the death chamber.

Tuna slaughter: a modern-day mattanza, Favignana Island, Sicily.
Jeorg Boethling/Alamy Stock Photo.

This is slaughter on a grand scale, sustainable only while tuna stocks remain abundant.

Whether the Romans used the death chamber system is unknown. They certainly used fixed-net installations anchored to the seabed with perforated stone weights, many of which have been discovered still in place.[14] All of these finds come from areas where tuna fishing has been practiced in modern times, like the north coast of Sicily. They confirm the use of long, fixed nets but not necessarily of death chambers. Fishermen may have taken the tuna by surrounding them with long nets suspended from boats, a method used historically in Spain and off Tuscany. It involved a number of rowing boats, crossing the path of the migrating fish, whether mackerel, tuna, or sardines. Lookouts stationed ashore would signal to two boats armed with nets, which would encircle the school. A third boat would deploy another net, joining the two others to form a trap. The crews of small boats would slap the water with their oars or drop stones overboard to keep the fish away from gaps in the nets. Then a second stage ensued: the encircling of the trapped fish with a much heavier net that was pulled toward the shore at the direction of the watchers on land, who ensured that the school was trapped.

Whatever the method used, the key role belonged to the watchers, who spotted the arriving school from higher ground or from crude structures of wooden scaffolding. Some towns even owned lookouts and permanent towers as well as rights to good fishing spots and rented them out to fishermen, a practice known in the Aegean as early as the first century BC. Assessing the size and direction of a tuna school required both experience and skill. The watchers would look for regular formations moving rapidly and try to assess not only the school's size but also its depth. They would count the number of Cody's shearwaters following the fish and feeding on the anchovies and other small fry swimming frantically in front of their predators. According to ancient writers, the watchers' estimates were remarkably accurate, even when tuna schools numbered as many as five thousand fish. The teamwork between the shore-based watchers, the helmsmen and oarsmen, and those who maneuvered the nets had to be exquisitely precise.

Many tuna harvests were conducted by business partnerships with a well-defined hierarchy of roles, among them a master of the net, scouts, and a mysterious worker called the loosener of the floats. The work could involve five or more boats and their captains, even an accountant, perhaps as many as thirty people all told. Medieval records show that some temporary tuna fishing spots yielded enormous numbers of fish. By the eighteenth century even the smaller tuna fisheries could yield as much as 300,000 kilograms in a good year. In 1824 a single fishery near Bizerte, Tunisia, landed more than ten thousand tuna. Given that the adult tuna of the day weighed between 120 and 150 kilograms, we can conservatively estimate that this one fishery brought in more than 1 million kilograms. Not that every year saw such yields. Long before industrial fishing methods caused a drastic collapse in tuna stocks starting in the 1960s, tuna migrations fluctuated significantly, notably during the mid-eighteenth century, when Spanish tuna fishermen moved their operations to more plentiful waters around Sardinia.

Salting the Catch

An even greater challenge than catching migrating fish was preserving them for the marketplace. The Roman author Marcus Aurelius, who clearly enjoyed dried fish, wrote a letter to his friend Fronto in which he described vineyard workers eating a meal of dried small fish, well soaked to restore the texture and flavor.

Salting was the best way of preserving fish, provided one had reliable sources of salt. While the basic methods were familiar to most fishing communities, it was the Greeks and Romans who applied them on a large scale, especially to tuna harvests and to smaller fish as well. Roman salting facilities are most famous for their production of garum, the fish sauce used widely throughout the empire and made largely from small fish like anchovies and sardines. Fish sauce was only a by-product of much larger salting operations that processed not only tuna but also mackerel and smaller species that could be taken as they fled the tuna schools. Fresh fish was a luxury even a short distance from a harbor: nobles and commoners alike ate their fish salted.[15]

The greatest concentrations of Roman fish-salting facilities occurred in places where mackerel and tuna schools came closest to shore. No one knows when fish salting first became commonplace. It may have begun in the second millennium BC, perhaps even earlier, and is chronicled by numerous Roman sites throughout the Mediterranean. Sicily was a major center of fish salting before Roman times. Archimedes is said to have built a large ship at the command of Hieron II of Syracuse that was sent as a gift to the Ptolemies in Egypt with a cargo that included grain, wool, and one thousand amphorae of salted fish.[16] Some small Punic salting workshops lie as far west as Cádiz, Spain, and date to the sixth and fifth centuries BC. Here, workers processed the fish in salting tanks, then packed them in amphorae for shipment throughout the Mediterranean. The salt tank method may have been developed there first and then spread into the Mediterranean, but it is more likely that salting developed independently in several areas, notably Italy, especially at the mouth of the Tiber River, where salt pans operated in fish-rich coastal lagoons.

Fish-salting establishments varied considerably in size. Small urban workshops were found at Pompeii and Sabratha, a city in northwestern Libya that produced an estimated sixteen thousand sixty-liter amphorae of packed fish per year. Belo Claudia, at the western end of the Strait of Gibraltar in southern Spain, was a small port town devoted entirely to fish and salting. Much larger factories developed in areas where the fish schools came close inshore, notably at Cotta in Morocco, just a few kilometers south of the western entrance of the Strait of Gibraltar. This facility, overlooking a beach and in use from the first century BC to the third century AD, consisted of a large, rectangular building housing a U-shaped layout of salting vats of various sizes as well as a central work area, a preparation section, and storage space. A tower at the southwestern corner probably served as a lookout for spotting and tracking the schools and for directing the men at their nets, who then brought the catch ashore for immediate salting.

Salting appears to have intensified during the first centuries BC and AD with the Roman annexation of territories in North Africa and the western Mediterranean. Lixus in Morocco was such a major fish center that it even minted coins bearing fish images. In Portugal a complex at Troia, on the Sado estuary, had a small town, an amphora factory, and at least fifty-two salting workshops that extended some four kilometers along the riverbank. Troia was unusual in that the fish-rich estuary provided catches year-round, not just during migrations. It flourished during the centuries immediately before and after Christ and then declined but continued production until the fifth century. The town may have had the advantage of direct trade routes to the Roman army in Britain and also into the Mediterranean. Other salting factories, smaller than the western workshops, flourished throughout the Mediterranean, in the Adriatic, and even as far as Turkey.

Fishing and fish preservation were a significant part of the Roman Mediterranean economy. During the first and second centuries AD the collective volume of Roman fish vats may have reached twenty-six hundred cubic meters, an impressive figure reached by catching thousands of small fish. The trade appears to have enriched the merchants who dealt in salted fish and fish sauce, many of whom owned villas and estates, while people of low social status, many of them slaves, carried out the actual production. The business could be especially profitable if the salt workshop lay close to coastal lagoons, where fishermen could work even outside of mackerel or tuna season.

By Roman times fish had long been a commodity, a common food that fed legions and galley crews, city dwellers and farmers. The wealthy lavished enormous sums on seafood, partly because they liked it but also because fresh, exotic fish were a mark of social standing if displayed and served at table. But even in the ancient world and even given the bounty of mackerel and tuna migrations overfishing diminished fish stocks in the Middle Sea. Like the Egyptians before them, the Romans turned to aquaculture.

Scaly Flocks

The pervasive inequality of Roman society expressed itself forcibly in, of all places, their fish pools. Marcus Terentius Varro (116–27 BC) was a Roman scholar and prolific writer. A genuinely learned man as well as a successful farmer, he set down his considerable wisdom on estate management in *Rerum Rusticarum Libri Tres* (*Three Books on Agriculture*), his only extant complete work. Varro owned two fishponds, and he took some space in the third book of the *Rusticarum* to explain the clear distinction between the saltwater pools of the wealthy and the freshwater ponds of ordinary citizens: "Those of the one kind, in which water is supplied to our home-fed fishes by the river Nymphs, are kept by men of the people, and are profitable enough; while the other sea-water ponds, which belong to the nobles, and get both water and fishes from Neptune, appeal more to the eye than to the pocket, and empty rather than fill the owner's purse. For they cost a great deal to build, a great deal to stock, and a great deal to feed."[1] The judicious and sober Varro was a prosperous farmer and rancher, but he proudly sided with the have-nots when it came to fish. He watched the frenzied competition over fishponds among wealthy coastal villa owners in the Bay of Naples and was glad not to be part of it.

Many preindustrial states depended on the labor of the many for the benefit of the few, the many being paid standardized rations, of which fish, caught on an enormous scale, were one. Any rationing authority must always have plenty of food on hand and deliver it on time. This meant that the supply had to be reliable and constant, but in the case of fish, catches fluctuated sharply from year to year. So, being pragmatic farmers, the Egyptians turned to aquaculture—fish farming. The Sumerians of Mesopotamia, the Chinese, and the Greeks and Romans did the same.

Fish farming was all about obtaining greater yields than those provided by wild fisheries. It undoubtedly began with minimal human intervention, for instance, in the Nile Delta and elsewhere upstream where marshes teemed with shallow-water fish, especially during the floods. Enormous stretches of the ancient Mediterranean coast consisted of saltwater lagoons and wetlands where fishermen could create barriers—generally made from reeds, wicker, and wooden poles—to pen fish into a specific area. Fish farmers might also dig additional channels to improve water circulation and to minimize the effects of silting. Fish might be controlled, but unless one fed them, the yields were small, although better and less risky than sea fishing.

No one knows when aquaculture began along the Nile, but it probably long predates the first evidence that has come down to us. A relief in the tomb of Aktihep, an official of the Middle Kingdom about 2500 BC, shows men removing tilapia from a pond. The early fish farmers raised immature fish and shellfish in carefully prepared pools, then brought them to maturity in artificial environments to ensure a steady supply for the court and the nobility. About 2000 BC farmers in Lower Egypt started to use a land reclamation method that is highly productive and still used today. During the spring they dig large ponds in saline soil and flood them with freshwater for two weeks. The lower salinity of the standing water forces the saline groundwater downward. They drain the ponds and repeat the process, discarding the second flooding as well. Then they fill the pond with thirty centimeters of water and stock it with mullet fingerlings caught in the ocean. The fish, harvested between December and April, yield about three hundred to five hundred kilograms per hectare. After the spring fish harvest, the farmers check the soil by inserting a eucalyptus cutting in it. If the twig germinates they know they can plant crops on the land. The process takes about three to five years to make salty soil arable again, much faster than the ten years required by other reclamation methods.[2]

Exactly when and where the first totally artificial ponds were built is a mystery, for none have been identified archaeologically. In the first century BC Diodorus Siculus described a huge enclosure built for aquaculture in Agrigentum, Sicily (see map 10 in chapter 13). The labor was carried out by chained prisoners of war working for the tyrant Hieron of Syracuse. "The Acragantini built an expensive kolumbethra," Siculus wrote, "seven stades in circumference and twenty cubits deep. Into it the waters from rivers and springs were conducted and it became a fish-pond, which supplied fish in great abundance to be used for food and to please the palate."[3]

Greek texts speak of extensive eel aquaculture, much of it in enclosures erected at strategic locations in rivers or natural basins. The eels from Lake Copais in Boeotia were famous for being so tasty that the people sacrificed large eels to gods unremembered today. Here as elsewhere aquaculture involved the construction of earthworks and called for considerable expertise. The building of enclosure walls and the preparation of the pond bottoms required much labor, time, and expense.

By the time the Romans governed Egypt people in places like the Faiyum Depression had a long tradition of containing and controlling floodwaters with semiartificial reservoirs that they carefully stocked with fish. These reservoirs represented a large capital investment, and fish farming rights in reservoirs owned by villages were strictly controlled. Aquaculture had become a regulated business requiring careful supervision, legal protections, and collective labor by villagers to maintain the reservoirs and ponds.

The Romans were the first in the Mediterranean to elevate marine aquaculture to a fine art. They used sophisticated technology such as underwater concrete and freshwater aeration, perhaps first in natural coastal lagoons like those at Ostia and Cosa near Rome, from which commercial fish farmers could stock their own ponds. Marine fish farming was most intensive along the Tyrrhenian coast, close to Rome's insatiable fish markets, where there was also a wealthy local population. Rome's dedicated fish market, the Forum Piscarium, was built before 210 BC and later destroyed by fire. Demand for fish of all kinds, especially exotic species, grew rapidly in the two centuries before Christ, driving prices ever higher. Supplying fresh fish to urban markets was a challenge in an era without refrigeration. Water tanks on carts and special barges with perforated holds provided a modicum of fresh catches, but many fish spoiled before they could be eaten.

Most people ate farmed fish for daily consumption. Only aquaculture could provide the yields needed to feed the growing population. Roman consumers ate a wide range of crustaceans, fish, and mollusks, both fresh and salted. Aristotle's *Historia Animalium* and Pliny the Elder's *Natural History* as well as frescoes and mosaics tell us what fish the Romans ate and farmed. According to Pliny, Alexander the Great arranged for artificial ponds to be built for Aristotle so that he could study the fish contained in them.[4] Roman authors described more than 260 types of fish, and Greek sources cited 400 varieties. Of these, about 10 were consistent favorites.

Most fishponds contained one or two of seven species. Roman fish farmers tended to exploit species that congregated in coastal waters, where freshwater and saltwater mixed, because they could tolerate a wide range of salinity. Coastal fisherfolk were well aware of the special conditions in which these fish flourished, but the yields were unreliable. A logical step to increase catches would have been to improve both the control and harvest of the fishing grounds, a process that would have led almost inevitably to primitive forms of aquaculture.

Eels, which can live in fresh, brackish, or salt water, were the most common farm fish and were popular in Rome as early as the second century BC. Gaius Hirrius supplied six thousand eels for Julius Caesar's triumphal banquets in 46 and 45 BC.[5] Some devoted, wealthy eel owners even adorned their pet eels with jewels. Eels were popular partly because their distinctive migratory habits made them easy to trap. Some impression of their immense self-propagating capacity comes from today's Italian eel farms. One thousand-square-meter pond at Orbetello, on the coast north of Rome (see map 10 in chapter 13), can produce four tons of eels from a mere ten kilograms of elvers (young eels) in just one year.

Pliny the Elder described the eel fisheries at Lake Benacus, inland from Venice, where eels and juvenile fish fed in coastal lagoons during the spring and summer, then left for the open sea in the fall. Like tuna migrations, this annual cycle was well known to local fishers, who harvested eels by the thousands in traps created by partitioning the Mincius River. Wooden posts and reed barriers in the Venice lagoons allowed for proper water circulation but prevented grown fish from departing in the autumn, so that they could be harvested instead. This practice endured until the late nineteenth century, when permanent dikes replaced the reed barriers. After that, a specialized fishery caught the juveniles in enormous numbers each spring to sell to fish farmers. According to one estimate, between twenty and twenty-five million juveniles were introduced annually into the fish farming enclosures of the Venetian lagoons. The young eels also traveled to other locations in barrels, along with young mullet.

Gray mullet were another favorite in Italy, as they were in Egypt. These small, blunt-nosed fish sometimes migrate into brackish lagoons, especially in fall and winter, and then return to the ocean to spawn. In Italy as in the Nile, they adapted readily to confinement. According to Pliny, their hearing was so acute that they would come when their names were called. Sea bass, sometimes called wrasse, were another favorite, especially those that swam up the Tiber from coastal lagoons. It was said that Roman foodies could tell from the taste whether a bass was farmed, caught in polluted freshwater, or taken from the sea. The second-century Greek physician Galen of Pergamon advised against eating fish from upstream on account of pollution from sewage and the waste from textile workshops. Pliny the Elder was also partial to parrot fish, which he called first-rate eating, more popular than mullet for those with refined tastes but hard to raise in ponds.

The first-century AD writer Lucius Junius Moderatus Columella, the most important writer on agriculture of the Roman Empire, writes that giltheads were among the first fish to be farmed.[6] They adapted readily to being raised in both freshwater and saltwater ponds and were much prized for their flavor. Red mullet, which flourished in both Mediterranean and Atlantic waters, were also valued for their flavor. Unusually large specimens weighing up to a kilogram were trophy fish at lavish banquets. Being rare and caught in deep water, they were so expensive, Columella wrote, that married men could not afford them. Exceptional mullet cost thousands of sesterces since they could not readily be raised in ponds, unlike the much smaller and more common gray mullet. Flat fish such as flounder and sole were also popular, as were tilapia, but the real subject of a food-conscious Roman's adoration was not any particular fish but garum.

Shipwrecks off southern France and northwest Italy contain fish sauce amphorae dating to the fifth century BC, suggesting that garum was at least as old as Rome itself. It was fermented from the blood and intestines of fish through autolysis, the destruction of cells by their own enzymes.[7] The fish were macerated in salt and cured in the sun for three months. The quality of the sauce was determined by the fish parts used to make it, the best being based on tuna intestines while poorer quality grades were made from inferior catches and small fish. The mixture fermented and liquefied in the heat, the salt inhibiting bacteria. A clear liquid that formed atop this mixture was carefully drawn off with a fine strainer and often flavored with concentrated herbs.

Hundreds of recipes passed through the Roman Empire as the fish sauce industry expanded exponentially.

Everyone had a favorite flavor. One of the most popular in Rome came from Cartagena and Gades in the southern Spanish province of Hispania Baetica and was known as the garum of the allies (see map 10 in chapter 13). Garum from Portugal was also very popular. Fossae Marianae in southern Gaul, the extreme southern tip of France, was a major garum distribution center for Gaul, Germania, and Britain. Garum was the mustard and ketchup of the Roman world, and fish sauce merchants could become very wealthy.

Unlike tuna-salting facilities, garum factories tended to be built at a distance from the water's edge, which means more of them have survived. Some of these facilities were enormous. One at Troia, in the Spanish province of Lusitania, had masonry vats and saltworks operating over an intermittent three kilometers (see map 10 in chapter 13). Large processing plants operated on the Atlantic and North African coasts as well as in Crimea. It was a huge industry by the standards of the day, requiring millions of kilograms of small fish and the detritus from butchering and salting those of all sizes.

Much fish sauce must have traveled in wooden boxes and leather containers, making it impossible to determine what volume of garum traveled through the Roman Empire. But it's certain, for example, that fish sauce from Gaul abounded at the Roman colony of Augusta Raurica in modern Augst, near Basel in Switzerland (see map 10 in chapter 13). Fish sauce from Gaul and Spain filled about a third of the amphorae in one sample from a local dump.

The fish sauce merchant Aulus Umbricus Scaurus was a major producer at Pompeii during the first century AD. His factories, probably located outside the city because of the foul smell, produced four kinds of sauce. From his house overlooking the sea he could watch ships carrying his product overseas. His very best garum was apparently mild with a subtle flavor, perhaps like a Thai or Vietnamese fish sauce, and was extremely expensive. Most of it was made with mackerel. Whatever its quality, the Romans used it to flavor and enhance all manner of dishes, sometimes mixing it with wine. It was also thought to cure dog bites and remove unwanted body hair.

Much commercial fish farming was relatively small-scale. Columella wrote that profiting from fish was very different from making money from crops, and he urged farmers who had unproductive soils near the shore to establish a revenue source from the sea. They should carefully consider the nature of the shore, he wrote, and then build ponds that would house fish accustomed to that environment. The pond owner should place seaweed-covered rocks in the ponds "as far as the wit of man can contrive, to represent the appearance of the sea, so that, though they are prisoners, the fish may feel their captivity as little as possible."[8] He warned owners to beware of taking anything but well-fattened fish to market, since unfattened catches, however fresh, brought lower prices. And he advised them to build "recesses near the bottom of some [ponds] . . . to which the 'scaly flocks' may retire, some of them twisted into a spiral and not too wide, in which the lampreys may lurk."

Many marine fishponds were small, simple facilities, and most of them were completely cut from rock. Inflow and outflow were controlled by at least one channel, sometimes two, carefully placed to take advantage of prevailing winds and currents. Some of these ponds were close to saltworks and may have been used during mackerel and tuna migrations to keep excess fish until they could be killed and salted. Nineteenth-century Greek tuna fishermen along the Argolid Coast of the Peloponnese would keep fish alive in coastal ponds for up to two weeks; the Romans likely did the same.

Once fish farmers had figured out that carefully placed channels were necessary to avoid stagnant water in fish enclosures, lagoon aquaculture became huge. The carefully engineered channels provided the inflow and outflow of water from tidal streams, whose strength varied significantly from place to place. But freshwater inflow was also needed, for tidal movement was not enough to maintain healthy oxygen levels or to flush out ammonia-rich fish waste. Once the Romans discovered its importance, freshwater inflow increased fish yields by 100 percent or more and made marine aquaculture far more than just a pastime for Marcus Terentius Varro's wealthy neighbors. A huge Roman fishpond still exists at Torre Astura near Anzio, encompassing about fifteen thousand square meters, the largest such installation known (see map 10 in chapter 13). Numerous smaller ones are known, all of them capable of producing far more fish than a villa would need.

The port and fishery at Cosa on the Tyrrhenian coast (see map 10 in chapter 13) became a large operation by taking advantage of a limestone promontory and a coastal lagoon where fish abounded both inside and outside the sheltered water.[9] According to the geographer Strabo, the high ground of the point served as a place for tuna spotting. The lagoon extended about twenty kilometers along the shore and was separated from the ocean by an eight-hundred-meter-wide sandbar, with the fisheries at the narrower western end, where springs supplied freshwater. Seawater entered the lagoon through several natural inlets, making for an ideal mix of fresh- and saltwater.

Cosa was a major commercial fishery for centuries, perhaps beginning with simple cane or wooden enclosures erected during the first century BC, followed by more permanent structures such as piers, carefully sited to avoid disturbing the water's natural circulation. Migrating fish would swim into the lagoon and could be caught in the inlets. In the late first century BC sluice gates were installed in the major inlet, and large concrete fishponds were built at the western end. A springhouse with a water-lifting device was installed sometime later; it fed the fishponds with freshwater that was aerated as it flowed onto a rock platform and also provided water for manufactories in the town.

Cosa harbor was also a major salting center, but the relationship between the pond and the salting operation is unclear. Certainly the lagoon was a superb natural environment for fish, whose entry and exit were controlled by traps and sluices that came into play during migration season. From all indications, a single engineer masterminded the entire harbor and fishing complex. He must have had a detailed practical knowledge of both hydraulics and fish farming. Cosa itself was an important trading port, perhaps for unspectacular staples like garum.

The Romans knew that raising freshwater fish in tanks was easier than farming saltwater species. Freshwater fish require less oxygen than their saltwater relatives and are also more disease resistant. Artificial fishponds were common features of Roman rural villas and city residences after the late first century AD. They not only provided fresh fish but also served as ornaments: Roman gardens as far afield as Asia Minor, North Africa, and Gaul featured decorative ponds. The Villa of the Piscina in Centocelle, a suburb of Rome, boasted a fifty-meter fishpond with amphorae set into its sides and a central fountain. Inset amphorae are commonplace in freshwater fishponds throughout the Roman Empire. Most likely they served as a sort of nest that allowed fish to hide from aggressive territorial behavior. Ponds with amphorae may have been used to farm the strongly territorial tilapia, which is otherwise easy to grow in captivity and was probably widely farmed.

The most intensive fish farming unfolded in custom-built masonry ponds. These were a different proposition from lagoon farming. They were designed to maximize yield per cubic meter, which meant that great efforts were needed to renew the water, both to ensure adequate oxygen levels and to keep the pond clean. If done right, the yields could be significant. Modern installations can hold as many as twenty thousand to fifty thousand fish in a seven-hundred-cubic-meter pond, depending on the age and species of the fish. By the first century AD advances in concrete technology made it easier for inland landowners to build small ponds that could provide fish for the household and perhaps a modest profit from selling the surplus.

Piscinae *and* Piscinarii

Piscinae were coastal ponds of the wealthy in the Bay of Naples and over long stretches of the Tyrrhenian coast. Expensive to maintain, these ponds were symbols of unrestrained gluttony and excess. Cicero contemptuously labeled their owners piscinarii, "fish fanciers," and "Tritons of the Fish Pool."[10] Nothing was too over the top. The most complex ponds extended into the Bay of Naples in front of imposing coastal villas. Constructing them usually involved extensive rock cutting as well as cement work, so the contractors had to employ skilled workers and also have the necessary design skills to combine function with aesthetics. Just positioning the enclosure relative to prevailing currents and winds required specialized knowledge and experience.[11]

Once such an elaborate pond was built, the owner had to employ a team of workers to stock and feed the fish, maintain the sluices, and clean the tanks. Stocking piscinae required capturing juveniles attracted to pond outlets when water ran out at low tide as well as fishing for them in coves and lagoons. Villa slaves may have done much of the hard work of stocking the pools. A savvy owner could reduce some of his expenses by selling fresh fish to nearby urban markets that had wealthy customers. It was no coincidence that the most intensive marine aquaculture was in areas like the Bay of Naples, along the coast north and south of Rome, and near other wealthy cities like Alexandria.

Many piscinae were carefully landscaped so that the owners and their guests could look down on clear pools internally subdivided into decorative shapes, sometimes adorned with statuary. Perforated sluices in the dividing walls separated the fish. The host and his guests would stroll among the tanks, watch the colorful fish, and sometimes even catch them with hook and line. Only the wealthiest could afford to own and maintain piscinae. They were often celebrities, people who went to extremes to maintain their positions. The orator Hortensius, one of Varro's friends, regularly entertained the scholar at his country house. While he often bought fresh fish from nearby Pozzuoli for

Fishpond at Hadrian's Villa, Tivoli, Rome, second century AD. De Agostini
Picture Library/W. Buss/Bridgeman Images.

his guests, he also kept pet eels and employed an army of fishermen to catch
small fry to feed the voracious denizens of his ponds. The heyday of piscinae
was an opulent age. Lucius Lucullus, a friend of Cicero's, had a tunnel bored
through a hill to provide saltwater to his ponds, and he erected a breakwater
at vast expense to ensure that the incoming tide brought cool water to them.

Elite private banquets were spectacles as much as meals. They were feasts
for the senses at which the host strove to impress his guests with extravagant
fare, lavish displays, and entertainment. Exotic fish, carefully prepared and
displayed for their rarity and especially the difficulty of their catching, were an
important element. Large fish adorned huge platters, were sometimes decorated with jewels, and were brought to table to the accompaniment of flutes
and pipes. When a fisherman gave the emperor Domitian (AD 238–55) a turbot of unusual size, the court had to make a special platter for it. Exotic sturgeon or turbot inspired the satirist Martial to an epigram: "Although a large
dish bears the turbot, the turbot is always wider than the dish."[12] He wrote of
the wealthy Calliodorus, who sold a slave for four thousand sesterces (about
$2,200) and used the money to buy a 1.8-kilogram farmed surmullet. Writers

like Juvenal complained of trophy fish that cost more than a cow, an estate, or a racehorse.

For the guests at a banquet, power and social standing were measured by one's place at the table and even by the different foods served to guests of varying social position. The Younger Pliny criticized a friend who "set the best dishes for himself and a few others and treated the rest to cheap and scrappy food."[13] Pliny himself made a point of serving the same food to everyone. Martial wrote of a social climber named Papylus, who sent expensive fish as gifts to make a social mark but dined on fish tails and cabbage at home. Tales of the conspicuous luxury and wealth, epitomized by the fishponds, spread far and wide, usually to the benefit of their owners but not always. Cicero railed privately in his letters against piscinarii for being obsessed with fishponds at the expense of affairs of state.

Like so many playthings of the wealthy, piscinae eventually went out of fashion. Most were constructed between the mid-first century BC and mid-first century AD. The end of the Republic and the crystallization of imperial power led the emperor Augustus, among others, to try to curb luxurious banquets and other wealthy excesses. Many lavish fishpond sites ended up as part of imperial estates. The emperor Nero is said to have coveted fishponds on the Bay of Naples belonging to his aunt Domitia, who had remodeled and maintained them with great care. He had her poisoned and seized her property.

The statesman Flavius Aurelius Cassiodorus Senator (c. AD 485–c. 585) founded the monastery of Vivarium on his estates on the shores of the Ionian Sea (see map 10 in chapter 13).[14] He intended the place to be a school whose students would be guided by his writings on Christian texts and a place where travelers and the poor could enjoy the irrigated gardens and fish in the nearby river. Special pools were created to keep ocean fish alive for the table. By then, fish farming as practiced in earlier centuries had become a largely forgotten art, as were the building techniques associated with its facilities.

Christian monasteries, mostly situated inland, became the greatest consumers of fish, partly because of the strictures of a monastic diet on holy days. The emphasis turned from marine fish to freshwater species found in streams, lakes, and monastic ponds, where they were safe from a constant menace of the ocean: brigands and pirates. The Christian doctrine of IXTHEUS, literally, the "Big Fish," symbolized fish eating as the most intimate link between Christ and the faithful. IXTHEUS was the greatest fish of all, larger than anything offered to emperors and accessible to everyone, whether aristocrat or commoner. The lavish feasts and magnificent catches enjoyed by rulers, nobles, and the newly wealthy receded into history. Instead, the newly expanding religion celebrated its faith with feast and fast, observances of Holy Days and Lent, which would come to have a profound effect on global fisheries.

15

The Fish Eaters

When fish became rations for sailor and soldier alike, as they did along the Nile and throughout the Mediterranean world in classical times, they became not only a commodity but vital ship's provisions for merchant vessels sailing beyond the boundaries of the routinely known world. A merchant skipper, however fast or seaworthy his vessel, had one constant worry when far from established ports and stopping places: Do we have enough food and water aboard? The problem was especially acute along the desolate coasts of the Red Sea and the Indian Ocean. Even remote fish camps were welcome sights when food was running short. Without dried fish and jars of freshwater, few ships would have coasted through the Red Sea or along Arabian shores. In an inconspicuous but very real sense fish shaped history along these coasts. They enabled the seafaring that opened up trade over wide tracts of the Red Sea and Indian Ocean.

The Red Sea is a vicious ocean, one cursed with headwinds, hidden coastal reefs, and extreme heat. Even if he had local knowledge, no sane seaman sailed these treacherous waters at night. Ships remained anchored after dark. Sailors learned where convenient anchorages lay, and the fishers on shore also knew them—as did pirates. Out of necessity, sea captains developed mutually profitable relationships with the fisherfolk who lived along these desolate shores.

The people Greek geographers called ichthyophagi, or fish eaters, dwelt in scattered communities along the arid coasts of the Red Sea, Arabia, and the

184

Persian Gulf. According to Diodorus Siculus, the fish eaters lived in shaded, north-facing caves, in whalebone shelters, or under crude lattices of branches but spent most of their time in the water. They set up their dwellings near narrow channels and in small ravines where they could use convenient boulders to build damlike fish traps. At high tide seawater would flow over the dam, allowing fish of all kinds into the basin behind it. As the ebb tide receded, trapping the fish, entire bands descended on the receding water, shouting loudly. The women and children gathered the smaller fish near the land and threw them ashore. Meanwhile, the young men went after the larger fish, even seals, dispatching them with sharpened goat horns or killing them with jagged rocks. Once the catch was safely ashore, the fish eaters laid the fish out to dry on sunbaked hot rocks, which quickly cooked them. Then they shook out the backbones and trod on the flesh, mixing it with "the fruit of Christ's thorn" (*Ziziphus spina-christi*, Christ's thorn, is a common evergreen tree with edible fruit and leaves attractive to bees. Tradition claims that it was used to make Christ's crown of thorns). The resulting mixture formed small, sun-dried bricks that, according to Siculus, provided "stores that are unfailing and ready for use, as though Poseidon had assumed the task of Demeter [the goddess of the harvest]."[1] During stormy weather or exceptionally high tides, the fish eaters turned to large mussels. "They break their shells," Siculus writes, "by throwing huge stones at them and then eat the meat raw, its taste resembling somewhat that of oysters." If all else failed, they scavenged the flesh adhering to decaying backbones shaken from earlier catches.

To Siculus and his contemporaries, the ichthyophagi were savages. Their diet may have scandalized an urbanized Greek or Roman or a prosperous farmer, but, as the geographer perceptively remarked, they never lacked for food. They knew how to trap fish and preserve their flesh, and they provided fresh and preserved fish to mariners passing through the Red Sea and the Indian Ocean for many centuries. Long before Asian rice and much more abundant grain made fish a less important part of maritime diet, the anonymous fish eaters may well have made early voyaging in the Red Sea and Indian Ocean possible. Even so, every vessel must have towed lines astern to catch fresh fish, as they did as recently as the 1930s.[2] Fresh fish were far more palatable than preserved fish, however well cured.

The importance of fish grew gradually after about 6000 BC when bitumen-reinforced vessels first coasted the desolate shores of the Persian Gulf. Dried, salted, or smoked fish were light and easily stowed in bulk, could be cooked or chewed raw, and were obtainable almost anywhere the fish eaters dwelt, especially when they were camped close to a convenient anchorage. Bartering for fish was no harder than obtaining drinking water, and for cargo skippers it was a matter of developing long-term relationships, sometimes for many generations, with chiefs and headmen at strategic places.

Down the Red Sea

Southward voyages from the Mediterranean world started at the northern end of the Red Sea, the name of which is a direct translation of the Greek Erythra Thalassa. Why red? No one knows, but it may refer to the seasonal blooms of the sea sawdust plant that grows near the water's surface. Or perhaps the name was an Asiatic reference to south, in contrast to the Black Sea in the north.

The Red Sea is a 2,250-kilometer-long seawater inlet of the Indian Ocean. Its center trench, about 2,200 meters deep, is an extension of East Africa's Great Rift Valley known as the Red Sea Rift. Extensive coastal shelves and coral reefs on both coasts provide habitats for more than one thousand invertebrate species. At least twelve hundred species of fish also thrive in these waters, including forty-two deepwater forms. As they do over much of the northern Indian Ocean, two monsoon seasons blow from the southwest and northeast, making the Red Sea waters very warm. Because it has high evaporation rates, is fed by few rivers, and has a limited connection with the larger ocean to the south, it is one of the saltiest stretches of water on earth. These attributes have always made it a formidable undertaking for vessels propelled by oars, paddles, or sails.

Nonliterate sailors were fishing and trading along Red Sea coasts long before fragmentary Egyptian records tell of their voyages. Knowledge of the coastlines, their hazards, and their inhabitants came through hard experience and was passed from skipper to skipper and generation to generation, a constellation of oral tradition and tough apprenticeship. Expeditions southward from the eastern shore of the Red Sea to the Land of Punt, known to the Egyptians as Puente, are recorded from the time of the pharaoh Khufu in the mid-third millennium BC. Punt became an established trading partner, supplying Egypt with gold, aromatic resins, and frankincense as well as ivory and other African products. While its precise location is unclear, it was probably a broad region somewhere around modern-day Eritrea, Ethiopia, and Somalia.

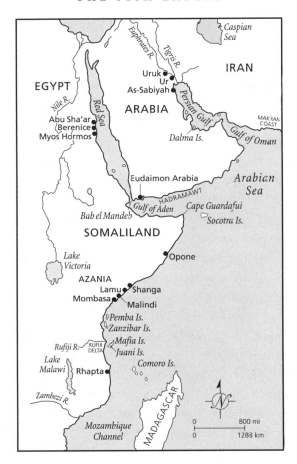

11. The Red Sea, Azania, and the eastern Erythraean Sea, showing fishing settlements and ports of call.

Most Egyptian voyages probably went unrecorded, with the notable exception of Queen Hatshepsut's five-ship expedition to Punt in the fifteenth century BC. The queen boasted loudly of its success on the walls of her mortuary temple on the west bank of the Nile, which suggests that such royal passages were probably rare.[3]

Sometime around the first century AD an anonymous Egyptian merchant who apparently had much voyaging experience around the Indian Ocean wrote one of the classics of early navigation, *The Periplus of the Erythraean Sea* (*Periplus* is a Latinization of the Greek word for "a sailing around," sometimes applied to navigational directions).[4] The first work to describe the coastlines and ports along trade routes that had already been in use for many centuries, it tells of the author's southward voyage through the Red Sea, then to the East Coast of Africa and, in another routing, along the Arabian coast to the Persian Gulf, India, and beyond. The *Periplus* is a matter-of-fact document, written by someone with firsthand experience of rugged desert coastlines where drinking water, food, and pirates were daily concerns.

The author begins, as any southbound skipper would, in the Red Sea. "Of the designated ports on the Erythraean Sea, and the market-towns around it," he writes, "the first is the Egyptian port of Mussel Harbor [Myos Hormos]. To those sailing down from that place, after eighteen hundred stadia [about 285 kilometers] there is Berenice. . . . On the right-hand coast next below Berenice is the country of the Berbers [or Barbaroi, barbarians]. Along the shore are the Fish-Eaters, living in scattered caves in the narrow valleys."[5] The author's description of these scattered caves has an immediacy that suggests he may have visited fish eaters on several occasions.

In Graeco-Roman times, when *The Periplus of the Erythraean Sea* was widely consulted, fish were a major component of the Red Sea economy, marketed fresh, dried, salted, or smoked as well as fermented into garum, the ubiquitous Roman fish sauce. Much of the fishing industry was based at the port of Myos Hormos, which came into being during Ptolemaic times, in the third century BC.[6] It became a well-established entrepôt after the Romans took over the Nile Valley in 30 BC and constructed a road linking the town to the Nile. Until the third century AD the port remained a hub for trade down the Red Sea.

According to the geographer Strabo, writing at the time of Christ, "as many as one hundred and twenty vessels were sailing from Myos Hormos to India, whereas, formerly, under the Ptolemies, only a very few ventured to undertake the voyage and to carry on the traffic in Indian merchandise."[7] The explosion in direct passages to the Indian coast resulted from the Greek navigator Hippalus's advocacy of a route across the Indian Ocean that took advantage of the alternating cycles of the monsoon winds. By all accounts, he did not discover them but merely publicized a phenomenon that had been closely held navigational wisdom for many centuries.[8]

Myos Hormos, a cosmopolitan city, had large communities of Romans, Egyptians, and even Indians. Judging from inscriptions found on potsherds, both desert nomads and fish eaters were active traders there. A lagoon with gradually sloping beaches, now filled with silt, framed the harbor behind shallow reef, beyond which the bottom plunged abruptly. The relatively uncomplicated entrance made the harbor a busy place: ships were repaired, hulls were sheathed with lead against voracious teredo worms, and rigs were maintained. It was here that fishers mended their gear, some of which are preserved in a waterlogged area near the former lagoon.[9] The evidence for fishing and fishers here was well preserved in the damp area of the site. It is only a small part of the complex archaeological record from the site, one that is normally virtually invisible owing to poor preservation.

The Myos fisherfolk made nets from bast fiber, probably flax. The finer-meshed ones were likely cast from boats or the shore to catch smaller fish such as sardines. Groups of male and female net makers may have sat amid piles of dried flax, deftly knotting twisted strands into uniform squares. Nothing was wasted. Some workers cut and shaped lead waste from the sheathing of ships' hulls into net weights; others fashioned floats from discarded wooden amphora stoppers.

Most Myos Hormos nets had relatively large meshes for catching large fish or for use as dragnets, often featured in Roman mosaics. The fishers also made extensive use of passive net traps—there are four surviving bag nets made of grass, palm, or bast fiber—which were trailed behind boats either to scoop up fish or to keep the catch alive. They used woven palm fiber to make baited basket traps, which they attached to a float for use in tidal waters. Examples of these traps were found at Abu Sha'ar, farther up the western coast. The second-century Greek historian and geographer Agatharchides recounts that the fish eaters took inshore species with stone traps in the form of barriers across pools and tidal inlets. Most fish were "easily subdued," he writes, but the enterprise could be dangerous when the traps caught seals, dogfish, or large eels.

As is true of most ancient fishing sites, at Myos Hormos fishhooks tell much of the story. Locally made barbed copper hooks are sometimes found grouped together, as if used for long lines. Larger fish were taken with bigger baited hooks and a single line. The fishers also made extensive use of gorges, a straight fragment of baited bone, shell, or wood laid parallel to a line. As the line went taut with the strike, the gorge would stick in the catch's mouth or body. Gorges were also used in the Persian Gulf but apparently not in the Mediterranean.

The fish eaters' watercraft remain a mystery. Writings on clay ostraka refer to *schediai*, rafts or flat-bottomed vessels propelled, according to mosaics, by oars. There are extensive references to these, for they were highly adaptive to the shallow-water fishing practiced not only near Myos Hormos but also throughout the Red Sea.[10]

Preservation conditions were so good that the city's middens yielded not only bones but also some flesh, even half of a sliced-open parrot fish. Myos Hormos lay close to a variety of marine environments, so the fishers could take pelagic fish such as barracuda and shark in open water, exploit local reefs for their parrot fish, and also fish for species that thrived on sandy bottoms. They also ate a wide variety of grouper, sea bream, jack, and trevally as well as snapper and wrasse.

Myos Hormos and other Red Sea ports lay in hot environments where fish, if not carefully preserved, spoiled almost immediately. There was strong local demand for fresh fish, but much of the catch was also sliced and dried, salted, or smoked. Garum was a staple of the marketplace. Effective preservation allowed the port to export fish across the desert to the Nile, while other places sent fish deep into the Eastern Desert and as far away as the Levant. The fish business in the major ports was large enough that fishers were probably able to specialize. Records hint at fishing permits and taxation of fish traders. Fishers based at major ports would also have sold preserved fish to merchant vessels as provisions. The smoked bundles could be compressed and stowed in compact spaces without spoiling. Many centuries later in the North Atlantic, the Norse carried the same kind of food: dried cod was a staple on their voyages west to Greenland and beyond.

Thousands of years of coastal voyaging along inhospitable, dangerous coasts up and down the Red Sea depended on strategic ports of call, where vessels could restock drinking water and fish. There was a close link between the long-distance monsoon-wind trade and the fish produced by sedentary coastal settlements where small boats exploited reefs and deepwater fisheries. Fishing is virtually invisible in many archaeological sites, but a convincing argument can be made for a close connection between coastal fishing along the length of the Red Sea and the rapid expansion of monsoon-wind voyaging after the first century BC, once Hippalus publicized the potential of direct passages to India.

South to Azania

Upon reaching the southern end of the Red Sea and passing through the narrows at Bab el Mandeh, a skipper using *The Periplus of the Erythraean Sea* had two choices. He could turn eastward toward the Arabian coast or head south to Azania. If he continued south, along the western shore of what is now the Gulf of Aden, he would eventually round Cape Guardafui, the so-called Cape of Spices, at the northeastern tip of what is now Somalia. He would then trend southward along a desolate coast with widely spaced market villages where cinnamon and slaves could be obtained in addition to foodstuffs, cotton, and other commodities from the Arabian coast and farther afield.

South of an entrepôt named Opone, according to the *Periplus,* the sailor would reach the "small and great bluffs of Azania," a coast with deep water close inshore.[11] He would encounter no safe ports for some days until he came to the Courses of Azania, a long shoreline of islands, rivers, and safe anchorages that began at the picturesque town of Lamu, in what is now Kenya, where coral reefs fringe the coastline.[12] These barriers corralled shallow, warm water in which a wide diversity of fish species thrived. Visiting sailors encountered a languid, humid shore of beaches and estuaries backed by dense woodland on the edge of a low-lying coastal plain that in some places extended as far as three hundred kilometers inland. On that shore, they would discover, "there are no wild beasts except the crocodiles, but there they do not attack men. In this place there are sewed boats, and canoes hollowed from single logs, which they use for fishing and catching tortoise. In this island they also catch them in a peculiar way, in wicker baskets, which they fasten across the channel-opening between the breakers."

An intrepid captain might sail for two days farther south to a place called Rhapta, meaning "sewn," a name apparently derived from local sewn boats. This remote but as yet unlocated place abounded with elephant ivory and tortoise shell. The ivory was especially valuable because African elephants have softer, less brittle tusks than their Indian cousins, making their ivory ideal for carving. Beyond Rhapta lay unexplored waters, where there were said to be man-eating people.

Apart from winds and navigational hazards, the classic problems in traveling to Azania were securing food and drinking water, not necessarily obtained at large ports like Berenice but from small tribal groups that camped and fished at water's edge. Dried and salted fish must have been staples for Azanian voyagers, for even those aboard well-provisioned vessels were at the mercy of local fish-eater chiefs, who exploited inshore fisheries and bartered the preserved catch to visiting ships. Just as in the Red Sea, along the Azanian coast word of the best places for watering ship and replenishing stores would have passed from generation to generation based on long-established relationships between individual captains and African chiefs dwelling in large villages as well as fisherfolk living in what must often have been little more than small fishing camps.

Long before the *Periplus* was written ships from the Red Sea and Arabia ventured down this desolate coast in search of ivory and other African commodities coveted by the outside world. Many voyages would have failed if not for individual ship captains' relationships with anonymous fisherfolk who plied the coastal waters in sewn plank canoes and placed their traps strategically. The East African trade, such as it was, thrived outside the footnotes of history long before Islam spread to Azania. There were no convoys of ships or powerful merchants orchestrating the trade. A scatter of imported potsherds, beads, and exotic glassware chronicle sporadic visits to what was then a remote shoreline.

People have lived on the East African coast since long before the first millennium BC, but the early inhabitants left few traces.[13] At the time of the *Periplus*, the coast was occupied by scattered hunter-gatherer bands. Given the rich fishery in later times, one can reasonably assume that a sizable number of these bands were fish eaters. Fish and mollusks were a central element in coastal diets by the seventh century AD. At Juani Island in the Mafia Archipelago, off the coast of central Tanzania, an important site on the grounds of the local primary school has yielded two phases of occupation, one between the fourth and sixth centuries AD and another between AD 880 and 1200. The earliest inhabitants consumed predominantly maritime foods, especially shellfish. They collected both edible and decorative mollusks, including *Nerita*, a common tropical sea snail, and cowries. Shellfish consumption dropped sharply during the second occupation, a trend also observed at two sites on Zanzibar dating from AD 600. The abundant fish in the earlier Juani diet included emperors, groupers, and other coral and bay species as well as parrot fish and other inshore species; the same fish appeared in the Zanzibar sites. The Mafia and Zanzibar sites do not necessarily prove that the occupants were full-time fishers. Rather, they chronicle a rapid adaptation to coastal environments in which the settlers focused on easily available fish and mollusks rather than on farming and domestic animals.

Nevertheless, at least some of the African coastal people were established farmers as well. A complex tapestry of hunting and farming communities flourished along the shore and far into the hinterland, a permeable conduit that brought ivory and slaves to the beach from far inland. Despite the appearance of artifacts and institutions derived from other lands, Azania was culturally purely African. Early sporadic contacts are documented not necessarily from artifacts such as imported porcelain but from the introduction of Asian animals and plants, including humped zebu cattle. Few of these early communities survive in the archaeological record. Many were submerged by rising sea levels, which also wiped out evidence of the coastal fisheries.

A settlement named Shanga on Pate Island, in the archipelago off Lamu, occupied as early as AD 750, offers a glimpse of fishing activity along a coast whose varied fisheries included estuaries, coral reefs, rocky habitats, and mangrove swamps.[14] Here, the fishers took large numbers of estuarine fish, reflecting the settlement's location, but reef species such as parrot fish were also common. They also caught marbled parrot fish, which prefer sheltered bays and lagoons where algae and sea grass abound, and the reef-loving, yellow-and-blue-striped emperor fish (*Lethrinus* sp.).[15] Shanga fishers worked inshore habitats and reefs, sometimes even the outer reefs, but they never ventured into open water until after the twelfth century, when their circumstances changed dramatically.

A handful of travelers throw light on the coast and its fisheries, notably Muslim geographers. The Arab historian and geographer Al-Masudi, visiting Azania in 916, noted that "there are . . . many . . . fish, with all sorts of shapes." Another geographer, Al-Idrisi, wrote a century later that the inhabitants of the town of Malindi "obtain various kinds of fish from the sea, which they cure and sell."[16] The fourteenth-century traveler Ibn Battuta reported that the inhabitants of Mombasa imported grain from farmers inland but subsisted for the most part on bananas and fish. By Battuta's time, Islam was well established along the East African coast, and a distinctive African society had developed based on a lively trade between the ivory- and gold-rich interior and the wider Indian Ocean universe. The reversing seasons of the monsoon winds made the open-water journey from Africa to India and back within a year a routine proposition.

In earlier times the coast had been a remote land on the very edge of the Mediterranean and Arab worlds. Now, with an insatiable demand for gold, iron ore, ivory, slaves, and even poles from mangrove swamps for use in house construction in Arabia, profound changes took place along the coast. Azania became a cosmopolitan marketplace. A network of small "stone towns" came into being, in which mosques and the houses of the elite were constructed of coral, using building methods first adopted in the Red Sea.[17] Each town had a hinterland of lesser settlements along the shore, on the islands, and in the interior, every one of them with deep cultural roots in the past. These were quiet, even serene communities where life unfolded at a languorous pace, except when trading vessels arrived with the monsoon and when they departed with the southwesterlies. At such times, tranquillity gave way to the bustle of loading. Docks and ships grew dense with stacks of elephant tusks, tightly lashed piles of mangrove poles, passengers crowded on deck with their possessions. Bundles of dried fish would be packed into the bowels of each ship, the hold stinking with the odor of previous journeys' provisions. Drums throbbed, the crew sang, the sail was raised, and the laden merchantman eased out to sea. Once the ships had sailed, quiet descended on the town until a load of ivory or a line of slaves arrived from up-country, ready for the next monsoon season.

After about 1000 BC coastal society became more hierarchical, the towns headed by powerful families. During the twelfth century there was a shift in fishing practices. For the first time, open-water fishing took hold at Shanga and other settlements; domestic animal bones begin to proliferate in excavated town garbage heaps at this time as well. No longer did coasting merchant ships seek fish from fish eaters. Something quite different was going on. Cattle and sheep had considerable prestige in African societies of the day, not only as symbols of wealth and power but also as social instruments used in feasting and as gifts for eminent visitors.

The archaeologists Eréndira Quintana Morales and Mark Horton have argued that those higher on the economic ladder had more access to domesticated animals and the capital to invest in boats and offshore fishing.[18] Coastal populations were rising, perhaps putting pressure on inshore fisheries. One response, especially in societies with emerging social hierarchies, would have been to use boats to fish offshore. Ownership of such vessels would have allowed powerful individuals to reinforce their social and political positions with carefully orchestrated hospitality and feasting.

All of these developments occurred as coastal society developed an increasingly maritime outlook, encouraged by a thriving international marketplace that was disrupted and eventually changed by the arrival of the Portuguese under Vasco da Gama in 1498. By then, Azania had long been part of a wider commercial world whose tentacles extended deep into the Red Sea, along the Arabian coast, into the Persian Gulf, and as far as the western Indian coast and even beyond. A voyager to these regions would discover another world of constant movement in which fish were an inconspicuous yet priceless commodity.

16

The Erythraean Sea

Emerging in 2000 BC from the mouth of the Red Sea, a sailor who chose to turn eastward rather than follow the African coastline south to Azania would enter a vast ocean that extended to distant lands far beyond the horizon. Called by the Greeks the Erythraean Sea, it is now known as the Indian Ocean. To Greek geographers the Erythraean defined the edge of the known world. The nearby lands were the realm of uncivilized foreigners whom they called Barbaroi, the babblers or barbarians, whom they thought of as poverty-stricken, primitive people with no interest in trade. Among them, however, were familiar folk: the fish eaters.

Heading eastward after the narrows at Bab el Mandeb and sailing along the Arabian coast, a skipper would have found his first port of call at what *The Periplus of the Erythraean Sea* called Eudaemon Arabia, probably what is now Aden (see map 11 in chapter 15). Long a convenient transshipment port for cargoes from India, Eudaemon Arabia lay at the west end of a "continuous length of coast . . . along which there are Nomads and Fish-Eaters living in villages."[1] Unlike the coast of the Red Sea, with its reefs and shallows, this shoreline's greatest challenge was not so much navigation as the procurement of sufficient food and drinking water. Every ship trailed fishing lines, but in the days before rice was available in the West a successful voyage here must have depended on fish bartered with fish-eater communities. As recently as the 1930s the Australian historian and sailor Alan Villiers, who spent a year sailing in an Indian Ocean dhow, reported numerous fishing places along this coast.[2] There is no reason to believe that fish were any less abundant in earlier times, perhaps caught from the same kinds of small, square-sailed fishing craft steered by the fisherman's foot on the tiller as he leaned over the leeward side to net small fish. Their presence was fortunate for traders, as the passage could take many days against the gentle northeast monsoon wind.

The Lower Sea and Mesopotamia

After what was likely a slow passage eastward that made use of familiar anchorages where fish and drinking water could be obtained, a ship would eventually reach the mouth of the Persian Gulf, called by the author of the *Periplus* "that very great and broad sea."[3] Another major defile on the trade route between India and the Red Sea, the Persian Gulf had at its head a port named Apologas, near the Euphrates River. North of the fretted, marshy delta of the Euphrates lay Mesopotamia ("The Land between the Rivers"), now southern Iraq, the tumultuous crucible of Sumerian civilization more than five thousand years ago.

In Mesopotamia, the Sumerians believed, the god Enki had mounted his storm chariot, forged order out of chaos in an incubator of extreme temperatures, dense marshes, deserts, and rising seas, and fashioned both the spiritual and human worlds. The periodic floods of the two great rivers, the Euphrates and the Tigris, made life possible on arid plains where summer temperatures can reach 49 degrees C. Mesopotamia's turbulent landscape of conflict between fresh- and saltwater passed into the head of the Persian Gulf, "the Lower Sea," through the Shatt-al-Arab river delta, a lattice of marshes and swamps where at least part of the history of fishing in the Indian Ocean began. As sea levels stabilized about seven thousand years ago, the enormous tract of marshes and wetlands at the head of the gulf became one of the richest, most biologically diverse environments on earth.[4]

Fishers thrived here long before farmers appeared on the flanks of the watercourses and swamps around 6000 BC, herding goats and sheep and planting wheat and barley in damp fields watered by river floods. Despite the abundant water, the marshes were a place of startling extremes of searing heat and bitter cold. Fast-moving floodwaters could wipe out crops and carry away livestock in just hours. Such realities ensured that fish remained a staple of the diet, that people dwelling near or within the marshes spent much of their lives aboard small, high-bowed reed canoes waterproofed with local tar, poling through quiet defiles in the dense reeds.

The earliest known Mesopotamian farming communities were small hamlets clustered along ridges, natural levees, and side channels formed by the great rivers. Their inhabitants made a distinctive painted pottery, the mark of the 'Ubaid tradition (named after the first such village discovered in the lowlands), which quickly became widespread. Ranged along the edges of the southern marshes, these villages became a cradle of Mesopotamian farming and permanent settlements that gradually spread upstream between the Euphrates and the Tigris, where fertile soils and simple irrigation canals made farming possible. There were always spiritual links to the marshes. It was here that Marduk, the patron god of Babylon, was said to have created the first human settlements by laying a reed upon the face of the waters, then forming dust and pouring it beside the reed to create a desirable habitation for the gods.

The reed huts of the fishermen and farmers eventually developed into mudbrick dwellings crowded into cities, the world's first. Among them was Uruk, west of the Euphrates, the home of the epic hero Gilgamesh from whom the Bible gets the story of Noah's flood (see map 11 in chapter 15). By 3100 BC several cities flourished in southern Mesopotamia, and a jigsaw puzzle of competing city-states developed into the Sumerian civilization.[5] Its rulers presided over an austere floodplain where extremes of nature confronted them on every side, including some of the hottest summer temperatures on earth. Sudden floods could sweep away irrigation canals in hours. The capricious Euphrates and Tigris changed their courses without warning; the spring inundations alternated between inadequacy and excess. Irrigation agriculture could be very productive, but there was only enough water for about 4,143 square kilometers of irrigated fields in a landscape with about 10,000 square kilometers of arable land. Feeding densely populated cities and their hinterlands was a persistent challenge, since the rivers could leave a city's canals and lush gardens high and dry within days. These conditions meant that fish were a vital part of the Sumerian diet. But the simple Sumerian fishing technology could not supply all the fish that were needed.[6]

The marshes in the lower reaches of the Euphrates and Tigris provided rich catches of giant and marsh carp, which thrive in muddy water. To catch them, fishers used elemental methods that changed little over the centuries. They took the fish with hook and line or speared them from light canoes using single- or multiple-headed spears, especially during the spawning season from

Marsh Arabs spearfishing in southern Iraq. Photo by Wilfred Thesiger,
Pitt Rivers Museum, Oxford, UK/Bridgeman Images.

March through May. They also set fire to small reed islands to drive nearby
fish into waiting nets. Toxic vegetable poisons stirred into calm pools would
kill or stun numerous fish, mainly by affecting their gills. Reliefs depict the use
of net barriers and weirs to catch fish in the rivers. They also used long lines
and gill nets, seines, and all the simple weaponry of ancient fisherfolk.

Sumerian and Babylonian scribes recorded about 324 fish names for at least
90 species. In the face of the constant specter of scarcity, large-scale fishing
became a competitive business governed by complex regulations and the leas-
ing out of fishing rights. Many fisherfolk belonged to guilds and often collab-
orated closely with bird hunters. Given the growing cities' insatiable demand
for fish, the processing and transport of catches were closely organized. Many
cities created freshwater ponds where catches netted from boats were kept
alive until needed. Most fish were sun-dried, the larger ones being hung on
lines; others were salted, smoked, or pickled. There was even a market for fish
roe processed into a form of cheese.

Sumerian fish markets would have been cacophonous, bustling places set
close to canals or the great rivers. A market at sunrise in the heart of Ur, one

of the great Sumerian cities (see map 11 in chapter 15), would already be filled with the smell of cooking fish and rotting catches, the smoke from the cooking fires wafting over a confused mass of reed-covered stalls huddled along the water's edge. The sellers shout and gesture amid the throng, touting the virtues of their wares. Children dart among the stalls, dodging porters carrying baskets laden with smoked catfish. Cats and dogs lurking in the background hoping to steal a morsel are kept at bay with shouts and sticks. Buyers poke and sniff at the butterflied or filleted fish, whisking away the flies that swarm over the merchandise. Some stalls lie close to freshwater ponds stocked with languidly swimming catfish. These are only for the elite, who pay high prices and bustle the fish away to be served in the cool of imposing residences before they spoil. The best fish have already been given to the palace or temple, where they swim in special ponds until needed. As the sky brightens, a constant stream of jostling boats and rafts brings new supplies.

All this activity took place outside the demands of ritual observance. So many fish were sacrificed to the gods that major temples employed fishers to supply their altars or else taxed everyone's catch. Priests and other temple personnel consumed large quantities of fish, especially carp, the surplus being sold to the public.

As one of the greatest Sumerian cities, Ur was a well-connected place. Such relationships were vitally important for lowland communities in Mesopotamia, which lacked good toolmaking stone and, later, metal ores, and so had to trade for them. Add to this a constant demand for fish and grain, livestock, and even firewood and trading links between widely separated communities are inevitable and indispensable. So are the resulting social connections. The proof of these links is the distinctive 'Ubaid painted pottery, which traveled enormous distances from its home kilns: all over the lowlands, into the distant mountains of the north and east, and to the Persian Gulf.[7] In the heart of Mesopotamia these pots were commonplace artifacts in palaces and households alike. Elsewhere, far to the north and along the shores of the gulf, such widely traded vessels assumed very different meanings, especially in isolated places, where they were exotic objects brought from afar by coasting skippers.

A fifth- and sixth-millennium village named As-Sabiyah at the northern point of the Persian Gulf was well integrated into the region's complex webs of interaction (see map 11 in chapter 15). The village lies on a low peninsula amid saline mudflats with a creek nearby. At the time of its occupation it was accessible from the sea, which is now some two kilometers away. Judging from shells and bird bones, there were freshwater lakes or marshlands nearby. With its abundant bird life and plant foods, the site was in a favorable position at a time when sea levels were higher than they are today.[8] No less than 67 percent of the total bone weight recovered from the site came from marine fishes, with a gradual decline in favor of mammals, which may reflect an increasing reliance on domesticated animals. The wide expanses of shallow water nearby allowed the inhabitants of As-Sabiyah to take smaller sharks and sawfish, also eagle rays, some quite large. The fishers mostly stayed in shallow water, but the bones of tuna and other pelagic species show that they also ventured out to reefs and deeper waters. Unsurprisingly, the site also yielded net weights and fish gorges.

The connection of As-Sabiyah and other coastal sites to wider exchange networks can be traced by their 'Ubaid pottery. These links may have been purely local or part of wider regional networks that entailed an increasingly broad economic base that included raising livestock, gathering plants, hunting, and fishing. By 4000 BC the fish eaters arrayed around the gulf had embraced quite distinct ways of subsistence. This is not to say that fishing was unimportant: it was certainly fundamental at a time when the exchange of prestige goods like pearls was gaining importance in the Mesopotamian world.

The earliest known human occupation in the south of the Persian Gulf region dates to the late sixth to early fifth millennium BC. A succession of communities lie on Dalma Island in western Abu Dhabi, about eighty kilometers east of the Qatar Peninsula (see map 11 in chapter 15).[9] The island, about nine kilometers long, is basically a salt dome with central hills that rise about ninety-eight meters above sea level. Permanent wells at its southern end made human settlement possible and also contributed to date cultivation, the earliest example of such consumption in Southeast Arabia. Dates were invaluable to mariners. The fruit could be dried and the stones ground and mixed with flour. Like fish, they could be carried over long distances in a ship's hold. The Dalma site yielded 'Ubaid pottery, as has another site one hundred kilometers west of Abu Dhabi. Several islands along the Western Region of Abu Dhabi have yielded scatters of Bronze Age pottery dating to the second millennium BC. These may be the remains of way stations for traders headed up the Gulf of Oman who stopped to take on water and supplies.

Gulf waters are generally shallow, so basket traps and intertidal fishing methods yielded the best catches. Hook-and-line fishing worked best in the deeper fishing grounds off Oman, where shell fishhooks appear as early as the late fifth millennium BC. The earliest examples, made of pearl oyster or large bivalve shell, are invariably unbarbed and sometimes have long shanks, effective against fish with sharp teeth.[10] By about 4000 BC fishermen were using barbless copper hooks; they turned to stronger bronze when it became available.

"Serpents Coming Forth from the Depths to Meet You"

The *Periplus* described inshore passages made in small vessels that would coast along the Arabian shore, then head directly east from the western side of the Gulf of Oman. Eastbound craft carried frankincense and pearls, while westbound craft transported cloth, semiprecious stones, dates, and slaves. The cargo traveled in boats assembled from sewn planks. This local boatbuilding technology was well established, probably before 3000 BC. The technology fashions the hull shape by sewing planks together with mangrove or other fibers. Ribs can be added later to strengthen what is a very flexible vessel. Sewn hulls were so effective that they are still in use in Indian Ocean waters today. In the Red Sea and the Gulf of Oman coasting merchantmen could anchor and acquire drinking water and dried fish but then they had to traverse the desolate Makran coast, backed by inhospitable foothills dissected by river valleys (see map 11 in chapter 15). Until dates and rice became available, few foods except fish and meat were suitable for salting or smoking. Preserved fish must have been a staple for the mariner coasting along this barely inhabited shoreline.

Among the ubiquitous sand dunes along Makran beaches fish bones and mussel shells lie buried alongside potsherds, proving that the detritus arrived in human hands. Fishing camps, now vanished, must have thrived along this arid coast for the benefit of passing ships looking for food. Two sites about 120 kilometers inland on what were at least semiperennial rivers show that at the end of the fifth and during the fourth millennium BC, people living in the humid Dasht Valley traded fish from the coast. The rugged trek inland from the shore would have taken about three days on foot over extremely hot terrain. There were apparently no draft animals at the time.

Inland, fish as well as numerous perforated mollusk shells were buried with the dead. A very ancient house destroyed by fire while still occupied yielded a five-meter-long sawfish saw, perhaps a prized trophy, that was dated to the fourth millennium BC.[11] Fishing communities along the Makran coast that

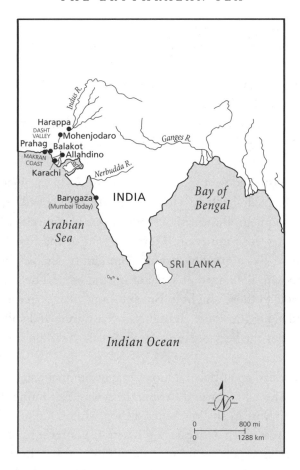

Harappa
DASHT
VALLEY ·Mohenjodaro
Prahag Balakot
Ganges R.
MAKRAN Allahdino
COAST
Karachi
Nerbudda R.

INDIA
Bay of
Bengal

Barygaza·
(Mumbai Today)

Arabian
Sea

SRI LANKA

Indian Ocean

0   800 mi
0   1288 km

12. The eastern coasts of the Erythraean Sea with ports of call and major Indus
cities, also the Bay of Bengal.

were close to safe anchorages were active at least a thousand years before the
great cities of the Indus Valley came into being. Since they supplied fish to
settlements far inland, it is only logical to assume that they traded with passing ships as well.

The *Periplus* described how, to the east, the coast made a wide curve along
a low-lying, marshy shore "from which flows down the river Sinthus [Indus],
the greatest of all the rivers that flow into the Erythraean Sea." Navigators
were warned that as they approached the Indus "there are serpents [probably
eels] coming forth from the depths to meet you."[12] Of the river's seven mouths,
only the center one was navigable. There the mariners could find a market

town named Barbaricum, where they anchored to load or offload diverse cargoes. While many vessels, especially those sailing direct from Arabia or the Persian Gulf, visited southern ports, it was the Indus Valley that generated much of the trade that developed between cities inland, the gulf region, Mesopotamia, and the Red Sea.

Even before the great civilization of the Indus Valley region came into being around 2700 BC there were fishing settlements clustered along the beaches and wetlands close to where the modern city of Karachi lies today, a short distance north and west of the Indus mouth. As usual, poor preservation conditions make fishing activity almost invisible. People had fished the shallow waters of Sonmiani Bay for thousands of years before cities like Harappa and Mohenjodaro rose upstream. From the end of the fourth millennium until about 2700 BC a growing fishing community, almost entirely dependent on the ocean, flourished at Balakot on the bay.[13] The fish taken there were comparable to those caught in Buleji fishing villages in the region today. Grunts, found along the entire Baluchistan coast, were and still are the most common fish; they can be taken in rocky areas a short walk from the site of the ancient village.

Much of the fishing at Balakot took place in summer and fall, when many species came inshore to spawn. Catching them was easy during those months, but the grunt spawns in shallow water during winter. Judging from modern practice, grunt were taken with cast or gill nets, the latter set close to the shore. Fixed nets were especially useful in deeper water, where larger fish could be caught; the fishers also set nets on the bottom for crabs and other crustaceans. Trolling with lines from boats was probably as effective in the past as it is today.

Balakot was most likely a subsistence fishing settlement in which each family processed its own catch. A tiny site at Prahag, west of Balakot along the Makran coast, yielded evidence of large-scale fish processing. Skate, grunt, catfish, drum, and other species were caught locally, presumably with hooks and lines from boats. The fish were cut open, the heads and tails removed, and the flesh preserved by salting and drying. The inhabitants seem to have eaten goat and sheep also and perhaps dolphins as well as gazelle, a small desert antelope. Judging from the systematic butchery, it appears that the fish were mainly for trading.

As centuries passed, Balakot found itself drawn into a wider world. The community lay in the shadow of the huge, fertile Indus Plain, where conditions were changing rapidly. At the time, two major rivers, the Indus and the

Saraswati to the south, provided water to a huge expanse of fertile soils between the foothills of Baluchistan to the west and the Great Indian (Thar) Desert to the southeast. The Indus is one of the great rivers of Asia, rising in southern Tibet and descending though Kashmir before flowing through the semiarid Indus Plain. Here, deep silt deposits provided soft, easily turned soils that could be cultivated on a large scale without metal tools. This is also a region of climatic extremes, very hot summers and sometimes very cold winters. Almost all of the water for farming came from rivers and streams flowing down from the distant mountains.

Like Mesopotamia, the often seemingly unpromising land of the Indus Plain was a cradle of early farming and animal domestication. Twelve thousand years ago the mountain borderlands were home to small-scale hunter-gatherer societies anchored to reliable water supplies. They were constantly on the move, except perhaps on the shores of the Indian Ocean, where coastal marshlands, estuaries, and shallows close inshore supported shallow-water fisheries that would assume ever-greater importance in later times.[14] No one could survive in these contrasting landscapes without maintaining connections with neighboring bands. Connections based on intermarriage, kin ties, and other such relationships endured into much later times and formed the basis of far more complex societies.

The economic ground shifted when farming took hold over a wide area of the Indus Plain between the fifth and third millennia BC, launching the region on a trajectory of increasingly rapid cultural changes. The floodwaters of the Indus were the driving force of this change. Between July and September the rising Indus transported an enormous volume of fine silt downstream, which cascaded over the plain as the river rose above its banks. Just like their contemporaries along the Euphrates and Nile, the local farmers built their villages and then larger communities near natural flood channels that overflowed onto the flat landscape, allowing the villagers to plant crops with minimal effort and no need for irrigation. At first, when the floodplains were densely forested and the impact of catastrophic flooding was much reduced, the farmers prospered. But circumstances changed as village populations rose, more and more land was cleared, and deforestation brought uncontrolled flooding. Survival required cooperation at the community level. Local chieftains and priests soon presided over an increasingly complex hierarchy of settlements large and small.

About 2700 BC a short period of explosive growth coincided with an increase in long-distance trade between lowlands and highlands and also along the ancient coastal routes linking the Indus and the Persian Gulf. By this time the Indus civilization spanned an area larger than present-day Pakistan. This society was very different from the predominantly urban Sumerian civilization of Mesopotamia. Indus people lived in a patchwork of major cities and smaller communities linked by loose cultural and religious ties.

As they did for the Sumerians, cities functioned for Indus leaders as a means of organizing and controlling their society. There were at least five urban centers, the largest being Mohenjodaro, which covered 250 hectares and had a population of up to one hundred thousand in and around the city. It was apparently a planned city, with a citadel at its west end and a grid of narrow streets and houses below. Unfortunately, all efforts to decipher Indus Valley script have so far failed, so nothing is known of the city's rulers and their history.

Harappa, Mohenjodaro, and other Indus cities were carefully built: they had drains, wells, and elaborate baked-brick fortifications that protected the cities from floods. Not that these worked all the time: Mohenjodaro was rebuilt at least nine times. Excavations have revealed artisans' quarters for bead makers and others, and there must have been precincts for fishers. The bones of their catches abound in these cities on a scale that suggests there were full-time fishermen living there.

For all the fertility of its soils, the Indus Plain was a high-risk environment. Tens of thousands of urban nonfarmers depended on grain generated by capricious floods. This uncertainty meant that foods like fish were of fundamental importance, provided they could be taken in bulk. Quite apart from the logistics of acquiring enormous catches, their preservation required careful management, especially since, in addition to relying on the harvest from the river, the cities imported enormous numbers of dried and salted fish from the distant coast. The Indus is a fast-flowing river whose soft banks were often too friable for stable fishing activity. Almost all freshwater fishing took place in calm backwaters, lakes, and smaller channels, where the current was slower and fish like carp and catfish could be taken, especially in winter and summer, when the Indus flowed more slowly.

The waters of the other great river, the Saraswati, were calmer, which may mean that more fishing took place there. Baluchistan's rivers and streams were also gentler, and their quiet pools yielded abundant catches. Calm oxbows and side channels were the places where people set nets, weighed down with terracotta sinkers that look like clay beads but show the distinctive wear from abrasion caused by the net. One painted potsherd from Harappa depicts a man standing among fish holding one or more nets. Along the bottom of the sketch is a large net that must have surrounded a body of water full of trapped fish. Not that nets were the only technology. Many fishers used simple hooks and lines. By 2700 they had begun to add barbs to metal hooks and were among the first people to do so.

Hundreds of thousands of dried fish traveled inland from the mouth of the Indus to Mohenjodaro and other cities, but one can only guess at the scale of the trade. Occasionally an archaeological dig throws up a fleeting mirror image like that from Allahdino, about forty-five kilometers east of Karachi, which thrived during the Indus civilization's heyday between 2700 and 1700 BC.[15] As at Balakot, at Allahdino nearly all the fish were marine species, but here the fishers specialized almost exclusively in silver grunt. In an area of the Allahdino excavation known as the High Mound, occupied after 2500 BC, almost all the fish bones lay in three rooms along the western side of a lane. Virtually all of them were from heads, suggesting that the bodies were dried and salted. This is exactly what commercial fisheries in the region do today. Fish kept for local consumption were treated differently: just as it is today, the head was eaten.

As Harappa, Mohenjodaro, and other cities along the Indus and Saraswati grew and grew, the demand for shells, beads, and dried or salted fish seems to have grown exponentially. As was the case in Egypt and Mesopotamia, fish became a near-industrial-scale commodity that fed not only humans but also goats, sheep, and even camels.

The west coast south of the Indus was shallow and dangerous, with powerful breakers when the southwest monsoon blew strongly. The narrow channel up to the major port at Barygaza (modern-day Mumbai) could be lethal, as its hidden rocks and forceful currents could cast an unwary skipper aground during a falling tide. According to the *Periplus*, "native fishermen in the King's service" were stationed at the channel entrance in well-manned large boats called *trappaga* and *cotymba* and stood ready to guide visitors through the shallows, using the strong flood tide to carry them in.[16]

The author of the *Periplus* also wrote of trading opportunities, ports, and fast-flowing tides all the way around the Indian peninsula as far as the mouth of the Ganges. The island country of Sri Lanka, off the southern tip of India, was a popular stopping-off place. Fed by 103 major rivers and two monsoons, its large floodplains were prolific spawning grounds where fish could be harvested for four or five months a year. Much of the fishing was opportunistic, taking place during the spawning season, just as it does in another floodplain country to the north, Bangladesh. Catfish, snakeheads, and all the familiar shallow-water fish were in Sri Lanka, provisions familiar to skippers from all parts of the Indian Ocean. The fishermen used spear and hooks but also relied heavily on toxic plants to poison fish trapped in drying pools. They do not seem to have used nets.[17]

North and east of Sri Lanka the merchant skipper entered an ocean where coastal fisheries had fed canoe sailors for more than forty thousand years. Apart from tropical cyclones that barreled up the Bay of Bengal and caused havoc in Bangladesh, these waters continued the familiar monsoon sailing that linked the Indian Ocean world to Southeast Asia. Farther on lay Thinae (China), where traders could obtain silk. "The regions beyond these places," the *Periplus* notes, "are either difficult of access because of their excessive winters and great cold."[18] The detailed advice, however, ends with Sri Lanka: beyond it lay a different, little-known world.

17

Carp and Khmer

Perhaps inevitably, because of the accidents of geology, the Jomon culture has become the poster child of early Asian fishing. Long-enduring and sophisticated in its adaptations and harvesting of fish and mollusks in diverse, rich coastal landscapes, Jomon thrived, albeit in various forms, until long after rice agriculture and more complex societies took hold in the Japanese archipelago. The ancient fishing traditions of China also date back to dynamic and changing maritime environments after the Ice Age, just as those of northern Europe and the Mediterranean did.

Early Chinese Fishing

Central and southern China offer a great contrast to the experience of Jomon fishers. Here, too, fishing was part of broad-spectrum hunting and foraging well before twelve thousand years ago.[1] The Lower Yangzi River basin supported communities that lived on wild rice and almost certainly ate carp that flourished in the floodplain's shallow pools and side waterways. Fishing grew in importance after rice cultivation began along the Yangzi around 7000 to 6000 BC. Carp abounded in floodplain areas like the Middle Yangzi valley, and their bones duly occur in archaeological deposits. Downstream, in the Lower Yangzi region, the Kuahuqiao site lies about a meter below sea level on the southern bank of the Qiantang River. At the time it was inhabited, the

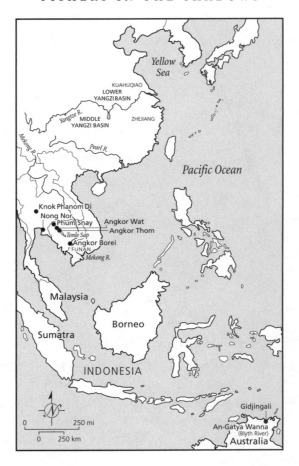

13. East and Southeast Asia, with the major Khmer cities and earlier sites.

area was bounded by mountains on one side and freshwater lakes on the other. The people lived in pile dwellings over the waterlogged ground but eventually abandoned the site owing to rising sea levels. Kuahuqiao may have been one of many settlements in this region, whose shallow waters made it rich in fish, but the others are invisible beneath the sea.

Over many centuries Chinese fisherfolk developed a constellation of simple but effective fishing methods.[2] Apart from the ubiquitous barbed spears, the fishers used cast nets deployed from dugout canoes, rafts, and planked boats, especially in shallow water. Some of these nets were little more than barriers with inset baskets to receive the fish, while others were seines that hauled in large numbers of fish. The fishers deliberately planted brush to at-

Chinese fishermen with cormorants. Watercolor by William Alexander (1767–1816). The Higgins Art Gallery & Museum, Bedford, UK/Bridgeman Images.

tract fish to shallow water for shade and shelter, where they could be encircled with nets or caught by skimming the water. A great deal of early Chinese fishing involved rafts, especially in the calm inland waters. Flat-bottomed, planked fishing boats and rafts morphed into the higher-sided junks of later times.

One famous technique used domesticated cormorants bred in captivity and trained to catch small fish for their masters. Often, well-trained birds did not require neck rings to prevent them from swallowing the fish. And sometimes several birds would even cooperate to land fish too large for a single cormorant to carry. The Ming Dynasty writer Su Fang commented, "Cormorants were raised by many people along the rivers being carried on small rafts. . . . The birds dived deeply into the water and swiftly brought up small fishes; . . . A small ring was tied around their necks so that they could not swallow fishes of large size. . . . The birds were greedy and insatiable, but the fishermen were satisfied and reaped a large profit."[3] It was not until after 1000 BC that seagoing junks came into use for coastal fishing, but endemic piracy inhibited large-scale operations.

The preindustrial Chinese were, above all, successful farmers for whom fishing was usually a sideline. As populations swelled and agricultural plots became smaller, people increasingly relied on wild plant foods and fish. In many places like the Yellow River valley and the Middle and Lower Yangzi freshwater fishing was part of a seasonal cycle in which fish and plant foods, including cultivated rice, were the primary forms of sustenance. In historic times many people on China's central plains fished during the summer monsoon, when their rice fields and reed dwellings were flooded. They dwelt afloat and ate fish for half the year, then returned to their fields when the monsoon floods receded. Their prehistoric ancestors likely did the same.

Along the more temperate Yangzi and farther south, freshwater fish, especially the Asian carp, which abounded in shallow river waters and lakes, were a critical resource. The monsoon was the critical time for taking carp: the receding floods created shallows where fish were stranded and could be easily caught with nets and spear. In the Pearl River Basin and along the Yangzi, extensive wetlands and shallow lakes fed by summer floods provided an ideal environment for wild carp.[4] It was only a matter of time until some farmers created ponds in which they kept carp alive until they were needed. The fish were soon bred in captivity.

Cyprinus carpio haematopterus, the common Amur carp, is native to eastern Asia. An omnivorous species, it prefers large bodies of slow-moving or standing water with soft, muddy sediment. Four species of carp—grass, black, silver, and bighead—occur in the Lower Yangzi, all of which migrate from lakes to rivers during the spawning season. They reproduce in the Yangzi and then grow in thousands of riparian lakes. All four have similar spawning environments but live at different depths. Most bred in the Middle Yangzi, where there were twelve spawning sites along a 380-kilometer stretch of the river until land reclamation and dam building caused drastic falls in their populations. Easily caught and kept in enclosed ponds, they were domesticated by the Chinese well before 3500 BC, at a time from which there are no written records of fishing or aquaculture.

Carp farming probably began when wild populations were washed into ponds and rice paddies during monsoons.[5] Prolific breeders, they grow fast and do not eat their young. As agricultural populations rose, carp farming became a viable supplemental food source for subsistence farmers in increasingly crowded landscapes. Domesticated carp grew much faster than wild ones, reaching weights of more than 40 kilograms and lengths of some 120 centimeters in two years. They are said to have been bred and grown on silk farms, where they were fed silkworm pupae and feces.

Carp aquaculture was commonplace long before the Chinese politician Fan Li wrote a classic primer, *Yang Yu Ching* (*Treatise on Fish Breeding*), which appeared in 475 BC. Fan Li, a minister of the state of Yu, now Zhejiang, in eastern China, started breeding and raising carp in large ponds. He is said to have planted mulberry trees on the margins, in which he placed apiaries, whose droppings fed the fish, while the leaves of the trees nourished silkworms and then goats. His book is anecdotal and at times mythic, but the advice on carp is prescriptively literal: "You construct a fish pond out of six *mou* of land. In the pond you build nine islands. Place into the pond plenty of aquatic plants that are folded over several times. Then collect twenty gravid carp that are three *chih* in length and four male carp that are also three *chih* in length. . . . Leave the water undisturbed and the fish will spawn." He put the fish into the pond during the "second moon" (March). He recommended the systematic release of six turtles into the pond between the fourth moon (May) and the eighth (September), creatures he described as "heavenly guards, guarding against the invasion of flying predators."

Swimming round and round in the pond, the carp behaved as if they were in a large river or lake. The yields after a year were striking. "By the second moon of the next year," Fan wrote, "you can harvest 15,000 carp of one *chih* each, 45,000 carp of two *chih* and 10,000 carp of three *chihs*," a total worth "1,250,000 coins." He recommended saving two thousand two-chih carp as parent stock and selling the remainder. By Fan's estimates, the increase in income from year to year would be enormous.[6]

Fishpond culture became quite sophisticated. Some ponds featured artificial depressions where the carp would segregate themselves by size. To grow big carp, pond owners collected spawn from the shores of lakes and rivers where larger fish gathered. A dozen loads of mud taken at water's edge and laid on the bottom of a pond would give a farmer large carp within two years. Fan Li, who had given all his wealth to the poor when he took up carp farming, made a second fortune from aquaculture.

The next thousand years marked the apogee of carp farming in China, as increasingly careful attention was paid to the fishes' diets and to prevention of parasites.[7] Since all waters in ancient China were publicly owned, fish culture became an integral part of rural life. In the south, farmers in Han Dynasty times (206 BC–AD 220), following what must have been an ancient practice,

dug their own ponds and tanks, in which they grew lotuses and water chestnuts and raised fish and turtles. On the banks they planted trees and tethered
water buffalo, which they used to till their fields. In the north contour irrigation canals along the tributaries of the Huang He River fed water to fields and
fish tanks via gravity.

The golden age of carp farming ended abruptly with the rise of the Tang
Dynasty (AD 618–906). The imperial family name was Li, which was also the
word for the most commonly farmed form of carp. An imperial decree
promptly forbade any carp farming and made consumption of carp an offense
punishable by fifty blows. The emperor's fiat turned out to be a blessing in
disguise for a society that was increasingly dependent on fish, for it prompted
pond owners to domesticate new species. The aquaculturists turned to the
big-head carp (*Hypophthalmichthys nobilis*), another freshwater species native to
large rivers and floodplain lakes throughout East Asia. These mottled silver-
gray fish are large, ranging between sixty and eighty-two centimeters long,
and fast growing, making them ideal for aquaculture. Their flesh is white and
firm, making them an excellent eating species.

The farmers also raised the silver carp (*Hypophthalmichthys molitrix*), now
the most commonly grown carp in the world. This filter feeder consumes
plankton and achieves high population densities. Silver carp can weigh more
than eighteen kilograms and leap aggressively from the water when scared, a
major hazard for fishers in canoes and, today, for pleasure boaters. Pond owners soon discovered that big-head carp and silver carp, along with grass or mud
carp, could coexist in the same body of water. Each species kept to its preferred environment. Grass carp are top feeders, silver and bigheads feed at
middle depths, and mud carp forage along the bottom. Productivity soared,
and the emperor's edict was apparently obeyed. A fortunate genetic mutation
also led to the appearance of goldfish, which were prized as ornamental fish in
nobles' gardens. The policies of the Tang led to another innovation: the seasonal collection of small fry along major rivers. These were accumulated, then
dispersed in natural waters via methods that became highly refined during the
Sung Dynasty (AD 906–1120).

The Ming emperors (AD 1368–1644) strongly encouraged aquaculture, in-
spiring farmers to provide the rulers and urban marketplaces with fresh fish.
Ming authorities also encouraged the use of more sophisticated aquaculture
techniques, such as disease control measures and the application of food and
fertilizer to ponds. Pond owners were told to maintain high productivity by

enriching the water with animal manure and organic wastes. In addition to planting mulberry trees that fed silkworms, as recommended by Fan Li, farmers built structures for pigs and chickens by the water, so that the manure did not go to waste. When a pond had to be drained for maintenance, the owner would dig out the sludge at the bottom and use it to fertilize his crops. In southern China fish were used to help clear fields on hillsides bounded by dikes. Once rain filled the field, the landowners would buy small fry and release them into the enclosures. Within two or three years the fish had consumed the roots of the weeds, and the field would be ready for planting. The owners sold the fish and planted rice in the cleared fields.

By 1500 collecting fry from rivers and raising them in ponds was big business in China. So was fermenting catches to make fish paste and sauce, using techniques remarkably similar to those that produced Roman garum. The sauce and fermented fish trade reached large proportions in central and southern China, as it did in Southeast Asia. The methods used to raise carp when fish farming was a family business were passed from generation to generation over many centuries, and aquaculture became a cornerstone of Chinese agriculture.

When the thirteenth-century Venetian traveler Marco Polo described the many shipping canals he saw on China's large rivers and lakes, he also noted that so much fresh fish was transported inland from the coast to local markets every day that he found it hard to believe they were all sold. He observed that the varieties in the markets changed with the seasons, but, remarkably, he never identified any of these varieties. Today, almost all fish one can buy in China are farmed.

Southeast Asia: Angkor and the Tonle Sap

The three major river systems of Southeast Asia, each with its own fertile delta, are greatly reduced versions of much larger ancient waterways. The Middle Thailand and Chao Prya Delta forms one such system, the Mekong River and Tonle Sap lake of Cambodia a second, and the Red, Ma, and Ca Rivers of Vietnam form the third.[8] The rivers flood seasonally, inundating large areas of farmland with shallow water where long-stalked, fast-growing rice can be cultivated. In the past each valley was a fertile enclave surrounded by higher ground where drought-resistant deciduous and moist tropical forests were watered by variable monsoon cycles and marked by considerable local climate and topographic variations. These valleys supported dense populations, nourished increasingly powerful and volatile kingdoms, and underwrote long-distance trade.

Rice was the foundation of these complex societies, which were well established across Southeast Asia from about 2000 BC. Rice-farming communities first appeared in China's Yangzi valley and spread southward along rivers and coasts. The cultivation of rice was among the first of many Chinese ideas that percolated down into Southeast and South Asia from the north. Bronze Age technology, also from the north, came into widespread use between 1000 and 500 BC, when increasingly aggressive long-distance trading helped fuel intense competition among a constellation of rich, warlike chiefdoms.

By 300 BC the sea-trading networks of Southeast Asia were part of a much larger commercial universe that extended from India as far east as the island of Bali. This maritime trade brought a vigorous exchange of ideas and new cultural influences. By the time of Christ some Southeast Asian societies had become kingdoms, presided over by an aristocratic class who maintained prestigious spiritual ties with revered ancestors. Some of these rulers became divine monarchs, especially those whose domains lay along the Lower Mekong and the Tonle Sap, a wide region the Chinese named Funan, "the port of a thousand rivers."

A second major center flourished at Angkor Borei in Cambodia.[9] Located about ninety-six kilometers southeast of the modern-day capital, Phnom Penh, the site was and still is accessed by a canal some eighty-five kilometers long. The remains of brick and earthen walls enclose about three hundred hectares of higher ground that is bisected by an artificial waterway and is set amid low-lying delta-like floodplains. These old walls marked a center that flourished between roughly 500 BC and 500 AD. The indigenous Khmer people, fourteen thousand of whom still live there, regard Angkor Borei as the cradle of Khmer civilization. A series of carefully excavated trenches dug into various parts of the site between 1995 and 2000 chronicle a sophisticated fishery. More than seven thousand fish fragments came from the excavations, together with mammal bones, birds, and shellfish. The fish bones come from at least twenty-four species, most commonly the snakehead murrel (*Channa striata*), climbing perch (*Anabas testudineus*), and catfish.

The snakehead is an elongated predatory fish that can grow up to a meter in length. It can breathe air through its gills, which allows it to migrate short distances over land, and it is a prolific breeder, mating as often as five times a year. Consummate predators, they are an aggressive, invasive species, aptly called Fishzilla in a National Geographic blog, and are considered excellent food. Climbing perch, which can grow up to twenty-five centimeters long, is another native Southeast Asian species that is highly marketable because it can survive out of water for prolonged periods, provided it is kept wet.

Rice agriculture, fishing, and hunting sustained Funan centers like Angkor Borei for many centuries, allowing their inhabitants to remain at the strategic locations where they could maintain exchange routes and maritime connections. The Mekong fishery was rich enough that large populations could be crowded into the heart of an enormous, often flooded, very fertile landscape. Fish were easy to catch in estuaries, rivers, and lakes, and, as elsewhere, they could be preserved with simple technologies that had been refined long before. The civilization of Angkor, close to the Tonle Sap, was the greatest and most enduring of the Funan kingdoms.

Few freshwater fisheries anywhere rivaled the bounty of the Tonle Sap, a huge lake that fed villages, towns, great temples, and entire states for centuries. Long before Angkor became a state, some Southeast Asian societies had become highly centralized kingdoms, presided over by an aristocratic class to whom formal display, feasting, and ritual were of paramount importance. Over many centuries the heads of these kingdoms tried to carve out ever-larger polities, ruling by charisma and force. At first their kingdoms flourished in riverside and lowland areas along the Lower Mekong River and farther upstream toward the Tonle Sap plains. The politics were highly volatile, but by the sixth century AD the center of economic and political gravity had moved inland to the Tonle Sap, a region the Chinese called Chenla.

The Mekong is the longest river in Southeast Asia. It rises on the Tibetan plateau and flows more than forty-two hundred kilometers through multiple countries, including China, Cambodia, and Vietnam, to the East China Sea. The Mekong is the world's most productive freshwater fishery, and Tonle Sap is its heart. Fish from Tonle Sap nourished the magnificent Angkor civilization and its thousands of farmers and artisans for centuries. Exactly how many people lived under its rule is impossible to calculate, although the numbers were certainly far smaller than those of the twenty-first century Khmer. In that already crowded landscape, the Tonle Sap fishery was sustainable. Most likely, aquaculture already played a major role in keeping it so. Today, given the roughly sixty million people living in the region and depending on the Mekong for more than five hundred fish species, the fishery is unsustainable without aquaculture and is endangered by ambitious hydroelectric dams far upstream.[10]

The Tonle Sap lies in central Cambodia and is connected to the Mekong by the 120-kilometer-long Tonle Sap River; the two rivers meet at Phnom Penh.[11] The lake itself occupies a depression in the vast floodplain of the Lower Mekong Basin, and the Tonle Sap River emerges from a mosaic of shifting channels at the basin's southern end. The rainy monsoon period from May to October causes the Tonle Sap to rise to its highest levels. A belt of freshwater mangroves surrounds the lake, part of a lattice of habitats that support a broad range of animal and plant species. Thanks to the Mekong floods and the monsoon, the Tonle Sap flows north from the Mekong from May to October and south, draining the lake, during the rest of the year. The sediment that flows into the lake contains nutrients that feed photoplankton and nourish a staggeringly rich fishery. At least 149 fish species thrive in the Tonle Sap, along with a multitude of birds and a prolific number of water snakes. The catches range in size from finger-long silverfish to Mekong giant catfish, one of the largest freshwater fish in the world. Adults are up to 3 meters long and weigh up to 230 kilograms. Easy to catch and now overfished, they are an illegal prey today but were a staple in earlier times.

As the Tonle Sap floods, the surrounding areas become prime fish-breeding grounds. Serious fishing begins at the end of the rainy season, when the water starts to drop. Outflowing water carries away the fish, mostly silver carp, which are caught in carefully deployed nets, often cone-shaped devices lowered from the fishers' floating houses. Tens of thousands of fish are caught this way, most of them cleaned, then salted and fermented to form a fish sauce called *prahok*, widely used as a relish. The detached heads of the fish serve as fertilizer for rice paddies.

Various Khmer rulers tried to unify the Tonle Sap region into one kingdom, but none were successful until a dynamic monarch, Jayavarman II, came to power in AD 802. He conquered his competitors, set up a series of tribute kingdoms, and proclaimed himself supreme king and the reincarnation of the Hindu god Shiva on earth. For forty-five years Jayavarman II presided over a powerful, highly centralized state that required enormous food surpluses and huge, carefully controlled labor forces to build canals, reservoirs, and elaborate temples to house each ruler's royal linga. The capitals built by dynasties of Khmer rulers were the hub of the universe, an area known today as Angkor.

A man-made dam for capturing fish on the Tonle Sap, 1918. Pictures from History/Bridgeman Images.

The centripetal society that resulted carried the cult of wealth, luxury, and divine monarchy to amazing heights.[12]

Another ambitious ruler, Suryavarman II, ascended to the Khmer throne in AD 1113. Four years later he ordered the construction of Angkor Wat, an extraordinary shrine that today is the largest ancient religious structure in the world. Rising more than sixty meters above the forest, it dwarfs even the largest Sumerian ziggurat and makes Mohenjodaro's citadel on the Indus look like a village temple. It would not have been possible to complete this remarkable edifice without the enormous quantities of rations provided by highly productive rice agriculture and the bountiful Tonle Sap fisheries.

Angkor Wat was the Khmers' supreme effort to reproduce a monument to the Hindu god Vishnu, preserver of the universe. Every detail of its design reproduces part of the Hindu heavenly realm in a terrestrial mode. The gods lived atop a cosmic mountain, Mount Meru, represented by a central tower. Four other towers are Meru's lesser peaks, and the temple is surrounded by an enclosure wall that replicates the mountains at the edge of the spiritual world. Long bas-reliefs covering 168 meters of the lower gallery walls show the king receiving high officials while riding on an elephant with his court. Elsewhere on the walls there are battle scenes and sensuous celestial maidens, naked to the waist and dancing in celebration of the delights of paradise. One wall depicts the Hindu legend of the Churning of the Sea of Milk, in which giants and gods together pull on the body of Vasuki, a great serpent coiled around Mount Mandara, to stir the primordial ocean. They churned for a thousand years and produced the elixir of immortality. The artists carved dozens of different fish turned topsy-turvy in a choppy sea. According to the legend, they had been poisoned and then cut in two by the sword of Suryavarman II acting in his role as Vishnu. Another little-known relief at the temple shows more prosaic activities: people fishing, hunting, and making music in a forested wetland where birds, fish, and crocodiles abound.

For years archaeologists thought of Angkor Wat and nearby Angkor Thom as stand-alone palace-temples. Now they have used light detection and ranging, or LIDAR, basically highly accurate light sensors mounted in helicopters, to record everything that lies at ground surface, whether covered by forest or not.[13] They now know that Angkor Wat rose amid a huge, engineered agricultural and aquatic landscape of bunded, or dike-surrounded, rice fields that covered about one thousand square kilometers and supported an estimated three-quarters of a million people. Angkor Wat was part of an enormous dispersed urban complex that was already in existence before it was built. The major shrines lay at the center of a huge network of channels, embankments, and reservoirs that managed, stored, and dispersed water from three small rivers down through the city and into the Tonle Sap lake. The scale of the waterworks is truly staggering. The West Baray (or reservoir), about two kilometers west of Angkor Wat, is about eight kilometers long and two kilometers wide, fed by water diverted from rivers to the north. Thousands of people served the temple, and thousands more grew rice and fished the Tonle Sap to support the temple staff. This was a spread-out urban landscape that grew and caught rations to feed the huge labor forces serving the divine king. The logistics were as complex and well organized as those of the pharaohs at Giza.

In 1181 another ruler, Jayavarman VII, erected a new capital at Angkor Thom nearby. When visitors walked inside, they entered a symbolic world at the center of which was the king's funerary temple, the Bayon. Some reliefs in the Bayon depict a market where crowds of common folk are gathered and men are spit-roasting large fish and boiling meat and rice. There are also scenes of men deploying nets, their spear-skewered catch lying on drying racks, and of women selling fish in the marketplace.

All of this lavish expenditure depended on the exceptional productivity of Angkor, on its rice fields, reservoirs, and canals and the exceptionally rich Tonle Sap fishery. The French explorer Henri Mouhot, who paddled across the Tonle Sap in January 1860, observed that "the fish in it are so incredibly abundant that when the water is high they are actually crushed under the boats, and the play of oars is frequently impeded by them."[14] Then, as today, most fishing took place between December and May, when fishers trapped, netted, and fattened tens of thousands of carp and catfish.

Given even this abundance, the Khmer state was so densely populated that aquaculture must have been a necessity. Unfortunately, aquaculture depends on perishable, organic raw materials that rarely survive to become fodder for archaeologists, so one can only guess at the extent of fish farming at the height of the Khmer state. Judging from other parts of the world, the simple but effective methods likely changed little over many centuries. So it is reasonable to look at recent preindustrial aquaculture from the region as opening a window into the deeper past.

It would have been easy for the people of the Khmer kingdoms to trap fish in the delta and the Tonle Sap, then allow them to graze in enclosures and ponds, an idea that may have spread southward from China, where aquaculture along the Yangzi and other low-lying coastal rivers and estuaries had been well established for many centuries. Fish farming would have been highly productive, and it may have been amplified by the raising of carp and other fish in rice paddies, a common practice today. Where water is abundant, as in Cambodia, there are major advantages to cultivating fish in flowing water, as it brings in oxygen and flushes away the fishes' wastes.

Yields in modern-day Cambodia are impressive.[15] Valuable fish like *Pangasius*, a medium- to large-sized freshwater shark catfish indigenous to South and Southeast Asia, are raised in bamboo or wooden cages measuring about 9 by 4.5 meters. The cages float at the surface, covered with straw mats or aquatic plants like water hyacinths to keep the fish cool, and can yield up to 100 to 120 kilograms per cubic meter of cage space in about eight months. Today, fishermen who specialize in catching fingerlings stock the enclosures.

Carp respond well to being enclosed in cages in running water, even heavily polluted sewers and rivers, but their cages are commonly anchored to the bottom and are often completely submerged. Often fed with soaked rice, they grow exceptionally fast and are usually sold as soon as they reach a marketable size.

Aquaculture has assumed growing importance in both China and Cambodia in reaction to their explosive population growth. The fish farming now feeding tens of millions of people in East and Southeast Asia has a direct ancestry in practices that were well established long before imperial China and Angkor Wat.

18
Anchovies and Civilization

At least twenty sonorous conch shell trumpets (*pututus*) have come from the temple at Chavín de Huántar in the Andean foothills, a testimony to the power of seashells in shrines far from their Pacific home. Chavín de Huántar is a maze of subterranean tunnels where water resonates through hidden defiles. When a modern expert blew his conch, researchers recorded the sound through tiny microphones placed inside his mouth and in the shell's mouthpiece, main body, and opening. The sound was like that of a French horn and was altered in the way similar wind instruments are, by muting: the pitch changed when the player put his hand inside the shell. By placing microphones inside the temple's ceremonial chamber, the scientists demonstrated that the murmur of the trumpet sounded as if it came from several directions simultaneously. The effect was a sense of droning confusion, which must have added to the awe and mythic fear listeners probably felt. Such trumpet sounds amplified the ancient temple's supernatural atmosphere.[1]

A granite monolith known as the Lanzón, a human–feline icon with snarling fangs, stands in a central chamber within the Old Temple. Lanzón was probably the major deity at Chavín, an oracle whose pronouncements emerged from a hidden chamber above its head. Elsewhere at Chavín, Lanzón carvings depict the god holding a conch in one hand and a spiny oyster shell in the other, perhaps a reference to fertility and the duality of the sexes. The same shells symbolized the constant interactions between the distant coast and the mountains, between highlands and lowlands, that were one of the central threads of Andean history.

The Chavín conches and spiny oyster shells traveled from their homelands off the coast of Ecuador on the backs of llamas for more than five hundred kilometers across the coastal plain and then up winding tracks to the mountain foothills. *Strombus*, the conch, served as a ceremonial instrument and was formed into inlays for fine jewelry and other ornaments.[2] It is easily altered for human use by cutting off the pointed end and grinding out a mouthpiece. Conch shells are among the most sacred artifacts of the Andean world, just as they were in many other ancient societies. *Strombus* trumpets entered musical history from as far afield as the Aegean Islands and South Asia. The *Bhagavad Gita*, an Indian "Song of God," describes how Lord Krishna and the prince Arjuna blew conch horns as they rode into battle seated in a giant chariot pulled by white horses. So established are conches as trumpets that the US Coast Guard lists them as legitimate sound-making devices in its official *Navigation Rules*.

Spondylus, the spiny oyster, was much harder to acquire. It clings to warm-water reefs between six and eighteen meters below the surface of both the Gulf of Mexico and the Pacific Ocean. Searching for these deepwater mollusks involved free diving, a hazardous occupation even for experts, who often suffered hearing loss as a result of their dives. The difficulties of collecting them must have added to their value. To the peoples of the Andes, *Spondylus* was the "blood of the gods," that is, meat that only gods could consume and whose hallucinogenic qualities can induce shamans' trances. This property made its flesh a conduit between the living and the supernatural worlds as well as a way of "feeding the ancestors," who controlled water sources and thus the future of human existence.

Like the conch and other shells, *Spondylus* was associated with the music that accompanied the chants and dances performed at public ceremonies. Sound was all-important in such rituals. Oyster shell pendants tinkled as their wearers moved; snail-shell bells, drums, gourd rattles, and rasps all made music. Spiny oyster shells made wavelike sounds when held to the ear, perhaps interpreted by listeners as a form of supernatural music. No one knows the precise spiritual meaning of *Spondylus*. Perhaps it was a symbol of agricultural fertility: high lords offered spiny oyster shell dust to the gods to avert drought. The mollusk's red colors linked it to blood, women, and sacrifice. It may also have symbolized spiritual transformation, the ability of Andean shamans to pass effortlessly from the living to the supernatural world.

Over the centuries an enormous volume of *Spondylus* shells traveled from Ecuador to the surrounding highlands and lowlands. Inka artisans fashioned figurines from the shells, and *Spondylus* beads abound throughout the lowlands. The trade was both lucrative and prestigious because of the spiny oyster's strong associations with water rituals, a central part of Andean beliefs. Spiny oyster shells were highly valued as late as the seventeenth century. They have become collectibles in modern times and, as ancient, venerated trade objects, are today a symbol of improved political relationships between Peru and Ecuador.[3]

Early Fishing Societies

Judging from a scatter of radiocarbon dates, people settled and fished along the Pacific coast of South America as early as fourteen thousand years ago, perhaps even earlier. The earliest well-defined fishing community on the continent is Quebrada, near the modern town of Camaná in southern Peru, established shortly after the first settlement of the Americas. At that time, when sea levels were lower, the camp lay 7 to 8 kilometers inland from the Pacific.[4] People lived at Quebrada, perhaps on several occasions, until about 6000 BC. Certainly not a permanent camp, it was part of the seasonal round of hunter-gatherers who moved from the highlands to the Pacific and back, perhaps traveling down natural drainages. They brought obsidian for toolmaking from a known source about 130 kilometers upstream. While at the ocean they ate almost exclusively marine foods. Excavations revealed that 96.5 percent of the animal bones were from fish, especially drums (*Sciaena*), a common species that formed a basis for ceviche, a kind of raw fish salad popular in Inka times and probably earlier.

Almost certainly the fishers took their catches with nets. As proof we have only a few fragments of what may have been nets and pieces of gourds that may have served as floats. They also foraged for surf clams, *Mesodesma donacium*, which grow in great abundance in the intertidal zone unless their habitat is disrupted by El Niño events. The resources of the coast were so easy to acquire that at some point before 6000 BC permanent settlement replaced temporary encampments. Obsidian at Quebrada becomes much scarcer, as if contacts with the highlands became less frequent. By 6000 BC no fewer than seventeen smaller camps surrounded the larger Quebrada site.

Around eleven thousand years ago permanent settlement began along the

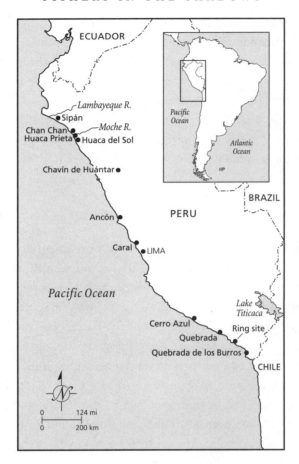

14. Anchovies and Andean states: Archaeological sites in western South America discussed in chapter 18.

coasts of the Atacama Desert of southern Peru and northern Chile. We know this from several locations, including the multilayer Ring site south of the modern Peruvian coastal town of Ilo. Here, a large, circular shell midden accumulated between about 9200 and 3850 BC contains thick masses of fish bones, mollusks, and remains of sea mammals and seabirds.[5] The only terrestrial mammals found in the dig were four mice. The Ring people were broad-spectrum hunters and foragers who focused entirely on the ocean.

So were the inhabitants of another coastal site, Quebrada de los Burros, where a small spring provided water for people there between 7700 and 5300 BC. They lived in small, semicircular dwellings, as most coastal peoples probably did at the time, and depended on the Pacific as their major food source. Large numbers of sardines were presumably caught with nets, other species with hooks. These people also hunted terrestrial game such as guanaco and deer as well as large seabirds, which they took with stone-tipped spears that may also have been used to impale sharks.

About one and a half kilometers inland lay a patch of edible plants known as *lomas* that obtain their moisture from dense fog between June and September and die during the sunny months. Seasonal growth rings on the surf clam shells from the site reveal that, in the earlier layers, people foraged for mollusks most intensively from October to May, when lomas were absent. During the later stages of occupation, the window for clam foraging narrowed to September to January. The mollusk shells suggest that Quebrada de los Burros was a permanent settlement in its early history but became more of a seasonal community in later times, when the inhabitants lived in the interior and came to the coast for lomas, hunting, and clams during the fog season. The reason for this alteration is a mystery, but it may be connected with changes in the permanent water supply.

Far to the north, people lived from about 4500 to 1000 BC at the Paloma settlement, forty-eight kilometers south of Lima, behind a bay fifteen kilometers north of the Chilca drainage.[6] Paloma covered fifteen hectares and lay close to extensive lomas vegetation. At first, it was a seasonal camp for somewhat mobile groups, but their descendants, some thirty to forty people, settled there permanently, living in dome-shaped houses built with cane supports and grass or reed thatch. The dry conditions in the garbage heaps have preserved fragments of fishing nets and also bone fishhooks. The Paloma fishers caught large fish, took seabirds and sea mammals, and collected mollusks, but most of their diet came from small fish like anchovies and sardines. Chemical analyses of the human bones revealed very low strontium levels, a sign of an unusually high protein component in the diet, which can only have come from the Pacific. Many Paloman men suffered from ear damage caused by diving in cold water. At first, men consumed more protein than women, but female protein consumption improved over the centuries. There are also signs that some individuals and families enjoyed a better diet than others, a hint that Paloman society was not egalitarian.

The Paloma people mostly lived off the ocean, but their diet also included loma plants. They practiced very limited cultivation in an environment where crops like beans, gourds, and squash could be grown only in local streambeds after they flooded. The land provided raw materials for clothing, dwellings, nets, baskets, and fishing floats as well as firewood for cooking and warmth. One can argue that the land produced the simple infrastructure for effective fishing to the point that marine- and land-based economies were interdependent from very early times. This interdependence increased when inland societies began constructing major ritual centers and society grew more complex. At the same time, fishing communities may have become more dependent on floodplains, as coastal populations rose and the lomas that had sustained earlier communities were no longer adequate.

"The Little Victims Crowded Each Other"

In 1865 the American archaeologist and diplomat Ephraim Squier, who would later provide some of the first descriptions of Inka ruins, landed on Peru's north coast. His ship's crew rowed him ashore through a sluggish swell, passing over "a solid mass of the little fishes [anchovies] . . . which were apparently driven inshore by large and voracious enemies in the sea. . . . The little victims crowded each other, until their noses, projecting to the surface, made the ocean look as if covered over with a cloak of Oriental mail. We could dip them up by handfuls and by thousands."[7] The belt of anchovies extended about a mile along the shore. Women and children scooped them up "with their hats, with basins, baskets, and the fronts of their petticoats." Squier had arrived at one of the richest coastal fisheries in the world.

The Peruvian anchovy (*Engraulis ringens*) is a pelagic species found in the southeastern Pacific Ocean. They live off larger zooplankton, among them krill and large copepods, and swim in enormous shoals in the upwelling waters of the Humboldt Current off the coast of Peru. Anchovies are small fish that live for three years and reach a maximum size of about twenty centimeters.[8] Today, they are one of the most heavily exploited fish in the world, with a yield that peaked at 10.5 metric tons in 1968.

The bounty of the anchovy fishery is legendary. Extending over two thousand kilometers from northern Chile to northern Peru, this strip of coastal water can yield as much as one hundred metric tons of anchovies per square kilometer year after year. Today, it produces more than one-fifth of the world's commercially taken fish, a wealth rivaled only by the Benguela Current off Namibia in southwestern Africa, where upwelling also occurs. There are well-known "hot spots" off Peru around 8 degrees, 11 degrees, and 15 degrees south latitude that can yield as much as one thousand metric tons per square kilometer. Not surprisingly, the largest early monuments in Peru occur along the six hundred kilometers of the coast bracketed by these hot spots. The most complex fishing societies arose where the fisheries were richest. At least in theory, the anchovy population in premodern times could support as many as six million people.[9]

The anchovies feasted on zooplankton, seabirds thrived on anchovies and mollusks, and humans ate all three, except in El Niño years, when warm waters flowed over the cold and the anchovies moved elsewhere, followed by the birds. El Niños were unpredictable events. The more severe ones brought unfamiliar tropical fish to the coast. These tended to be years of suffering, years when the people ate less fish, mollusks when they could find them, and whatever they could obtain on land.

Invariably, fishing intensified as populations rose. Coastal communities raised their catch in various ways. Along the Peruvian coast, with its hot spots, fishers wove more nets and used reed canoes to gather ever-larger anchovy harvests. They could not have done this without growing cotton, a fiber with the rare characteristic of being able to survive long exposure to seawater, which made it exceptionally useful for making fine-meshed nets. Mass harvesting of small fish intensified as cotton cordage and nets came into widespread use after about 2500 BC, when fishers switched from larger fish almost entirely to anchovies and sardines, the latter, apparently, during El Niños. At that time, coastal Andeans were growing far more plants for tool manufacture—such as cotton for net making and gourds for floats—than for food.

Fishing technologies differed from one location to another. Where there were sandy beaches people tended to favor nets set from reed canoes. Along rockier lengths of coast, for example, south of the Santa River, they relied on hooks and lines to catch larger fish close to shore. The densest populations along the Pacific were at the backs of sandy beaches, where anchovy harvests were the largest. Some experts believe the coastal population may have grown as much as thirtyfold in the four centuries before 1800 BC, a time of massive construction projects along the coast during which local societies became less egalitarian and socially more complex.[10]

The explosive growth in human settlement in the valleys also resulted in some of the most elaborate irrigation systems in the ancient world.[11] The Andeans began to cultivate maize, beans, chilies, squash, and other crops by carefully husbanding river floodwater, first in small-scale irrigation systems and

A Peruvian totora reed boat. De Agostini Picture Library/Bridgeman Images.

later in much larger ones. Between 1800 and 400 BC short and longer canals irrigated no fewer than forty-one hundred hectares of farmland. When even small-scale irrigation came into common use and the proportion of plant foods in people's diets began to rise, the dynamics of coastal life changed dramatically. Food supplies, from the combination of the coastal fishery and river valley crops, became more reliable. Eventually, many coastal communities moved inland, leaving the fishing to those who remained by the Pacific. Some coastal villages became specialized fishing communities, supplying fish as a commodity to the increasingly powerful inland centers.

The yield of the anchovy fisheries increased considerably with the development of coastal watercraft. Having no trees from which to build dugouts, the fishermen fashioned light canoes with sharply raised bows out of bundles of tied *totora* reeds, which abounded close to shore and were used for thousands of years to build simple dwellings. Known today as *caballitos de totora*, "little reed horses," these canoes ride low in the water, so an occupant can straddle it. The fisherman uses his legs to push off from the sand into the surf, where the high bow allows the totora to cut through swells into deeper water, where larger fish can be taken.

Once in deep water, the totora riders bring several of their canoes together to lay fine, weighted gill nets that could catch thousands of anchovies and sometimes larger fish like mullet. Once the gill net lay in place, individual fishers would have laid baited reed traps for lobster and other crustaceans or fished with hook and line. Judging from modern practice—some totoras are still in use—each fisherman would have had two canoes, one drying out on land to prevent waterlogging while the other was in use. There is a remarkable similarity between the totora and the modern-day paddle board.

Fishing and the Origins of Andean Civilization

The enormous anchovy catches were dried, probably by being laid out on reed mats. As a product, dried anchovies and sardines had numerous advantages: they were easily caught and dried in enormous numbers, they were a reliable food source, and they were light enough to be carried inland in bulk, in baskets or nets on peoples' backs or in llama saddle packs. The new emphasis on anchovy and sardine fishing coincided with the development of large ceremonial centers and the expansion of irrigation agriculture. These large public works and the increasingly elaborate social and ritual environment required great numbers of people who were neither farmers nor fishermen. Workers laboring on adobe structures and those digging increasingly large-scale irrigation works all required rations.

How important were fish and other marine products in the emergence of Andean civilization? Generations of archaeologists have assumed that pre-industrial civilizations arose only when intensive agriculture was available to support rapidly growing urban populations. This assumption does not necessarily apply to the Peruvian coast and its associated river valleys, where major ceremonial centers and growing populations flourished before 2000 BC. Many years ago the archaeologist Michael Moseley, working in the Ancón–Chillón area of the north coast, documented the rapid pace of economic change after about 2000 BC.[12] He pointed out that farming the desert required cultivated plants and knowledge of how to grow them, workforces to construct irrigation canals and field systems, and social institutions capable of organizing workers. The social mechanisms to build these large structures must have been already in place.

Long before they began irrigating river valleys, the people living along the Pacific had built complex ritual structures that required large numbers of workers. This labor was supported by the maritime economy, not by irrigation agriculture, which came into practice on a large scale only later. There was no sudden change to farming; instead, an increasingly powerful corporate authority arose to order and maintain elaborate ceremonial structures erected long before intensive floodplain agriculture. Moseley argues that this corporate authority came into being when fishing communities submitted willingly and voluntarily to some form of control. He believes that the unique maritime resources of the Pacific coast provided sufficient calories to support rapidly growing sedentary populations of nonfarmers clustered in increasingly larger communities on the coast and in inland river valleys. If Moseley is right—and his theory has survived a long time—then fish were the ultimate economic basis for the elaborate Andean state-organized societies that developed in later times.

The change can be seen in the quantities of fish brought ashore. Judging from modern yields, if ancient coastal populations had lived at 60 percent of the carrying capacity of the fisheries and eaten nothing but small fish, the coast could have supported more than 6.5 million people. This does not necessarily mean that it did so, but the figures show that the exploitation of small fish would have established a more than adequate economic base for the emergence of complex societies.

One cannot argue, of course, that fishing caused the rise of Andean civilization. But fish were certainly part of a cultural change that unfolded in both the highlands and lowlands over many centuries. The reliance on coastal resources led to the formation of large, densely concentrated coastal populations whose leaders were able to organize labor forces not only to build large ritual centers but later to transform river valleys by building extensive irrigation works to grow cotton and gourds for nets as well as other crops. Under this scenario, irrigation agriculture was in the hands of a small, well-defined group with powerful religious authority, elites who took advantage of the existing simple technology and local populations to create new economies. This transformation, based on trade, maize agriculture—which reached the coast around 4500 BC—and a maritime diet, were an impetus of radical changes in Andean society. But it depended on ancient fishing traditions that can be documented thousands of years earlier at early coastal villages. For millennia most shoreline populations drew more than 90 percent of their subsistence from the ocean.

The exponential growth in the size and complexity of coastal societies is apparent all along the six hundred kilometers where the richest fisheries lay. Dozens of ancient settlements in the Supe and neighboring river valleys some two hundred kilometers north of Lima flourished between 3100 and 1800 BC. One of them, Caral, arguably the earliest city in the Americas, was occupied between about 2876 and 1767 BC.[13] Six large mounds and at least thirty-two public buildings form the core of the city. Its Great Temple, a massive construction thirty meters high, has a large, sunken circular court in front of it. The Peruvian archaeologist Ruth Shady Solís believes that Caral was the hub of a network of eighteen settlements in the Supe Valley that formed a cluster of major sites, along with numerous villages and smaller communities scattered along the edge of the valley. Their inhabitants had access to *Spondylus* shells from more than twelve hundred kilometers away in coastal Peru and Ecuador. Possession of these was a telling measure of the Supe Valley's importance in the wider Andean world. The central city of Caral is estimated to have absorbed more than a quarter of all the labor invested in the valley during these centuries. Many Supe Valley communities played specialized roles in the local network. Some were fishing villages; others cultivated beans, cotton, squash, and other crops that were later supplanted by maize. Caral and other Supe settlements were vulnerable to both major earthquakes and storms from El Niño events, both of which heavily damaged the main temple. The city was abandoned about 1767 BC.

After 1800 BC ever-larger sites and ceremonial centers grew alongside the irrigation systems as society became more formalized. Farmers working under increasingly close supervision modified river valley landscapes for maize agriculture. Fishers became an anonymous background to elaborate, volatile river valley kingdoms.[14] On the north coast the Moche state developed in coastal river valleys in two major regions, the Moche and the Lambayeque Valleys, between AD 200 and 800. The Mochica are best known for their spectacular warrior-priest burials at Sipán in the Lambayeque Valley and for their magnificent ceramics and metallurgy. Their artists, masters of realistic portraiture, left us a vivid impression of a colorful society ruled by a wealthy elite. To what extent there was centralized authority is a matter of controversy. But the rulers built spectacular temples, like the Huaca del Sol and Huaca de le Luna in the Moche Valley, which were settings for the kind of elaborate public ceremonies that tend to validate elite authority. Densely packed neighborhoods on the flat ground between the two great *huacas,* or shrines, housed artisans who produced gold objects, textiles, and sophisticated ceramics. Exotic gold ornaments and fine cotton textiles passed from lowlands to the highlands, as did coastal products like seaweed, the only source of iodine for highland famers, who exchanged crops such as ulluco and potatoes for it.

The subsistence world of farming and fishing became overlain by the cut and thrust of elite politics and territorial ambitions. The Sicán dynasty, under a lord named Namlap, rose about AD 750 to 800 and thrived for five centuries. Sicán was a closely organized society in which artisans produced enormous quantities of fine metal objects, many of them fabricated with thin gold alloy sheets. The riches were staggering. A principal burial in the intact East Tomb at Huaca Loro yielded 1.2 tons of grave goods, including a golden face mask, gauntlets, and sheets of gold foil once sewn to cotton garments. The Sicán engaged in a massive long-distance trade of metal objects with the highlands and along the coast, from which they obtained numerous *Spondylus* shells from far to the north. By this time water control and large-scale irrigation works were central to coastal subsistence, with fish providing a supplement that became especially important in El Niño years.

The Chimú, successors of the Sicán dynasty after about AD 900, developed a state that presided over the coast from the Moche Valley to the Lambayeque. Their leaders ruled from Chan Chan, a sprawling city that covered more than twenty square kilometers. This was a controlling domain, one which governed not only valley towns and irrigation schemes but outlying villages that grew cotton and edible crops or caught large quantities of fish. At their height Chimú farmers had 30 to 40 percent more land under cultivation than is farmed today. Everyone, fisher, farmer, or artisan, was part of a much larger enterprise. Chimú rulers were careful to maintain strategic monopolies on the trade of key exotics and other commodities. Nowhere is this more apparent than at Cerro Azul, an important fishing community of the Warku kingdom, on a promontory some 130 kilometers south of Lima. Here, tens of thousands of anchovies were harvested, dried, and traded to inland farmers and perhaps even farther afield.[15]

In 1470 the coast became part of the vast Inka empire, Tawantinsuyu, "The Land of the Four Quarters," which came into being through conquest in a century or less, spanning highland and lowland environments from the Lake Titicaca region to Ecuador.[16] The Inka were accomplished warriors and brilliant organizers who used both administrative skill and draconian force to hold their empire together. Now the coastal fisherfolk served remote masters.

The Inka erected an imposing stone fortress overlooking Cerro Azul. The local economy became a highly organized production line based on the anchovy fishery, whose harvests far exceeded the supplies needed to feed the locals.[17] Thousands of anchovies and sardines were dried, packed tightly into storage rooms, and covered with dry sand to preserve the harvest. They were inventoried and taxed by ubiquitous officials with their *quipus,* knotted strings used to record numbers. The volume of the trade must have been enormous. Some idea of the numbers of people involved comes from contemporary descriptions of a polity in the neighboring valley to the south, home to twelve thousand farmers, ten thousand fishers, and six thousand merchants.

In 1532 Francisco Pizarro captured the Inka ruler Atahualpa, beginning a Spanish *entrada* that, with the help of epidemics of exotic diseases that decimated the native population, destroyed Tawantinsuyu. The Inka empire collapsed in the face of the conquistadors, but, as usually happened in history, the ancient rhythms of field and fishery continued unchanged. People have to eat. Colonial farmers mined guano on offshore islands; anchovies passed by the basket- and wagonful into Lima and other cities. But the fishery was still preindustrial, much of it conducted in small wooden boats or from reed canoes identical to those of earlier times. It may have yielded millions of fish and significant weights of fishmeal, used, like guano, as fertilizer, but now it was for purely local markets. Five centuries were to pass before anchovies and guano would become two main staples of the Peruvian economy, a status that anchovies would maintain until industrial-scale fishing brought about the collapse of one of the richest fisheries in the world.

PART THREE

The End of Plenty

Humans exploited freshwater and marine fish close to shore and also mollusks for tens of thousands of years to feed their families, kin, and households. Then came the early civilizations, culminating in the West with the Roman Empire, all of which relied heavily on rations for hundreds, sometimes thousands, of people laboring on public works, serving as officials, or engaged in campaigns with armies or naval forces. Long before medieval times people had heavily exploited the world's inshore waters, sometimes to the point of overfishing. Their activities also caused natural environmental shifts and habitat alterations. Fishing in ancient times had already profoundly affected the world's inshore marine ecosystems. What happened after the Romans was even more dramatic.

The intricate dissolution of Roman rule in the East and West coincided with a lessening of commercial fishing except in northern Europe, where cod, herring, and other fish abounded close to shore. Most medieval Europeans ate predominantly cereal diets and preferred meat to fish—a classification that at the time included all creatures living in water. Fish were a dietary substitute associated with health, prestige, and penitence, the latter closely defined by the Christian church. Fresh fish were expensive and generally reserved for the rich or self-sufficient monastic communities. Until about AD 1100 people relied on local fish that were eaten fresh or lightly preserved. By 1200, prompted in part by the increasing number of meat-free holy days, many commoners were eating marine fish that had been dried, salted, or brined, often in places considerable distances away. The nobility and the wealthy, meanwhile, preferred fresh fish, especially an exotic fish, the common carp, which was farmed in ponds.

In addition to changing social conditions, Europe's fishers had to respond to environmental changes. The relatively mild centuries of the Medieval Warm Period led to a rise in populations and created an increasing dependence on fish. By the tenth century people were catching fish for sale to consumers at local markets, often as a form of artisanal fishing, and fishing communities were making a living supplying fish to growing cities and towns. Three centuries later there were networks of carts carrying fish across southern England and relays of horses transporting fresh catches from Normandy to Paris. By 1300 regions far inland were farming carp, pike, and other species on a large scale. Overfishing, human activities like barrier construction across rivers, and environmental change all reduced salmon runs in parts of western Europe. Slow-breeding sturgeon populations declined sharply in the face of rising demand. The response was to intensify efforts to exploit fisheries at the periphery, especially herring.

The complex spawning patterns of herring in the Atlantic and North Sea allowed thousands of fish to be caught close inshore. But there was a problem. Herrings are oily fish, and they rot within hours. Still, the herring fishery expanded rapidly, especially in the southern North Sea and along the Pomeranian shore of the Baltic. The fish were salted on the beach, a treatment that let them keep for a few months and then be sold in bundles. By the thirteenth century the exploitation had reached a large commercial scale, especially of inshore spawning shoals in the southern North Sea and, in the Baltic, off Scania in southern Sweden. Huge catches were brined in sealed barrels that were carried far inland and traded in standardized units. A century later the Dutch were the major players in what had become the first truly international fish industry. By 1520 they were supplying herring to Rome. These developments coincided with the beginning of the Little Ice Age, which brought cooler ocean temperatures at the time of year when young herring are especially sensitive to colder water. Heavily fished herring stocks in the Baltic and North Sea collapsed, and fishers turned to other species. The changes were apparently permanent. Baltic herring runs today are 20 percent smaller than those of a thousand years ago.

Salted herring were not very appealing, so fishers turned to Atlantic cod, a white ocean fish with flesh that was readily dried or salted and that kept for long periods. These fish were exploited in Norway as early as the Bronze Age, when they became a staple in the Lofoten Islands. When dried into stockfish, they were an invaluable ration for people at sea and for the devout observing Lent. An insatiable demand arose, seized upon by Hanse merchants in the Baltic and North Seas, who had the bulk carriers to transport the fish. The relentless search for cod stocks sent English fishermen to Icelandic waters by 1412, where the hazards were frightening but the profits enormous. Then, by 1497, came the discovery of the Newfoundland cod fishery, where fish could be gathered in baskets from the surface. The cod industry was already an international business in Europe, its tentacles stretching far inland and to the Catholic nations of the Mediterranean. But the Newfoundland and New England fisheries turned the exploitation of cod into a vast commercial enterprise. Cod became part of the triangular commerce that linked Britain with the slave plantations of the Caribbean and the ports of New England. The long-term profits were staggering, cumulatively larger than those from all the gold found in the Americas. But even as early as the eighteenth century there were signs of overfishing. The average size of cod began to fall.

What is astounding is that this huge international trade, the first truly global fish industry, was based on methods and equipment that had hardly changed from medieval times. Despite this, the centuries-long devastation of the North Atlantic cod fisheries was well under way by the nineteenth century. As demand ashore rose and fish became harder to find, fishing became more efficient, with the development of long-lining, the use of open dories and mother ships in the open Atlantic, and the deploying of large seine nets close inshore. The depletion of stocks continued unabated. Trawls, weighted nets that were dragged along the sea bottom, had been in use since the fourteenth century, but with the invention of the beam trawl, whose wooden beam kept the net's mouth open, catches skyrocketed. The devastation to the seabed was immense. With the adoption of steam power in the 1830s and 1840s and then, a century ago, the diesel-powered trawler, fishermen could stay far offshore for much longer periods, icing their catch as they worked. By the 1890s catches by steam trawlers were as much as eight times larger than those made under sail. Diesel landings were sometimes 40 percent larger than those of steam trawlers. With the development of modern-day trawls and purse seines, encircling nets first used in the 1850s, fishing became not a matter of opportunism but an efficient way of exploiting the ocean on an industrial scale.

These developments took hold in European waters, but the technology spread far and wide as fishermen followed the classic strategy of ancient times: if a fishery becomes depleted, move elsewhere. The Japanese adopted purse seines for taking small pelagic fish in 1882. By the 1930s the French were operating factory ships far offshore. Demand for Peruvian fish meal exploded as its use as animal feed expanded dramatically. Fishermen now operated in formal companies with the financial resources to purchase and maintain vessels and their new electronic fish finders. After World War II fishing became a fully industrial business, with Japan leading the way. Fleets of trawlers ventured as far afield as Antarctica, depleting hitherto unfished areas within fifteen years, then moving on. Today, we face the challenge of feeding more than nine billion people by 2050, at a time when climate change threatens fisheries already under severe stress. In 2014, for the first time, more fish for human consumption were farmed than caught in the wild.

The modern fishing industry should not get all of the blame for the current state of the world's fisheries. The present condition of the world's fishing grounds is the culmination of thousands of years of exploitation of the oceans, exacerbated by the assumption that fish were a limitless resource. Today, population growth, technological innovation, and relentless searches for profit have stripped the oceans of potential seafood almost beyond recovery. All of this is a result of that most human of qualities—the ability to exploit opportunities as they arise.

19

Ants of the Ocean

The implosion of the Roman Empire did not have much of an effect on the routines of subsistence fisherfolk in western Europe. They went about their seasonal routines just as they had for centuries. Subsistence fishing is hard to detect in archaeological sites, so evidence for either freshwater or sea fish is rare for the early Middle Ages. There are scattered finds of sea fish in rural settlements between the sixth and mid-seventh centuries both in Britain and in France and the Low Countries, but no signs of intensive fishing. Cargo capacities at sea were small; trade focused more on valuable goods than on basic commodities. Whatever the reasons, fish were not prominent features of western European menus after Roman times.

Scandinavia, in environments where agriculture was either high risk or impracticable, was another matter. Between the fifth and mid-seventh centuries, cod, herring, and related species were important catches in Norway, especially in the Lofoten Islands of the north, later to become a major cod fishery; the Danish and Swedish islands of the western Baltic were also productive. At Sorte Muld on the island of Bornholm, thirteen thousand herring bones date to the sixth to seventh centuries, 96 percent of the fish in the deposits. Throughout the north ancient traditions of maritime culture and ready access to huge stocks of marine fish laid the foundations for the dramatic changes in ocean fisheries in later centuries.[1]

As early as the first century AD Christians were urged to practice penance with days of abstinence, especially on Wednesdays and Fridays and during Lent, when one ate grain, vegetables—and fish. Abstinence acquired impetus with the gentle and highly disciplined Saint Benedict (c. 480–543/47). His *Regula Benedicta,* the Rule of St. Benedict, advocated fasting and a meatless diet for religious houses. As Benedictine communities spread through Europe beginning in the sixth century, the meatless doctrine extended into secular society as a basic tenet of Christian observance. Over several centuries the demand for fish by the devout rose exponentially.[2]

Fish eating in periods of abstinence was routine in Holland by the end of the Middle Ages. During Lent people ate herring, flatfish, mussels, eels, and vegetables. When it came to fasting there was some confusion as to what constituted a fish. A celebrated sixteenth-century fish expert, Adriaen Coenen, classified seals as fish, directly below herring, in his widely read *Visboek* (Fish book), published in 1578.[3] In the end about 40 percent of the days of the year required abstinence, creating an insatiable demand for fish among both rich and poor.

In early medieval times practically everyone subsisted almost entirely on a carbohydrate diet of fruit, grains, legumes, and vegetables. Meat was rare, fish even more so, except for the ubiquitous eel, *Anguilla anguilla,* which crowded ponds and streams and was easily taken with spear or trap.[4] Even better, eels could be smoked over high heat to a dry, sticklike consistency in a couple of hours, after which they would keep for long periods. Eels were so abundant that they became a form of currency, used to pay for services rendered or for fishing rights. In 970 the abbot of Ely Abbey in Fenland in eastern England received a gift of ten thousand eels annually from the nearby villages of Outwell and Upwell.

Farming Cyprinus carpio

Until the eighth century, when monasteries acquired land grants and rights to fish in lakes, ponds, and rivers, both freshwater and sea fish were far too expensive for most people.[5] At first, only monastic houses near well-established fisheries could consume seafood, but as religious communities strove for self-sufficiency and diets improved fish became increasingly important. The elite lived well if they had access to fresh- or saltwater fish. Fresh fish, especially pike and big trout as well as anadromous species like salmon, were a central part of elites' diets until at least the thirteenth century. Sturgeon from the great rivers, fish that could be 3.5 meters long and weigh 300 to 400 kilograms, were the ultimate luxury. Sturgeon are valued today for their caviar, but in medieval times they were a prized fish. They were prestigious gifts, presented at courts, sometimes pickled in barrels.

Large eels, pike, and salmon had considerable value, especially larger specimens, which were given to city leaders and high nobles as gestures of esteem. Some species, like the bony pike, could be boiled and made into soup but were often presented between courses at banquets purely for display. A cookbook from 1420 by the head chef to Duke Amadeus of Savoy described a recipe for pike gilded to resemble pilgrims. A lamprey headed the procession, symbolizing the pilgrims' staff, and some pike were covered in gold leaf.

As water mills became more refined, people living inland experimented with fish farms to cater to a privileged clientele.[6] Such ponds began to appear between the Loire and the Rhine Rivers around the eleventh century, stocked with local species like bream or pike. Yields were small until carp farming took hold over a wide swathe of inland Europe. *Cyprinus carpio* is a heavy-bodied form of minnow that thrives in shallow, warm water every spring and can grow to considerable size. Wild carp flourish in the warm waters of the lower Danube and in rivers flowing into the Black Sea. Farmed carp, perhaps transported by monks, arrived in central and western Europe sometime after 1000 and spread rapidly across the continent, especially between monasteries. They did not arrive in England until the fourteenth century, perhaps for climatic reasons. The monks would introduce adult carp into warm, heavily overgrown ponds in spring and allow them to breed before removing them. They would then relocate the young into growing ponds in a system of rotation through nutrient-rich enclosures for between four and six years, until the fish were ready for the table. At harvest time the farmer drained the pond and crowded the fish into its deep middle, where they could easily be removed.

By the mid-fourteenth century carp farming was big business. One religious house, Chaalis Abbey near Paris, had a fish farm that extended over more than forty hectares at different locations, all to feed the monks. Such monastic operations, however, paled into insignificance beside the efforts of the barons Rozmberk of Trebon in southern Bohemia. By 1450 they controlled seventeen small ponds and three large ones, covering more than seven hundred hectares, and sold carp to Prague and other cities. There are about four hundred square kilometers of carp ponds around Trebon to this day. Carp were never cheap. For much of the fifteenth century a kilogram of carp cost the equivalent of just

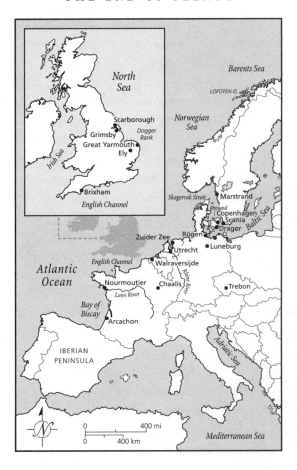

15. Herring fisheries: The major ports and locations of the Baltic and North Sea herring fisheries and also other western European locations discussed in chapter 19.

under nine kilograms of beef or twenty loaves of bread. The demand was so great that central France after 1400 supported forty thousand hectares of carp ponds, almost all located farther inland than fresh sea fish could be transported without spoiling.

The tightly controlled carp business was highly profitable, especially for landowners and religious houses, but it waned inexorably once sea fish became more readily available after 1300. After the fifteenth century virtually all of France's busy carp farms became dry land in the face of political unrest, relaxed monastic diets, higher labor costs, and a preference for sea fish over the muddier taste of carp.

Clupea harengus, *A Most Prolific Fish*

Clupea harengus, the Atlantic herring, is the ant of the ocean. None other than Karl Linnaeus called it the most prolific of fish, this in northern waters that abounded with variety in the North Atlantic and North Sea.

There are both spring and autumn spawning herring stocks in the North Sea. The northern stock, Buchan herring, spawn in the area between the Shetland Islands and the Scottish east coast off Aberdeen. The Bank herring has spawning grounds off the English coastline between Yorkshire and Norfolk and on the Dogger Bank in the central North Sea. The third and southernmost herring stock is the Downs, which spawns in the Southern Bight of the North Sea and the English Channel. The Buchan herring usually spawn first, followed by the Dogger, while the Downs herring spawn in late autumn. In winter and spring all three populations drift around the North Sea in a counterclockwise movement, wintering in the eastern part of the North Sea. Around June the Buchan herring reach the Shetlands, where Dutch fishers, in their deepwater boats known as *busses,* would await the start of the fishing season, which arrived on the night of St. John, June 24.[7] By September and October herring were thick off England's East Anglian coast, where they laid eggs on shallow parts of the seabed close to land and in the huge nursery area off the Dogger Bank. The exhausted fish then drifted northward off the Low Countries during the winter, until the entire cycle began again.

A food source from heaven, one might think. Unfortunately, herring flesh is oily, especially at autumn spawning time, which means that they spoil within a few hours. Northern Europe is cool and damp, making wind drying impractical for herring in most places, unlike the less oily cod. Salt was in short supply, and salting methods were crude at best. Most salt came from coastal marshes and was made by dissolving peat through filters, then boiling and evaporating the liquid. The resulting *zelle* was expensive and often scarce. The salting of herring in early medieval times often involved little more than covering the fish with salt, then turning them regularly to ensure an even cure, a process that lasted about two weeks.

Clupea harengus was a significant catch for local communities in the western Baltic for thousands of years. Except on the coast, however, the marine component in early medieval diets was relatively small. Fish were an important staple on the island off Gotland, off eastern Sweden, and for Norse communities. Men buried with weapons in a cemetery may have been warriors who ate fish as rations while traveling. After a slow beginning the Baltic fisheries expanded gradually, as demand for fish increased. The busiest herring fishery was in the western Baltic. People on Bornholm ate numerous herring as early as the sixth century. By the tenth to thirteenth centuries archaeological finds in northern Germany and Poland testify to extensive herring fisheries, presumably caught with nets. Simultaneously, commercial herring fishing expanded in sheltered coastal inlets and estuaries along western Baltic coasts, as demand increased in growing urban settlements. Across the North Sea, Anglo-Saxon chroniclers tell us that both English and continental herring fishers were active off East Anglia in late summer and autumn.[8]

A major breakthrough came in the thirteenth to fourteenth centuries, when herring fishers in Denmark's Roskilde Fjord near Copenhagen began using a small knife to remove the gills behind a herring's head and then immediately salted the fish. The running blood allowed the salt to penetrate the intestines, making for a much better, more durable cure. Quite when or where this processing method came into being is unknown. Earlier Norse fish bones from Roskilde do not show evidence of the method.[9] Better quality salt was also more commonplace. By the ninth century Norse ships were sailing south to Nourmoutier at the mouth of the Loire River in the Bay of Biscay, where evaporated, sun-dried salt had been traded since ancient times.

The earliest known herring fishery in the Baltic Sea to serve a wider market developed off the island of Rügen, close to the Lüneburg salt mines in northern Germany. Salt gave the merchants of nearby Lübeck a privileged position in the Baltic herring trade and tight control of the herring landing sites. They also imposed strict quality controls on the curing and barreling of herring. During the thirteenth century the dealers of Lübeck and Straslund, 215 kilometers east on the mainland opposite Rügen, dominated the fish trade over a huge area from Silesia in the east to central and southern Germany in the west.[10]

The Rügen trade withered after 1290 in the face of competition from the much larger fishery off the Scanian coast of southwestern Sweden, where good quality Lüneburg salt was also abundant. The late twelfth-century Danish historian Saxo Grammaticus, the author of the first history of Denmark, claimed that spawning herring were so closely packed off Scanian beaches that rowing was nearly impossible, and you could pick up the fish with your hands. The Scania fishery came into prominence just as barreling became part of new curing methods in which the curers laid tightly packed, gutted herring in wooden casks between layers of salt. The salt sucked the moisture out of the herring, which were then repacked in fresh brine, in which they could keep for up to two years. Typically, a barrel of salt cured three barrels of herring, each weighing a standard 117 kilograms. With barreling, the long-distance herring trade took off.

Pickling in barrels was an ideal way to store heavily salted herring. They remained edible for up to ten months at 10 to 12 degrees C, and even longer at lower temperatures. The brining system soon became rigorously standardized to ensure uniform quality. At last there was a solution to the preservation issue. Herring became an international industry within a few generations, driven not only by religious considerations but also by the needs of growing urban populations and requirements for military provisions. By 1390 herring were so commonplace, even far from the ocean, that the French soldier and traveler Philippe de Mézières remarked that anyone "can have a herring who cannot afford a big fish."[11]

Barreling raised the economic stakes: now the Baltic fishery supplied cities far inland. From the beginning, herring fishing had been in the hands of farmers, who turned to herring after the harvest. Villagers over a large area of the Øresund, the sound between Denmark and Sweden, closed their houses and left churches empty during the spawning season. As demand accelerated beyond the Danes' ability to satisfy it, hundreds of people from as far away as Flensburg in Jutland and from other Baltic lands converged on what became known as the Scania fairs.[12] Many were wage-earning seasonal fishers who moved around the Baltic and North Sea from one fishery to another.

The fishermen formed informal groups of five to eight men known as *notlags*, who fished with fixed or drift nets from a single boat. Provided there was a net and a boat, the notlag was viable for a season, to be reconstituted each year. The fishermen worked from small boats called *schuten*. Some worked with set nets during daylight, others used torches at night. No one was allowed to deploy ground nets, perhaps out of a concern for maintaining fish stocks. Notlag membership was open to all. All the group had to do was pay a catch tax, usually in herring, to the local lord twice a season.

At their height in the fourteenth century the Scania fairs took place on an enormous scale between August 15 and October 9. Over seventeen thousand

Scania herring market during the late nineteenth century. An inspector stamps a barrel. After C. Reohling. Interfoto/Alamy stock photo.

people are said to have attended the fishery around 1400, with a further eight thousand engaged in related trades. At daybreak one might see a silent crowd of waiting merchants standing on the beach among the fishing huts, looking seaward at the flickering lights bobbing on the waves. They are forbidden to buy fish or even discuss prices while the boats are still in the water. As the laden craft approach the beach, a horn sounds. The merchants rush to water's edge, jostling and shouting to acquire the best fish in what is essentially a highly disorganized auction. Once bargains are struck, fish transporters carry the herring to special huts behind the seawall, for no one is allowed to process fish on the beach. Teams of specially selected women gut the fish, while other women pack them in waiting barrels and cover them with a brine of Lübeck salt and water. The established number of fish is around nine hundred herrings per barrel. The *grtumkjeri,* an inspector under oath, examines the packed barrels and brands them with a quality control symbol that guarantees the place of origin, the time of packing, and the quality of the content. A merchant's mark was branded onto the barrel to allow demands for compensation to be met, even when the container was hundreds of kilometers inland.[13]

The production system was so refined that the quality and consistency of Scania herring surpassed those of all competitors. In 1384 the same production standards crossed the North Sea to Scarborough in northwest England, making the British fishery competitive. Meanwhile, the Rügen markets were devastated when Lübeck vendors discovered that the farmers who flocked to fish at the Scania fair were a natural and expanding source for all manner of consumer goods. A general market developed alongside the fishery, which caused the fishers to gather not at widely scattered beaches but at specific points that served as temporary markets, locations like Dragør on Amager Island in Denmark and Skanör and Falsterbo in extreme southwestern Sweden.

By the middle of the fourteenth century merchants from different cities could own property for their warehouses and workshops, structures known as *vitte*. Vitte were privately owned temporary trading stations, complete with stores, churches, monasteries, and brothels. All the cities of the Hanseatic League, a merchants' guild, and others as far away as the Zuider Zee in the Low Countries maintained them. Even English and Flemish merchants retained a presence at Scania. Unlike the merchants, who had complex legal protections, the fisherfolk lived in *fiskelejer,* crude settlements of wood or rush-mat huts where they dried their nets and maintained their gear.

Between 1370 and 1380 Scania dominated the European herring market, from northern Norway to Spain and Italy and from Wales to central Germany and farther east. Lübeck merchants alone imported 76,000 barrels of herring in 1368. Total imports of Scania herring by Baltic cities may have been as many as 225,000 barrels annually.[14] Supplies fluctuated without warning. Some years saw the water literally boiling with fish, while in 1474 and 1475 virtually no herring arrived. Fortunately, preserved herring stocks were apparently sufficient to satisfy the demand of the European markets.

By the beginning of the fourteenth century merchants from as far away as England and from throughout the Baltic region converged on the city of Marstrand, in modern-day Sweden, to purchase and process herring. Dutch and German merchants shipped fish up the Rhine to Köln, the central herring marketplace for all of Germany. Here, sworn testers checked the quality of the fish and marked the barrels, which were then traded south as far as Zurich and Basel. The entire network bound the producers to the consumers in southern Germany in a large-scale, long-lived marketplace. Herring was the lubricating oil for all kinds of trade across Europe, including cloth and furs from the east, all kinds of luxury goods, and agricultural products. The Danish scholar Carsten Jahnke has estimated that the value of Danish fish exports in the late fourteenth and early fifteenth centuries was two or three times that of cattle and half again as much as that of all agricultural exports.

The Scania fairs reached their zenith between 1370 and 1380. The Hanseatic cities, which controlled sources of Lübeck salt, took over the administration of the fairs after 1370 and tried to restrict their North Sea competitors' access to Scania. Their exclusionary policies worked against them. Fisherfolk from England, Scotland, and the Low Countries realized they had underexploited herring fisheries at their doorsteps. The English began trading directly with Prussian cities in the heart of Europe, with such success that Scania became a regional fair of much-reduced economic importance. Not only were North Sea processing standards now equal to those of the Baltic fisheries, but also the processors there developed more appetizing *matjes* ("maids")—mild-tasting, soused herrings processed from young, immature fish that have not spawned—caught off Denmark and Norway and ripened for about five days in oak barrels filled with a mild brine. They became popular because they could be served in all manner of ways and were more appetizing than the sticklike salted herring.

As the Scania fishery declined, Danish merchants prospered from the herring trade based on the Limfjord in northern Denmark. They traded barrels of cheaper, somewhat lower quality herring for local consumption, in contrast with the Hanse trade from Scania, which was concerned purely with export. Norwegian fishers caught Atlantic herring off the Bohuslen coast north of modern-day Gothenburg, at the time part of Norway. The Bohuslen fishery, which relied on seine nets cast from shore, had been active as early as the twelfth century and peaked at 75,600 barrels in 1585. The herring population was affected by the North Atlantic Oscillation, which caused major fluctuations on a roughly centennial scale. The fishery literally appeared and disappeared with irregular landings, with the exception of a remarkable boom during the 1780s. By 1810 herrings were so rare that exports ceased.

Scania's merchants were well capitalized, their control of barreling exquisitely precise. They turned a perishable commodity into a high-quality product that appealed to consumers over a far wider world than just the Baltic cities. This was the largest commercial fishery of medieval Europe, complete with a well-organized infrastructure behind it.

Fishers Take a Buss

Much of the economic gravity of the herring trade passed to the North Sea during the fifteenth century. Most early North Sea fishers had operated out of seasonal encampments and settlements dotting the shores of the Low Countries. Some, like Calais and Ostend, were large ports, while others were smaller towns and tiny fishing villages. Apart from coastal fairs, the oldest city markets in Antwerp and Ghent were devoted to fish.

The fishing settlements where these fisherfolk lived are now almost invisible, but Walraversijde, in what is now Belgium, situated by a tidal inlet, is an exception.[15] Originally a temporary camp, it soon became a permanent community. Excavations there have revealed dispersed groups of wattle-and-daub houses with thatched roofs, each with a brick hearth in the center. Nearby stood small sheds, presumably for storing gear of all kinds, possibly also serving as boathouses. Written records of the day describe the inhabitants as engaged in sea fishing and the trading of salted fish and other goods. Peat extraction pits are discernible close to the houses; the peat was dried and then burned, and the ashes were mingled with seawater to produce brine that was then heated in pans to create salt.

The fourteenth century was a difficult time for fishers and coastal farmers, who were completely dependent on city markets at a time when landholdings and water rights were being consolidated, to the impoverishment of many rural communities. The poverty of the coastal towns caused a belt of dunes that had protected the communities from rising waters to be poorly maintained. When, inevitably, a severe gale and high tide coincided in the notorious Saint Vincentius sea surge and flood of January 1394, most of the city of Ostend was submerged and Walraversijde suffered heavy flooding and silting. After the flood the village ended up in front of, instead of behind, the coastal dunes. The dwellings were rebuilt farther inland in parallel or perpendicular rows, perhaps using people displaced by the flood as laborers to build a protective dike or to serve in the herring fishery.

Walraversijde became a large, nucleated coastal settlement that had the support of powerful interests with far more than fishing in mind. Local nobles and officials actively encouraged the inhabitants to serve as privateers preying on merchant ships and English craft, which they did with considerable success. The fishers were so aggressive that in 1404 the alderman of the countryside around Bruges warned them against setting sail to plunder without orders from their superiors. Walraversijde was now a classic fishing community in which half of the inhabitants were absent for long periods of time. The owners of fishing vessels were the principals of the village. Each of their ships was crewed by up to twenty independent fishers, each of whom brought his own nets and had a share in the profits. Judging from contemporary documents, their expertise on such esoterica as navigating tidal inlets and salting herring was valued. But the community was also the domain of violent individuals actively involved in piracy. So Walraversijde, like other such villages, remained on the margins of society.

Walraversijde was part of a revolution in North Sea fisheries that came about during the fifteenth century with the introduction of a new fishing vessel known as the buss. The *groote visserij,* or "great fishery," organized by a group of towns, depended not only on rigidly enforced quality standards but also on a large fleet of deep-sea fishing vessels.[16] The towns formed an association, which held a monopoly over the catching, processing, and marketing of salted herring from the 1560s to the 1850s. There were as many as eight hundred busses in the year 1600. A herring buss was a decked vessel of seventy to one thousand tons' burden. A skipper and between ten and fourteen crew members manned the ship for months on end. At sea, they filled barrels with their partially cured catch, which they off-loaded onto special vessels that carried them to land for further processing if needed. By the seventeenth century between six thousand and ten thousand fishers, in addition to processors and other workers, were working aboard herring busses. The catches were enormous. In the first decade of the seventeenth century about 31,000 lasts, that is, 372,000 barrels, came to land.

Buss fleets were constantly busy during the herring season. They began in the Shetland Islands off northern Scotland, where the fish swarmed in February and March, and followed the herring gradually southward into the North Sea. By September and October the busses preyed on spawning herring off the English coast and on the Dogger Bank. In November and December they congregated off Great Yarmouth in East Anglia, where the herring trade had long been established. The Great Yarmouth fish fair attracted buyers from all over Europe. An enormous sandbank created by fast-running tides in a local estuary was firm enough to support a multitude of temporary fishing camps, where the men went out fishing and the women and children gutted and processed the fish, packing them in barrels. The gutters toiled at filthy gutting tables as the laden boats arrived at dawn. Rows of packed barrels stood back of the beach. A nineteenth-century fish gutter toiling at a gutting table from dawn till dark could process about forty fish a minute. Medieval practitioners must have been just as adept. It was dangerous work, for a slipping knife could maim a worker for life and destroy her livelihood. Nothing was wasted: the discarded guts were turned into fertilizer.

In 1310 alone foreign merchants exported no fewer than 482 lasts of herring, about 5 million fish. By 1342 as many as five hundred continental and domestic boats paid harbor dues at Great Yarmouth, most of them coming from the Low Countries in the herring season. The port was especially famous for its red herrings, processed by a combination of smoking and salting. Thirty to fifty Yarmouth boats carried barreled herrings as far as Bordeaux, trading their cargoes for wine. The Elizabethan writer Thomas Nash observed in 1599, "The puissant red herring . . . is most precious merchandise because it can be carried through all Europe."[17] What had begun as a cottage industry had developed into a vast enterprise on both sides of the North Sea.

How did smaller communities like Walraversijde fare? Busses were much more expensive than earlier vessels, requiring wealthy fish merchants to be involved in the actual fishing operation. Instead of sharing in the profits, most Walraversijde fishers now became wage men. The village had at least a hundred houses, with an open space for making cordage, a brewery, and an inn and brothel. The local elite donated the funds for a chapel. Stained-glass windows depicted the wealthy families' weapons and other gifts as a symbol of the loyalty and links they shared with the fishers. These ties were vital to both the nobility and the humble inhabitants of the settlement, who provided them with ships, a workforce, and privateering services.

By the fifteenth century Walraversijde was a settlement of brick-built, plastered houses with thatched roofs. The village was still clearly oriented toward the sea and toward fishing, but now the sea brought it such exotic commodities as cloves, pepper, ivory combs, and luxury Spanish wares from Valencia in eastern Spain. Such items occur throughout the settlement, indicating that the community had tapped into the general flow of goods through maritime networks. This is a characteristic of much later fishing communities, like seventeenth-century Newfoundland. Among the more prosaic items the village abounded with were wooden net needles, many of them marked with the individual owner's symbols. Judging by these artifacts, most net meshes were about 2.2 to 3.8 centimeters, suitable for coastal trawls and also for herring nets equipped with lead weights and cork floats. The fishers used iron hooks, most of them up to 14 centimeters long, presumably to catch larger species like cod and haddock.

The fish brought ashore at Walraversijde were mainly herring, cod, flatfish, and eels, all species typical of the southern North Sea. The villagers used barrel-lined water wells fabricated from oak barrels. Tree-ring analysis of the oak used to make some of the barrel staves shows that they came from the Gdansk region of northern Poland and that the trees were felled between 1380 and 1430, meaning they most likely were made to hold Scania herring. At that time the Hanse controlled a monopoly on Scanian herring exports to the Low Countries. The moment the monopoly was abolished, in 1441, the community stopped using barrel wells. After 1475 Walraversijde suffered from the general political instability of the day and greater insecurity at sea. A century later the community lay waste, ravaged by war. Only the chapel tower survived, and it collapsed in a nineteenth-century storm.

Walraversijde rose and fell with the vicissitudes of the North Sea herring industry. The herring fisheries were a vital part of the Netherlands economy at the beginning of the sixteenth century, comprising as much as 8.9 percent of the gross domestic product. By the nineteenth century the figure was just 0.3 percent. In those three hundred years both the volume and profitability of the fishery had declined progressively. Surviving accounts of fishing companies show that a minimum catch of about forty lasts was needed to keep a ship in business and cover one year's expenses. These included the price of Spanish salt, the purchase of barrels (four barrels of salt were needed to pickle each last of herring), and taxes levied by local and provincial governments. Then there was the depreciation cost of vessels, spread over an average life of about twenty years, plus purchase and maintenance of nets and wages and food for the crew. With substantial fixed costs and highly uncertain harvests, investment in the herring industry more and more brought substantial losses. By the 1750s the waters off Marstrand and East Anglia no longer churned with vast shoals of fish; lean years grew more common, and the herring industry went into a final decline. The Dutch turned their attention instead to the enormous profits that had long flowed from the cod fisheries of the North Atlantic.

2 0

The Beef of the Sea

The medieval version of salted herring, especially low-quality herring, was distinctly unappetizing: a hard, oily stick with a strong fishy taste. During the twelfth century rations like these fed four thousand poor people in Paris alms-houses during Lent and also provisioned armies. For the devout who lacked access to fresh fish, they were one of the few sources of protein on holy days until a new player, the Atlantic cod, entered the marketplace in significant quantities. Unlike that of the oily herring, the flesh of the cod was white and firm, much easier to cure, and had a potential shelf life of five to seven years. The dried fish was hard to the touch and resembled a piece of wood, but it was light and easy to transport in quantity, making it an ideal food for sailors and the military. Dried cod were known as stockfish, while cod preserved in lower latitudes were salted and dried. Cooking a piece of dried cod was simple, if time-consuming. In his guide *Salt and Fishery* (1682) John Collins offered this culinary advice: "Beat it soundly with a Mallet for half an hour or more, and lay it three days in soaking."[1] Dried, salted cod soon became a staple through-out Europe, especially when meatless holy days numbered as many as 150 a year.

Gadus morhua, the Atlantic cod, is a member of the family Gadidae, which also includes such popular fish as haddock, pollock, and whiting. Cod thrive in circumpolar to temperate Atlantic waters from Cape Hatteras to Green-land and from the Arctic Ocean to the Bay of Biscay. A heavy-bodied fish with a large head, cod stay within a couple of meters of the ocean floor except when coming to the surface to feed. They can grow to a length of two meters and weigh up to ninety-six kilograms. Even in today's depleted seas, twenty-seven-kilogram individuals are not uncommon. These are cold-water fish, most comfortable in water temperatures between 0 and 13 degrees C, and voracious feeders, with white, relatively oil-free flesh that is easy to dry in the cold winds and sun of the northern late winter and early spring. Readily caught with hook and line, *Gadus* has been a northern European catch since the end of the Ice Age.[2]

The waters between the Lofoten and Vesterålen Islands off northern Norway are a major winter spawning ground for cod. Moving south from the cold Barents Sea in January every year, they arrive at the Vestfjord, which is encircled by the arm of the Lofotens. The islanders harvest the fish for the rest of the winter. This cod fishery has thrived for at least two thousand years and probably much longer. The harvest persists to this day. Large wooden racks laden with decapitated cod whose carcasses have been hung out to dry stand on Lofoten headlands and behind harbors.[3]

Norse colonists traveled restlessly south and westward from their homeland in their lightly built, seaworthy sailing ships, merchant vessels capable of carrying twenty tons of cargo, including cattle and entire households. They settled the Orkney and Shetland Islands by 800 and the Faroes shortly afterward. Around 874 a man named Ingólfr Arnarson and his wife landed in Iceland, a land with forests between mountain and shore. He found Irish monks there, hermits who had arrived from the south in skin boats but who soon left rather than share the land with pagans. The Norse brought herd animals with them but relied heavily on seal hunting and inshore cod fishing. Most farmers likely spent as much time aboard a boat as in the fields.

The Norse voyages continued, taking the quarrelsome Eirik the Red to Greenland in about 985, where Norse colonists found better grazing than at home. The settlers were aware of snow-clad mountains to the west, but some fifteen years passed before Leif Eiriksson, the son of Eirik the Red, crossed the Davis Strait and coasted southward along an increasingly forested coast until he reached northern Newfoundland. None of these voyages would have been possible without the cured fish from Iceland that kept for five to seven years and provided light, nutritious protein, not only for mariners but for farmers. Dried cod was the beef jerky of Norse sailors.

Between the seventh and tenth centuries lake and river fish, also eels,

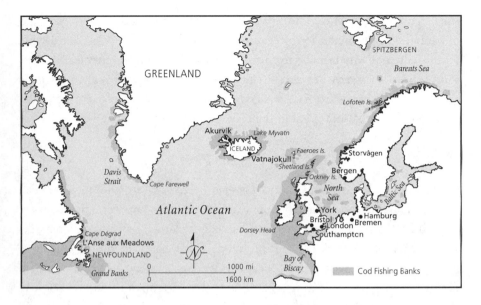

16. The major ports and locations of the North Atlantic cod fisheries.

dominated fish diets in England and Europe, except where marine fish were readily accessible, notably in southern Norway and on the herring-rich islands of the western Baltic.[4] In excavations in places like York and Southampton remains of herring have been dated to as early as the eighth century. Their importance increased during the eleventh and twelfth centuries, but cod were virtually unexploited. Before the Norman conquest of England the Anglo-Saxon language did not even have a word for cod. Interest in cod came from the north. Before Norse settlers reached Scotland in the ninth century, people there fished on a limited scale, mainly for species that could be caught from shore. During the ninth and tenth centuries, when the migrants increased in number, the Scots turned to cod and the related ling and saithe, perhaps because the Norse visitors brought their own dietary preferences as well as their expertise in cod processing.

Norse preservation revolved around two methods. Stockfish were dried in the round with most of the vertebral column left intact. *Klipfish* were decapitated and butterflied, their upper vertebrae removed, and then dried flat. The Lofoten and Vesterålen Islands, where temperatures remained around freezing for months on end, were ideal for curing stockfish. Klipfish could be cured in a broader temperature range by drying and salting them, partly by spreading the fish on beach cobbles. The best stockfish come from cod between sixty and one hundred centimeters long because plenty of flesh is preserved after drying. Klipfish are best when made from fish between forty and seventy centimeters long. These seemingly arcane statistics are of great importance when one is examining fish bones from archaeological sites and contemplating the piscatory revolution that unfolded in the eleventh century.[5]

The Fish Event Horizon

Between about 950 and 1000 what had been a widespread, informal fish trade in Norway and Iceland suddenly developed into an international enterprise. The British archaeologist and fish expert James Barrett calls this dramatic turnaround the Fish Event Horizon, which can be identified in ancient garbage heaps by changes in how catches were processed.[6] Why did the Fish Event Horizon occur? Was it because of a general growth in trading activity? Actually, the factors involved were complex. One may have been a decline in the availability of freshwater fish because of the silting of streams and lakes caused by extensive agriculture, the proliferation of milldams, and intensified inland fishing. Then there was late Anglo-Saxon law surrounding fasting and holy days, which by the seventh century applied to both religious and secular people. In England, the Benedictine reforms of the tenth century culminated in the translation of the Rule of St. Benedict into Old English about 970. This may or may not have affected fish consumption, but the rule was commonly observed long before then.

The main impetus of the fish revolution may have been the growth of cities and towns. When herring and cod first appear in archaeological sites, it is in towns rather than villages. Herring occurred almost entirely in urban settlements until the eleventh century. Cod entered the English diet around AD 1000, but neither herring nor cod were widely consumed in the countryside until long after they were commonplace in towns. The growth of sea fishing coincided with a significant increase in the capacity of northern European cargo ships, which rose from about twenty tons around 1000 to about sixty by 1025. The clumsy, slow-moving Hanse *cog* and the equally slow *hulc* moved goods and fish through Baltic waters from Scandinavia south into the English Channel. These elephantine ships were the medieval equivalent of bulk carriers, designed to transport large cargoes of tightly packed barrels of cured herring and huge bundles of stockfish. Most likely the dense urban populations of early cities and towns across Europe produced an insatiable demand for seafood, especially during fasting periods.

The fish revolution began in the far north, where dried cod were a crucial food source during the long winter months. Given the abundance of cod and the Lofoten region's prime drying conditions, a flourishing local fish trade developed over many centuries, just as it did in Iceland, where some of the best fish bone collections have survived.[7] Meticulously studied bone assemblages have come from both coastal and inland sites. The Lake Myvatn region of the northeastern Iceland highlands, some seventy kilometers from the sea, has yielded fish remains dating from the ninth and tenth centuries AD. Judging from the surviving bones, the fishers ate local lake catches but also subsisted on some processed fish from the coast, mainly cod and haddock dried as klipfish.

Fish commerce in northern Norway and Iceland was local, probably based on social mechanisms such as kin ties, mutual obligations, gift exchanges, and ties between chieftains living in different landscapes. A web of such interconnections moved fish inland, along with sea bird eggs, sea mammal meat, and other commodities. Similar mechanisms drove trade between subsistence fishers and others in many parts of the world. Processed fish were light and easily transported inland on packhorses. Perhaps from the earliest days of settlement, the trade became integral to life in the harsh landscapes of the north. The inspiration for these fish distribution systems almost certainly came from the homeland, from systems based on household and family connections. The fish belonged to many species; there was no common standard; ties were ongoing but informal. Nonetheless, these humble beginnings were the ancestry of the highly organized fish industry that developed rapidly during the tenth century.

Early archaeological sites on the Westfjords Peninsula in northwestern Iceland chronicle the changeover. At the Akurvik site, dating to as early as the twelfth to thirteenth centuries, people occupied small boothlike structures for many fishing seasons. This was certainly not a year-round farming and fishing settlement but a specialized, seasonal camp. Its inhabitants discarded smaller fish in their entirety, but most middens produced a surplus of thoracic and precaudal vertebrae, as if the inhabitants were producing klipfish and stockfish in large numbers. The processors cut off most of the skull and mouth when the fish was gutted. Part of the backbone was also thrown out, the remainder helping keep the body together as it was dried. The thirteenth- and fifteenth-century bones at Akurvik come mostly from fish that were of optimal length for both klipfish and stockfish production, again a clear sign of the industry's standardization. Sites from the Lofoten and Vesterålen Islands off Norway support these observations. Earlier sites reveal a wide diversity of catches that were landed and processed. But Storvågen, an important medieval fish trade post, reveals an almost total focus on cod with far less diversity in the catches.

And there is more—a sign of long-term overfishing. Counting the growth rings on the face of the centrum of the atlas vertebra and using sophisticated statistical analyses, researchers have shown that the Akurvik cod were between 6 and 12.5 years of age, fairly old individuals by the standards of today, when fish are landed when between 2 and 10 years old and nearly three-quarters are between 4 and 5 years, as opposed to 6 to 10 years for the Akurvik catches. Thus the average age of the cod population has dropped by almost half since the fifteenth century. This age falloff is extremely important, for larger, older individuals lay millions more eggs than younger fish. A depleted population of older individuals offers an early perspective on the overfishing of cod stocks that occurred five centuries later in the North Atlantic.

Truly commercial cod fishing was well under way in the north around 1100, when stockfish exports suddenly boomed.[8] The Lofoten islanders shipped their dried fish south from the end of May until August, most of it to Bergen, which became the major center of the stockfish trade. In 1191 Danish visitors to the city reported that dried fish was so abundant that it was hardly worth weighing. Bergen had many advantages: it was a sheltered port well to the south and about halfway between the fisheries and the main importers: the Baltic regions, England, Germany, the Low Countries, and northern France. When Iceland became part of Norwegian domains during the thirteenth century Bergen became even more pivotal. Stockfish was a vital export that was exchanged for grain, which was always in short supply in western and northern Norway.

Isotopes, Kontors, and Hammers

Modern science provides fascinating insights into the international fishery of medieval times. For instance, English and Flemish settlements of the eleventh and twelfth centuries have provided fish bones with an isotopic signature typical of the southern North Sea, suggesting that fishing was done in relatively local waters. But as demand from growing urban populations rose, especially in London, local supplies could not satisfy it, and thirteenth- and fourteenth-century fish bones match Arctic Norwegian, Icelandic, and northern Scottish signatures. By the fifteenth and sixteenth centuries the signatures come from fish landed far beyond the North Sea.

Since the heads were cut off before fish were processed in large numbers, the frequency of head bones in a major city like London is an invaluable signpost. Ninety-five London area sites, from Roman to postmedieval times, have documented major changes in cod usage. Apart from about seventy Roman cod and a handful from Saxon London, cod became common only around AD 1000. During the thirteenth century the number of cod surged, but the frequency of skull fragments falls away, marking a major shift from locally caught fish to imported, processed ones. This moment coincides with the change in the bones' isotopic signature, from locally caught to northern fish. The Hanseatic League would not come to dominate the Anglo-Norwegian fish trade until the early fourteenth century. Why, then, do Lofoten fish start showing up in London quite suddenly around 1250? We don't know: perhaps it was a matter of fishers shifting markets or the depletion of cod stocks in the southern North Sea.

Bergen dominated the stockfish trade for centuries. Some Bergen traders were locals, while others came from as far afield as England. Most were Germans, first from the Rhine area and then, by the thirteenth century, from Lübeck and Wendish towns. By the fourteenth century the merchants belonged to the Hanseatic League and had privileges from specific towns. The Hanse operated in Bergen with great efficiency, backed by ample capital and long-established trade networks that guaranteed supplies of grain and other commodities vital to the north. Bergen Hanse maintained a *kontor,* a trading post, after the 1360s, which was for all intents and purposes an independent colony that provided credit to Norwegian fishermen through trading firms associated with it. The buildings still survive. The Hanse firms were popular with fishermen, for they guaranteed supplies of grain even in lean fishing years. By 1560 the kontor traded with three hundred fishers. The stockfish went from Bergen to Lübeck and also to England.

The English were the second largest customers from the twelfth century until the early fifteenth, when they began their own fishing off southern Iceland. The stockfish trade ebbed and flowed, with two climaxes, one in the twelfth century, when Norwegians began exporting fish to English ports, and the other in the sixteenth century, when there was a major technological change in the European stockfish business.

Ingenious people in southern Germany invented a device that the Hansards called a mill, the largest of which may have been powered by water. It was a machine for hammering fish to soften them, a task that had been done by hand. Mills allowed many more fish to be processed than were needed purely for domestic use and caused southern Germans to prefer Icelandic cod to Norwegian because it became softer when processed with the hammers. Another long-term change saw Icelandic fish going not only to Bergen but also directly to England, satisfying much of the demand there. By the late fifteenth century the fish were going to Hamburg, Bremen, and Lübeck. An ardent commercial rivalry arose, as the Dutch moved into the northern trade and others competed with the Hanse for fish from north of Bergen.[9]

All this stockfish went to northwest and northeast Europe and continued to do so long after the Newfoundland cod trade supplied fish to western Britain and Western Europe south of Normandy. As late as the 1470s a kilo of stockfish was worth six to seven kilos of rye, a huge profit margin for Norwegian fishers. Hanse merchants certainly did not exploit them. During the sixteenth century, some two thousand tons of stockfish departed annually from Bergen. By the 1620s falling prices caused economic distress and the abandonment of many permanent fishing villages.

"Comodius Stokfysshe"

Medieval fishers thought the ocean was inexhaustible. If one fishery declined and catches withered in the face of too many boats, they would simply move on. Christian dogma held that humans had a divine sanction to clear forests, plant the soil, and catch fish in lakes, rivers, and oceans. Such labor, they believed, brought them closer to God. In more extreme interpretations, fishing was a way of expiating sin while providing sustenance to the faithful. Those who fished the oceans felt an obligation to expand their ventures into more hazardous fishing grounds as those nearer home became overfished.

Apart from spiritual obligations, insatiable demand in the face of overfishing sent fishing boats to new, unexploited sources. Iceland was already known for its stockfish, but little of its medieval cargo left local waters. Most local fishing was inshore, a part-time activity traditionally combined with farming. Then, around 1412, English fishers from the North Sea, barred from the lucrative Bergen marketplace by the Hanse, sailed northward to Iceland in deep-draft, two-masted fishing vessels known as doggers, about which little is known.[10] Even the Norse prudently stayed at home between November and March, but not the doggers, which sailed north during February in response to an economic imperative: more fish. These fishing craft were developed from hard experience by fishermen who knew that success depended on staying in open water and in constant movement to follow the cod. Doggers were probably half-decked boats about eighteen meters long with a small cuddy in the bow for sleeping and cooking, the rest open for fishing and salting the catch. The men would have stood at the gunwales, each with hook and line, hauling in fish with mindless repetition.

The Icelandic fishery was tough and demanding, requiring voyages that lasted as long as sixty days. To harvest what was then known as the beef of the sea, men and boys endured frightful hardships, clad only in leather and wool, fishing in snow and rain, in gales and squalls, subsisting on hardtack or, often, on the very stockfish they sought. Death could come at any moment: the casualty rate among doggers may have been as high as 60 percent. But this was an era when life was cheap, when Christian doctrine and constant wars—with the resulting need to feed troops—made cod an indispensable commodity. One winter storm off Iceland in 1419 brought strong winds and snow. "Far and wide around the land," reported an anonymous writer in the Icelandic Annals. "English ships had been wrecked, no fewer than twenty-five. All the men were lost."[11] Despite the dangers, the fishers persisted, for the profits were enormous. English merchants paid about 50 percent more for cod than those in Bergen.

The Iceland cod fishery, famous for its "comodius stokfysshe," attracted both English and Scottish fishing boats. For the most part they stayed offshore, where the mind-set engaged with the far horizon rather than with the confines of narrow seas. The fishers would sail past the Orkneys and head northwest to make landfall on the Vatnajojkull region of eastern Iceland before heading to the fishing grounds off the west coast. The fishermen were a tough, unruly breed who jealously guarded their knowledge of where fish could be caught. On the whole they had little to do with the Icelanders, keeping well clear of a coastline of strong riptides and jagged rocks. Some landed at sheltered locations on the southwestern coast, where they set up camps to process their catches. These were unscrupulous people, sometimes little more than pirates, who thought nothing of robbing and murdering.[12]

Eventually this profitable fishery became better organized. By the sixteenth century some doggers were also engaged in trading. Their crews' fishing methods, described by John Collins in the seventeenth century, now involved 165-meter lines with lead weights and baited hooks. Shorter hooked lines hung from each long line, making fishing so effective that the Icelanders complained that the long-lining was keeping cod away from the shallower waters where they fished. Landings were enormous, brought in by as many as 150 boats by the sixteenth century, some displacing as much as ninety tons. They shipped out with thousands of iron hooks, long-line "strynges," and large quantities of salt.

Waters Swarming with Fish

Bristol, in southwestern England, lies at the head of the long and sometimes treacherous Bristol Channel. It was not a fishing port, but it was a cosmopolitan trading center, actively engaged in the Lenten fish trade. In the fifteenth century its merchants were restless entrepreneurs, willing to risk capital on bold ventures and deeply involved in the western fisheries—especially off Ireland, where fishers were bringing in species like pilchard, a relative of herring, preserved in barrels, and hake. In the North Sea the herring spawn and the Icelandic summer season governed the fishery, but in these waters fishing vessels worked year-round, adding profit to the lucrative wine and wool trade with Spain. Cloth, mining, and bountiful agriculture provided the capital for commercially risky fishing expeditions to Iceland and beyond.

Bristol's merchants, thriving in an era of restless discovery, were always alert for fresh opportunity. A polyglot community of sailors and fishermen, many from distant lands, frequented the city's taverns. These men had an intimate knowledge of the coasts and deep waters of Europe. They included deepwater seamen who had weathered midwinter storms in the Icelandic cod fishery and sailed far south along the African coast. Searching for new fishing grounds, many had sailed great distances from the crowded waters of the English Channel, the North Sea, and Iceland. For the most part they kept their counsel, for fishermen are secretive by nature. In their cups they might have told tales of sea monsters, of fish so large they could sink a ship, and of western lands dripping with gold. The mysterious Island of Brasil was said to be a kind of paradise, floating elusively on the far horizon clothed in perpetual mist. Not only fishermen were venturing far offshore. The French sailed to the Canary Islands in 1402, European ships reached Madeira sixteen years later, and the Portuguese colonized the Azores in 1432.

A profound curiosity about what lay over the horizon, with its promise of lands of untold wealth, culminated in the classic voyages of Christopher Columbus to the Caribbean in 1492 and John Cabot to Newfoundland in 1497. For all the talk of unimaginable wealth, the currency of the North Atlantic was one of Bristol's major commodities, fish. By the 1480s long trading voyages down the Atlantic coast and out to the Canary, Madeira, and the Azores islands had become routine. The mariners who sailed offshore used vessels that differed greatly from doggers. Their caravels originated among lateen-rigged fishing ships used by Arab and Berber fishers off western North Africa and the Spanish coast. These were two- and three-masted vessels that were later rigged with square sails. They were fast by contemporary standards, were capable of sailing reasonably close to the wind, and could carry much heavier cargoes than Norse *knarrs*. Caravels took Columbus to the Caribbean and became the workhorses of Bristol's maritime trade and of the sporadic expeditions that the city sent westward during the 1480s. No skippers' logbooks or passengers' accounts survive, so where these vessels traveled and what they discovered remains a mystery. That the crews were fishing seems almost certain. Customs records report that two ships sailed west from Bristol in 1480 with large quantities of salt, presumably for salting their catches.

By this time Bristol skippers habitually sailed to Iceland's western shores to fish and trade. When easterly gales passed through and the wind blew strongly out of a clear sky, they would have glimpsed the snow-clad mountains of Greenland on the western horizon, which are clearly visible only a day's sail westward. People in Iceland who had firsthand experience of Greenland may have provided what the historian Kirsten Sever has called an information chain that may have caused English fishing boats to sail west to fish for cod. The evidence of this, however, is scarce at best.[13] For one thing, cod are notably absent from meticulously studied Norse garbage heaps in Greenland. Furthermore, the settlers appear to have had a stronger preference for fattier seal meat, and in summer cod fishing would have competed with dairying and seal hunting.

Nevertheless, a few ships must have sailed west. Every skipper working open water knew the technique of latitude sailing, a time-tested way of crossing open water habitually used by the Norse. If bound for waters to the west, a skipper would have sailed northward until he reached about 60 degrees north and then turned west, using the easterly winds that everyone knew prevailed in these waters in spring and early summer. He would have sailed well

south of the pack ice and Cape Farewell, at the southern tip of Greenland, taking advantage not only of the easterlies but also of the west-flowing Irminger
and East Greenland currents. There may have been occasional severe gales,
but once past Greenland it was only another one thousand kilometers or so to
Labrador, a coastline known to exist from the oft-recited Norse sagas.

Why people fishing off Iceland looked westward is unknown. Perhaps conditions in the fishery had become too competitive or the political conditions
ashore too taxing. Whatever the case, to people accustomed to fishing in North
Atlantic waters in midwinter, the open water passage to the west was not a
formidable barrier. The risks were considerable—fog, icebergs, severe gales in
deep water—but restless fishermen in search of unexploited fishing grounds
would have accepted them. The waters were not, after all, very much different
from the maritime environments in which they had served their apprentice-
ships, apparently finding such risks acceptable.

Proof will always be elusive, but it seems virtually certain, at least on theo-
retical and logical grounds, that a few European cod fishermen visited the
Newfoundland fishery before the Venetian Zoane Caboto, aka John Cabot,
an expert seaman and navigator, received sponsorship from King Henry VII
of England to sail westward in search of a route to spice-rich Asia and came
on Newfoundland instead.[14] After an abortive effort in 1496, he sailed northward from Bristol toward Iceland the following year in a small caravel named
the *Mathew*, then turned westward with the prevailing easterlies. On June 26,
1497, he made landfall on Cape Dégrad, just eight kilometers from L'Anse aux
Meadows, the original Leif Eiriksson settlement on the Strait of Belle Isle.
Cabot coasted down the eastern shore of what is now Newfoundland, where
ice conditions were more favorable. So many cod teemed around the *Mathew*
that the crew gathered them in baskets. Cabot received an enthusiastic welcome back in Bristol. The Milanese envoy to England, Raimondo de Soncino,
reported to his patron, the duke of Milan, "They say that the land is excellent
and temperate. . . . They assert that the sea there is swarming with fish, which
can be taken not only with the net, but in baskets let down with a stone, so
that it sinks in the water."[15] The crew, he added, boasted that they could bring
home enough fish to make the Iceland fishery unnecessary. Cabot never discovered a route to Asia, and on his second voyage he vanished without a trace.

In 1502 the merchant Hugh Elyot's ship *Gabriel* returned to Bristol with
the first recorded cargo of Newfoundland cod, for which he received the then-

colossal sum of £180. News of the Newfoundland fishery's incredible riches spread rapidly through European fishing circles. With rising cod prices and exploding city populations, fishermen flocked to Terra Nova, the "new land." By 1510 Bretons and Normans were fishing Newfoundland coasts every summer, and the rush for highly profitable cod was under way.

"Inexhaustible Manna"

When news of the new cod fishery reached Europe, experienced fishermen flocked across the Atlantic. The teeming waters of Newfoundland and adjacent coasts, thick with nearly the same fish they had always known, must have seemed like a Promised Land compared to their depleted home seas. The French explorer Jacques Cartier, sailing up the St. Lawrence River in 1535, described it as the richest fishery he or his crew could remember. Half a century later the English merchant Anthony Parkhurst wrote of the sea near Newfoundland, "As touching the kindes of Fish beside Cod, there are Herrings, Salmons, Thorneback [skates], Plase, or rather wee should call them Flounders."[1]

Parkhurst knew what he was about, having fished off Newfoundland in 1575–78 in his own boat. He found himself pursuing familiar catches in waters beset with unpredictable weather and endemic fogs, just like the seas off Ireland and Scotland. American waters were a revelation. They provided what European seas had yielded in prehistoric times. Salmon, even large sturgeon, were plentiful, the latter once the dish of kings but by then sadly overfished. Far to the south in the Caribbean, Columbus's successors found plenty of colorful but completely unfamiliar reef fish and none of the riches of the northern fishery.

The fishers who voyaged to Newfoundland's gray waters came strictly for the catches.[2] Their interest in the rocky, forested coast was minimal. Nor had they any interest in the local Native Americans, who were expert fisherfolk by any standards. The Mik'maq, who occupied the whole of present-day Nova Scotia and Prince Edward Island, much of New Brunswick, and Quebec's southern Gaspé Peninsula, relied heavily on maritime foods, especially clams, oysters, and anadromous fish, which they harvested in large numbers and cleaned and smoked on low racks over smoky fires.³ They considered themselves part of the natural world, partners with animals and fish in the business of existence. Like all ancient fishing societies, that of the Mik'maq resulted from the cumulative experience of innumerable generations, profound environmental and cultural wisdom passed down by example and word of mouth. Had European fishers and fur traders not arrived on their shores, the Mik'maq might have continued to enjoy a comfortable and sustainable lifeway indefinitely. The Mik'maq and other local fishing societies were irrelevant to visitors, who were interested only in the fish that swarmed close offshore. The one distinguishing feature of this fishery was that the voyage to get there was longer than usual. But both Breton and English fishermen were used to being on the move, so a longer passage to the fishing grounds was only a slight change in their routine.

The enormous stretch of ocean between northern Europe and North America is known to oceanographers as the North Atlantic Boreal Zone. Climatic conditions were broadly similar on both sides; the fish were basically similar throughout the zone, especially cod, herring, and salmon. Fish were so abundant in the eastern North Atlantic that comfortable profits were almost guaranteed. So a routine soon developed: sail west in early spring and return in autumn with loaded holds. The historian Jeffrey Bolster quotes several contemporary observers to show how truly remarkable, by European standards, the Newfoundland fishery was. Charles Leigh, a veteran skipper, wrote of the Gulf of St. Lawrence in 1597, "In little more than an hour we caught with four hooks two hundred and fifty [cod]." Another gentleman explorer, John Brereton, reported that, compared with Newfoundland waters, "the most fertile part of all England is (of its selfe) but barren." So many similar descriptions of the incredible richness of the fishery have come down to us that they must be credible. Captain John Smith, on a visit to Maine in 1614, wrote, "He is a very bad fisher, [who] cannot kill in one day with his hooke and line, one, two, three hundred Cods." Observer after observer commented not only on the number of fish but also on their quality, "well fed, fat, and sweet in taste."⁴

Fishermen from several nations were soon at work in the Newfoundland

17. The major Newfoundland and New England fisheries (shaded) and key
locations in chapter 21.

waters: the Portuguese in 1501, Normans and Bretons by 1504.[5] Other French
fishers and the Basques from northern Spain were quick to follow, the latter
taking whales in the Strait of Belle Isle off the west coast of the newly found
land. The fishery expanded dramatically after 1540. Dozens of boats made the
voyage to Newfoundland, the Gulf of St. Lawrence, and the Gulf of Maine
year after year. In 1559 at least 150 ships sailed for Newfoundland from Bordeaux, La Rochelle, and Rouen alone. By 1565 French boats were fishing on
the Grand Banks offshore. The English had claimed the land but were slow
to harvest the newly discovered inshore riches, being content to fish off Iceland and closer to home. But when the Iceland fishery faded after 1565 they

promptly turned their attention to Newfoundland. Newfoundland fishermen, half a world away from Europe's dynastic and religious wars, harvested cod unmolested to serve as rations for military campaigns. Long before English colonists settled at Jamestown or elsewhere thousands of European fishers had firsthand experience of the Newfoundland fishery.

After 1580 the English moved in on Portuguese and Spanish fisheries, which had imploded because of conflict at home, and began supplying the lucrative southern European Catholic markets. Lightly salted, hard, sun-dried cod for military provisions and for the southern marketplace required land-based operations. The English processed their fish in an area on Newfoundland's eastern shore between Cape Freels in the north and Cape Pine in the south, the closest shoreline to the fishery. Between February and April fleets of boats sailed from English and French ports. The English often sailed southward to Portugal to pick up salt on the way. The passage took about five weeks, sometimes less, meaning that the boats were in place by April or May. The fishermen returned in August or September, accompanied by large ships used solely for transporting bulk cargoes. Known as sack ships, these large vessels may have been so named because they also carried sack, or fortified wine. The slaughter was epochal. As late as 1744 the French explorer and colonizer Nicholas Denys wrote of Cape Breton and the Gulf of St. Lawrence that "scarcely an harbor [exists] where there are not several fishing vessels taking every day 15,000 [to] 30,000 fish . . . this fish constitutes a kind of inexhaustible manna."[6]

The fishers themselves were the sixteenth-century equivalent of today's migrant farmworkers, moving from fishery to fishery—one year to Iceland, the next to Newfoundland, then perhaps back to the north again. The merchant and writer Lewes Roberts wrote of the fishermen in 1638, "Their lives may be compared to [that of] the Otter, which [is] spent halfe on lande and halfe in Sea."[7] The entire Newfoundland cod fishery had minimal impact in America. It was a European business, a migratory fishery with little material connection to the forested coastline except for a few isolated processing stations.

The riches seemed inexhaustible. Perhaps 350 boats fished off Newfoundland in 1615, a year of massive catches in which the average ship landed some 125,000 fish, many up to two meters long and weighing about ninety-one kilograms—gargantuan compared with today's cod. Western English ports like Dartmouth and Plymouth became major players in the cod trade. When the Reformation triggered a decline in observance of the Catholic church's ancient rules, wars on land and sea more than took up the slack. Salted herrings and stockfish were important staples for soldiers, sailors, and cargo ships. Still, given that a shortfall in landings would have had serious economic and political consequences, the British Parliament passed legislation establishing meatless fish days in England. As long ago as 1563 Secretary of State William Cecil of England had strongly encouraged fish days "so the sea-coasts will be strong with men and habitations and the fleet flourish more than ever."[8] These efforts became academic during the seventeenth century, when Britain finally became self-sufficient in food, thanks to cold-tolerant crops and new cattle- and sheep-raising practices. By then the English exported nearly all their lightly salted dry cod to the Catholic countries of the south.

Sedentary, dry cod fisheries close to shore, where less salt was required, were the English specialty. The fishers anchored, unrigged their large vessels, and fished from small, prefabricated boats they assembled on the beach. They set up processing shelters and drying racks ashore. Come September, everything would be dismantled and the ships would return home. While fishing methods remained much the same, the ships grew ever larger, some displacing as much as three hundred tons and carrying 150 people: fishers, processors, and artisans. Their shallops, double-ended rowing boats, were used to fish in places where cod fed on crustacea and smaller fish like capelins, which ate plankton close inshore. The boat would be anchored or allowed to drift while the crew set mackerel-baited lines with paired hooks. The fish were so abundant that the simple medieval technology of iron hooks and lead weights worked like a charm. By afternoon some boats had landed as many as one thousand fish. Once they were brought ashore, processors known as heads and splitters would decapitate, gut, and split each fish in seconds, then lay them on a salt pile to stabilize the carcasses before they were washed in saltwater and dried on racks or platforms of stones. After four or five days the fish were carefully stacked in enormous, layered piles. The average catch per fisher was said to be about ten tons per season.

As holdings ashore increased and competition for favored spots intensified, the English began leaving caretakers behind, especially at the best locations. These men were responsible for having everything ready for the next season. They and deserters from the departing ships were Newfoundland's first permanent European residents. The population varied from year to year owing to wars and other events back home. There were even years when all the migratory fishers were marooned for the winter. By 1700 about two thousand people were overwintering.

"Processing the Fish. The Inshore Newfoundland Fishery," by G. Bramati, c. 1825.
Private Collection/The Stapleton Collection/Bridgeman Images.

The population fluctuated every year until the Treaty of Utrecht in 1713
ended the War of Spanish Succession, which happened to coincide with a
serious faltering of the Newfoundland fisheries.[9] As early as 1683 the crowds
of boats had raised concerns about depletion of fish stocks. The men on these
boats were, after all, predominantly fishermen with experience in Europe's
much-ravaged fisheries. One observer wrote, "There is not fishing ground that
can constantly provide fish enough for so many Boats . . . were there but half
so many Boates fish here, they could not make so great a destruction One Year
as to prejudice the next years fishery."[10] The overcrowded waters were a problem apart from the pressure to acquire shore space close enough to the fishing
grounds to avoid excessive rowing, often against wind and heavy seas. There
was vigorous competition to be the first to reach favored places.

The English tended to fish inshore, north of the much larger coastal fisheries of the French. Many French boats never landed but fished on the offshore banks, exploiting a different cod stock and reducing competition close

to land. Fishing skippers sailed across the Atlantic, then located shallow water with lead and line. This was a challenging task in the foggy, often stormy weather of the Grand Banks in late winter. Once on the banks, the ship would drift while the crew manned crude fishing galleries built on both sides of the boat. The men stood in barrels lashed to the ship, the tops stuffed with straw to protect them from the sharp hooks. As they hauled in the fish, processors, also standing in barrels, would decapitate and gut the catch, throwing the cod into the hold, where a salter would lay them in thick salt. The fish remained there for two or three days before being stowed away.

This work was brutally hard, with no breaks even on the roughest days. The novelist Pierre Loti served as a naval officer on French ships working with cod fishermen off Iceland. He wrote in 1886 of the exhausting monotony of the fishery, where the men caught heavy cod with hook and line, hauling them inboard rapidly and incessantly. The fishers on one boat brought in more than one thousand cod in thirty hours. "At last their strong arms were wearied," Loti wrote, "and they fell asleep. Their bodies alone kept vigil and, of their own volition, carried on the action of fishing, while their minds floated in blissful unconsciousness."[11] The French had this fishery almost to themselves until the Treaty of Utrecht of 1713 was signed, when English vessels joined them on the Grand Banks.

Until the late seventeenth century the Newfoundland fishery lay in the hands of private interests, especially in England's West Country, where captains and land-based fishing admirals maintained rough-and-ready order over their unruly crews. Cod had become a strategic commodity, and the fishery was regarded as a tough nursery for potential naval seamen. Between 1620 and 1650 the mercantile nations of Europe turned the Atlantic basin into a huge trading area in which salted fish, slaves, and sugar flowed along distant trade routes. Newfoundland, New England, and other American colonies formed part of an intricate lattice of interactions with the *Gadus morhua* trade at its heart.

King Charles I had issued a Western Charter in 1634 that proclaimed Newfoundland an English domain and stipulated harsh punishments for offenders against English law. But as time went on, New England merchants assumed an increasingly important, sometimes rapacious role in the fish trade, especially in the West Indies, where they sold poor-quality fish as slave rations. By the 1650s Boston was a prosperous community of more than three thousand inhabitants, many of them affluent merchants. These traders were not averse to cheating Maine fishers by getting them drunk and entangling them in debt, and they flooded Newfoundland with food, cheap rum, timber, and tropical products. They were merely interested in a quick profit, with the inevitable result that the quality of fish cures declined, especially in the inshore fishery.

Hundreds of fishing boats made the trip across the Atlantic, many of them twice a year, harvesting a seemingly infinite bounty of cod. There were no signs of depletion. The Jesuit explorer Pierre-François-Xavier de Charlevoix wrote in 1720, "The number of [cod] seem[s] to equal the grains of sand that cover the bank." Then he added a veiled note of caution: "But they would do well to discontinue the fishery now and then" to replenish it.[12] His concern was not conservation but the potential wealth swimming on the Grand Banks. In 1747, 564 French fishing boats crewed by 27,500 fishers landed cod in France worth a million pounds, a massive sum for the day. Adding to this a burgeoning New England fishery, the catches were enormous.

New England: "The Blessings of the Deep"

From Newfoundland, the American coast trended southwest in a fractured topography of rolling hills. The same broken, formerly glacial landscape continued underwater, hosting a magnificent abundance of sea creatures, not only whales and other sea mammals but swarms of cod and mackerel as well as lobsters. Bartholomew Gosnold, sailing from Falmouth, England, in 1602 aboard the *Concord* in search of fragrant sassafras, made landfall in Maine and then sailed southward, where he reached a "mighty headland." Gabriel Archer, an adventurer aboard, wrote, "Near this cape we came to anchor in 15 fathoms, where we took great store of codfish, for which we altered the name and called it Cape Cod."[13] Bristol merchants soon followed with two ships and reported that Gosnold had not exaggerated. There was ample space ashore for processing the catch. The New England fishery was born.

The first New England colonists came as farmers, but food shortages forced them to take advantage of the wealth at their doorstep. As the historian Jeffrey Bolster puts it, "Staid newcomers of the middling sort who had been landsmen in England . . . were forced into the arms of the sea."[14] New towns rose close to fisheries and by streams and rivers where alewives and smelt spawned. The colonists followed common European practice and built weirs and dams to capture spawning fish across almost every river up and down the coast. They collected seabird eggs, pursued right whales off Cape Cod, and built fleets of small boats for inshore cod fishing. Soon local fish stocks became depleted and the productivity of estuaries declined. The colonists' magistrates responded with regulations to conserve "the blessings of the deep." The new rules revolved around spawning fish, especially striped bass, but also forbade the promiscuous use of cod or bass as fertilizer in cornfields.

Despite common assertions to the contrary that persisted for centuries, the local authorities did not believe the incredible abundance of New England waters was infinite. As milldam and weir building proceeded apace from southern Maine to Cape Cod, spawning fish predictably declined rapidly. Bolster notes that the weir building between 1621 and the 1640s had more impact on the region's anadromous fish than all the fish harvesting of the preceding three thousand years. The settlers faced a dilemma: fish promiscuously or conserve.

The New England colonists were especially concerned about fish like alewives, sea bass, and mackerel. Atlantic mackerel are oily-fleshed fish like herring, hard to preserve and much desired for their flavorful meat. A staple of the North Atlantic boreal fisheries, mackerel tend to swim deep in huge clusters by day and surface during the night, when they can be netted. During spring and summer especially they swarm near the shore in shoals of up to 750 million fish. From the fisherman's perspective, these shoals were unreliable, prompting concerns about overfishing as early as 1660, especially over the use of seine nets. Today, we know mackerel are among the world's most abundant fish, along with herring and menhaden. Yet colonist fishers of the day, using small boats, worried constantly about a potential decline of mackerel stocks, perhaps because some of them had firsthand experience in the English Channel and other depleted fishing grounds on the eastern side of the Atlantic.

By the mid-seventeenth century the seemingly inexhaustible cod had become the staple of the growing New England fish business. Commercial cod fishing got off to a slow start, owing partly to the need for abundant credit and also because of the complex logistics of processing, storing, and marketing the preserved fish. The English Civil War of 1642–51 caused a sharp decline in the number of English fishing boats coming to North American waters. The New England merchants promptly moved to take advantage of rising cod prices in southern Europe by investing in their own fleet. Now American ships carried *Gadus* to Spain, Portugal, and the Caribbean, where cod became rations for plantation slaves.[15] Between 1645 and 1675 production of salted cod rose dramatically to become a staple of the New England economy. In 1653 the Gen-

eral Court of Massachusetts Bay established a fisheries management commission, while laws were passed to exempt fishing boats and equipment from
taxation. The Massachusetts legislature also moved to set standards for the
quality of processed fish and to close the cod and mackerel fisheries during
spawning season. In 1668 the General Court forbade cod fishing during the
December–January spawning period, a sign of concern about the fishery's
long-term future. It is not clear how long the regulations remained in effect.
Most fishermen worked within a day's sail of home, but thousands of Yankee
fishermen traveled to the Grand Banks off Newfoundland each year.

The Treaty of Utrecht of 1713 required the French to relinquish all claims
to Newfoundland. They were allowed to land to process fish but could not
settle there permanently.[16] The English, meanwhile, as the number of permanent settlers increased steadily, rapidly expanded into French fishing areas.
Catch rates fluctuated wildly, from about 400 quintals or more per day down
to about 150 quintals (a quintal is 51 kilograms of split, salted, and dried cod),
and did not recover until fishing eased. Nevertheless, inshore waters were the
mainstay of the Newfoundland fishery between 1760 and 1775, yielding as
many as 775,000 quintals of fish annually until the War of Independence drastically reduced the catch.

Meanwhile, the French concentrated on the Gulf of St. Lawrence and especially on the Grand Banks, where as many as twelve hundred boats fished
but never came ashore. They salted their fish onboard in what was known as
a wet cure, processing them according to size. Great cod weighed forty-one
to forty-five kilograms, while middling individuals were twenty-seven to forty-
five kilograms and small specimens less than twenty-seven kilograms.

Even before 1713 New England boats had begun traveling to the Nova
Scotia banks in response to the depletion of local fish stocks in Massachusetts
waters, where there were as many as six thousand fishers. After Utrecht a small
number of New Englanders and a nominal garrison set up a permanent site
on the Canso Islands at the northeastern end of Nova Scotia, which lay close
to the offshore fishing grounds. Every summer hundreds of fishermen, mostly
from New England, descended on the Cansos. New England–owned sack
ships loaded the catches in fall and then sailed to England and Mediterranean
ports, returning to the islands with salt, provisions, and other supplies. They
also supplied fish to the Caribbean. During the 1720s and 1730s the Canso
fishery produced as many as 50,000 quintals of cod a year, preserved with
5,000 hogsheads of salt. The market appeared to be open ended. By 1745 New

England was producing an estimated 220,000 quintals of the fish a year. The Spanish market alone consumed 300,000 quintals annually, the Italian peninsula about as much. So much cod reached Europe that a glut ensued, causing the Canso fishery to decline, partly because of widespread complaints about the quality of the hastily cured fish. During the nineteenth century fishing boats from Gloucester, Massachusetts, mainly fished on the Georges Bank alongside European vessels. The Massachusetts fishers enjoyed such success that the statehouse made the cod a symbol of the state's prosperity.

Local cod stocks were unable to support intensive inshore fishing. Agricultural activity, marsh drainage, and weirs had degraded the food supplies for predatory fish like cod and haddock, which preyed on anadromous species close inshore. Cod had not been eradicated but the larger fish, the most productive spawners, were long gone. The technology the fishers used was hardly changed from that of their remote medieval ancestors across the Atlantic. Its simplicity tended to limit catches to the point that it was more profitable to sail to distant fishing grounds than to eke out a catch closer to home. This was exactly what the English had done when they sailed north to the Icelandic fishery in the early fifteenth century. The strategy was as ancient as fishing itself—move toward more plentiful catches.

Among those who remained untroubled by the disturbing signs of depletion were the natural philosophers of the day, who argued that the fish of the sea were there for humans to take, without limit. Many colonists even believed that the very act of fishing improved stocks. Nowhere could the catastrophic effects of wholesale fishing and hunting be seen more clearly than in the rapid decimation of the whales that had once flourished by the thousands in the Gulf of Maine and along the New England coast. Basque whalers had begun hunting here at least a century before the *Mayflower* arrived, killing thousands of right whales and bowheads in the Strait of Belle Isle between 1530 and 1620. From 1660 to 1701 Basque and Dutch whalers slaughtered between thirty-five thousand and forty thousand whales in the western Arctic, after which the New Englanders began decimating their inshore stocks in search of "oyl" for lighting. Within a few generations the inshore whale population was gone.

Whales were not the only source of oil. Walruses yielded one or two barrels of rendered oil each, and their tusks and hides were highly valued as well. They congregated in enormous numbers at haul-outs like those on the Magdalen Islands in the Gulf of St. Lawrence and as far south as Sable Island off Nova Scotia. During calving season, between April and June, they spent a considerable time ashore. Bands of hunters used dogs to separate the beasts, and then slaughtered them in enormous numbers. So intense was the destruction that walruses vanished from Sable Island to Labrador and now flourish only in arctic waters.

The cataclysm extended to seals and porpoises. Hunters entangled seals in bottom nets, often in specially chosen places where they could be killed at leisure. A seal hunt in Newfoundland in 1795, for which schooners carried crews to the ice, slaughtered thirty-five hundred seals in a week.[17]

By the time of the War of Independence the New England fishery had expanded considerably, notably in response to demand for fish for West Indies plantation workers.[18] The merchants behind the fishery sent their best fish to Europe and their "rubbish" fish, often improperly cured, to the Caribbean. In 1763 three hundred vessels carried 192,255 quintals of good-quality product to Europe and 137,794 quintals of refuse fish to the West Indies. In the Caribbean they loaded sugar and rum and transported them to Europe, then often sailed south to Africa to buy and ship slaves to the plantations. The problem with the cod fishery was its volatility: boom years could be followed by abrupt crashes. In 1788 the catch was so large, both inshore and on the Grand Banks, that a cod glut caused prices to fall sharply. Three years later the Gulf of St. Lawrence yielded only sixty quintals. No one could explain the drastic seesaws in cod stocks, which probably resulted from a complex combination of water temperature changes, changes in populations of their prey fish, and gross over-exploitation of the fisheries. What had happened in Europe appeared destined to repeat itself in North America.

No one could predict when the fleets would suffer a lean year. The season of 1592 was poor; so were 1620 and 1651. What prompts these crashes is still little understood. Whatever the causes, the poor years sometimes lasted for two seasons or even more. Still, between the mid-seventeenth and mid-nineteenth centuries the northwestern Atlantic cod fisheries showed great resilience, yielding between 150,000 and 250,000 tons of fish annually for many years. This level seemed sustainable, but there are hints of local stock crashes. In a sure sign of depletion Newfoundlanders in the mid-eighteenth century abandoned the inshore areas they had fished for generations and sailed considerable distances to locations like the Strait of Belle Isle between Labrador and Newfoundland to fish.

By the Napoleonic Wars of 1803–15 the migratory fishery had declined considerably. Meanwhile, the inshore fishery, where hand lines and small boats

Cod fishing from a dory on the Grand Banks, 1880s. Drawn by M. J. Burns.
North Wind Picture Archives/Alamy Stock Photo.

were used, continued in local waters right into the twentieth century. Despite
this underlying conservatism, technological innovations were afoot, some of
them due to American fishers' asserting their rights after independence. Between 1790 and 1810 as many as twelve hundred New England fishing boats
sailed to the Grand Banks and as far as Labrador. After 1835 halibut fisheries
using hand lines developed on the Georges Bank, as demand in the Boston
markets skyrocketed and inshore stocks became depleted. Within fifteen years
the Georges Bank stock was so seriously reduced that the fishers turned to
haddock. Meanwhile, cod catches had declined catastrophically by the 1850s.
Because hand-lining from schooners was producing inadequate numbers, in
the mid-1850s some skippers sent out their crews in their stern boats to hand-
line over a larger area. The new strategy worked, and the schooners began
carrying stacked dories. These were unloaded every day at dawn, allowing the
fishers to fan out over a wider area before returning each night to their mother
ship. Such fishing was hazardous in the extreme, but it increased catches, as
did line trawls, or bultows, long lines with several hundred baited hooks. The
Americans adopted such devices, as did large French vessels that set tub trawls

with as many as four thousand hooks, but the Canadians proscribed them out of a prophetic fear of depleted stocks. Attempts to ban them on American vessels failed. Yields increased dramatically in consequence, with a record 133,336,000 kilograms of cod landed in 1880.[19]

In 1865 Captain W. H. Whiteley invented the cod trap for use in the Strait of Belle Isle. Unlike the seine, which was pulled around a shoal, the trap was a stationary device to which the fish were led by netting. Cod traps came into widespread use during the late nineteenth century in inshore fisheries, where long lines were often prohibited. At the same time, steam-powered ships began to be employed for seal hunting and, later, in the cod fishery. The new technology had little effect on efficiency inshore, but it enabled much larger cargoes to be carried to market, creating the inevitable cycle of gluts and rapidly falling prices, followed by crashes and rising prices.

The market itself was changing rapidly. Salt cod production reached its peak in the 1880s before declining in the face of weakening markets for cane sugar from Caribbean plantations, competition from other food products, and the rapid expansion of outlets for fresh fish. By the 1870s lobstering was overtaking the traditional cod industry in many areas as the Northwest Atlantic fisheries, now sadly depleted, came under yet another new threat.

22

Depletion

Georges Bank, off the Gulf of Maine, c. 1845: A fishing schooner ghosts through the fog under a scrap of canvas. The skipper peers intently into the gloom, drizzle trickling from his hat brim. Up forward a sailor swings the lead-and-line. He calls the depth as the ship moves ahead slowly. "By the mark, six [fathoms]," he cries. "By the mark, five." The captain gestures to the steersman, who turns the bow into the wind. "Drop," he cries, and the anchor courses into the calm water. Minutes later the crew are at the rail with hooks and lines. After an hour, with few fish in hand, they raise anchor and resume their search. The skipper and mate watch the limpid ocean as the vessel ghosts ahead. Four down-anchors later they finally hit the jackpot and haul hundreds of cod over the rail.

Catching cod on Atlantic offshore banks sounds easy in historical retro-spect, where so much of the talk is about record catches in some of the richest fisheries in the world. But here, as everywhere else, the fishers had to outwit their quarry. Their failure or success depended on experience and observa-tional skill, sometimes on trickery. It also hinged on the habits and whims of the fish. This kind of fishing was and still is a meld of skill and opportunism. No one could look at fish below the surface, nor did they have the electronic devices that now peer hundreds of meters into ocean depths.

Subsistence fishing still thrives. Villagers today still cast hand nets off southern Indian beaches, rainforest people net large arapaima in the Amazon

River, and Native Americans gaff salmon running upstream from the Pacific. Millions of people rely on rivers, lakes, and oceans for food. Inasmuch as many more fishers are pursuing freshwater and inshore fish than in the past, over-fishing is now commonplace despite stringent regulations in many parts of the world.

It is virtually impossible to detect depletion by examining archaeological sites. Diminishing fish sizes and changing proportions of diverse species offer clues. The same applies to mollusks, whose size diminished in some South African coastal middens as the foragers stripped shell beds and shifted from one form of bivalve to another. Inhabitants of the ancient world followed the classic strategy for combating overfishing: simply move to new fishing grounds or fresh oyster beds. In the much less densely populated world of old, this strategy worked fine. On the whole, subsistence fisheries in the absence of cities were sustainable, the greatest hazard being the failure of a seemingly predictable salmon run or the sudden disappearance of anchovies or herrings.

The Revolution

In the Western world the great revolution in human fishing began about a thousand years ago with the sudden emergence of an international market for cod and herring in Europe. The "fish event horizon," as James Barrett called it, transformed the face of European fishing within generations. It began with the first intensive herring fishing in the North Sea and with the wind- and sun-dried cod of the Lofoten Islands in northern Norway. Religious dogma and war fueled the demand for cod and herring that gave birth to the North Atlantic cod fishery. The promiscuous exploitation of that and other species, both inshore and on the Grand Banks, began the centuries-long devastation of North Atlantic cod populations.

Sporadic concerns about diminishing fish stocks sometimes led to well-intentioned but usually ineffective laws and regulations, especially after the seventeenth century, when human coastal populations rose.[1] The people who raised such misgivings had to confront the popular assumption that fish in the ocean were limitless and that overfishing was a myth. As long ago as 1609 the Dutch jurist Hugo Grotius stated a common and persistent belief of the day: "For it is a universal law that the sea and its use is common to all. . . . For every one admits that if a great many persons hunt on the land or fish in a river, the forest is easily exhausted of wild animals and the river of fish, but such a contingency is impossible in the case of the sea."[2] As noted above, many argued even that fishing improved the ocean, a sentiment that persisted until the largest, most accessible fish had vanished.[3] The widespread depletion extended to the damage done by weirs and other human structures that impeded fish runs.

By the start of the nineteenth century the effects of overfishing were felt from Norway to New England. Finding fish was a matter of long experience, knowledge of the fishing grounds, and trial and error. Information about rich catches was closely held, passed from skipper to skipper by word of mouth. Once on the offshore banks New England fishing skippers took soundings with a lead-and-line, sampled the depths with hand lines, and anchored when they found themselves among the cod.

Perhaps inevitably in an age of widespread innovation fishing became more efficient as demand rose and fish became harder to find. French fishers developed a technique originally called set-lining. They set very long lines near the bottom, some with as many as four thousand hooks, and monitored them from small boats based on a factory ship. The Americans hated the new system, which, combined with traditional hand-lining, increased the already severe pressure on cod populations. At first catches rose, but the longer-term effects were catastrophic. Lines set just above the bottom depleted cod stocks even more drastically. Diminishing yields on the offshore banks also led skippers to send their crews out in open dories to hand-line, thereby covering a larger area. This was some of the toughest fishing imaginable and very dangerous in an area of unpredictable weather. Also by the 1850s highly efficient seine nets were commonplace along Cape Cod shores. The depletion inshore and offshore continued unabated.

Loud outcries from fishing interests in European waters led the British government to establish a Royal Commission to study the problem in 1863. The biologist Thomas Huxley was one of the members.[4] Despite testimony from hundreds of fishers and other experts and in the face of overwhelming evidence to the contrary, the commission concluded that if catches became too small, fishers would cease fishing and the stocks would recover in due course. Unrestricted fishing was thus entirely in order. The effect was to open the door for more uncontrolled fishing, at a time when a highly destructive technology, the bottom trawl, long in sporadic use, became commonplace.

Trawls and Trawlers

Fishing trawls had been developed centuries earlier when seine nets, operated in shallow waters from boats and from shore in northern Europe, were turned into nets towed on or close to the bottom. This greatly increased the catch.[5] In the Baltic, where flat-bottomed boats were ideal for deploying trawls, they were used as early as 1302. Fishers soon complained about the highly destructive effects of dragging nets across the seabed. In 1341 small-meshed nets known as *wonderkuil* towed between two boats close inshore off Holland were prohibited. The use of similar devices, made like oyster dredges but larger, in the Thames estuary prompted a House of Commons petition to King Edward III in 1376. Fishers complained about "a net so close meshed that no fish be it ever so small which enters therein can escape."[6] Subsurface growth and shellfish were ravaged. Surplus small fish caught in the trawls became pig feed. The monarch appointed a commission, which examined what was effectively the beam trawl and recommended it be deployed only in deep water. From the beginning there were some fishermen who were well aware of the dreadful waste caused by dragging the complex habitat of the seabed.

The first true beam trawls—nets with a wooden spar across one end to keep them open—may have come into use in the shallow waters of the Zuider Zee and the Low Countries.[7] The controversy surrounding these devices is known mainly from efforts to restrict their use in Flanders as early as 1499. France made their use a capital offense in 1584. There was strong opposition to them, but they yielded such large catches that they remained in use.

Beam trawls became popular along the south coast of England during the seventeenth century. The oak beams were about four meters long, and trawl heads kept the beam about sixty centimeters off the bottom. They were so effective that Parliament passed a law in 1714 banning the use of fine-mesh trawl nets for any fish except herrings, pilchards, sprats, or sand eels. Brixham, an important fishing harbor in the southwest, became the center of the early English trawl fishery. The trawls were towed by small boats with wide, deep sterns and were propelled by two masts with square sails, a rig design that probably dated back to medieval times. During the seventeenth century square sails gave way to a more efficient cutter rig with fore-and-aft sails that made maneuvering easier.

Trawling remained limited, partly because of the difficulty of preserving large numbers of small fish. Nevertheless, by the 1830s about 112 trawling boats

"Pilchard fishing in Cornwall: Emptying the seine." Study for a painting by
C. Napier Hemy (1841–1917), 1895. © Tyne & Wear Archives and
Museums/Bridgeman Images.

were registered at Brixham alone. The practice began to spread widely along
the English Channel and into the North Sea in response to rapidly increasing
demand for sea fish of all kinds. Many new fishing boats came on line, especially after new railroad lines facilitated rapid transport of fresh fish packed
in ice from major ports into London. By the 1850s ice was also widely used to
preserve catches, which both allowed boats to fish greater distances from shore
and expanded the market for seafood on land. The northeast England harbor
of Grimsby had 800 smacks in operation after 1860.

During the early nineteenth century fishers using hand lines could easily
catch two hundred fish per man a day, not only cod but also halibut and skate.
By late in the century many trawlers operated in fleets of as many as two hundred smacks working in groups under the command of an "admiral." They
stayed at sea for weeks on end while fast-sailing cutters and, later, steamships
transported the fish to the markets on land. The smacks' nets were shot over
the side and towed for three to five hours before being winched laboriously
aboard by hand. Sometimes trawls were so full of fish that they could stop a

boat in its tracks. Unlike those of hand-line fishing, the trawling catches were promiscuous samples of life on the bottom—fish, their predators, mollusks, and all.

Steam Changes the Equation

Then came steam power, and everything began to change. James Watt invented his steam engine in 1769, but it was nearly a century before steam came to the fisheries. The earliest known specially constructed steam trawlers came into service at Arcachon in France in 1836 and 1838. Bordeaux had them less than a decade later, and experiments were under way in England by 1856 and the United States by 1866.[8] The defining moment came at Grimsby in 1881 with the launching of a thirty-four-meter trawler named *Zodiac*, which proved to be an economic proposition, not just a crazy experiment. By 1882 steam trawlers were working in Scottish waters, but most fishing there still involved lines and drift nets worked under sail. The English, meanwhile, adopted the steam-hauled beam trawl with enthusiasm. Sailing trawlers were broken up or sold to fishers on the other side of the North Sea. Dutch and German trawler fleets also grew rapidly.

Steam trawlers made a huge difference. For the first time, a fishing craft could power against the wind. Their skippers did not have to worry about shortening sail or fighting their way off a lee shore in a gale. Tides and currents were much less important. Before steam, nineteenth-century fishers rarely sailed into deep water to fish in winds of more than forty-eight kilometers an hour. Steam trawlers stayed offshore far longer and in much tougher conditions. They could tow trawls in much deeper waters, to a depth of four hundred meters, four times the limit for sailing vessels, and their nets soon reached a width of fifteen meters or more. Steam winches fitted with steel cables made hauling up a loaded net a much shorter process. The fishers tied chains around the ground rope of the trawl, which enabled them to exploit rougher seabeds. By the 1890s ice plants had solved the problem of long-term preservation. On average, catches made by steam trawlers were six to eight times larger than those taken under sail.

And yet the yields from the North Sea declined, especially of prime fish like sole, turbot, and brill. The ruthless fishers turned their attention to plaice and haddock, but yields continued to decline. Raucous complaints by fishermen working inshore or without trawls resulted in the creation of yet another

British Royal Commission in 1883, which heard eloquent testimony about wasted, dead fish floating on the surface and about the catastrophic disturbance of the seabed.[9] The commission members, whose number included no fishermen, were ignorant of the ocean's depths, but the fishers who testified knew a great deal. They realized full well that deep trawling removed precious invertebrates, that the ground ropes cleared away everything in their path, much of it—including clams, mussels, and scallops—caught up in the nets and discarded. Indignant fishers of vast experience pointed out that trawls destroyed the foods the fishes ate, this before talking about the damage to spawn. The marine conservation biologist Callum Roberts rightly calls the commission's report a whitewash. The commissioners' deductions were controversial, indeed outrageous. They stated that beam trawls caused insignificant damage to the food devoured by fishes and that "there is no evidence of any unnecessary or wasteful destruction of immature food fishes by the use of the beam-trawl."[10] This conclusion caused enduring resentment.

Not that the commission's work had much effect. Technological changes were once again making a huge difference, among them the introduction of the Granton trawl, on which otter boards attached to the net spread the net by means of water pressure. The boards kept the mouth of the trawl open constantly, allowing it to be deployed over rougher terrain and opening vast new tracts of ocean to deep trawling. Catches rose by about 35 percent over the standard beam trawl. Yields rose, but the figures were misleading. The cost of trawling was rising sharply as the effort to catch fish increased because of diminished stocks. Fish were so scarce in some areas that the traditional hook and trap fisheries vanished. Despite the closure of some bays and estuaries to trawling to allow rebuilding of stocks, the efforts failed because hook-and-line fishermen, who moved in with a vengeance, kept stocks low.

Purse Seines and Diesels

Steam was one thing; internal combustion engines were another. Gasoline engines came into general use after 1900 and gave way to diesel power in the 1920s. Because oil required much less space than coal, the range of fishing vessels now extended far into the Atlantic. Diesel-powered ships produced catches as much as 40 percent higher than steam trawlers of the same size and had the space to process fish onboard. This development led to factory ships working far offshore. Fishers had traditionally salted fish onboard; now they had access to deep freezers and to machines for producing fish meal while at sea. Today, trawling is an extremely efficient way of harvesting fish on an industrial scale.

Most commercial fishing is now conducted with trawls or with purse seines, which first appeared in Rhode Island's mackerel fishery around the 1850s. The purse is an encircling net with a line running through rings in the lower edge, enabling the fisher to close it like a bag. After it proved highly effective for catching mackerel and smaller schooling fish, use of the purse seine soon spread to the menhaden fisheries and to Europe in the 1880s.[11]

Atlantic menhaden (*Brevoortia tyrannus*), members of the herring family, provided both bait for the cod fishery and oil for a rapidly industrializing economy. At the time of the Civil War six fish oil factories in Peconic Bay, New York, were processing about 2 million menhaden a week. Small purse seining boats could catch 150,000 of the fish a day at a rate of one dollar per thousand fish, enough for a profitable business. The oil-rendering industry grew and grew despite complaints about seines decimating the fishery. Steamers entered the menhaden scene in the 1870s, with massive investment not only in new boats but also in factories in New England, which soon numbered sixty-four. Maine became the center of menhaden processing, partly because the fish arrived off the coast, which was at the northern limits of their range, in June, when they were fat and well fed.

The slaughter was enormous, and protesters said that the fish population would soon be devastated. When the menhaden failed to arrive north of Cape Cod in 1879, fishers and factory workers were thrown out of work for six years. Natural fluctuations in the coastal ecosystem and human exploitation both contributed to the crash. As inshore stocks became depleted, the fish moved offshore, an event now known to be a sign of overfishing by vessels with oversize seines. In the end not only menhaden but also mackerel, halibut, and lobster populations crashed during the late nineteenth century as a direct result of the assumption that nature would replenish whatever stocks humans took. Nature operated quite independently of humans.

Meanwhile, European motorized fishing boats took purse seines offshore near Iceland in search of herring. In 1882 the Japanese adopted purse seines for small pelagic fish and then developed equivalent nets for catching skipjack. Efficient purse seining also helped satisfy a rising demand for fish oil and, above all, for meal, which became a highly lucrative product. In 1876 German farmers began experimenting with fish meal to feed their sheep. Fish meal consumption soon rose rapidly as animal feed markets developed in both Europe and North America. Meal made from anchovies became a major export in Peru. By the mid-1930s the French were operating factory ships at sea that were equipped not only to cure, deep-freeze, and store fish but also to produce oil and fish meal.

As North Sea waters became depleted, the fishermen—now operating in formal companies capable of the high capital outlays needed for vessels and equipment—followed the classic strategy: they moved elsewhere, extending their trawling to fishing grounds off Iceland and the Faroes. These operations were not particularly profitable until the 1930s, when much more powerful engines and larger vessels with greater cargo capacity came into use. By the end of the decade catches from those waters surpassed those of the North Sea.

As fishing became a global enterprise, many countries entered the game, exploiting fisheries far from Europe. Japan became self-sufficient in fish and rice about two thousand years ago and remained so until the nineteenth century, when its population was around thirty million. In 1900 the Japanese, now numbering around fifty million, helped fuel an increasing demand for fish that made their country a major player in the international fish industry. By 1914 Japan was landing more fish than Britain, including many salmon caught off the Kuril Islands, the Siberian coast, and Kamchatka.

The Japanese especially prized tuna as a delicacy. Once tuna boats were motorized their fishing range expanded dramatically, and the fishers, who had used long lines since the seventeenth century, now deployed them more intensively. After the 1920s deepwater tuna fishing thrived year-round instead of just during the annual migrations. Mother ships led fleets of small boats that recovered tuna from lines up to 150 kilometers long. Demand rose with the Japanese population, which by 1940 had reached seventy-eight million.[12]

The great intensification of industrial-scale fishing occurred after the Second World War, when the complexion of fishing changed yet again. Japan had long been the world's busiest fishing nation, catching twice the tonnage of the United States. The Japanese used trawlers to catch crabs in the Bering Sea and pursued whales in Antarctica and lesser fish in the China Sea. The war years brought fishing to a halt, allowing Japanese and European inshore fisheries to recover. Once the war ended, both Japan and the Soviet Union were desperate for fish and possessed large fleets; technology spawned larger nets, engines with greater range, and ever more capacious onboard freezers. Skippers soon found that much better catches lay far offshore, especially in virgin areas where fish were abundant and the seabed was untouched. By the mid-1950s Japanese fishers were working the entire western Pacific, from the Sea of Japan to Australia and eastward to Hawaii. A decade later they were across the Indian Ocean and in the Atlantic. The 1970s saw Japanese and Korean fishing become a global enterprise, so much so that many nations declared 200-nautical-mile (370-kilometer) exclusion zones off their shores. These restrictions merely pushed the fishermen into deeper water. At first the long lines and trawls brought in enormous catches, but the bounty soon withered. One study showed that catch rates in virgin areas fell by 80 percent within fifteen years. The obvious and traditional response was simply to move on to another area. Today, the oceans are festooned with long lines, some of them 100 kilometers long and fitted with thirty thousand hooks.

People have caught fish for more than a million years, yet only in the past century and a half, with the growth of industrialized fisheries, has the quest become unsustainable. Now that insatiable demand from rising populations is coming into ever-greater conflict with decimated fisheries, the world is turning to another classic palliative: aquaculture. Fish farming is growing exponentially, but it may not be sufficient to feed everyone, and its ecological consequences are little understood.

Industrialized fishing has deep roots in conscious decisions, hard-won experience, and government actions affecting people who made their living from the ocean. Many lived at the obscure margins of society, anonymous, hardworking, and laconic, and largely outside the dramas that interest historians. But their contribution to history has been enormous. The ancient Egyptians netted tens of thousands of fish from the Nile to feed the armies of workers laboring on public works. Caravans of mules carried dried and salted fish to Roman legions in the field. Norse sea captains and their crews lived off dried cod, cured by the thousands in northern Norway and Iceland. As noted earlier, a great deal of the decimation of the oceans occurred as a result of that most human of qualities: the ability to exploit opportunities when they arise.

The harvesting of salmon runs, of tuna migrations through the Mediterranean, and of anchovy swarms off South America took place long before the steam trawler and bottom trawl burst onto the stage. People fished, on the whole, with technology that had hardly evolved from medieval or even prehistoric times. There have always been people urging restraint, both fishers and others, such as seventeenth-century New England magistrates, who were concerned with preserving resources for future generations. Unfortunately, any caution regarding fishing stocks could not stand up to rising demand and the profits and livings to be made from satisfying it, or to the assumption that fish were a limitless resource.

Even in the modern age industrial-scale fishing, with its huge trawlers, advanced electronics, and powerful deck winches, copies the prehistoric strategy. For thousands of years one could always deal with depletion simply by moving to new fishing grounds, as trawlers still do on the high seas today. But that strategy eventually fails, and then the only option is to close the fishery to allow stocks to recover. The Canadian government did this with its cod fisheries in 1992 after that year's catch came in at 1 percent of the peak level of 1968. Here and in many other fisheries depletion has struck home.

23

More in the Sea?

The Tsukiji fish market in central Tokyo was the largest such emporium in the world. More than fifty million tons of 480 varieties of fish and other seafood were sold there between 1935 and 2016. Inside, there was a wholesale market where about nine hundred licensed dealers maintained small stalls and where bluefin tuna were processed and auctioned. Outside, the chaotic retail market sold kitchen equipment, groceries, and seafood. For those who didn't want to wait, numerous restaurants served the freshest possible sushi. Tsukiji was crowded, run-down, and swarming with fishmongers, auctioneers, and three-wheeled motorized vehicles piled high with fish. Beyond its unimpressive entrance, the twenty-three-hectare market was a maze of narrow, blood-stained alleyways lit by bare electric lights where about eighteen hundred tons of seafood changed hands daily. About forty-two thousand people worked or visited here on a typical day, many of them tourists, as I was one day when I rose before dawn to witness the bluefin tuna auction. Row upon row of massive tuna lay on wooden pallets, gutted and carefully tagged. Auctioneers walked from one huge fish to the next, tasting the tail meat to assess quality, then selling them one by one in a cacophony of shouts and hand signals. On the day I was there the prices ranged between $40,000 and $200,000 per fish, although much higher prices are common.

The dilapidated market, a remnant of an older Tokyo of narrow, often enigmatic streets, lay close to the ritzy Ginza district with its financial houses

Frozen tuna for auction at the Tsukiji fish market, Tokyo, 2008. The tails are cut open so the buyers can see the quality of the meat. Majority World/UIG/ Bridgeman Images.

and fashionable boutiques. In 2016 the legendary market closed to make way for the communications center for the Olympic Games of 2020; it was moved three kilometers south to Toyosu, an artificial island in Tokyo Bay. Many fish merchants and other citizens bitterly opposed the move, but it was probably long overdue. The state-of-the-art Toyosu market, one and a half times larger than the raucous Tsukiji, is air-conditioned, totally enclosed by glass, designed with wide passageways that are utterly clean, and surrounded by a highly organized outer precinct of restaurants and stores. Only one thing is unchanged: Large bluefin for auction still lie on wooden pallets on the floor. But tourists now must watch the auctions from behind glass windows. The new market distances the visitor from the noise, the smell, the reality of the largest fish market in the world. Perhaps this is just as well, for the blood and intestines of a tuna fish auction do not mesh with the sanitized worldview of mass tourism. The new market also separates the visitor from the harsh realities of today's global fish industry.

The Japanese crave fish more than any other nation on earth. Their insatiable demand is one of the reasons the Japanese government invested huge sums in Toyosu. The investment also reflects the gargantuan scale of the world fishing industry in a time of exploding population growth, expanding mega-cities, and humanly caused global warming, and it comes at a time when ocean fisheries are becoming unsustainable. In 2012 an estimated 4.72 million fishing vessels were in use, some 57 percent of them engine powered. Some 3.23 million, or 68 percent, of these vessels operated in Asia.[1]

Global fish landings dwarf those of earlier times. The tentacles of industrial fishing fleets extend into ever more remote tracts of virgin ocean. We face a future of decimated fisheries and devastated seabeds ripped apart by the destructive technologies descended from the beam trawls and other devices of the Industrial Revolution.

Given how vital the fish catch is to global food security, precise figures on the volume of the annual harvest are surprisingly difficult to acquire. The leading source of data on global landings is the United Nations Food and Agriculture Organization (FAO), which estimates that global marine fisheries produced a peak of 86 million tons of ocean fish in 1996.[2] This figure (which does not include discarded fish) then leveled out before falling to about 71 million tons in 2010. Fisheries data collected over many years by the scientists Daniel Pauly and Dirk Zeller of the University of British Columbia have produced different and even more sobering figures. Pauly and Zeller calculate the peak harvest at 130 million tons, with a markedly sharper decline since then: they estimate that actual catches, including recreational and subsistence fishing, are some 53 percent higher than the FAO-reported data but falling by about 1.2 million tons a year.[3] Industrial fisheries, they calculate, contributed 87 million tons in 2000, a figure that fell to 73 million in 2010. According to the FAO, 76 percent of global marine catches came from the efforts of eighteen countries, each of which landed more than 1 million tons of fish annually. Eleven of these countries are in Asia (including the Russian Federation, which mainly fishes in the Pacific). The greatest increases in landings came from China, Indonesia, and Vietnam, while Japan has been gradually reducing the size of its fishing fleets since the early 1980s. Globally, the greatest increase in catches has been in the Indian Ocean.

While industrial catches have been declining, artisanal, small-scale catches and recreational landings have increased from about 8 million tons annually in the early 1950s to 22 million tons in 2010. Official figures rarely include artisanal fisheries, but they are estimated to have caught about 3.8 million tons between 2000 and 2010. Recreational landings, insofar as they are recorded, are thought to be just under 1 million tons a year and are declining in developed countries—perhaps as a reflection of catch-and-release practices—but increasing in developing ones.

These numbers are approximations, albeit carefully argued ones. The Pauly and Zeller findings have generated considerable debate. One thing is clear: subsistence fishing is still fundamentally important to the food security of developing countries, especially in tropical southern and Pacific regions. So is recreational fishing, which is said to generate some $40 billion a year in global revenues, involve between fifty-five and sixty million people, and support about a million jobs globally.

The decline in industrial catches was inevitable given the historical trajectory of ever more rapacious deep-sea fishing generated by the combination of dramatic technological advances and the insatiable demand of a world population that will reach some nine billion by 2030. The local fisheries of industrialized countries can no longer satisfy this demand, so fish merchants have responded either by importing fish from developing nations that are often far away or by sending their trawlers to fish in their waters. Small local fisheries that once supplied seafood to nearby coastal communities and traded some of their catches far inland cannot compete with the industrialized fleets—and their governments do not assist them. The catches from industrialized fishing may be declining globally, but the scale of the trade as well as the profits are truly gargantuan. This is why the Japanese government invested so heavily in Toyosu.

As the FAO is well aware, international catch statistics form a patchy record at a time when both food security and poverty eradication policies depend heavily on both large- and small-scale fisheries. It's clear today that the high catches of the 1990s were not sustainable. The FAO recently calculated that 29 percent of fish stocks were being fished at biologically unsustainable levels in 2011, down from a peak of 32.5 percent in 2008.[4] In 2011, 71 percent were being fished at a sustainable level, a sharp decline from 90 percent in 1974. Unsustainable stocks can be rebuilt to sustainable levels only by strict stock management. Even populations fished within biologically sustainable levels have to be managed carefully. There is little room for expanded production. Underfished stocks, which have been subject to low fishing pressure, need careful management in advance to prevent overfishing.

Stock rebuilding is a painstaking enterprise in a world where ten productive species account for about 24 percent of world marine catches. Sharks, swordfish, and other large pelagic species have been decimated and became smaller as the older, larger fish were harvested. Anchoveta in the Southeast Pacific are considered fully fished, with no room for expanded catches, as are Atlantic herring in both the Northeast and Northwest Atlantic. Atlantic cod are overfished in the Northwest Atlantic and fully fished in the northeast part of the ocean. In 2011 4.5 million tons of the most marketable tuna species were taken, 68 percent of them in the Pacific. A third of the tuna stock was fished at biologically unsustainable levels, nearly 68 percent fully or underfished. The demand for tuna is growing, and the business is extremely lucrative. There are too many tuna fishing fleets with no effective management plans.

The declines in global marine catches have led to numerous efforts at re-building stock. Some countries, like Australia, New Zealand, the northwest-ern European region, and the United States, have well-established quota man-agement systems. In the United States, legislation mandating the restoration of overfished stocks has worked quite well, having raised 79 percent of Amer-ican stocks to acceptable levels. In 1992 the Canadian government, after the northern cod biomass had fallen to 1 percent of its earlier level, declared a complete moratorium. The cause was massive overfishing owing to electronic and fishing technology that stripped the seabed and caught numerous capelin as well as noncommercial fish of ecological importance. The initial Canadian moratorium was for two years, but the damage was irreversible, and the cod population has still not fully rebounded. The social consequences were cata-strophic. Over thirty-five thousand fishers and fish plant workers were thrown out of work, especially in Newfoundland. Some have turned to catching inver-tebrates like snow crab, which rebounded when the cod vanished. Newfound-land as a whole has had to make drastic adjustments to its way of life. But here there are grounds for some optimism. Early signs of recovery began in 2005. Five years later the Grand Banks stock had increased by 69 percent since 2007. But it was still at only 10 percent of the original stock. There is a long way to go, especially given the added complication of rising water temperatures owing to global warming.[5]

We no longer live in an era when we can assume that fish stocks are limit-less. The North Sea herring fishery collapsed during the 1970s, at a time when the entire North Sea was a free fishing area except within territorial bound-aries.[6] At least fourteen nations fished without restriction. Catches declined, prices rose, but any form of drastic cutback was seen as potentially disastrous for the fishing industry and the animal feed market. Change came when all countries around the North Sea extended their exclusion zones to 200 nautical miles (370 kilometers), eliminating the free fishing area and allowing national governments to impose their own conservation measures. The European Union (EU) also agreed to a common fisheries policy and assumed responsibility for management in EU members' waters. The consequences were immediate: the German canning industry was hit hard, numerous fishing companies went bankrupt, and the Dutch herring trawler fleet fell from fifty boats to twelve. In Britain many people stopped eating kippers (smoked herring) for breakfast.

The EU's management seems to have worked well in the short term, but the long term is another matter. Scientific understanding of the wider ecosystem is still poor. Still, North Sea fish stocks generally are in better shape. Herring stocks are considerably stronger, despite occasional poor years. In 2012 the International Council for Exploration of the Sea (ICES) recommended a 16 percent quota increase to 555,086 tons.[7] Stocks of North Sea cod and haddock are improving significantly. Compare this with ICES' recommended reduction of 62 percent in the southern hake quota in Spanish waters, where fishing pressure has been intense. The huge sacrifices made by many European fishers appear to be paying off.

Elsewhere in the world there are strong hints of overfishing in unmanaged, heavily exploited fisheries. This has serious ecological consequences, but overfished stocks could be rebuilt systematically by about 16.5 million tons globally, especially if high-seas fisheries far from land could be policed and managed to ensure maintenance of their productivity. This requires a level of international political will that has yet to manifest itself. Another potential strategy is creating marine reserves. At this writing, barely three-fifths of 1 percent of the ocean is protected from fishing. The marine biologist Callum Roberts believes that fifty times more reserve area is needed to protect fish stocks, a figure that will likely never be achieved given the many groups with economic interests in the oceans.[8]

Fish having become the most traded commodity in the world, the fish business employs millions of people worldwide. Careful management and the creation of ocean reserves are thus vital to jobs and trade as well as to nutrition. The most important emerging player in this business is aquaculture, long a staple of preindustrial civilizations. The farming of fish for human consumption continues to grow internationally, although expansion has slowed in recent years. In 2012 farmed food fish were 42.5 percent of the world's total fish production, up from 25.7 percent in 2000 and 13.4 percent a decade earlier. China alone produced 43.5 million tons of farmed fish in 2013. Asia has produced more such fish than wild catch since 2008, as much as 54 percent in 2012. Contrast this figure with Europe's 18 percent, which perhaps reflects its intense efforts to manage wild stocks. Aquaculture production has actually fallen in the United States, Japan, and France because production costs are lower overseas.[9]

There's no question that aquaculture is here to stay. Global food fish aquaculture doubled from 32.4 million tons in 2000 to 66.6 million tons in 2012. Twenty-five countries across the world produced 96.3 percent of all farmed fish in 2014. There are both inland and marine forms of aquaculture. China's farming of freshwater fish is a staple of its huge domestic marketplace. In 2012, 55 percent of humanity lived in densely populated countries like China, India, Bangladesh, Indonesia, and Japan. Countries in South, Southeast, and East Asia produced 87.5 percent of the world's farmed fish production in 2012, making it possible to feed millions of people.

The threat of climate change hangs over global fisheries. Climatic shifts like the North Atlantic Oscillation and El Niños in the Pacific have always affected fish populations. The information on the climate change threat is patchy at best and sometimes little more than rhetoric, which makes it hard to assess fisheries' vulnerability. Fish are often sensitive to changing water temperatures and changing acidity, Atlantic herring and cod being good examples of this phenomenon. Coral reefs suffer from bleaching; rising sea levels alter shallow-water, estuarine, and mangrove swamp fisheries. Even small climatic shifts can affect subsistence and artisanal fishing in myriad ways. Deepwater fishers are less affected, largely because they have the vessels and the resources to shift their areas of operation.

Perhaps the most effective weapon against climatic change is aquaculture, generally in sheltered waters. Even fish farmers, however, have to be alert for temperature changes and other inconspicuous factors that affect their productivity. Changing ocean temperatures have caused fish populations to wax and wane for thousands of years. But the warming future that lies ahead will generate more severe and more frequent hurricanes and tornadoes, with sea surges that can decimate shell beds and estuaries within hours. Those who are concerned about the impact of climate change on fisheries need to pay careful attention to paleoecological records and to the experience of much earlier fishers, who adapted smoothly to environmental changes.

The north coast of Peru is a case in point. The Peruvian anchovy fishery has a convoluted history, complicated by the country's once-powerful guano industry (bird guano was exported as a fertilizer), which clearly had an interest in maintaining seabird populations that feed on anchovies. When the California sardine fishery collapsed in 1950, Peruvians acquired the fishing boats at bargain prices just when a huge demand for poultry and swine feed was making fish meal attractive as a low-cost protein source. The first Peruvian fish meal plant was constructed secretly in 1950, but it was not until 1959 that the government lifted restrictions that the guano interests had gotten imposed on the fishery. Once the government realized that fish meal was worth about five times more than guano, fish meal production expanded dramatically.

What followed was a by-then-familiar scenario. Much larger steel fishing vessels replaced wooden ones; technological devices such as sonar and suction pumps came into use; nylon nets replaced cotton ones. The lure of easy profits brought new investors into the industry. Anchovy catches rose dramatically, far beyond the sustainable yield. By 1970 there were about 1,450 purse seiners in the fishing fleets, theoretically capable of harvesting 13 million tons of anchovy in 175 days versus the 7.5 million tons recommended by fisheries experts. Recognizing that the industry was headed for trouble, the government nationalized it and cut the harvest in half. This caused suffering among fishing communities. Although sustainability was clearly still at risk, the government denationalized the fishery in 1976. The coast suffered through a series of powerful El Niños, leading to the occasional implementation of fishing restrictions to allow stocks to recover. Current production is potentially about 7.6 million tons, close to the tonnage recommended years ago by fisheries panels. But there are dramatic fluctuations as well as drastic overfishing: only 2.2 million tons caught in 2014, even less with the El Niño of 2015. Perhaps with careful management the fishery can remain sustainable if those who administer it pay careful attention to climatic perturbations. This is, however, one of the most overexploited fisheries on earth.

People have always assumed they were meant to fish, and this has been a powerful motive not only for commercial but also recreational fishing. We have also, throughout our history, been largely heedless of environmental concerns. The issue now is how to continue fishing in a depleted ocean while also conserving it. Explosive population growth and the insatiable demand for fish, especially in Asia, have prompted numerous efforts to slow the rate of destruction and restore fisheries worldwide. How successful these efforts will be on a global scale is unknown, but the future is already here. Within a few generations almost all the fish eaten on earth will be farmed. A strategy developed by Egyptian officials, Roman sybarites, and Chinese carp fishers may finally supersede well over a million years of fishing in the wild.

More than three and a half centuries ago, as I noted at the beginning of this book, Izaak Walton wrote, "The *Water* is more productive than the *Earth*."[10] Industrial fishing, population growth, and technological innovation have almost brought us to the point where this is no longer true. One can only hope that widespread, strict management and large networks of marine reserves combined with systematic habitat protection will serve the interests of both the fish trade and conservation. Such an approach requires a highly unfashionable degree of long-term thinking. It calls for reviving the qualities of fishers that Walton praised: "Diligence, and observation, and practice."[11] For thousands of years people followed this precept. But over the past few centuries diligence has given way to destructive harvesting. Unless we want to turn the formerly vast richness of the oceans into a permanent desert, we would do well to remember that sustainable fishing is just as much an art as Walton's quiet angling. Otherwise we will find that there are no more fish in the sea.

Glossary of Fishing Terms

ANADROMOUS Running up rivers in large numbers to spawn.

ANGLING Fishing with a rod and line, especially recreationally.

AQUACULTURE Fish farming.

BAIDARKA A kayak made of sea lion skin, used for thousands of years by the Aleuts for fishing and hunting.

BARB A backward-facing point on a spear head or hook, intended to keep the caught animal from slipping off. Originally invented for terrestrial hunting, barbs proved highly effective in the water.

BASKET TRAPS Small, generally round traps of cord or fiber and other materials used to catch fish in shallow water.

BEAM TRAWL A trawl (q.v.) with a beam set across one end to keep the net open. The beam added great efficiency and permitted the trawl to be used in much deeper water, especially when deployed by steam power.

BIDENT A two-pronged fish spear.

BUSS A deepwater Dutch herring fishing vessel.

BUTTERFLYING After a fish has been cut along its belly and cleaned, opening it flat for drying, salting, or smoking, with the backbone left in for stability.

CAST OR CASTING NET A light net usually used by a single fisher, thrown into shallow water from a canoe or the shore. Sometimes cast between two canoes.

DRAGNET A large mesh net towed behind a fishing vessel, used in the Red Sea in ancient times.

FISH SPEAR A long stick with a point, generally barbed and made of stone, bone, or metal, at one end. Probably the most common ancient fishing device other than the

hook, fish spears came in many forms and were used predominantly in shallow
water.

FISHHOOK A hook attached to a line to catch fish. Fishhooks have been in use for at
least twenty thousand years and come in both barbed and unbarbed forms. They
achieved great elaboration in the Pacific and Pacific Northwest, among other places,
and were used in both deep and shallow waters.

FORESHAFT A short antler, bone, or wood shaft that linked a harpoon with its line to
the main spear. When the harpoon struck its prey, the foreshaft would detach, allowing the user to fit another harpoon or point to the shaft, thereby allowing him to
attack more prey. Useful with larger fish.

FYKE NET A Danish bag-shaped fish trap kept open with wooden frames or posts for
catching large numbers of fish, mostly in shallow water.

GAFF A wooden shaft with a hook or barbed spear for landing large fish.

GARABY A cone-shaped fish trap used along the Nile.

GARUM Roman fish sauce made by fermenting large numbers of small fish or parts of
larger ones.

GILL NET A curtain-like net hung in a straight line and weighted at the base. Fish
swim through the mesh and their gills become entangled when they try to withdraw.
Commonly used to catch salmon and other species, their use is now tightly regulated
in parts of the United States.

GORGE A short stick or bone, sharpened at both ends, which caught in a fish's mouth.
Gorges were invented before fishhooks.

GRANTON TRAWL A trawl with otter boards, metal or wood plates set at an angle to
keep the trawl open and the net spread using water pressure.

GRTUMKJERI (DANISH) An inspector under oath to ensure a uniform quality of barreled Scania herrings.

HARPOON A barbed fish spear attached by a line to a shaft. When it strikes its prey, the
harpoon detaches from the shaft, the fisher hauling in the catch with the line.

HERRING LAST A standard unit of ship's lading that varied by commodity. In the case
of herring it represented about twelve thousand fish.

KING TIDE An exceptional equinoctial tide.

KLIPFISH Cod butterflied and decapitated, their upper vertebrae removed, and then
dried flat.

KONTOR A Hanse trading post in major ports.

LEISTER A barbed spear with two opposing barbed tips, and sometimes three set at
equal angles. They were especially effective in shallow water, came into use during
the late Ice Age or soon after, and are still used in Pacific island lagoons.

LINE TRAWL A long line with several hundred or more baited hooks. Also called a
bultow.

LOKO KUAPA (HAWAIIAN). An arc-shaped coastal fish pond constructed of lava
boulders.

LONG-LINING The practice of employing long lines with multiple hooks, commonly used by late nineteenth-century cod fishers.

LURE An artificial bait designed to attract a fish's attention through color, flashing light, movement, or vibration. Lures are often equipped with more than one hook.

MATTANZA (ITALIAN) The mass harvesting of migrating tuna in Mediterranean waters, practiced in classical times and almost certainly earlier.

NEAP TIDE A tide that is of less than average range, occurring during the first or third quarter of the moon.

NET GAUGE A device used to create standard-sized meshes in fishing nets. Used by almost all net-using societies.

NOTLAG (DANISH) An informal group of herring fishers at the Scania herring fair.

PASSIVE NET TRAP A net, usually a bag net, left in place on the bottom to attract fish.

PURSE SEINE An encircling net with a line running through rings on the lower edge, allowing the fisher to close it like a bag. Highly effective for schooling fish like mackerel and menhaden.

QUINTAL A unit of mass in the Atlantic cod trade that is equivalent to 51 kilograms of split, salted, and dried cod.

SACK SHIP A large ship that carried cargoes of cod from Newfoundland to Europe during the seventeenth and eighteenth centuries AD.

SCOOP NET Often called a dip or hand net, basically a mesh basket held open by a loop. Useful for catching fish near the surface.

SEINE NET A large, often heavy-duty net used to trap large numbers of fish, typically operated by groups of fishers in shallow water either standing or from two boats.

SHELL MIDDEN A heap of discarded mollusk shells, sometimes accumulated over many decades or even centuries by prehistoric peoples living by the shore.

SMACK Traditional fishing boats with fore-and-aft rigs used off Britain and the Atlantic coast of North America. Smaller smacks had cutter rigs, larger ones were two-masted ketches.

SMALL FRY Small, immature fish.

SMOKING A preservation method that dries fish over fires.

SPEARTHROWER A throwing stick with a hook that could flick a spear longer distances with great accuracy. Used mainly on land by many hunter-gatherer societies.

SPONDYLUS The spiny oyster, whose mildly hallucinogenic flesh had powerful supernatural importance in Andean life.

SPRING TIDE A tide that is of greater than average range, occurring at full or new moon.

STOCKFISH Cod dried in the round with most of their backbone intact.

STROMBUS The conch, a sacred shell widely used as a trumpet in Central America, the Andes, and elsewhere.

THROAT GORGE A baited, double-ended gorge (q.v.) sometimes used in deeper water. Much used in southern Florida.

TICKLING Catching a fish by massaging it with one's hands.

TIRA (TAHITIAN) A long, curved pole with a bifurcated end that carries two lines with pearl shell hooks, deployed from a canoe and rigged so that the hooks lie close to the surface. Bunches of feathers attached to the pole move with the canoe and mimic the movement of birds that follow the fish upon which the prey (usually albacore) feed.

TOMOL (CHUMASH) Planked canoe used by the Chumash Indians of the Santa Barbara Channel, California.

TONNARA (ITALIAN) The so-called death chamber, an enclosed space defined by nets where tuna are trapped and slaughtered.

TOTORA (QUECHUA) A reed canoe used for fishing on the Peruvian coast.

TRAWL A large ocean-fishing net that is dragged across the seabed, originally developed from seine nets.

TROLLING LINE A line with one or more baited hooks towed behind a canoe or boat.

VITTE (DANISH) A privately owned temporary trading station at a medieval herring fair such as Scania.

WEIR An artificial barrier, usually made of posts and saplings, used to block a creek or stream to trap fish so they can be easily netted or speared.

WET CURE The process of salting cod aboard ship, especially on the Grand Banks.

Acknowledgments

I have been working on this book all my life, albeit unconsciously. I've been around fisherfolk and boats virtually all my life, so the research for these pages has been at the back of my mind for decades. Much of my spare time has been spent under sail in small boats, sometimes with an engine, often without. Some years ago this time on the water prompted me to write a history of early seafaring, *Beyond the Blue Horizon.* The central theme of that book was the intimate relationship between ancient sailors and the ocean in its many moods. Both from my own sailing experience and from writing this book I've acquired a profound admiration for those who fish, whether in the ocean or in freshwater. Their insights into their prey and the waters in which they seek them are far more than the opportunism that drove so much very early fishing. I'm deeply grateful to the many fishers, both professional and amateur, who shared their experiences with me, took me along to observe their fishing, and told me off forcibly when I was wrong.

This book is a history that draws on a wide range of academic and not-so-academic sources, ranging from archaeology and history to such esoterica as fisheries statistics, fishing traps, and mollusk foraging. I thoroughly enjoyed putting together what turned out to be a complex historical puzzle. Doubtless I will hear in short order from those kind, often anonymous individuals who enjoy pointing out errors large and small. Let me thank them in advance.

The research for this book drew on a rapidly expanding academic literature, much of it extremely obscure, often contradictory, sometimes brilliantly insightful. Inevitably, it involves the research of dozens of scholars. Years of discussion with colleagues over the past half century have also contributed to the story, but these conversations extend back so far that I cannot possibly remember them all. Please forgive me if I offer only a collective thank you. Your friendship and comments are deeply appreciated. Special thanks are due to John Baines, Xavier Carah, Alison Crowther, Nadia Durrani, Lynn Gamble, Charles Higham, John Johnson, Danielle Kurin, William Marquardt, George Michaels, Peter Rowley-Conwy, Daniel Sandweiss, Stuart Smith, Wim Van Neer, Karen Walker, Wasantha Weliange, David Wengrow, and the late Professor Grahame Clark, among many others. I owe a special debt to Jeff Bolster, whose comments and masterly account of the North Atlantic cod fishery, *The Mortal Sea,* opened my eyes to the complexities of the historical fishing world.

My agent, Susan Rabiner, has encouraged me from the beginning and is always there for me. It is a pleasure to have worked once more with William Frucht, the best of editors, who is possessed of a notably critical pen and is a source of profound wisdoms. I've learned much about good writing from him over many years. As always, my friend Shelly Lowenkopf has given me the benefit of his vast editorial experience and saved me from many literary disasters. Kathy Tomlinson went through every line of the manuscript with great skill and insight. My old friend Steve Brown drew the maps and drawings with his customary expertise. Last, and as always, my profound thanks to Lesley and Ana, who have always been supportive and made me laugh at the right moments. And I owe thanks to our cats, relentless supervisors of my work. Maybe they're mellowing. This time they sat in my outbox rather than on my keyboard.

Notes

The literature on the history of fishing is enormous. In the interest of brevity I have kept specialized references to a minimum, especially of site reports and obscure monographs or papers. Interested readers will find rich bibliographies in many of the works cited here.

Chapter 1. Bountiful Waters

1. Brian M. Fagan and Francis L. Van Noten, *The Hunter-Gatherers of Gwisho* (Tervuren, Belgium: Musée Royal de L'Afrique Central, 1971).

2. Adam Boethius, "Something rotten in Scandinavia: The world's earliest evidence of fermentation," *Journal of Archaeological Science* 66 (2016): 175.

3. William H. Marquardt, "Tracking the Calusa: A Retrospective," *Southeastern Archaeology* 33, no. 1 (2014): 1–24.

4. Mike Smylie, *The Perilous Catch: A History of Commercial Fishing* (Stroud, UK: History Press, 2015), chap. 3. See also John Dyson, *Business in Great Waters* (London: Angus and Robertson, 1977), 171–83.

5. Daniel Sandweiss, "The Development of Fishing Specialization on the Central Andean Coast," in Mark G. Plew, ed., *Prehistoric Hunter-Gatherer Fishing Strategies*, 41–63 (Boise, ID: Department of Anthropology, Boise State University, 1996).

6. Anadromous fish spawn in freshwater, migrate to the ocean to mature, then return to freshwater to spawn.

7. Mark Lehner, *The Complete Pyramids* (London: Thames and Hudson, 1997).

8. David Livingstone, *Missionary Travels and Researches in South Africa* (London: John Murray, 1857), 206. Ingombe Ilede: Brian M. Fagan et al., *Iron Age Cultures in*

Zambia, vol. 2: *Dambwa, Ingombe Ilede, and the Tonga* (London: Chatto and Windus, 1969), 65–66, 138.

9. Alison C. Paulson, "The Thorny Oyster and the Voice of God: *Spondylus* and *Strombus* in Andean Prehistory," *American Antiquity* 39, no. 4 (1974): 597–607.

10. Quote from Izaak Walton and Charles Cotton, *The Compleat Angler,* ed. Marjorie Swann (New York: Oxford University Press, 2014), 27.

Chapter 2. Beginnings

1. Kathlyn M. Stewart, "Early hominid utilization of fish resources and implications for seasonality and behavior," *Journal of Human Evolution* 27, nos. 1–3 (1994): 229–45.

2. J. C. A. Joordens et al., "Relevance of aquatic environments for hominins: A case study from Trinil (Java, Indonesia)," *Journal of Human Evolution* 57, no. 6 (2009): 658–71. See also J. C. A. Joordens et al., "*Homo erectus* at Trinil used shells for tool production and engraving," *Nature* 518, no. 7538 (2015): 228–31.

3. Nita Alperson-Afil et al., "Spatial Organization of Hominin Activities at Gesher Benot Yy'aqov, Israel," *Science* 326, no. 5960 (2009): 1677–80. See also Irit Zohar and Rebecca Bitgon, "Land, lake, and fish: Investigation of fish remains from Gesher Benot Ya'aqov (paleo-Lake Hula)," *Journal of Human Evolution* 30, no. 1 (2010): 1–14.

4. Curtis W. Marean, "Pinnacle Point Cave 13B (Western Cape Province, South Africa) in context: The Cape Floral kingdom, shellfish, and modern human origins," *Journal of Human Evolution* 59, nos. 3–4 (2010): 425–43.

5. Daniella E. Bar-Yosef Mayer et al., "Shells and ochre in Middle Paleolithic Qafzeh Cave, Israel: Indications for modern behavior," *Journal of Human Evolution* 56, no. 3 (2009): 307–14.

6. Quote from Izaak Walton and Charles Cotton, *The Compleat Angler,* ed. Marjorie Swann (New York: Oxford University Press, 2014), 6. (First published in 1673.)

7. John E. Yellen, "Barbed Bone Points: Tradition and Continuity in Saharan and Sub-Saharan Africa," *African Archaeological Review* 15, no. 3 (1998): 173–98.

8. Joris Peters and Angela von den Driesch, "Mesolithic fishing at the confluence of the Nile and the Atbara, Central Sudan," in Anneke Clason, Sebastian Payne, et al., eds., *Skeletons in Her Cupboard: Festschrift for Juliet Clutton-Brock,* 75–83 (Oxford: Oxbow Books, Monographs 34, 1993).

9. Randi Haaland, "Sedentism, Cultivation, and Plant Domestication in the Holocene Middle Nile Region," *Journal of Field Archaeology* 22, no. 2 (1995): 157–74.

10. L. H. Robbins et al., "Barbed Bone Points, Paleoenvironment, and the Antiquity of Fish Exploitation in the Kalahari Desert, Botswana," *Journal of Field Archaeology* 21, no. 2 (1994): 257–64.

Chapter 3. Neanderthals and Moderns

1. A general, up-to-date description is in Dimitra Papagianni and Michael A. Morse, *The Neanderthals Rediscovered: How Modern Science Is Rewriting Their Story*, rev. ed. (London: Thames and Hudson, 2015).

2. Quote from Claudius Aelianus, *De Natura Animalium*, book 14, chap. 3, A. F. Schofield, trans., *Aelian: On the Characteristics of Animals* (Cambridge: Loeb Classical Library, Harvard University Press, 1958).

3. William Shakespeare, *Twelfth Night*, 2.5.

4. Miguel Cortes-Sanchez et al., "Earliest Known Use of Marine Resources by Neanderthals," PLOS One, September 14, 2011. http://dx.doi.org/10.1371.pone.0024026.

5. Marie-Hélène Moncel and Floret Rivals, "The Question of Short-term Neanderthal Site Occupations," *Journal of Anthropological Research* 67, no. 1 (2011): 47–75.

6. Bruce L. Hardy et al., "Impossible Neanderthals? Making string, throwing projectiles and catching small game during Marine Isotope 4 (Abri du Maras, France)," *Quaternary Science Reviews* 82 (2013): 23–40.

7. Herve Bocherens et al., "Were bears or lions involved in salmon accumulation in the Middle Palaeolithic of the Caucasus? An Isotopic investigation in Kudaro 3 cave," *Quaternary International* (2013), DOI: 10.1016/j.quaint.2013.06.026.

8. C. B. Stringer et al., "Neanderthal exploitation of marine mammals in Gibraltar," *Proceedings of the National Academy of Sciences* 105, no. 38 (2008): 14319–24.

9. This passage is based on Brian Fagan, *Beyond the Blue Horizon: How the Earliest Mariners Unlocked the Secrets of the Oceans* (New York: Bloomsbury Press, 2012), chap. 2.

10. Sue O'Connor et al., "Pelagic Fishing at 42,000 Years Before the Present and the Maritime Skills of Modern Humans," *Science* 244, no. 6059 (2011): 1117–21. The notion of deepwater (pelagic) fishing at Jerimalai has been challenged by Atholl Anderson, "Inshore or Offshore? Boating and Fishing in the Pleistocene," *Antiquity* 87, no. 337 (2013): 879–95. A series of comments by others accompanies Anderson's paper.

11. This passage is based on Brian Fagan, *Cro-Magnon: How the Ice Age Gave Birth to the First Modern Humans* (New York: Bloomsbury Press, 2010).

12. Nuno Bicho and Jonathan Haws, "At the land's end: Marine resources and the importance of fluctuations in the coastline in the prehistoric hunter-gatherer economy of Portugal," *Quaternary Science Reviews* 27, nos. 23–24 (2008): 2166–75.

13. Gema E. Adán et al., "Fish as diet resource in North Spain during the Upper Paleolithic," *Journal of Archaeological Science* 36, no. 3 (2009): 895–99.

14. Eufrasia Rosello-Izquierdo et al., "Santa Catalina (Lequeitio, Basque Country): An ecological and cultural insight into the nature of prehistoric fishing in Cantabrian Spain," *Journal of Archaeological Science Reports* 6 (2016): 645–53.

Chapter 4. Shellfish Eaters

1. Vincent Gaffney et al., *Europe's Lost World: The Rediscovery of Doggerland* (York, UK: Council for British Archaeology, 2009).

2. A general source is Geoff Bailey and Penny Spikins, eds., *Mesolithic Europe* (Cambridge: Cambridge University Press, 2008).

3. Marek Zvelebil, "Innovating Hunter-Gatherers: The Mesolithic in the Baltic," in Bailey and Spikins, eds., *Mesolithic Europe*, 18–59. A general source on stabilized sea levels is John W. Day et al., "The Influence of Enhanced Post-Glacial Margin Productivity on the Emergence of Complex Societies," *Journal of Island and Coastal Archaeology* 7, no. 1 (2012): 23–52.

4. Quotes from Charles Darwin, *The Voyage of the Beagle: Journal of Researches into the Natural History and Geology Visited During the Voyage of HMS Beagle Round the World, Under the Command of Captain FitzRoy, RN* (Knoxville: WordsWorth Classics, 1977), 202, 206.

5. Quoted from J. G. D. Clark, *Prehistoric Europe: The Economic Basis* (London: Methuen, 1952), 48.

6. Betty Meehan, *Shell Bed to Shell Midden* (Canberra: Australian Institute of Aboriginal Studies, 1982).

7. Passage based on Nicky Milner, "Seasonal Consumption Practices in the Mesolithic: Economic, Environmental, Social or Ritual?" in Nicky Milner and Peter Woodman, eds., *Mesolithic Studies at the Beginning of the 21st Century*, 56–68 (Oxford: Oxbow Books, 2005).

8. This section is based on Meehan, *Shell Bed to Shell Midden.*

9. In the interest of accuracy, when I describe Meehan's research I refer to everything in the past tense, although the Anbarra are very much a living people.

Chapter 5. Baltic and Danube After the Ice

1. Anders Fischer, "Coastal fishing in Stone Age Denmark—evidence from below and above the present sea level and from human bones," in Nicky Milner et al., eds., *Shell Middens in Atlantic Europe*, 54–69 (Oxford: Oxbow Books, 2007).

2. Adam Boethius, "Something rotten in Scandinavia: The world's earliest evidence of fermentation," *Journal of Archaeological Science* 66 (2016): 175.

3. Inge Bødker Enghoff, "Fishing in Denmark During the Ertebølle Period," *International Journal of Osteoarchaeology*, no. 4 (1994): 65–96.

4. Soren H. Anderson, "Ringkloster: Ertebølle trappers and wild boar hunters in eastern Jutland: A survey," *Journal of Danish Archaeology* 12, no. 1 (1995): 13–59.

5. Quote from J. G. D. Clark, *Prehistoric Europe: The Economic Basis* (London: Methuen, 1952), 48.

6. Caroline Wickham-Jones, "Summer Walkers: Mobility and the Mesolithic," in Nicky Milner and Peter Woodman, eds., *Mesolithic Studies at the Beginning of the 21st Century*, 30–41 (Oxford: Oxbow Books, 2005).

7. Clive Bonsall, "The Mesolithic of the Iron Gates," in Geoff Bailey and Penny Spikins, eds., *Mesolithic Europe*, 238–79 (Cambridge: Cambridge University Press, 2008), is a good general summary on which much of this section is based.

8. Láslό Bartosiewicz et al., "Sturgeon fishing in the middle and lower Danube region," in Clive Bonsall, ed., *The Iron Gates in Prehistory,* 39–54 (Oxford: British Archaeological Reports, Book 1893, 2009).

9. Description of Lepenski Vir based on Bonsall, "The Mesolithic of the Iron Gates," 255–59. See also J. Srejovíc, *Europe's First Monumental Sculpture: New Discoveries at Lepenski Vir* (London: Thames and Hudson, 1972).

Chapter 6. Rope-Patterned Fisherfolk

1. Junko Habu, *Ancient Jomon of Japan* (Cambridge: Cambridge University Press, 2004), has a summary of recent research.

2. Akira Matsui, "Postglacial hunter-gatherers in the Japanese Archipelago: Maritime adaptations," in Anders Fischer, ed., *Man and Sea in the Mesolithic: Coastal Settlement Above and Below Present Sea Level,* 327–34 (Oxford: Oxbow Books, 1995).

3. Keiji Inamura, *Prehistoric Japan: New Perspectives on Insular East Asia* (Honolulu: University of Hawaii Press, 1996), 60–61.

4. Akira Matsui, "Archaeological investigations of anadromous salmonid fishing in Japan," *World Archaeology* 27, no. 3 (1996): 444–60, has a summary of the theory and a critique based on recent research.

5. Ibid., 452–53.

6. Tetsuo Hiraguchi, "Catching Dolphins at the Mawaki Site, Central Japan, and Its Contribution to Jomon Society," in C. Melvin Aikens and Song Rai Rhee, eds., *Pacific Northeast Asia in Prehistory,* 35–46 (Pullman: Washington State University Press, 1992).

7. Habu, *Ancient Jomon,* 61–72.

8. An enormous literature surrounds Jomon pottery. Inamura, *Prehistoric Japan,* 39–52, summarizes the debates.

9. Junko Habu, *Subsistence-Settlement Systems and Intersite Variability in the Moroiso Phase of the Early Jomon Period of Japan* (Ann Arbor: International Monographs in Prehistory, Archaeological Series 14, 2001).

10. Inamura, *Prehistoric Japan,* 127–46.

11. Summarized in Matsui, "Archaeological investigations," 455–57.

Chapter 7. The Great Journey Revisited

1. Brian Fagan, *The Great Journey* (London: Thames and Hudson, 1987).

2. William W. Fitzhugh and Chisato O. Dubreuil, eds., *Ainu: Spirit of a Northern People* (Washington, DC: Smithsonian Institution Arctic Studies Center and University of Washington Press, 1999).

3. David W. Meltzer, *First Peoples in a New World: Colonizing Ice Age America* (Berkeley: University of California Press, 2009), has a detailed account of controversies, data, and theories.

4. D. H. O'Rourke and J. A. Raff, "Human genetic history of the Americas," *Current Biology* 20, no. 3 (2010): R202–R207.

5. This passage is based on John F. Hoffecker et al., "Beringia and the Global Dispersal of Modern Humans," *Evolutionary Anthropology* 25, no. 2 (2016): 64–78.

6. A botanist, Erik Hultén, coined the term *Beringia* in 1937. David Hopkins et al., eds., *The Paleoecology of Beringia* (New York: Academic Press, 1982), is the classic source, although it is now somewhat outdated. An update appears in John F. Hoffecker and Scott A. Elias, "Environment and Archaeology in Beringia," *Evolutionary Anthropology* 12, no. 1 (2003): 34–49.

7. John F. Hoffecker et al., "Out of Beringia?" *Science* 343, no. 6174 (2014): 979–80.

8. John F. Hoffecker et al., "Beringia and the Global Dispersal of Modern Humans," *Evolutionary Anthropology* 25, no. 2 (2016): 64–78.

9. Carrin M. Halffman et al., "Early human use of anadromous salmon in North America at 11,500 years ago," *Proceedings of the National Academy of Sciences* 112, no. 40 (2015): 12334–47.

10. Summarized by John F. Hoffecker, "The Global Dispersal: Beringia and the Americas," in John F. Hoffecker, ed., *Modern Humans: African Origins and Global Dispersal*, 331–32 (New York: Columbia University Press, 2017).

11. John R. Johnson et al., "Arlington Springs Revisited," in David R. Brown et al., eds., *Proceedings of the Fifth California Islands Symposium*, 541–45 (Santa Barbara: Santa Barbara Museum of Natural History, 2002).

12. Daniel H. Sandweiss, "Early Coastal South America," in Colin Renfrew and Paul Bahn, eds., *The Cambridge World Prehistory*, 1:1058–74 (Cambridge: Cambridge University Press, 2014). Huaca Prieta: Tom D. Dillehay et al., "A late Pleistocene human presence at Huaca Prieta, Peru, and early Pacific Coastal adaptations," *Quaternary Research* 77 (2012): 418–23.

Chapter 8. Fishers on the Pacific Northwest Coast

1. Jean Aigner, "The Unifacial Core, and Blade Site on Anangula Island, Aleutians," *Arctic Anthropology* 7, no. 2 (1970): 59–88.

2. George Dyson, *Baidarka* (Seattle: University of Washington Press, 1986).

3. Waldemar Jochelson, *History, Ethnology, and Anthropology of the Aleut* (Salt Lake City: University of Utah Press, 2002).

4. Kenneth M. Ames and Herbert D. G. Maschner, *Peoples of the Northwest Coast: Their Archaeology and Prehistory* (London: Thames and Hudson, 1999), was a fundamental source for my description of the Northwest coast.

5. Quote from Hilary Stewart, *Indian Fishing: Early Methods on the Northwest Coast* (Seattle: University of Washington Press, 1977), 25. This is a definitive source with lavish illustrations.

6. Michael J. Harner, *Pacific Fishes of Canada* (Ottawa: Fisheries Research Board of Canada, 1973), is a primary source on the fish. See also Roderick Haig-Brown, *The Salmon* (Ottawa: Fisheries Research Board of Canada, 1974).

NOTES TO PAGES 93–110

7. John K. Lord, *A Naturalist in Vancouver Island and British Columbia* (London: R. Bently, 1866), describes Indian sturgeon fishing.

8. This passage is based on Ames and Maschner, *Peoples of the Northwest Coast*, chaps. 3, 4.

9. Erna Gunther, "An Analysis of the First Salmon Ceremony," *American Anthropologist*, n.s. 28, no. 4 (1926): 605–17.

10. Chad C. Meengs and Robert T. Lackey, "Estimating the Size of Historical Oregon Salmon Runs," *Reviews in Fisheries Science* 31, no. 1 (2005): 51–66.

11. Discussion based on Ames and Maschner, *Peoples of the Northwest Coast*, 120–21.

Chapter 9. The Myth of a Garden of Eden

1. Brian Fagan, *Before California: An Archaeologist Looks at Our Earliest Inhabitants* (Walnut Creek, CA: Altamira Press, 2003), has a general account.

2. Edward Luby and Mark Gruber, "The Dead Must Be Fed," *Cambridge Archaeological Journal* 9, no. 1 (1999): 1–23.

3. Torben C. Rick et al., "From Pleistocene Mariners to Complex Hunter-Gatherers: The Archaeology of the California Channel Islands," *Journal of World Prehistory* 19, no. 3 (2005): 169–228.

4. Torben C. Rick et al., "Paleocoastal Marine Fishing on the Pacific Coast of the Americas: Perspectives from Daisy Cave, California," *American Antiquity* 66, no. 4 (2001): 595–613.

5. Travis Hudson and Thomas C. Blackburn, *The Material Culture of the Chumash Interaction Sphere* (Los Altos, CA: Ballena Press, 1982–87).

6. Chester D. King, *The Evolution of Chumash Society: A Comparative Study of Artifacts Used for Social System Maintenance in the Santa Barbara Channel Region Before A.D. 1804* (New York: Garland, 1990).

7. Torben C. Rick, "Historical Ecology and Human Impacts on Coastal Ecosystems of the Santa Barbara Channel Region, California," in Torben C. Rick and Jon M. Erlandson, eds., *Human Impacts on Ancient Marine Ecosystems*, 77–101 (Berkeley: University of California Press, 2008).

8. Douglas J. Kennett and James P. Kennett, "Competitive and Cooperative Responses to Climatic Instability in Coastal Southern California," *American Antiquity* 65, no. 2 (2000): 379–95.

9. Lynn Gamble, *The Chumash World at European Contact* (Berkeley: University of California Press, 2008).

10. Travis Hudson et al., *Tomol: Chumash Watercraft as Described in the Ethnographic Notes of John P. Harrington* (Los Altos, CA: Ballena Press, 1978).

11. Quoted from Travis Hudson and Thomas C. Blackburn, *The Material Culture of the Chumash Interaction Sphere III: Clothing, Ornamentation and Grooming* (Los Altos, CA: Ballena Press Anthropological Paper 28, 1985), 135.

12. D. Davenport et al., "The Chumash and the swordfish," *Antiquity* 67, no. 1 (1993): 257–72.

Chapter 10. The Calusa

1. A popular account is in Jerald T. Milanich, *Florida's Indians from Ancient Times to the Present* (Gainesville: University Press of Florida, 1998). See also Milanich, *Archaeology of Precolumbian Florida* (Gainesville: University Press of Florida, 1994).

2. The discussion that follows is based on William H. Marquardt and Karen J. Walker, eds., *The Archaeology of Pineland, A Coastal Southwest Florida Site Complex, A.D. 50–1710* (Gainesville: Institute of Archaeology and Paleoenvironmental Studies Monograph 4, 2013). The bibliography in *The Archaeology of Pineland* is a comprehensive source on Calusa archaeology and history.

3. Karen J. Walker, "The Pineland Site Complex: Environmental Contexts," in ibid., 23–52.

4. William H. Marquardt, "Tracking the Calusa: A Retrospective," *Southeastern Archaeology* 33, no. 1 (2014): 1–24.

5. This passage is based on Walker, "The Pineland Site Complex: Environmental Contexts."

6. G. M. Luer and R. J. Wheeler, "How the Pine Island Canal Worked: Topography, Hydraulics, and Engineering," *Florida Anthropologist* 50, no. 1 (1997): 115–31.

7. Laura Kozuch, *Sharks and Shark Products in Prehistoric South Florida* (Gainesville: Institute of Archaeology and Paleoenvironmental Studies Monograph 2, 1993).

8. Karen Walker, "The Material Culture of Precolumbian Fishing: Artifacts and Fish Remains from Southwest Florida," *Southeastern Archaeology* 19, no. 1 (2000): 24–45, was the major source for this section. See also Susan D. DeFrance and Karen J. Walker, "The Zooarchaeology of Pineland," in Marquardt and Walker, eds., *The Archaeology of Pineland*, 305–48.

9. Quote from Walker, "The Material Culture," 33.

10. Summarized and discussed by Marquardt, "Tracking the Calusa: A Retrospective," 6–7.

11. Ibid., 13–16.

12. Merald R. Clark, "A Mechanical Waterbird Mask from Pineland and the Pineland Masking Pattern," in Marquardt and Walker, eds., *The Archaeology of Pineland*, 621–56.

13. Marion Spjut Gilliland, *The Material Culture of Key Marco, Florida* (Gainesville: University Presses of Florida, 1975).

14. John E. Worth, "Pineland During the Spanish Period," in Marquardt and Walker, eds., *The Archaeology of Pineland*, 767–92.

Chapter 11. The Great Fish Have Come In

1. P. V. Kirch, *The Lapita Peoples: Ancestors of the Oceanic World* (London: Blackwell, 1997). See also P. V. Kirch and T. L. Hunt, eds., *Archaeology of the Lapita Cultural Complex: A Critical Review* (Seattle: University of Washington Press, 1988).

2. Ritaro Ono, "Ethno-Archaeology and Early Australonesian Fishing Strategies in Near-Shore Environments," *Journal of the Polynesian Society* 119, no. 3 (2010): 269–314. See also Virginia L. Butler, "Fish Feeding Behavior and Fish Capture: The Case for Variation in Lapita Fishing Strategies," *Archaeology in Oceania* 29, no. 2 (1994): 81–90.

3. P. V. Kirch, *On the Road of the Winds: An Archaeological History of the Pacific Islands Before European Contact* (Berkeley: University of California Press, 2000), has a general account.

4. P. V. Kirch, *The Evolution of the Polynesian Chiefdoms* (Cambridge: Cambridge University Press, 1984).

5. Quote from William Ellis, *Polynesian Researches,* 2 vols. (London: Fisher, Son and Jackson, 1829), 2:290–91.

6. Douglas L. Oliver, *Ancient Tahitian Society,* 3 vols. (Honolulu: University Press of Hawaii, 1974), 1:281–314.

7. Charles Nordhoff, "Notes on the Off-shore Fishing of the Society Islands," *Journal of the Polynesian Society* 39, no. 2 (1930): 137–73, and no. 3 (1930): 221–62.

8. J. Frank Stimson, "Tahitian Names for the Nights of the Moon," *Journal of the Polynesian Society* 37, no. 4 (1928): 326–27.

9. P. V. Kirch, *Feathered Gods and Fishhooks: An Introduction to Hawaiian Archaeology and Prehistory* (Honolulu: University of Hawaii Press, 1985).

10. Quote from Samuel Kamakau, *The Works of the People of Old* (Honolulu: Bulletin Papers of the Bishop Museum, Special Publication 61, 1976), 74.

Chapter 12. Rations for Pharaohs

1. Fred Wendorf et al., *Loaves and Fishes: The Prehistory of Wadi Kabbaniya* (Dallas: Southern Methodist University Press, 1980). See also Wim Van Neer, "Some notes on the fish remains from Wadi Kubbaniyah (Upper Egypt, Late Palaeolithic)," in D. C. Brinkhuizen and A. T. Clasen, eds., *Fish and Archaeology,* 103–13 (Oxford: BAR International Series, 294, 1986).

2. Douglas J. Brewer and Renée F. Friedman, *Fish and Fishing in Ancient Egypt* (Warminster, UK: Aris and Phillips, 1989), 60–63.

3. Wim Van Neer, "Evolution of Prehistoric Fishing in the Nile Valley," *Journal of African Archaeology* 2, no. 2 (2004): 251–69.

4. Gertrude Caton Thompson and E. W. Gardner, *The Desert Fayum* (London: Royal Anthropological Institute, 1934), is the classic account. For later research, see Van Neer, "Some notes."

5. Brewer and Friedman, *Fish and Fishing,* 74–75.

6. Ibid., 72–73.

7. Leonard Loat and George Albert Boulenger, *The Fishes of the Nile* (1907; repr. Charleston, SC: Nabu Press, 2011).

8. Veerle Linseels and William Van Neer, "Gourmets or priests? Fauna from the Predynastic Temple," *Nekhen News* 15 (2003): 6–7.

9. Erik Hornung, *Conceptions of God in Ancient Egypt,* trans. John Baines (Ithaca: Cornell University Press, 1982).

10. Stan Hendricks and Pierre Vermeersch, "Prehistory: From the Palaeolithic to the Badarian Culture (c. 700,000 to 4000 BC)," in Ian Shaw, ed., *The Oxford History of Ancient Egypt,* 37–39 (Oxford; Oxford University Press, 2000).

11. Brewer and Friedman, *Fish and Fishing,* 42–46.

12. Mark Lehner, *The Complete Pyramids* (London: Thames and Hudson, 1997), has a comprehensive overview.

13. Ibid., part 4, has a useful description.

14. Jean-Christophe Antoine, "Fluctuations of Fish Deliveries in the Twentieth Dynasty: A Statistical Analysis," *Studien zur Altagyptischen Kultur* 35 (2006): 25–41.

15. James H. Breasted, *Ancient Records of Egypt* (Chicago: University of Chicago Press, 1906–7), 4:466.

16. Wim Van Neer et al., "Fish Remains from Archaeological Sites as Indicators of Former Trade Connections in the Eastern Mediterranean," *Paleorient* 30, no. 1 (2004): 101–48.

17. Diodorus Siculus, *The Library of History,* trans. C. H. Oldfather (Cambridge: Loeb Classical Library, Harvard University Press, 1933), book 1, line 36.

Chapter 13. Fishing the Middle Sea

1. Cyprian Broodbank, *The Making of the Middle Sea* (London: Thames and Hudson, 2013), 126ff., summarizes early fishing activity. See also Arturo Morales Muñiz and Eufrasia Rosello-Izquierdo, "Twenty Thousand Years of Fishing in the Strait: Archaeological Fish and Shellfish Assemblages from Southern Iberia," in Torben C. Rick and Jon M. Erlandson, eds., *Human Impacts on Ancient Marine Ecosystems,* 243–78 (Berkeley: University of California Press, 2008).

2. A. Tagliacozzo, "Economic changes between the Mesolithic and Neolithic in the Grotta dell'Uzzo (Sicily, Italy)," *Accordia Research Papers* 5 (1994): 7–37. For the marine shells, see M. K. Mannino et al., "Marine Resources in the Mesolithic and Neolithic at the Grotta Dell'Uzzo (Sicily): Evidence from Isotope Analyses of Marine Shells," *Archaeometry* 49, no. 1 (2007): 117–33.

3. Richard Ellis, *Tuna: A Love Story* (New York: Vintage, 2008), is a good general account of this remarkable fish.

4. Broodbank, *The Making of the Middle Sea,* 171–72.

5. This section is based on Annalisa Marzano, *Harvesting the Sea: The Exploitation of Marine Resources in the Roman Mediterranean* (Oxford: Oxford University Press, 2000), chaps. 1, 2.

6. Homer, *The Odyssey*, 12:355—56.

7. James N. Davidson, *Courtesans and Fishcakes: The Consuming Passions of Classical Athens* (London: HarperCollins, 1997), 4.

8. Quoted from ibid., 5.

9. Archestratus was a Greek poet and gastronome who lived in Syracuse in the mid-fourth century BC. His poem *Hedypatheia*, or "Life of Luxury," described where to find food and discussed fish extensively.

10. Quotes from Davidson, *Courtesans*, 8.

11. Quotes from ibid., 19.

12. Theresa Maggio, *Mattanza: The Ancient Sicilian Ritual of Bluefin Tuna Fishing* (New York: Penguin Putnam, 2000), describes modern-day *mattanzas*.

13. Quote from Oppian, *Halieutica*, trans. A. W. Mair (Cambridge: Loeb Classical Library, Harvard University Press, 1928), book 33, lines 643—44.

14. Marzano, *Harvesting the Sea*, 69—79.

15. Fish salting: ibid., chaps. 3, 4. See also Athena Trakadad, "The Archaeological Evidence for Fish Processing in the Western Mediterranean," in Tønnes Bekker-Nielsen, ed., *Ancient Fishing and Fish Processing in the Black Sea Region*, 47—82 (Aarhus, Denmark: Aarhus University Press, 2005).

16. Hieron II was the Greek Sicilian king of Syracuse from 270 to 215 BC and an important figure in the First Punic War. He became a strong ally of Rome. Cargo figures from Marzano, *Harvesting the Sea*, 109.

Chapter 14. Scaly Flocks

1. Marcus Terentius Varro, *Rerum Rusticarum Libri Tres* (Cambridge: Loeb Classical Library, Harvard University Press, 1934). English translation published on penelope .uchicago.edu/ Thayer/Varro, book 3, chapter 8, p. 347.

2. Mark J. Spaulding et al., "Sustainable Ancient Aquaculture," *Ocean Views*, July 11, 2013, voices.nationalgeographic.com.

3. Diodorus Siculus, *Library of History*, volume 11, books 21—32, trans. Francis R. Walton (Cambridge: Loeb Classical Library, Harvard University Press, 1957). Quote from chapter 25, line 4.

4. Pliny the Elder, *Natural History: A Selection*, trans. John F. Healey (New York: Penguin Books, 1991), book 8, line 44.

5. James Higginbotham, *Piscinae: Artificial Fishponds in Roman Italy* (Chapel Hill: University of North Carolina Press, 1997), 45.

6. James Higginbotham, *Piscinae*, chap. 2, describes the fish species kept in piscinae.

7. Robert I. Curtis, *Garum and Salsamenta* (Leiden: E. J. Brill, 1991), is a definitive source on this complex subject.

8. Lucius Junius Moderatus Columella, *De Re Rustica, Books 5—12*, trans. E. S. Forster and E. Heffner (Cambridge: Loeb Classical Library, Harvard University Press, 1954—55). Quotes from book 8, chapter 8, lines 1—4, chapter 17, lines 1—4.

9. Anna Marguerite McCann et al., *The Roman Port and Fishery of Cosa* (Princeton: Princeton University Press, 1987).

10. Higginbotham, *Piscinae,* 60.

11. Today, many Roman fishponds are underwater, thanks to rising sea levels. They have been used as markers to measure changes in sea levels.

12. Marcus Valerius Martial, *Epigrammata,* trans. E. W. Lindsay (Oxford: Oxford Classical Texts, Oxford University Press, 1922), book 13, chapter 81, line 13.

13. Gaius Plinius Caecilius Secundus (Pliny the Younger), *Letters of Pliny,* trans. William Melmoth, book 2, line 6. Gutenberg.org.

14. J. J. O'Donnell, *Cassiodorus* (Berkeley: University of California Press, 1979), is the definitive biography.

Chapter 15. The Fish Eaters

1. Quotes in this paragraph from Diodorus Siculus, *The Library of History,* trans. C. H. Oldfather (Cambridge: Loeb Classical Library, Harvard University Press, 1935), book 3, lines 15–21.

2. Alan Villiers, *Sons of Sinbad* (London: Arabian Publishing, 2006). Villiers gives a vivid portrait of life on sailing dhows in the Indian Ocean and Red Sea when traditional lifeways were still widespread during the 1930s.

3. Peter A. Clayton, *Chronicle of the Pharaohs* (London: Thames and Hudson, 1994), 104–7, summarizes Hatshepsut's rule and her expedition.

4. Lionel Casson, *The Periplus Maris Erythraei* (Princeton: Princeton University Press, 1989), is the definitive translation and commentary, which I relied on throughout.

5. Ibid., 51 (chap. 2, 6–7).

6. Davis Peacock and Lucy Blue, eds., *Myos Hormos-Queir Al-Qadim: Roman and Islamic Ports on the Red Sea* (Oxford: Oxbow Books, 2006). See also Ross J. Thomas, "Port communities and the Erythraean Sea trade," *British Museum Studies in Ancient Egypt and Sudan* 18 (2012): 169–99. See also Steven E. Sidebotham, *Roman Economic Policy in the Erythra Thalassa 30 BC–AD 217* (Leiden: E. J. Brill, 1986).

7. Quote from Strabo, *Geography,* trans. Horace Leonard Jones (Cambridge: Loeb Classical Library, Harvard University Press, 1918), book 2, chapter 5, line 12.

8. Hippalus was a Greek merchant and navigator who lived in the first century BC. He may have been the first Greek geographer to realize that the west coast of India extended southward, not in a straight line east from Arabia, thereby making an ocean crossing a viable possibility.

9. Ross J. Thomas, "Fishing equipment from Myos Hormos and fishing techniques on the Red Sea in the Roman period," in Tønnes Bekker-Nielsen and Darío Bernal Casasola, eds., *Ancient Nets and Fishing Gear,* 139–60 (Aarhus, Denmark: Aarhus University Press, 2010).

10. Thomas, "Fishing equipment," 139ff.

11. Quotes in this paragraph from Casson, *The Periplus,* 61.

12. Adriaan H. J. Prins, *Sailing from Lamu: A Study of Maritime Culture in Islamic East Africa* (Assen, Netherlands: Van Gorcum, 1965), gives an excellent impression of the place, in many respects little changed from medieval times.

13. Alison Crowther et al., "Iron Age agriculture, fishing and trade in the Mafia Archipelago, Tanzania: New evidence from Ukunju Cave," *Azania* 49, no. 1 (2014): 21–44. Juani: Alison Crowther et al., "Coastal Subsistence, Maritime Trade, and the Colonization of Small Offshore Islands in Eastern African Prehistory," *Journal of Island and Coastal Archaeology* 11, no. 2 (2017): 211–37.

14. Mark Horton, Helen W. Brown, and Nina Mudida, *The Archaeology of a Muslim Trading Community on the Coast of East Africa* (Nairobi: British Institute in Eastern Africa Memoir 14, 1996).

15. Marbled parrot fish: Eréndira M. Quintana Morales and Mark Horton, "Fishing and Fish Consumption in the Swahili Communities of East Africa, 700–1400 CE," *Internet Archaeology* (2014), doi:10.11141/ia.37.3.

16. Quotes in these paragraphs are from G. S. P. Freeman-Grenville, *The East African Coast: Select Documents from the First to the Earlier Nineteenth Century* (Oxford: Clarendon Press, 1962), 14, 20.

17. Nicole Boivin et al., "East Africa and Madagascar in the Indian Ocean World," *Journal of World Prehistory* 26, no. 3 (2013): 213–81.

18. Quintana Morales and Horton, "Fishing and Fish Consumption."

Chapter 16. The Erythraean Sea

1. Quote from Lionel Casson, *The Periplus Maris Erythraei* (Princeton: Princeton University Press, 1989), 63, 65.

2. This coastline is described by Alan Villiers, *Sons of Sinbad* (London: Arabian Publishing, 2006), chap. 15.

3. Quote from Casson, *The Periplus,* 67.

4. Douglas J. Kennett and James P. Kennett, "Early State Formation in Southern Mesopotamia: Sea Levels, Shorelines, and Climate Change," *Journal of Island and Coastal Archaeology* 1, no. 1 (2006): 67–99.

5. Samuel Kramer, *The Sumerians* (Chicago: University of Chicago Press, 1963), is still an invaluable popular account. See also Harriett Crawford, *Sumer and the Sumerians,* 2d ed. (Cambridge: Cambridge University Press, 2004).

6. Laith A. Jawad, "Fishing Gear and Methods of the Lower Mesopotamian Plain with Reference to Fishing Management," *Marina Mesopotamica* 1, no. 1 (2006): 1–37.

7. Robert A. Carter and Graham Philip, eds., *Beyond the Ubaid: Transformation and Integration in the Late Prehistoric Societies of the Middle East* (Chicago: Oriental Institute of the University of Chicago, Studies in Ancient Oriental Civilization No. 63, 2010).

8. Mark Beech, "The Animal and Fish Bones," in Robert Carter and Harriet Crawford, eds., *Maritime Interactions in the Arabian Neolithic: Evidence from H3, As-Sabaniyah, an Ubaid-related Site in Kuwait,* 130–56 (Leiden: Brill, 2010).

9. Mark Beech, "In the Land of the Ichthyophagi: Prehistoric Occupation of the Coast and Islands of the Southern Arabian Gulf: A Regional Review," *Adumatu* 27 (2013): 31–48.

10. Sophie Méry, Vincent Charpentier, and Mark Beech, "First evidence of shell fish-hook technology in the Gulf," *Arabian Archaeology and Epigraphy* 19 (2008): 15–21.

11. J. Desse and N. Desse-Berset, "Les Ichthyophages du Makran (Belouchistan, Pakistan)," *Paléorient* 31, no. 1 (2005): 86–96.

12. Quotes from Casson, *The Periplus,* 73.

13. W. R. Belcher, "Marine Exploitation in the Third Millennium BC—The Eastern Coast of Pakistan," *Paléorient* 31, no. 1 (2004): 79–85. Balakot is described on pages 80ff.

14. This section relies on Jane R. McIntosh, *A Peaceful Realm: The Rise and Fall of the Indus Civilization* (Boulder: Westview, 2002).

15. Belcher, "Marine Exploitation," 80–82.

16. Casson, *The Periplus,* 79.

17. Wasantha S. Weliange, "Prehistoric fishing in Sri Lanka," in P. Perera, ed., *Festschrift in Honour of Professor S. B. Hettiaratchi: Essays on Archaeology, History, Buddhist Studies and Anthropology,* 211–28 (Nugegoda, Sri Lanka: Sarasavi Publishers, 2010).

18. Casson, *The Periplus,* 93.

Chapter 17. Carp and Khmer

1. Li Liu and Xingcan Chen, *The Archaeology of China: From the Late Paleolithic to the Early Bronze Age* (Cambridge: Cambridge University Press, 2012).

2. Francesca Bray, "Agriculture," in Joseph Needham, ed., *Science and Civilization in China,* vol. 6, part 2: *Biology and Biological Technology,* 1–673 (Cambridge: Cambridge University Press, 1984).

3. Quotes from Berthold Laufer, *The Domestication of the Cormorant in China and Japan* (Chicago: Field Museum of Natural History Anthropological Series, Publication 300), 18, no. 3 (1931): 225.

4. Yangzi carp: Rafael Murillo Muñoz, *River Flow* (Boca Raton, FL: CRC Press, 2012), 1102–3.

5. C. F. Hickling, *Fish Culture,* 2d ed. (London: Faber and Faber, 1971).

6. Quotes in these two paragraphs are from Ted S. Y. Moo, trans., *Chinese Fish Culture by Fan Lee* (Solomons, MD: Chesapeake Biological Laboratory Contribution 459, n.d.), 2, 4. A *mou* was a measure of area: 6.6 mou equal 1.6 kilometers. A *chih* is 0.3581 meters.

7. Bray, "Agriculture," 1–673.

8. Charles Higham, *Early Mainland Southeast Asia: From First Humans to Angkor* (Bangkok: River Books, 2014).

9. Vuthy Voeun et al., "Faunal Remains from the Excavations at Angkor Borei, Kingdom of Cambodia." Manuscript. I am grateful to Miriam Stark for sharing this document with me.

10. Michele Nijhuis, "Harnessing the Mekong or killing it?" *National Geographic Magazine* 227, no. 5 (2015): 102–29.

11. Ian Campbell et al., "Species diversity and ecology of Tonle Sap Great Lake, Cambodia," *Aquatic Sciences* 66, no. 3 (2006): 355–70.

12. Charles Higham, *The Civilization of Angkor* (Berkeley: University of California Press, 2001), was the source for this section. See also Michael D. Coe, *Angkor and the Khmer Civilization* (London: Thames and Hudson, 2003).

13. Described for general readers by Brian Fagan and Nadia Durrani, "The secrets of Angkor Wat: How archaeology is rewriting history," *Current World Archaeology*, no. 77 (2016): 14–20.

14. Quote from Henri Mouhot, *Voyage dans les royaumes de Siam, de Cambodge, de Laos et autres parties centrales de l'Indochine* (1868; repr. Geneva: Editions Olizane, 1999), 172.

15. Food and Agriculture Organization of the United Nations, Fishery and Aquaculture Country Profiles, Cambodia. Country Profile Fact Sheets (Rome: FAO Fisheries and Aquaculture Department, 2011). http://www.fao.org/fishery/facp/KHM/en.

Chapter 18. Anchovies and Civilization

1. Richard L. Burger, *Chavín and the Origins of Andean Civilization* (London: Thames and Hudson, 1992). The trumpet research is being carried out by the Center for Computer Research in Music and Acoustics (CCRMA), Stanford University.

2. Alison C. Paulson, "The Thorny Oyster and the Voice of God: *Spondylus* and *Strombus* in Andean Prehistory," *American Antiquity* 39, no. 4 (1974): 597–607. See also Marc Zender, "The Music of Shells," in Daniel Finamore and Stephen D. Houston, eds., *The Fiery Pool: The Maya and the Mythic Sea*, 83–85 (New Haven: Yale University Press and the Peabody Essex Museum, 2010).

3. Daniel Sandweiss, "The Return of the Native Symbol: Peru Picks *Spondylus* to Represent New Integration with Ecuador," *SAA Bulletin* 17, no. 2 (1999): 8–9.

4. Daniel Sandweiss, "The Development of Fishing Specialization on the Central Andean Coast," in Mark G. Plew, ed. *Prehistoric Hunter-Gatherer Fishing Strategies*, 41–63 (Boise, ID: Department of Anthropology, Boise State University, 1996).

5. Jerry D. Moore, *A Prehistory of South America: Ancient Cultural Diversity on the Least-Known Continent* (Boulder: University Press of Colorado, 2014), has general descriptions of the sites discussed in these paragraphs.

6. Jeffrey Quilter, *Life and Death at Paloma: Society and Mortuary Practices in a Preceramic Peruvian Village* (Iowa City: University of Iowa Press, 1989).

7. Quotes in this paragraph are from Ephraim Squier, *Travels in Peru* (New York: Harper, 1888), 110, 129.

8. Anchovy fishery: Edward A. Laws, *El Niño and the Peruvian Anchovy Fishery* (Sausalito, CA: University Science Books, 1997).

9. Michael E. Moseley, *The Inca and Their Ancestors: The Archaeology of Peru*, rev. ed. (London: Thames and Hudson, 2001), chap. 4.

10. Daniel H. Sandweiss, "Early Coastal South America," in Colin Renfrew and Paul Bahn, eds., *The Cambridge World Prehistory*, 1:1058-74 (Cambridge: Cambridge University Press, 2014). See also D. H. Sandweiss et al., "Environmental change and economic development in coastal Peru between 5,000 and 3,600 years ago," *Proceedings of the National Academy of Sciences* 106, no. 5 (2009): 1359-63.

11. Moseley, *The Inca*, chap. 5; Moore, *A Prehistory of South America*, 106-15.

12. The classic but now somewhat outdated work is Michael E. Moseley, *The Maritime Foundations of Andean Civilization* (Menlo Park, CA: Cummings Publishing, 1975). For a discussion, see Moore, *A Prehistory of South America*, 219-36. See also Daniel Sandweiss, "Early Fishing and Inland Monuments: Challenging the Maritime Foundations of Andean Civilization?" in Joyce Marcus, Charles Stanish, and R. Williams, eds., *Andean Civilizations: Papers in Honor of Michael E. Moseley*, 39-54 (Los Angeles: Cotsen Institute of Archaeology, UCLA, 2009).

13. R. Shady Solís, "America's First City: The Case of Late Archaic Caral," in W. Isbell and H. Silverman, eds., *Andean Archaeology*, vol. 3: *North and South*, 28-66 (New York: Springer, 2006).

14. For a general description of Moche, Sicán, and Chimú, see Moore, *A Prehistory of South America*, 331-38.

15. Joyce Marcus, *Excavations at Cerro Azul, Peru: The Architecture and Pottery* (Los Angeles: Cotsen Institute of Archaeology, UCLA, 2008). See also D. H. Sandweiss, *The Archaeology of Chincha Fishermen: Specialization and Status in Inka Peru* (Pittsburgh: Carnegie Museum of Natural History, 1992).

16. Izumi Shimada, *The Inka Empire: A Multidisciplinary Approach* (Austin: University of Texas Press, 2015), is a definitive account.

17. Sandweiss, *The Archaeology of Chincha Fishermen*.

Chapter 19. Ants of the Ocean

1. The essays in James H. Barrett and David R. Orton, eds., *Cod and Herring: The Archaeology and History of Medieval Sea Fishing* (Oxford: Oxbow Books, 2016), were fundamental sources for this chapter. For herring: Paul Holm, "Commercial Sea Fisheries in the Baltic Region, c. AD 1000-1600," in Barrett and Orton, eds., *Cod and Herring*, 13-22.

2. *The Rule of St. Benedict*, English Version, Chapter 29, lines 31-33, www.osb.org.

3. Adriaen Coenen (1514-87) was a fishmonger at Scheveningen and an official seafood auctioneer as well as an imaginative illustrator. He began his 410-page-long *Visboek* at the age of sixty-three, basing it on his wide knowledge and collection of dried fish. The book is housed in the National Library of the Netherlands.

4. Friedrich-Wilhelm Tresch, *The Eel: Biology and Management of Anguillid Eels*, trans. Jennifer Greenwood (New York: Wiley, 1977). For a general survey: Richard C. Hoffman, "Economic development and aquatic ecosystems in medieval Europe," *American Historical Review* 101 (1996): 631-69.

5. Quoted from Brian Fagan, *Fish on Friday: Feasting, Fasting, and the Discovery of the New World* (New York: Basic Books, 2004), 178.

6. Richard C. Hoffman, "Carp, cods and connections: New fisheries in the medieval European economy and environment," in M. J. Henninger-Voss, ed., *Animals in Human Histories: The Mirror of Nature and Culture*, 3–55 (Rochester: University of Rochester Press, 2002). See also Richard C. Hoffman, *An Environmental History of Medieval Europe* (Cambridge: Cambridge University Press, 2014).

7. Holm, "Commercial Sea Fisheries in the Baltic Region," summarizes recent research.

8. J. Campbell, "Domesday herrings," in C. Harper-Bell et al., eds., *East Anglia's History: Studies in Honour of Norman Scarfe*, 5–17 (Woodbridge, UK: Boydell Press, 2002). See also James H. Barrett, "Medieval Sea Fishing, AD 500–1550," in Barrett and Orton, eds., *Cod and Herring*, 250–72.

9. Holm, "Commercial Sea Fisheries in the Baltic Region," 15.

10. Carsten Jahnke, "The Medieval Herring Fishery in the Western Baltic," in Louis Sicking and Darlene Abreu-Ferreira, eds., *Beyond the Catch: Fisheries of the North Atlantic, the North Sea, and the Baltic, 900–1850*, 157–86 (Leiden: Brill, 2009). See also Inge Bodker Enghoff, "Herring and Cod in Denmark," in Barrett and Orton, eds., *Cod and Herring*, 133–55.

11. Quote from Fagan, *Fish on Friday*, 99.

12. This passage is based on Jahnke, "The Medieval Herring Fishery," 161ff.

13. Ibid., 168–70.

14. Holm, "Commercial Sea Fisheries in the Baltic Region," 16.

15. This passage is based on Dries Tys and Marnix Pieters, "Understanding a Medieval Fishing Settlement along the Southern North Sea: Walraversijde, c. 1200–1630," in Sicking and Abreu-Ferreira, eds., *Beyond the Catch*, 91–122.

16. Bo Poulsen, *Dutch Herring: An Environmental History, c. 1600–1860* (Groningen: Aksant Academic, 2009). This is a definitive summary of the subject and an invaluable source. See also Christiaan van Bochove, "The 'Golden Mountain': An Economic Analysis of Holland's Early Modern Herring Fisheries," in Sicking and Abreu-Ferreira, eds., *Beyond the Catch*, 209–44.

17. Quote from Charles L. Cutting, *Fish Saving: A History of Fish Preservation from Ancient to Modern Times* (New York: Philosophical Library, 1955), 54.

Chapter 20. The Beef of the Sea

1. Quote from Brian Fagan, *Fish on Friday: Feasting, Fasting, and the Discovery of the New World* (New York: Basic Books, 2004), 67.

2. Mark Kurlansky, *Cod: A Biography of a Fish that Changed the World* (New York: Walker, 1997). For definitive academic papers, see James H. Barrett and David C. Orton, *Cod and Herring: The Archaeology and History of Medieval Sea Fishing* (Oxford: Oxbow Books, 2016), chaps. 3–21.

3. Arnved Nedkvitne, "The Development of the Norwegian Long-distance Stockfish Trade," in Barrett and Orton, eds., *Cod and Herring,* 50–59.

4. James H. Barrett, "Medieval Sea Fishing," has an authoritative survey of the subject. Fish bone evidence: James H. Barrett et al., "'Dark Age Economics' Revisited: The English Fish-Bone Evidence, 600–1600," in Louis Sicking and Darlene Abreu-Ferreira, eds., *Beyond the Catch: Fisheries of the North Atlantic, the North Sea, and the Baltic, 900–1850,* 31–60 (Leiden: Brill, 2009).

5. Sophia Perdikaris and Thomas H. McGovern, "Codfish and Kings, Seals and Subsistence: Norse Marine Resource Use in the North Atlantic," in Torben C. Rick and Jon M. Erlandson, *Human Impacts on Ancient Marine Ecosystems, 187–214* (Berkeley: University of California Press, 2008).

6. See Barrett et al., "Dark Age Economics," 31–46.

7. This passage is based on Sophia Perdikaris and Thomas H. McGovern, "Viking Age Economics and the Origins of Commercial Cod Fisheries in the North Atlantic," in Sicking and Abreu-Ferreira, eds., *Beyond the Catch,* 61–90.

8. Justyna Wubs-Mrozewicz, "Fish, Stock, and Barrel: Changes in the Stockfish Trade in Northern Europe, c. 1360–1560," in Sicking and Abreu-Ferreira, eds., *Beyond the Catch,* 187–208. See also Nedkvitne, "The Development of the Norwegian Long-distance Stockfish Trade," in Barrett and Orton, eds., *Cod and Herring,* 50–59.

9. Mark Gardiner, "The Character of Commercial Fishing in Icelandic Waters in the Fifteenth Century," in Barrett and Orton, eds., *Cod and Herring,* 80–90. See also Mark Gardiner and Natascha Mehler, "English and Hanseatic Trading and Fishing Sites in Medieval Iceland: Report on Initial Fieldwork," *Germania* 85 (2007): 385–427.

10. Evan Jones, "England's Icelandic Fishery in the Early Modern Period," in David J. Starkey et al., eds., *England's Sea Fisheries: The Commercial Sea Fisheries of England and Wales since 1300,* 105–10 (London: Chatham Publishing, 2000).

11. Fagan, *Fish on Friday,* 183.

12. Ibid., chap. 13, summarizes a complex literature.

13. Kirsten Seaver, *The Frozen Echo: Greenland and the Exploration of North America, A.D. 1000–1500* (Palo Alto: Stanford University Press, 1997).

14. A classic account is Samuel Eliot Morison, *The European Discovery of America: The Northern Voyages* (New York: Oxford University Press, 1971).

15. Quote from English translation in Daniel B. Quinn, ed., *New American World: A Documentary History of North America from 1612,* vol. 1: *America from Concept to Discovery: Early Exploration of North America* (New York: Arno/Hector Bye, 1979), 97–98.

Chapter 21. "Inexhaustible Manna"

1. Anthony Parkhurst (fl. 1561–83) was an advocate for English settlement in New-foundland. He was the first Englishman to draw attention to the potential of the Gulf of St. Lawrence and the river beyond. Quote from a letter by Parkhurst to Richard

Hakluyt, in Richard Hakluyt, *The Principal Navigations, Voyages, Traffiques and Discoveries of the English Nation,*" ed. Ernest Rhys (London: Hakluyt Society, 1907), 5:345.

2. This chapter draws heavily on W. Jeffrey Bolster, *The Mortal Sea: Fishing the Atlantic in the Age of Sail* (Cambridge: Belknap Press, 2012), especially chaps. 1, 2. Also on Daniel Vickers, *Farmers and Fishermen: Two Centuries of Work in Essex County, Massachusetts* (Chapel Hill: University of North Carolina Press, 1994).

3. Harold E. L. Prinz, *The Mikmaq* (New York: Holt, Rinehart and Winston, 1996), has a general description, which I used here. See also Wilson D. Wallis and Ruth Sawtell Wallis, *The Micmac Indians of Eastern Canada* (Minneapolis: University of Minnesota Press, 1955).

4. Quotes in this paragraph from Bolster, *Mortal Sea,* 39–41.

5. This section draws on W. H. Lear, "History of Fisheries in the Northwest Atlantic: The 500-Year Perspective," *Journal of Northwest Atlantic Fisheries Science* 23, no. 1 (1994): 41–73.

6. Quote from Farley Mowat, *Sea of Slaughter* (New York: Atlantic Monthly Press, 1984), 168.

7. Lewes Roberts, *The Marchants Map of Commerce* (London: R. Mabb, 1638), part 1, p. 57.

8. Quote from Charles L. Cutting, *Fish Saving: A History of Fish Processing from Ancient to Modern Times* (New York: Philosophical Library, 1955), 33. These paragraphs and the following section rely on Peter E. Pope, *Fish into Wine: The Newfoundland Plantation in the Seventeenth Century* (Chapel Hill: University of North Carolina Press, 2004).

9. The Treaty of Utrecht was actually a series of treaties signed by the participants in the War of the Spanish Succession. Under the terms of these agreements France ceded Newfoundland, Nova Scotia, and some territories of the Hudson's Bay Company to Great Britain.

10. Lear, "History of Fisheries," 46.

11. Pierre Loti was a pseudonym. His actual name was Julian Viaud (1850–1923), and he was a French naval officer. Quotes in this paragraph are from Pierre Loti, *An Icelandic Fisherman,* trans. Guy Endore (Alhambra, CA: Braun, 1957), 8.

12. Pierre de Charlevoix, *Journal of a Voyage to North America* (London: R. and J. Dodsley, 1761). Reprinted by University Microfilms, Ann Arbor, 1966, 1:56.

13. Quote from A. C. Jensen, *The Cod* (New York: Thomas Y. Crowell, 1972), 66.

14. This passage relies on Bolster, *The Mortal Sea,* chap. 2, quote from p. 51.

15. Bernard Bailyn, *The New England Merchants in the Seventeenth Century* (Cambridge: Harvard University Press, 1955).

16. The Treaties of Utrecht are summarized at http://www.heraldica.org/topics/france/utrecht.htm.

17. Bolster, *The Mortal Sea,* 74–75.

18. Richard Pares, *Yankees and Creoles: The Trade Between North America and the West Indies Before the American Revolution* (Cambridge: Harvard University Press, 1956).

19. Bolster, *The Mortal Sea*, 137–38.

Chapter 22. Depletion

1. W. Jeffrey Bolster, *The Mortal Sea: Fishing the Atlantic in the Age of Sail* (Cambridge: Belknap Press, 2012), chap. 4, has a comprehensive discussion, which I relied on here. The references in Bolster are an invaluable guide to the very complex literature glossed over here.

2. Hugo Grotius (1583–1645) was a Dutch jurist who helped lay the foundations of international law. His book *Mare Liberum* (The free sea), published in 1609, established the principle that the sea was international territory and free for all nations to use. Quote from Hugo Grotius, *The Freedom of the Seas*, trans. Ralph Van Deman Magoffin (New York: Oxford University Press, 1916), 49.

3. Bolster, *The Mortal Sea*, chap. 2.

4. Callum Roberts, *The Unnatural History of the Sea* (Washington, DC: Island Press/Shearwater Books, 2007), 140–44, 163–64.

5. Dietrich Sahrhage and Johannes Lundbeck, *A History of Fishing* (New York: Springer-Verlag, 1992), 104.

6. Quote from Callum Roberts, *The Unnatural History*, 131.

7. Ibid., 132–36, 141–42, 154–60.

8. Ibid., 147ff.

9. Ibid., 157.

10. Ibid.

11. Bolster, *The Mortal Sea*, 113–14, 125–29.

12. Roberts, *The Unnatural History*, 279ff.

Chapter 23. More in the Sea?

1. The statistics in this chapter are drawn from the Food and Agriculture Organization (FAO), *The State of World Fisheries and Aquaculture* (Rome: Food and Agriculture Organization of the United Nations, 2014). As various authorities have pointed out, the figures are conservative and reflect incomplete reporting by many nations.

2. D. Pauly and D. Zeller, eds., "Catch reconstructions reveal that global marine fisheries catches are higher than reported and declining," *Nature Communications*, 2016, doi: 10.1038/ncomms10244, p. 9.

3. Callum Roberts, *The Unnatural History of the Sea* (Washington, DC: Island Press/Shearwater Books, 2007), chap. 26.

4. The statistics in this section are from FAO, *State of World Fisheries*, chap. 1.

5. Ibid., 181–92.

6. This passage is based on Mark Dickey-Collas et al., "Lessons learned from stock

collapse and recovery of North Sea herring: A review," *ICES Journal of Marine Science* 67, no. 9 (2010): 1875–86.

7. www.http://europeche.chil.me.

8. Roberts, *The Unnatural History,* chap. 26. FAO, *State of World Fisheries,* 18–26.

9. Daniel Pauly et al., "Fishing Down Marine Food Webs," *Science* 279, no. 5352 (1998): 860–63. See also K. T. Petrie et al., "Transient dynamics of an altered large marine ecosystem," *Nature* 477, no. 7362 (2011): 86–89.

10. Izaak Walton and Charles Cotton, *The Compleat Angler,* ed. Marjorie Swann (New York: Oxford University Press, 2014), 27.

11. Ibid., 147.

Index

Note: Page numbers in italics indicate maps and illustrations.

aquaculture: ancient Greeks and, 174;
ancient Romans and, 172, 174–76,
177–83, *181;* in Cambodia, 221–22;
carp, 245–47; in China, 10–11, 212–15,
301; Hawaiian, 11, 137–39, *138;* in-
creasing importance of, 300–301,
303; land reclamation and, 173;
monasteries and, 245; on the Nile
River, 11, 173; and rising city and
rural populations, 144–45
Archer, Gabriel, 277
Archestratus, 166
Archimedes, 170
Aristotle, 174–75
Arlington Springs site, 85
Arlington woman, 102
Arnarson, Ingólfr, 258
Asian carp, 212–15
As-Sabiyah, 200–201
Atbara region, 29–30
Atlantic bluefin tuna, 162–63, 167–69, *168*
Atlantic cod, 257–69; Bristol trading
center, 266–67; Canadian morato-
rium on, 299; cooking, 257; descrip-
tion of, 257–58; fishing conditions,
276, 284; Greenland fishery, 267–68;
as international enterprise, 260–64;
Lofoten Islands (Norway), 5, 55, 239,
243, 258, 259–60, 261, 262, 263; New
England fishery, 277–82; Newfound-
land (*see* Newfoundland cod fishery);
Norse colonists and, 258–60; overfishing and depletion, 239–40, 262,
275, 278, 280, 282–83, 285–86, 299
Atlantic herring: Baltic Sea fisheries,
238–39, 248–52; North Sea fisheries,
253–56, 299–300; red herrings, 255;
at Sorte Muld site, 243
Atlantic menhaden, 291
Atlantic salmon, 33, 41–42, 238
Atlit-Yam, 161

Augusta Raurica, 177
Augustus, Emperor, 182
Aurelius, Marcus, 169
Australia, Gidjingali Aborigines, 50–53
Azania, *187,* 191–92, 193–94

baidarkas (kayaks), 87–89
Bajondillo Cave, 34–35
Balakot, 204
Baltic Sea: Ertebølle people, 56–60;
formation of, 47; herring fisheries,
238–39, 248–52; map, *46;* mollusks,
47–49; Norje Sunnansund site, 3,
55–56; Sorte Muld, 243
Baluchistan, 204, 205, 206
Bank herring, 247
barbel, 24
barreling, 249, *250*
Barrett, James, 260, 285
barricade traps, 152
Barygaza (Mumbai), 207
Battuta, Ibn, 193
Bay of Bengal, *203*
Bay of Naples, 11, 172, 180, 182
Belgium, Walraversijde settlement,
253–56
Bell-Cross, Graham, 1
Belo Claudia, 170
Benedict, Saint, 244
Benguela Current, 26, 228
Bergen, 262, 263, 264
Bering Land Bridge/Beringia, 74,
77–83, *78*
big-head carp, 214
Bismarck Archipelago, 125
bivalves, 27, 49–50, 52, 285
boats. *See* watercraft
Bodrum, 164
Bohuslen herring fishery, 252
Bolster, Jeffrey, 271, 277, 278
bonito, 135